Avant-Folk

Avant-Folk

Small Press Poetry Networks
from 1950 to the Present

by Ross Hair

LIVERPOOL UNIVERSITY PRESS

for Elodie, Lily, and Amelia

First published 2016 by
Liverpool University Press
4 Cambridge Street
Liverpool
L69 7ZU

British Library Cataloguing-in-Publication data
A British Library CIP record is available

ISBN 978-1-78138-329-2 cased

Typeset by Carnegie Book Production, Lancaster
Printed and bound by CPI Group (UK) Ltd, Croydon CR0 4YY

Contents

Acknowledgements

For the practical help and support, advice, and/or encouragement I have received over the course of writing this book I sincerely thank: John and Olga Janssen, Alistair Peebles, Anthony Cond, Robert Sheppard, Thomas A. Clark, Laurie Clark, Simon Cutts, Erica Van Horn, Colin Sackett, John Bevis, David Bellingham, Páraic Finnerty, Jeffery Beam, Elizabeth Matheson, Whit Griffin, Thomas Meyer, Steven Manuel, Hannah Neate, Helen Mitchell, Les Buckingham, Tim Craven, Elspeth Healey and her colleagues at the Spencer Research Library, The Poetry Library (Southbank Centre), Clément Oudart, Bob and Sue Arnold, Roger Conover, Pia Maria Simig, Lucy Douglas, Autumn Richardson, Richard Skelton, and Sam Ward.

I would also like to thank the editors, journals, and presses who published earlier versions of work included in *Avant-Folk*. Material from the introduction and chapter 1, 'The Avant-Folk Ways of Lorine Niedecker,' was originally published in *Among Friends: Engendering the Social Site of Poetry* by the University of Iowa Press. Editors: Anne Dewey and Libbie Rifkin © 2013. Used with Permission. An earlier version of chapter 3, 'Jonathan Williams: Beyond Black Mountain,' appeared in *Black Mountain College Studies* 3 (2012). Chapter 4, 'Opening the Folds: A Pastoral Vanguard' is an expanded version of an earlier essay, 'Opening the Folds: Thomas A. Clark, Ian Hamilton Finlay, and Pastoral,' which was published in the *Journal of British and Irish Innovative Poetry* 5.2 (2013). The book's coda, 'Certain Trees,' develops ideas originally presented in 'Thick as Trees: Kinship and Place in Transatlantic Small Press Poetry Networks,' an article that was published in the journal *Anglophonia/ Caliban* 35 (2014).

Permissions

Grateful acknowledgement is made to the following authors, publishers, and copyright holders for permission to reproduce material.

Thomas A. Clark, *Folding the Last Sheep*, published by Moschatel Press 1973; 'It is afternoon,' from *Pauses & Digressions*, published by Moschatel Press 1983; *Pastoral*, published by Moschatel Press 2010. Copyright © 1973, 1983, and 2010 by Thomas A. Clark. Reprinted with the permission of Thomas A. Clark.

Simon Cutts, 'As for verse' and 'Les coquelicots' from *A New Kind of Tie: Poems 1965–68*, published by Tarasque Press, 1972. Copyright © 1972 by Simon Cutts. Reprinted with the permission of Simon Cutts.

Simon Cutts, 'After Samuel Palmer's version of Virgil's "Eclogues",' from *Piano Stool: Footnotes*, published by The Jargon Society, 1982; 'Eclogues 1984–2000: After Samuel Palmer's Virgil,' from *If It Is At All*, published by Granary Books and Coracle, 2007. Copyright © 1986, 1982, and 2007. Reprinted with the permission of Simon Cutts.

Stephen Duncalf, 'A Rusty slab lies upon the landscape,' from *Good Hoofs*, published by Coracle 1976; 'Orchard' from *Huts By-way Engine Orchard*, published by Coracle 1977. Copyright © 1976 and 1977 by Stephen Duncalf. Reprinted with the permission of Simon Cutts.

Ian Hamilton Finlay, 'Giraffe,' 'Scene,' 'Poet,' 'Mansie Considers the Sea in the Manner of Hugh MacDiarmid,' and 'Angles of Stamps' from *The Dancers Inherit the Party* published by Polygon. Copyright © 2004 by Ian Hamilton Finlay. Reprinted under fair use and acknowledgement to Polygon/Birlinn, Ltd.

Ian Hamilton Finlay correspondence to Ronald Johnson, from the Ronald Johnson Archives courtesy of Special Collections, Spencer

Abbreviations

AMO Ian Hamilton Finlay, *A Model of Order: Selected Letters on Poetry and Making*, ed. Thomas A. Clark Glasgow: WAX366, 2009.

BD Jonathan Williams, *Blackbird Dust: Essays, Poems, and Photographs*. New York: Turtle Point Press, 2000.

BYHM Lisa Pater Faranda, ed., *'Between Your House and Mine': The Letters of Lorine Niedecker to Cid Corman, 1960 to 1970*. Durham, North Carolina: Duke University Press, 1986.

CW Lorine Niedecker, *Collected Works*, ed. Jenny Penberthy. Berkeley: University of California Press, 2002.

D Ian Hamilton Finlay, *The Dancers Inherit the Party and Glasgow Beasts: Early Poems and Stories*, ed. Ken Cockburn. Edinburgh: Polygon, 2004.

'DG' Alec Finlay, 'The Dewy Glen,' in Ian Hamilton Finlay, *The Dancers Inherit the Party and Glasgow Beasts*, ed. Alec Finlay. Edinburgh: Polygon, 1996.

JT Jonathan Williams, *Jubilant Thicket: New and Selected Poems*. Washington: Copper Canyon Press, 2005.

MB Jonathan Williams, *The Magpie's Bagpipe: Selected Essays*, ed. Thomas Meyer. San Francisco: North Point Press, 1982.

NCZ Jenny Penberthy, *Niedecker and the Correspondence with Zukofsky 1931–1970*. Cambridge: Cambridge University Press, 1993.

SFA Simon Cutts, *Some Forms of Availability: Critical Passages on the Book and Publication*. New York: Granary Books, 2007.

Introduction

We are what the seas
have made us
longingly immense

—Lorine Niedecker

In *Beautiful Enemies*, Andrew Epstein challenges 'the Romantic myth of the poet as solitary genius' (10) and argues that 'aesthetic and cultural forms cannot be fully understood through the study of individual authors in isolation' (5). Epstein makes this claim in the context of the New American Poetry that rose to prominence in the 1950s and 1960s, proposing that the lyric 'should not be seen as an utterance issuing from an isolated subjectivity but as a social text, caught in a web of interpersonal and intertextual relations' (15). For the first generation of New York poets, the main subject of Epstein's book, their interpersonal relations were supported by a social infrastructure comprised of numerous New York City coffeehouses, loft spaces, galleries and bars, all of which reified their sense of group identity. Such venues were, Epstein suggests, 'densely interwoven cultural, intertextual, interpersonal spaces' that ensured tangible, if often fractious, notions of poetic community (15). But where do geographically remote, isolated or solitary poets lacking the 'highly social environments' and urban enclaves fit in relation to these metropolitan networks (Kane, 1)? Do they simply reinforce the myth of 'isolated subjectivity' that Epstein is keen to dispel, or, as I argue, do they indicate that there are alternative means for establishing and sustaining 'interpersonal relationships' outside of the geographical conveniences and proximities of the city? These questions of remoteness, distance and the question of 'interpersonal relationships' are especially pertinent in the context of the 'transatlantic drift' of American and British poetry that occurred during the 1960s and 1970s (Blanton 134). As I intend to show via the examples of Lorine Niedecker, Ian Hamilton Finlay, Jonathan Williams and a younger generation of poet-publishers

1

that include Stuart Mills, Simon Cutts, and Thomas A. Clark, this was an important time when many poets on both sides of the Atlantic 'found parallel practices or significant models via transatlantic communication,' particularly through the channels of small press publishing which, as we shall see, continues to flourish (Tuma 41).

As a vital taproot for the 'transatlantic communication' examined in the following chapters, Niedecker offers a compelling example of how a networked poetry community can operate not only outside of the familiar cosmopolitan centres of literary activity such as New York or San Francisco, but also transnationally. Niedecker was a poet whose relations with the broader poetry world were largely remote and marginal. 'She shuns the public world, lives, reads, and writes, very quietly near the town of Fort Atkinson, Wisconsin, by the Rock River on its way to Lake Koshkonong,' Jonathan Williams writes on the dust jacket to her Jargon collection *T&G*: 'Her importance—and remove from—the urbane literary establishment is the rank of Miss Dickinson's' (n. pag).

Although frequently labelled an Objectivist poet, Niedecker's relation to the 'fluctuating boundaries' of this group was largely peripheral (Kenner, *A Homemade World* 163). So much so, in fact, that Niedecker is entirely absent from Kenner's survey of that particular group in *A Homemade World*, just as she is in L. S. Dembo's 'groundbreaking recovery of the Objectivist poets at the University of Wisconsin-Madison in April and May 1968 [where] he conducted interviews with Louis Zukofsky, George Oppen, Charles Reznikoff, and Carl Rakosi' and later published them in *Contemporary Literature* (DuPlessis, 'Lorine Niedecker's 'Paean to Place' 393). Yet, despite (or because of) its peripheral status, Niedecker's poetry constitutes a compelling 'social text,' to recall Epstein's phrase, which is defined by, and responsive to, a poetic network that claims no geographical centre and which does not advance any specific group identity.

Despite her relative isolation in Wisconsin, Niedecker was widely published. As Peter Middleton has noted, 'over half the books Lorine Niedecker produced in her lifetime were published in Britain' by small poetry presses ('The British Niedecker' 247). These include some of the most important and influential imprints of the period such as Wild Hawthorn Press (Scotland), Fulcrum Press (London), and The Jargon Society which operated from two remote locations: Highlands, North Carolina and Dentdale in England's Yorkshire Dales. These were the presses that were primarily responsible for situating Niedecker's poetry in a 'larger eastward drift of American poetry publications to Britain between about 1962 and 1973' ('The British Niedecker' 247). The 1960s and 1970s were a particularly vibrant time when 'American avant-garde poems of the 1960s became migrants,' as Middleton explains, 'because for a short period an elective affinity between American and British poets, readers, and publishers emerged to shape the reception of this poetry' ('The British Niedecker' 247–248). This 'elective affinity' is the principal subject of *Avant-Folk*, which examines the development of a loose-knit, transatlantic collective of poets, publishers, and artists that evolved in the late 1950s and early 1960s around the activities of Jonathan Williams and The Jargon Society and which continues up to the present day. Via the mutual concerns and sensibilities of these individuals, as well as the small presses and little magazines that they shared, occurred a rich amalgamation of vernacular and avant-garde poetics that, following in a broader tradition of modernist-folk aesthetics, incorporated modernist poetry forms and strategies with discerning uses of regional dialect, demotic culture, and craft practices. This merging of the vernacular with the avant-garde is but one of the many consequences of this vibrant period of creative exchange when poets on both sides of the Atlantic, working in close collaboration with artists, printers and book designers, expanded considerably the creative and social possibilities of small press publishing.

Critical interest in transatlantic small press poetry networks and the fruitful exchanges that they have facilitated has increased in recent years. In particular, Stuart Montgomery's Fulcrum Press and Gael Turnbull's and Michael Shayer's Migrant Press have attracted critical attention and been recognized as major forces within this transatlantic milieu.[1] One American poet who was published by both presses who has received substantial attention in this context is Edward Dorn, who was closely allied with Olson and Black Mountain, lived in the UK (from late 1965 to 1970) while teaching at the University of Essex, and formed a strong friendship with J. H. Prynne. Indeed, according to Neil Pattison, Dorn's friendship with Prynne 'is one of the defining alliances of the period' (viii). By comparison, The Jargon Society, and Williams's own poetry, has been largely ignored, despite the active presence of Williams on both sides of the Atlantic from the 1960s onwards. One possible reason is Jargon's reputation as a Black Mountain press. For example, in Pattison's summary of the transatlantic 'alliances of the period,' Jargon's extensive involvement with British poetry from the 1960s onwards is largely overlooked in favour of presses and scenes that emerged in response to 'the greater grandeur of Olson's reputation' in and around Cambridge, Worcester, Newcastle upon Tyne, and Bristol (vi). Another explanation of the absence of Williams's press in Pattison's

---

1 See C. B. Blanton's 'Transatlantic Currents,' in *A Concise Companion to Postwar British and Irish Poetry*, eds. Nigel Alderman and C. D. Blanton (Chichester: Wiley-Blackwell, 2009), pp. 134–154; Peter Middleton's 'The British Niedecker,' in *Radical Vernacular: Lorine Niedecker and the Poetics of Place*, ed. Elizabeth Willis (Iowa City: University of Iowa Press, 2008), pp. 247–270; and Richard Price's 'Migrant the Magnificent,' *PN Review* 33.4 (March–April, 2007), pp. 29–33.

account of Anglo-American poetry relations might be because despite Olson being of 'principal importance' to the largely Cambridge-focused poets that concern Pattison, Williams interacted with a more disparate group of British poets who, while drawing on Black Mountain and New American poetry, cast their nets more widely, drawing on concrete poetry, contemporary Scottish poetry, and the historical avant-garde of the early twentieth century (iii).

Additionally, in choosing to publish 'people as bizarrely disconnected as say Alfred Starr Hamilton and Charles Olson,' Williams positioned Jargon outside the transatlantic Olson–Prynne/Black Mountain–Cambridge axis to present an alternative perspective on the development and interactions of New American and New British poetry from the 1960s onwards (Alpert 59). As Williams explains to Barry Alpert in 1973:

> These days, many people in the academic world finally have some sense of Black Mountain and yet they're not willing to take up the cudgels on behalf of somebody who's just one poet. For instance, I think Alfred Starr Hamilton is a very curious and interesting poet and yet Alfred Starr Hamilton is strictly on his own, as Lorine Niedecker was strictly on her own, and I cannot seem to generate any interest, any enthusiasm. Nobody bothers to write about these people. (59)

The resurgence of interest in Niedecker's work over the past two decades suggests that this is now certainly not the case.[2]

A major claim of *Avant-Folk* is that Niedecker was not 'strictly on her own' as a poet, but rather a vital link within a transatlantic network of poetry and publishing activity that has, until now, largely eluded critical attention. There are two possible reasons for this elusion: firstly, this *sui generis* network does not readily cohere as a particular movement, school, or group; and secondly, in contrast to the New York School, for example, it is not specifically tied to one particular location. Indeed, *Avant-Folk* aims to explicate the ways in which the small press publication has helped facilitate community, dialogue, exchange and collaboration amongst a geographically and stylistically disparate network of poets, publishers, and artists.

The scope of the network concerned in *Avant-Folk* is extensive and defines an informal 'society' of kindred spirits operating on the fringes

---

2   The publication of a comprehensive selection of Alfred Starr Hamilton's poetry, *A Dark Dreambox of Another Kind*, edited by Ben Estes and Alan Felsenthal (The Song Cave, 2013), which builds on the earlier 1970 Jargon collection of Hamilton's poetry, would indicate that Hamilton's work is also ripe for similar reassessment.

of the more established poetry movements and groups from the late 1950s up to the present day. Furthermore, this 'society' covers a broad transatlantic terrain, encompassing various, and mostly provincial, parts of North America, England, and Scotland. Unlike contemporaneous currents in British and American poetry—such as the New York School or the Cambridge poets—there is no convenient name or label to define the individuals within this society, and neither is there a supporting manifesto that readily categorizes it as a collective. The word 'society,' however, does to an extent help nominate this collective that, as that word implies, emerges from what is perhaps one of the most instrumental presses within this transatlantic milieu, The Jargon Society of Jonathan Williams.

As Kyle Schlesinger suggests, 'Jargon's spirit has moved through dozens, perhaps hundreds of small presses, leaving a living legacy in its wake' (para 28). This is a result of Williams's extensive and tireless networking activities on both sides of the Atlantic that, according to Guy Davenport, makes him 'an ambassador for an enterprise that has neither center nor hierarchy' (*Geography* 181). Williams is perhaps best known as a publisher of Black Mountain poets such as Charles Olson, Robert Creeley and Robert Duncan, all of whom he befriended while studying at Black Mountain College in the 1950s. However, Williams's ambassadorial role in the remote relations concerning *Avant-Folk* can also be perceived in his important relationship with Niedecker whose poetry, and its transatlantic reception, saliently encapsulates this current of late twentieth-century Anglo-American poetry.

Lorine Niedecker
Jargon might be easily dismissed as an 'eccentric' press, partly because of the unorthodox list of authors and subjects it published over the decades, but also because, to recall the etymological sense of the word, of the way it deliberately situated itself 'out of the way' and made itself 'remote from the centre' (*OED*). This eccentricity is reflected in the way that Jargon strategically located itself 'on the margins of the Modern World' in Appalachia and Cumbria (*MB* 132). Williams considered himself a 'metrophobe,' 'peripheral in [...] vision,' and someone who was constantly 'looking for edges' and 'for the stuff on the outside' of what he considered a venal urban, culture industry (*BD* 38; Dana 220). This 'stuff' comprises neglected modernist poets including Mina Loy and Bob Brown, maverick 'outsider' folk artists and poets such as Alfred Starr Hamilton and Mason Jordon Mason, photographers, artists, and poets involved in the new British and American poetry that came to prominence in the 1960s.

Williams's enthusiasm for Niedecker may initially appear to reiterate what many critics consider an inaccurate perception of Niedecker as 'an anomalous rural savant' (Willis, 'Introduction' xiii). As Elizabeth Willis notes, and as chapter one discusses in more detail, as much attention has been put on Niedecker's 'working-class Wisconsin identity as to her poetics; we are told that Niedecker was isolated, washed hospital floors, lived most of her life in a small cabin, and sewed her clothes by hand' ('Introduction' xiii). Considering his penchant for 'the stuff on the outside,' it is easy to forget the important role that Williams played in securing Niedecker's reputation by facilitating the 'eastward drift' of her poetry toward the United Kingdom and assume instead that Niedecker was simply another maverick or savant that he collected for Jargon. Williams's assessment of Niedecker, however, is more astute.

Williams expressed interest in publishing Niedecker as early as 1957, but it took another 12 years before Jargon published its first Niedecker book, *T&G: Collected Poems (1936–1966)*, which was followed by *From This Condensery: The Complete Writings of Lorine Niedecker* in 1985. In 1961 Williams visited Niedecker for the first time at Niedecker's Fort Atkinson home. 'I was so happy to talk an hour or so this past fall with Jonathan Williams who stopped at my place on his trip thru the mid-west,' Niedecker writes to Corman (*BYHM* 31–32). A friendship formed which was sustained mainly through the mail, although Williams visited Niedecker again in February 1967 when she accompanied him to a reading he gave at the University of Wisconsin, Milwaukee. It is especially illuminating how Niedecker describes the event to Corman:

> I couldn't help as I looked around at that quiet little gathering of somewhat select persons [wonder] what it would be like to live in a community of poets! a little too cold to speculate while there and now each one of us is an isolate dot on the page again. (*BYHM* 114)

Considering the tenacious image of Niedecker as a solitary poet, her analogy is striking as it is not only herself but all of the poets gathered together that evening who are 'isolate dot[s] on the page.' Furthermore, this analogy—particularly the emphasis it puts on the page as a social medium for such a broad community of individuals—makes the process of publication a pertinent synecdoche of the broader infrastructure of small presses, little magazines, and correspondence that connects the otherwise isolate dots comprising Jargon's 'society' of poets.

But just how much Niedecker desired 'to live in a community of poets' is unclear. Taking advantage of the multiple meanings of the word 'impossible' in her poem 'T. E. Lawrence,' Niedecker implies that 'to be alone' is both an unbearable situation and an untenable one. 'How impossible it is / to be alone,' she writes, noting that it is the 'one thing' that humanity 'has never really / moved towards' (*CW* 198). The poem is deliberately ambiguous: has humanity never succeeded in overcoming the problem of loneliness? Or, has it never had to? Suggesting social inclination *and* evolution, the poem's claim that humanity has never 'moved towards' reconciling this question of loneliness only exacerbates its ambiguity.

Clearly, Niedecker did at times feel alone. 'Lonesome is such a physical thing,' she writes to Zukofsky on one occasion (*NCZ* 284). And, to Corman she remarks: 'I wish you and Louie and Celia [Zukofsky] and I could sit around a table,' adding: 'Otherwise, poetry has to do it' (*BYHM* 48). However, as Niedecker intimates, poetry makes aloneness emotionally untenable because of its considerable social scope. Referring to Niedecker's friendship with Zukofsky, who was living at 'a cool distance' in New York, Jenny Penberthy draws attention to this important fact by noting how the two poets found 'companionship' and 'sociability in poetry': 'They delighted in sharing space in little magazines and being published at the same time and by the same publishers—another form of companionship-in-poetry' (*CW* 160; *NCZ* 6). Private correspondence was an additional element of this 'companionship-in-poetry,' Penberthy explains: 'Letters brought material for poems while poems continued the conversations letters began' (*NCZ* 9). In particular, it was the 'mutual quoting' and 'pilfering' of each other's letters in their poems, Penberthy suggests, that reaffirmed the poets' friendship (*NCZ* 15).

The social implications of such practices are apparent throughout Jargon's broader transatlantic society. Indeed, to recall Epstein's ideas regarding the 'social text' of poetry and the 'web of interpersonal and intertextual relations' that it comprises, it is possible to see how important social affinities, filiations, and fellowships have been established via reciprocal borrowings, appropriations, and elaborations of material. Pastoral, as chapter five discusses, is one of a number of prominent themes that have facilitated such socially motivated, intertextual relations across Jargon's 'society.'

The necessity for these and other similar practices in sustaining the remote relations examined in *Avant-Folk* can also be seen in Williams's review of Niedecker's selected poems, *My Friend Tree*, which Ian Hamilton Finlay's and Jessie McGuffie's Wild Hawthorn Press published in 1961. In his review, Williams draws attention to Niedecker's remoteness: 'No phone, almost no neighbors—I'm sure none with whom she can talk about poems, about the latest book from Louis Zukofsky off in Brooklyn Heights' (*MB* 22–23). On first impression, Williams appears to reiterate the popular 'misperception that Niedecker worked in isolation and that her work was unmediated by cultural forces beyond the local' (Willis, 'Introduction' xiv). Williams, for example, on the jacket blurb for her collection *T&G*, describes Niedecker as 'faithful and recurrent, as beautiful and homely, as my favorite peony bush' (n. pag). According to Willis, this 'unintentional slight' is typical of Niedecker's publishers' 'paternalistic' attitudes toward her (Willis, 'Introduction' xiii). However, Williams's botanical allusion can also be read as an acknowledgement

of his and Niedecker's mutual regard for solitary Japanese poets such
as Issa, Buson, and Bashō, whose haiku frequently invoke, among other
flowers, the peony.[3]

'To see Niedecker as tree or flower is lovely and not inaccurate,' Jane
Augustine suggests: 'It reflects the influence of haiku on her short forms
and the Asian use of the natural object as "always the adequate symbol,"
as Pound noted' (n. pag). Although Augustine recognizes that botanical
allusions are significant of the transtextual 'society' that both Niedecker
and Williams kept, she still questions 'the suggestion of limitation
and feminine stereotype, "woman" equals "nature,"' that readers of
Niedecker have made (n. pag). Botanical allusions and imagery might,
however, also be seen as the means for overcoming the very 'suggestion
of limitation' that Augustine questions.

In the case of Williams's own poetry, his invocation of flowers
and botanical imagery is not gender-specific, but rather used as the
means for articulating a social vocabulary. In his poem 'Enthusiast,'
for example, Williams claims that 'we flower in talk,' quoting Edward
Dahlberg's assertion that literature is 'the way we ripen ourselves / by
conversation' (*JT* 250).

Niedecker expresses a similar sentiment in 'Wintergreen Ridge' in
which she recollects her meeting with the British poet Basil Bunting:

>   When visited
>   by the poet
>
>   From Newcastle on Tyne
>   I neglected to ask
>   what wild plants
>
>   have you there
>   how dark
>   how inconsiderate
>
>   of me (*CW* 254)

Noting the pun in 'dark,' Middleton believes that the poem 'affirms
that it is polite or *light*, and considerate to acknowledge the wild
plants indigenous to a poet's location' ('The British Niedecker' 263).

---

3 Both Niedecker and Williams were especially fond of Nobuyuki
Yuasa's translation of Bashō's travel writings, which includes, for
example, the following haiku: 'Mid-winter peonies / And a distant
plover singing. / Did I hear a cuckoo / In the Snow?' (Basho 58).
Williams considers Yuasa's Bashō 'an excellent translation' and
Niedecker refers to Yuasa in her correspondence to Corman (*MB*
153; *BYHM* 145).

Furthermore, as an integral part of photosynthesis, light is also what most plants need in order to thrive.

But why should one acknowledge another's plants? Geoffrey Grigson offers a possible answer when he notes that the 'enjoyment of plants does involve their history and their associations':

> What names have these plants be given? Are they native or have they been introduced? If they have been introduced, where did they come from? Or why, or how, were they introduced? If they are natives, when were they first discovered? And what have they meant, generation after generation, to the Englishman in his daily life, in his ceremonies of spring, summer, and winter, his practice of magic and medicine, his feeding of body and mind? (*Englishman's Flora* 16, 13)

By enquiring about the wild plants of Bunting's homeland, the speaker in Niedecker's poem might also be expressing an interest in the poet's culture. After all, plants, as Grigson notes, have their own stories to tell. Perhaps those stories may find some mutual ground between Newcastle upon Tyne and Wisconsin. In respect of the 'Darwinian' concerns of 'Wintergreen Ridge' and the 'oneness of all life, human, animal, and vegetable' that it explores, Niedecker might be intuiting common, transatlantic affinities—evolutionary, biological, and/or cultural—between the Old and the New worlds via the social language of plants (Cox 305). Or, as Niedecker writes elsewhere in *North Central*, plants, like poetry, might be seen as testimony of 'waters working together / internationally' (*CW* 232).

The recurrent use of botanical imagery to articulate Niedecker's work emphasizes its extensive reach. Like the peonies flowering in Fort Atkinson, Niedecker's poetry is very much rooted in its environment, 'feeling it as a living center and source' (*NCZ* 76). However, and again like a flower, her poetry is also far-reaching. It travels. It is perhaps for similar reasons that many publications by or relating to Niedecker have incorporated plant imagery in their designs. For example, the image of bracken on the cover of Niedecker's Fulcrum book, *North Central* (1968) or the plant prints by the typesetter and book designer A. Doyle Moore included in her first Jargon title *T&G* (1968), as well as in the Jargon tribute, edited by Williams, *Epitaphs for Lorine* (1973). Considering the herb's associations with the sovereignty of women ('Where rosemary flourishes the lady rules,' claims one folk proverb), as well as its 'emblematical' associations with 'remembrance,' Doyle's print of rosemary sprigs in *Epitaphs* is especially apposite for a collection of tributes to the poet (Thiselton-Dyer 84, 96).[4]

---

4   See also Erica Van Horn's postcard in her Living Locally series: 'A

Botanical distribution is the subject of Niedecker's poem 'Consider' which explores how flowers traverse their immediate locales and disseminate over considerable geographical and cultural distances:

> *Consider*
>
> the alliance—
> ships and plants
>
> The take-for-granted bloom
> of our roadsides
>
> > Queen Anne's Lace
> > Black Eyed Susans
> > rode the sea
>
> 'Specimens graciously passed
> between warring fleets'
>
> And when an old boat rots ashore
> itself once living plant
>
> > it sprouts. (*CW* 283–284)

'Consider' shows how trees, by providing timber for ships, not only transport botanical cargos but also themselves. Thus, 'when an old boat rots ashore' its decomposing timber encourages a new cycle of growth to begin. However, the nouns 'ships' and 'plants' also function as verbs so that it is also human culture that *ships* to, and *plants* itself in, new soils.

As Richard Caddel notes, it is the transplanted people who take with them the 'take-for-granted,' the familiar, everyday names to new shores and climates, if not always the plants themselves:

> In the case of Queen Anne's Lace, a little used name for one (English) umbellifer became transferred to another, in New England, 'in memory' perhaps ironically, of an English Queen left behind (the English name is associated with St Anna): the name in other words, came with the people who named it. So too the native [Black Eyed Susan], a compositae with yellow petals and a black center, takes a name from an imported English folk song [...] about taking ship. (285)

---

healthy rosemary plant / growing by the kitchen / door shows that a strong / woman lives in the house' (n. pag).

Names, as well as plants, may therefore be considered akin to what botanists call 'anthropophytes,' a neologism, as Grigson explains, that refers to plant species '"which have followed the spread of civilization to the temperate and sub-tropical zones of both hemispheres, and to high altitudes in the tropics, until their present distribution is world-wide"' (*Gardenage* 31). One might therefore see Niedecker's poetry as an equivalent to the 'anthropophyte,' but one which is permanently in the throes of distribution: 'I sent University of Wisconsin a copy of *T&G* way back in Sept,' Niedecker writes wryly to Corman: 'A few days ago I wrote: Did you fail to receive? They answer they've placed it with regional materials. I should ask: What region—London, Wisconsin, New York' (*BYHM* 208)? Wisconsin may very well provide the soil and native habitat of Niedecker's poetry but, as she implies, it has travelled much further and found nourishment in other soils.

The theme of botanical distribution in 'Consider' is developed further when Niedecker quotes the popular scientific thinker Loren Eiseley. In his book *Darwin's Century* (1958), Eiseley refers to the eighteenth-century French scientist Georges-Louis Leclerc, Comte de Buffon who 'had his specimens passed graciously through warring fleets' and 'corresponded with Franklin' (45). According to Eiseley, Buffon's major contribution to evolutionary theory was his awareness of 'the significance of animal and plant distributions':

> He said of the New World species which differed from those of the Old Continent: 'They … have remote relations, which seem to indicate something common in their formation, and lead us to causes of degeneration more ancient, perhaps, than all others.' (44)

Buffon uses the term 'degeneration' in his discredited theory that species from the Old and New worlds derived from one common stock but through migration, time, and the effects of changing environments 'degenerated' from their originating *genus*. However, it is Buffon's term 'remote relations' that resonates pertinently with Jargon's society and Niedecker's position within it.

Utopic Spaces, Elsewhere Communities

'Consider' is a prime example of how 'remote relations' have operated in the context of late twentieth-century transatlantic small press poetry networks as the poem's publication history enacts similar distributive processes to those that it describes. Initially published without a title in *Origin* in 1970, Niedecker's poem was later reprinted as 'Consider' in the posthumous collection, *Harpsichord & Salt Fish* that Richard and Ann Caddel's Pig Press published in 1991. Thus, under the auspices of an 'alliance' of kindred poets, publishers and readers, 'Consider' forms part of an 'expatriated' small press book 'graciously passed' across the Atlantic like the flowers and names it invokes (Middleton, 'The British Niedecker' 248).

Harpsichord & Salt Fish might therefore epitomize what Anne Moeglin-Delcroix has called the 'utopic potential' of the small press publication ('Little Books' n. pag). Moeglin-Delcroix conceives the small press publication as an 'alternative' and 'free space' that exits 'outside established institutions' ('Little Books' n. pag). Indeed, the artist's book bears a close and longstanding relationship with literature and small press publishing. As Johanna Drucker has suggested, these publications 'appear in every major movement in art and literature and have provided a unique means of realizing works within all of the many avant-garde, experimental, and independent groups whose contributions have defined the shape of twentieth-century artistic activity' (*Century* 1). However, 'as a named phenomenon,' Lucy Lippard writes, the artist's book 'surfaced with conceptual art in the sixties, part of a broad, if naive, quasi-political resistance to the extreme commodification of artworks and artists' ('Conspicuous Consumption' 50).[5] 'Accessibility and some sort of function were an assumed part of their *raison d'être*,' she proposes, and were usually 'portable and replicable,' 'durable and intimate,' 'non-precious and inexpensive' ('Conspicuous Consumption' 50). According to Drucker, 'the paradigm' of this kind of artist's book is Ed Ruscha's *Twentysix Gasoline Stations* (1963), which reproduces in a small unostentatious format 26 photographs of American gasoline stations situated between Los Angles and Oklahoma City, accompanied by captions indicating the gasoline brand and the station's location (*Figuring* 176).

Although, the 'indifferent' and 'artless' quality of artists' books such as Ruscha's show affinities with certain small press publications examined in *Avant-Folk*, it is Drucker's broader definition of the artist's book, as an activity, rather than as a category, that is perhaps most pertinent (Godfrey 97). 'If all the elements or activities which contribute to artists' books as a field are described,' Drucker proposes, 'what emerges is a space made by their intersection, one which is a zone of activity, rather than a category':

> There are many of these activities: fine printing, independent
> publishing, the craft tradition of book arts, conceptual art,

---

5   Clive Phillpot dates the term a little later, suggesting that 'The first time the term "artist's book" was used to include modest, cheap, unlimited booklets conceived by artists, was probably on the occasion of the exhibition *Artists Books* [sic] at Moore College of Art in Philadelphia in 1973' (146). More specifically, in John Perrault's essay for the exhibition catalogue that describes these publications as 'practical and democratic' (Phillpot 146).

painting and other traditional arts, politically motivated art activity and activist production, performance of both traditional and experimental varieties, concrete poetry, experimental music, computer and electronic arts, and last but not least, the tradition of the illustrated book, the *livre d'artiste*. (*Century* 2)

As the following chapters will show, the small press publishing activities that occur in the milieu of Jargon and its transatlantic 'society' encompass (and blur) many of these activities, creating similar intersectional spaces to those that Drucker attributes to the artist's book.

In addition to these intersectional spaces, the small press publication also establishes an autonomous *elsewhere* space that, according to Moeglin-Delcroix, bears 'a close relationship to utopia':

Whatever we my think, utopia, in fact, was not originally a temporal notion referring to the imagination of the future, but a spatial notion, indeed, a geographical one. It is, we must remember, the name of an island, an autonomous world that is confined, lateral, marginal and far away. It is 'without' place because in proposing another organisation of life, it situates itself outside the ordinary functioning of the world. ('Little Books' n. pag)

The small press publication is also '"without" place' because it becomes the site of an indeterminate interspace—a utopic 'nowhere' or 'elsewhere'—where geographically remote poets, artists, and readers might intersect. This 'utopic potential' is evident, for example, in the supranational influence of Corman's influential Kyoto-based magazine *Origin* which, as Alan Golding notes, 'in the absence of a literal, physical community, established a metaphorical one' through its transnational readership (698).

The 'spatial notion' of the small press publication and the utopian interspaces it affords has had considerable social and creative implications for the otherwise remote poets examined in *Avant-Folk*. It also significantly revises the modernist trope of the expatriate, especially Hugh Kenner's notion of 'Elsewhere Communities.' Kenner's concept is based on travel ('"Elsewhere" because you must travel to find it,' he proposes), and the absorption of the experiences that travelling elicits: '"Community" because you become part of it by incorporating it into yourself' (*Elsewhere* 30). According to Kenner, Ezra Pound is the 'greatest example' of the Elsewhere Community and its personification because of his extensive travels in Europe (*Elsewhere* 29).

'We thrive in Elsewhere Communities,' Kenner suggests, 'and there are many ways to search for them' (*Elsewhere* 28). The 'Mimeograph

Revolution' of the 1960s and 1970s—when, as Jerome Rothenberg notes, small presses and little magazines became 'the vortex, the vital center, of their own time & place'—present a later manifestation of Kenner's concept (11). The spreading 'terrain' of small press networks during these decades, which reached 'all the way to Highlands, North Carolina & Kyoto, Japan,' meant that poems could travel even when their authors could not (Rothenberg 10–11). As Stephen Bann suggests, this was a period of considerable movement, 'a movement between countries and continents, undertaken in privileged cases by the poets themselves but in all events by the proliferating little magazines that celebrated international poetic brotherhood' ('Tarasque' 133). During this period the small press publication was as, if not more, likely to become expatriated as much as the poet; particularly so for poets such as Niedecker, whose economic circumstances limited her opportunities for travelling on the scale enjoyed by Pound.

Modest publications also created opportunities for what Kenner considers another notable aspect of Elsewhere Communities, namely 'human collaboration' (*Elsewhere* 124). This, Kenner suggests, 'can sometimes be unconscious, or else as simple and sustaining as the knowledge that we're not alone' (*Elsewhere* 124). The knowledge of not being alone is crucial to the broader dynamics of Jargon's society, as Niedecker's example has indicated. This 'knowledge' is also keenly felt in the work of Niedecker's one-time publisher, the Scottish poet and artist Ian Hamilton Finlay. Wild Hawthorn Press and its flagship magazine, *Poor. Old. Tired. Horse.*, both of which Finlay established with Jessie McGuffie in 1961, are pertinent examples of the collaborative, social, and utopic possibilities of small press publishing. In her letter to Gael Turnbull (6 July 1961), McGuffie writes of wanting 'to try and counteract the terrible depressing kind of writing that always gets published here in Edinburgh these days. I want the series to be non-provincial, but *Scotch* or *American or Wherever-from* art, looking all beautiful with lino cuts too. It's to be called The Wild Hawthorn Press' (cited in Turnbull 35).

As chapter two discusses, the original ethos of the Wild Hawthorn Press was to resist what McGuffie and Finlay, like many of their contemporaries, considered the insular nationalism and parochialism of the poetry associated with the Scottish Renaissance. By publishing an international range of poets that included Niedecker, Zukofsky, Ronald Johnson, Gael Turnbull, Robert Lax, Franz Mon, Ferdinand Kriwet, Pierre Albert-Birot, and Hungarian-French Op-artist Victor Vasarely, Wild Hawthorn established itself as an important cosmopolitan press at the intersection of modern poetry and art.

Although Wild Hawthorn Press would eventually focus on publishing solely Finlay's work, it nevertheless encapsulates the idea of 'Aloneness, yet being part of a community' that Kenner attributes to Elsewhere

Communities (*Elsewhere* 28). The importance of the Wild Hawthorn Press for the remote relations examined in *Avant-Folk* is particularly pronounced when Finlay's long-term agoraphobia and his geographical isolation are considered.[6] Finlay's situation, however, did not prevent him from engaging with, and influencing, an international range of poets and artists:

> Though he does not travel at all in person—he stays at home and minds his own business, that hardest of creative ways of life—his work influences poets everywhere at once. He is a real man of letters in the most exact and useful meaning of the term, and his publishing effort (The Wild Hawthorn Press) is uniquely valuable. (*MB* 12)

'I am only a wee Scottish poet on the outside of everything,' Finlay told Nagy Rashwan in 1996 (n. pag). However, the 'utopic potential' of small press publishing not only made it possible for this 'wee Scottish poet' to influence poets 'everywhere' at the same time, but it also made it possible to facilitate much of the transatlantic dialogue that occurred during the 1960s. Indeed, other than private correspondence, the publication is a place that made it possible for Finlay to not only disseminate his work, but also enter into fruitful dialogue with other peoples'. As Ken Cockburn suggests, Finlay's 'publications formed a crucial part of his engagement with the wider world' and provided 'a "support structure" of like-minded practitioners' (Introduction xvi).

The notion of a utopic 'elsewhere' community is implicitly evoked in the title of Finlay and McGuffie's magazine, *Poor. Old. Tired. Horse.* Although the title might initially suggest the traditional folk song 'Poor Old Horse,' the name actually derives from Robert Creeley's poem 'Please'—'a poem about a horse that got tired. / Poor. Old. Tired. Horse.' (*Collected Poems* 156). Adumbrating the open ethos of Finlay's publishing ventures and their utopian aspirations, Creeley's poem is 'a poem for everyone' whose speaker wants 'to be elsewhere, elsewhere' (*Collected Poems* 156).

The encompassing scope of *Poor. Old. Tired. Horse.*—its openness to 'everyone' and its tacit evocation of a utopian 'elsewhere'—has also been noted by one of its regular contributors, the poet and translator Edwin Morgan:

> Its main aims were (i) to introduce a variety of foreign poets in translation to Scottish readers, (ii) to present a selection of

---

6   With the exception of a brief period in Edinburgh, Finlay lived in various rural parts of Scotland to eventually settle in the remote locality of Dunsyre in Lanarkshire.

good poetry, mainly lyrical, wherever it came from (Scotland, England or America), and (iii) to explore aspects of the visual presentation of poetry through a series of illustrated numbers using drawings, woodcuts, calligraphy, and typographic design. (*'Poor. Old. Tired. Horse.'* 26)

From 1961 to 1967, over the course of 25 issues, Finlay published a diverse selection of 'new' British and American poets that included Niedecker and Williams. It also featured the work of contemporary artists such as Bridget Riley and Ad Reinhardt, concrete and visual poetry, earlier avant-garde icons like Guillaume Apollinaire and Kurt Schwitters, as well as forgotten writers such as Hamish Maclaren. 'In all this,' Morgan proposes, 'there was the desire to keep certain lines of communication open, in particular those from country to country, but also those between poet and artist, and those between present and past' (*'Poor. Old. Tired. Horse.'* 26). Finlay's efforts are pivotal in what Robert Crawford identifies as the 'strand of internationalism' in twentieth-century Scottish literature that 'point[s] not only to the English speaking world, but also to Europe' (and, in Finlay's case, beyond to Brazil and Japan) and which resists 'a narrowing of the imaginative or ideological arteries' (327). Indeed, the scope of *Poor. Old. Tired. Horse.* makes it a prime example of how the small press publication brings together, in terms of time and space, a 'longingly immense' (to invoke Niedecker) range of contributors (*CW* 240).

Mapping Jargon's Society

The 'eastward drift of American poetry' noted by Middleton in relation to Niedecker was reciprocated by a westward drift of British poetry to North America. Charles Tomlinson's collection of poems *Seeing Is Believing*, for example, was initially published in 1958 by the New York publisher McDowell Obolensky, and it was the Chicago magazine *Poetry* that in 1966 first published Bunting's *Briggflatts*. Migrant's publication of Finlay's mimeographed chapbook *The Dancers Inherit the Party* in 1960 also brought him to the attention of American readers: 'The book was great for putting me in touch with people overseas,' Finlay would later tell Williams: 'I remember that Lorine Niedecker wrote, Robert Creeley and Cid Corman also. And you and Robert Duncan' (cited in Hair, 'Models of Order' 182). Finlay's reputation in America would continue with the inclusion of his poetry in little magazines such as Corman's *Origin* in Kyoto, Aram Saroyam's *Lines* in New York City, and Raymond Federman's and Helmut Bonheim's Santa Barbara-based *Mica*. Tellingly, the 'Notes on Contributors' in *Mica* states that 'I. H. FINLAY's reputation in the U.S. is growing every day' (28). Although it would continue to do so steadily throughout the decade, Michael Gardiner's suggestion that there is 'a close relation between Finlay and the Olsonian-Creeley circles' is not strictly accurate (132). Despite his close relations with Williams and

Creeley, as the following chapters discuss, Finlay's poetics contrast considerably with those of Olson and the so-called 'Black Mountain School' of poetry that Olson has become synonymous with. Finlay's work, as we shall see, moved increasingly away from the popular American idioms of the time in favour of a poetry that emphasized order and purity and valued objective construction over subjective expression.

Finlay's early publisher, the aptly named Migrant, is another Westward migrant whose aim was 'to cross-fertilize poetry' and 'encourage English-speaking poets in Britain, Canada, and the US, in particular, to read each other's work' (J. Turnbull, 'The Migrant Years' n. pag). Migrant's founder, Gael Turnbull, had himself experienced a 'migratory past,' living and working as a medical doctor in Canada, the United States, and the United Kingdom (J. Turnbull n. pag). Reflecting on Migrant in the early 1980s, Gael Turnbull admits that he 'was more interested in what might be done with the British end of it' (25). 'I felt exiled in Ventura and it was a way of keeping something going for myself, in contact with poets in both England and Scotland," he writes, although Turnbull was also keen to "create a context that was not narrowly national' (25). Migrant reflected its name by operating from Ventura, California, under Turnbull's care, and from Worcestershire, England where his co-editor, Michael Shayer, was based.

It seems fitting that Migrant's first book, Robert Creeley's *The Whip* (1957), was co-published by three small presses: Migrant, in the United Kingdom, Jargon in the United States, and Contact Press in Canada. Not only did this ensure more extensive distribution for Creeley's book, but it also reaffirms the ways in which poets, publishers, and readers were, in the broadest sense, *co-respondents* of the new poetry. Thus both Migrant press and its eponymous magazine, Richard Price claims, 'became an early and key bridge across the Atlantic between British and American avant-garde writers,' publishing books by a number of American and British poets including Edward Dorn and Roy Fisher ('Migrant The Magnificent' 30). 'The magazine provided an even more focused cross-section of this transatlantic traffic and must,' Price imagines, 'have been an extraordinary eye opener to its readers, welcoming both European and North American poetry in the same breath as it asserted the value of new English and Scottish poetry' ('Migrant The Magnificent' 31). Thus, in 'juxtaposing such figures as Fisher, Finlay, and Edwin Morgan against a work like Olson's *Maximus*,' C. D. Blanton suggests, Migrant not only 'advanced two critical narratives at once, insisting on both the persistent relevance of a modernist style and the linguistic fact of a transatlantic connection,' it also 'recapitulated the founding gesture of a modernist avant-garde, chartering a series of alternative institutions outside the narrower boundaries of canonical taste' (148).

Jonathan Williams's similar traversals between the United Kingdom and North America are evident in *Epitaphs for Lorine*. Williams's poignant introduction is signed with his British address, 'Corn Close, Dentdale, / Sebergh, Yorkshire / England' but the place of publication, printed on the book's title page, is 'Penland North Carolina,' which reflects his own dual residency as well as the scope of Jargon's orbit (n. pag).

The contributions to *Epitaphs* are equally diverse and varied, with British contributors, including Roy Fisher, Christopher Middleton, Stuart Montgomery, Dom Sylvester Houédard, and Gael Turnbull, rubbing shoulders with American writers such as Allen Ginsberg, Denise Levertov, James Laughlin, Charles Reznikoff, and Mary Ellen Solt. One thousand copies of the book were published and privately distributed which, along with the range of contributors, gives some indication of the size of the international readership that Niedecker had accrued by this time.

As well as providing mutual support, the transatlantic exchanges in Jargon's society also prompted the cross-fertilization of poetic modes and styles. Furthermore, these transatlantic exchanges also prompt further questions about regional and national identity. Williams is a prime example of how familiar demarcations become blurred in such a densely networked society such as Jargon's. Is Williams simply an American tourist ensconced in rural Cumbria? A dilettante of its culture, dialect and natural history? Or, is he in fact a transplanted poet? Because of Williams's annual residency in the United Kingdom, we might also consider what effect this might have on the 'American side' of his work, much of which concerns the cultural and topographical environs of the Southern Highlands. Are these dual or, perhaps, competing concerns in Williams's poetry, or are they complementary components of a greater whole that transcends national distinctions? We might also ask whether The Jargon Society is an American or British press, or whether such a question even matters. Perhaps the dual residency of Williams and Jargon is better understood in the context of the 'glocal,' a neologism derived from the world of Japanese business (*dochakuka*), that, according to Robert Eric Livingston, makes visible 'the mutual articulation of [...] two spatial coordinates,' the local and the global, 'and insists 'on the need for a careful rereading of the means of [their] articulation' (147). Thus, unlike his older namesake, William Carlos Williams, Williams's concern is not for the 'intimate, even messy creative contact with specific localities in order for anything like a "national" literature to emerge' (White 68). Indeed, the networked remote relations examined over the course of the following chapters frequently question the very possibility of a national literature. A picture gradually emerges of a utopic network of small presses that, much like Grigson's botanical 'anthropophytes,' is both place-specific yet indefinitely *elsewhere*, thus complicating familiar assumptions regarding regional versus national identity, community, and belonging.

Avant-Folk

The botanical tropes that Williams and Niedecker share not only demonstrate how societal bonds might be reaffirmed within the broader Jargon milieu, but also indicate the prominent role that 'folk' assumes within it.

'Folk' tends to suggest cultural and aesthetic forms such as music, handicrafts, and stories, that are usually transmitted or learnt orally/ aurally and which belong to, or derive from, non-industrial, rural, or proletarian communities. The folklorist Richard M. Dorson has suggested more specifically that the primary concerns of 'folklore and folklife may be placed under four groupings' which 'are not all-inclusive or mutually exclusive': *oral culture* ('spoken, sung, and voiced forms of traditional utterance,' including folksong and folk poetry); *material culture* ('How men and women in tradition-oriented societies build their homes, make their clothes, prepare their food, farm and fish, process the earth's bounty, fashion their tools and implements, and design their furniture and utensils'); *social folk custom* (that emphasizes 'group interaction rather than [...] individual skills and performances'); and *performing folk arts* (the performance of 'traditional dance, music, and drama') (2–5).

All of these 'tradition-oriented' forms, traditions, and practices, as Dorson indicates, fall under the more general term 'folklore,' which also denotes the academic study of them. According to Georgina Boyes, it was E. B. Tylor's two-volume book, *Primitive Culture: Researches Into the Development of Mythology, Philosophy, Religion, Art, and Custom* (1871) that helped create the discipline that is now known as 'folk-lore' (7). Tylor's thesis, Boyes explains, is that 'all cultures evolve in unilinear sequence through stages of savagery and barbarism to civilisation' (7). Consequently, Tylor endeavoured to show how 'residual expressive culture from early stages of the progression "survived" into the civilised era in the form of traditional songs, games, narratives and customs' (Boyes 7).

Tylor's study operates via an essentialist binary of the civilized versus the primitive in which 'folklore' denotes the vestiges of a primitive culture enduring within the civilized present. This perception of folklore illustrates how, as Colin Rhodes explains, the word 'primitive' is often used to distinguish 'someone or something less complex, or less advanced, than the person or thing to which it is being compared':

> It is conventionally defined in negative terms, as lacking in elements such as organization, refinement and technological accomplishment. In cultural terms this means a deficiency in those qualities that have been used historically in the West as indications of civilization. (13)

Although the idea of the primitive is a Western construct for defining non-Western art forms, societies, and technologies, 'the West has long believed that it contains its own primitives—peasant populations, children and the insane' (Rhodes 7). Drawing on Tylor's work, T. F. Thisleton-Dyer in his book *The Folklore of Plants* (1889), for example, distinguishes between 'cultured' and 'lower' or 'savage races' and compares British folk customs and beliefs to 'primitive and uncultured tribes' of the non-Western world (15, 10, 23, 27).

The conflation of folk and primitivism has also been cast in a more romantic light that expresses belief in the 'cultural and spiritual superiority of rural as opposed to town life, the peasant as opposed to the factory worker, the spontaneous simplicity of the folksong as opposed to the sophistication of art music,' frequently lapsing into condescension and essentialism (Boyes 7). 'The folk and their customs,' as Jane S. Becker has shown with regard to the American Folk Revival of the late nineteenth century, were commonly 'identified not only with the past but with groups of racially and ethnically marginalized peoples, generally deemed inferior and backwards' (20).

Hal Foster identifies a similar rhetoric of the 'primitive' in the avant-garde art of the early twentieth century that denotes 'an association of racial others with instinctual impulses' (71–72). 'Primitivism,' however, has informed and shaped the avant-garde in more subtle ways; from the incipient avant-gardism of the Fauves and Cubists and *Der Blaue Reiter Almanach* (*The Blue Rider Almanac*) of Franz Marc and Wassily Kandinsky (which, Jed Rasula notes, included 'Children's drawings; "primitive" artifacts from African, American, and Oceanic cultures; Russian folk icons; and Bavarian glass paintings' alongside examples of Western high art) to Vorticism, Dada, De Stijl, and Constructivism (38). As we shall see, it is this more eclectic line of primitivism and its confluence with avant-garde innovation that has subsequently influenced many of the poets, artists, and publishers examined in *Avant-Folk*.

Niedecker, for example, has claimed Eugene Jolas's avant-garde magazine *Transition* and surrealism as early influences that 'always seemed to want to ride right along with the direct hard, objective kind of writing' that she drew from Pound, Williams, and Zukofsky ('Extracts from Letters to Kenneth Cox' 36). She also told Pound that she felt 'close to Tristan Tzara,' one of the founding figures of Dada and a later affiliate of Surrealism (cited in Niedecker, *New Goose* 9). Niedecker's surrealist mode, according to Peter Nicholls, 'is closer to what has frequently been called "Literary Cubism," a tendency best represented by the poems of Piere Reverdy' than André Breton (198). Nicholls suggests that Niedecker's 'surrealism' is 'a sort of portmanteau word' that conveys 'an alternative non-image based poetics' which runs 'from Gertrude Stein to the Language writers' (196). These distinctions between an Imagist and Objectivist 'direct hard, objective' mode and a 'non-image based poetics' with its roots in the broader avant-garde adumbrate Matei Călinescu's suggestion that, by the second decade of the twentieth century, the avant-garde 'as an artistic concept had become comprehensive enough to designate not one or the other, *but all the new schools*, whose aesthetic programs were defined, by and large, by their rejection of the past and by the cult of the new' (117).

Călinescu's conception of the 'avant-garde' usefully reflects the eclectic avant-garde sensibilities running through *Avant-Folk*. Nevertheless, in over-emphasizing the avant-garde's rejection of the past, as Călinescu does, there is perhaps a danger of forgetting its important backward glances. These glances are especially evident in the Russian avant-garde of the early twentieth century that, as chapter two discusses, influenced Finlay's early poetry. As we shall see, writers and artists such as Natalia Goncharova and Mikhail Larionov found in the Eastern roots of Russian folk art and customs instructive ways for moving beyond the domineering influence of modern Western art.

Folk Revivalism

The confluence of surrealism, objectivism, and folk in Niedecker's poetry reiterates an abiding relationship between modernist literature and folk tradition that can be found in the work of a number of writers including W. B. Yeats, Federico García Lorca, Langston Hughes, Claude McKay, William Carlos Williams, and Hugh MacDiarmid. Niedecker, Finlay and Williams not only continue in this modernist vein but they also revise it, tacitly subverting many of the reductive constructions of 'folk' that gained currency as a result of the various folk revivals that occurred in the late-nineteenth and twentieth century. Indeed, the three folk revivals that occurred in the late nineteenth century and throughout the twentieth in Britain and the United States are especially relevant to the intellectual milieu of *Avant-Folk*.

The first significant period of revivalism that emerged in the last decades of the nineteenth century marks a period when musicologists such as Cecil Sharp and John Avery Lomax were documenting the songs and tunes of disappearing oral folk traditions and cultures. Such activities led to the establishing of folklore as an academic subject and the foundation of scholarly societies such as the American Folklore Society in 1888 and, in the United Kingdom, the Folk-Song Society in 1898. In the case of the British revival, folk song became the raw material and 'major source of the new British [art] music'—particularly the 'pastoral school' associated with composers such as Ralph Vaughan Williams, Arnold Bax, George Butterworth, and Percy Grainger—and helped in cultivating 'a neo-rurality, reworking the heritage of villages, country houses, the rural and the pre-industrial' into idealized images of Englishness (A. Blake 45). Out of this Englishness a 'kind of musical monument was erected,' Michael Brocken suggests, 'upon which a shadow of real and untainted symbolic phantom was projected (but in a constant state of disappearance)' that could all too easily lapse into 'escapist whimsy' or 'hagiography' (3, 10). Nevertheless, as Brocken notes, it was from this 'historical subsoil of folk music revivalism' that 'so much twentieth-century music thought grew,' including the revivals that followed this first phase (3). This 'subsoil' was also a literary one that had its roots, particularly for Vaughan Williams, in English Romantics such as William Blake who, as we shall see, would later become a figurehead for Jonathan Williams's American imaginings of a forgotten English tradition that re-invested the pastoral with a visionary potency.

Niedecker's career spans two periods of American folk revivalism. The first takes place during the 1930s and 1940s and the second occurs approximately from the mid-1950s up to the early 1970s. These periods, as chapter one discusses, are roughly concurrent with the publication of Niedecker's first book, *New Goose*, in 1946 and the renaissance (or 'revival') of her work in the 1960s and 1970s.

The Depression and its aftermath was a motivating force in the first of the two American revivals. According to Jane S. Becker, in the climate of the Depression 'the folk and their traditions seemed to offer Americans the foundations for a way of life that did not rely on material wealth' (5). Gillian Mitchell likewise suggests that during this period 'a mood of introspection and self-analysis prompted a new focus on American culture, particularly that of the "ordinary" people' (26). Such focus was directed emphatically in the projects borne out of the New Deal programme under the auspices of the Works Progress Administration (WPA). As Mitchell notes, many painters, writers, and musicians working for the WPA such as Claude McKay, Zora Neal Hurston, Harry Partch, Kenneth Patchen, and Niedecker, 'drew inspiration from folk idioms and local cultures' (26). Despite, or perhaps because of, this 'thirst for self-knowledge' and a 'desire to learn more about the past as a means of understanding the difficulties of the present,' the revived interest in American folk culture, handicrafts, and music during the 1930s and 1940s also exacerbated the idealization of a vanished rural past (Mitchell 39). However, as we shall see, the poetry that Niedecker produced during this period subverted many of these popular assumptions by invoking folk culture as a contemporary phenomenon that addressed, rather than evaded, the modern world.

As Elizabeth Willis notes, 'Niedecker's renaissance' in the 1960s—'the period of nearly all her book publications, the repeated re-editing and re-arrangement of her poems, and the development of her longer serial works'—parallels the second revival of 'folk and labor concerns' that burgeoned in the late 1950s ('Possessing Possession' 97). Folk dovetailed with poetry considerably during this period as Allen Ginsberg's friendships with Bob Dylan and Harry Smith—the filmmaker, artist, musicologist, and compiler of *The Anthology of American Folk Music* (Folkways, 1952)—attest.[7]

The confluence of folk revivalism and poetry is also evident on the other side of the Atlantic during the 1960s.[8] Echoing the folk revivalist spirit of the period, Tina Morris and David Duncliffe in their magazine *Poetmeat* 'proposed' the name 'The British Poetry Revival' to nominate the wide range of innovative poetry emerging in the United Kingdom on the fringes of the literary mainstream (Sheppard 35). An incipient example of this new British poetry was the Beat-inspired poetry championed by Michael Horovitz in his anthology, *Children of Albion: Poetry of the Underground in Britain* (1969). The provenance of this British equivalent of Allen's *The New American Poetry* can be traced back to the Royal Albert Hall Poetry Incarnation of 1965 where Ginsberg, along with 20 other poets and writers, read to an audience of 8,000 people who, Robert Sheppard notes, were 'predominantly educated (often art-school and working class) [...] with interests in CND, drugs, modern jazz, and street life' (41). However, as guitarist Davy Graham's performance at the event would suggest, folk was another popular interest; no doubt due to its close associations with grassroots protest and political activism as well as its oral nature. Indeed, the latter dovetails markedly with the Beat's preoccupations with the perceived authenticity of the individual's voice and his or her unique speech-rhythms. It is also evident in the spirit of communality and solidarity that spoken performances such as Ginsberg's reading of *Howl* in San Francisco in 1955, and the Poetry Incarnation a decade later, promoted. Indeed, the confluence Beat and folk sensibilities is evident in Horovitz's assertion in *Children of Albion* that although 'none us may be "folk" in 1968' the new poetry retains an 'oralism' that links back to Langston Hughes, the 'long lamented father of jazz-poetry' (335).

Niedecker's rediscovery in the United Kingdom also occurs within the milieu of the postwar Scottish poetry revival, which was at its peak when the Wild Hawthorn Press published *My Friend Tree* in 1961. In the decades following the end of the Second World War, as Richard Blaustein notes, 'Nationalistic feelings were stirring once again in Scotland' and this 'renewed desire for political and cultural autonomy'

---

7   The dovetailing of folk and poetry is also apparent in the figure of Jack Spicer who, in the late 1940s, helped Smith collect records for the *Anthology of American Folk Music* while hosting a weekly folk-ballad radio show on KPFA. 'In the early 1950s, when [Smith's] anthology was released,' as Kevin Killian notes, 'it had the same kind of impact on the music world as *The New American Poetry* did among poets a decade later' (para 10).

8   A later example of this confluence is Gael Turnbull, who was an enthusiast of English folk dance and a member of a Morris troupe.

found expression and confirmation in the country's vernacular heritage and folk music (117). As one of the major proponents of the Scottish Folk Revival, Hamish Henderson suggests, the renewed interest in traditional music and song 'woke many young people, woke them up to the beauty of this vernacular heritage,' including his friend Finlay (cited in Blaustein 117). For Finlay, however, as much as folk confirmed the unique qualities of his country's culture, it would also play a decisive part in his critique of the myopic Scottish nationalism that he believed the Scottish Renaissance promoted.

Despite the close relations that exist between the two key twentieth-century folk revivals and the folk poetry and poetics of Niedecker, Finlay, and Williams, all three of these poets show a more prospective understanding of folk tradition. The work of all three poets confirms Georgina Boyes's claim that 'tradition' is, ultimately, 'a function not of origin, but of continuance' (12). Indeed, Boyes's observation provides a tacit leitmotif throughout the course of *Avant-Folk* with that sentiment of 'continuance' informing the work of Niedecker, Finlay, Williams, and the younger generation of Scottish and English poets, artists, and publishers operating predominantly outside of 'the Children of Albion' axis. These include Stuart Mills, Simon Cutts, and Thomas A. Clark, the main subjects of the last three chapters of *Avant-Folk*.

Out of these poets it is perhaps only Clark, a Scottish poet influenced considerably by Finlay and Niedecker, whose poetry has drawn consistently on folk tradition and music. In contrast, as chapter four explains, Mills and Cutts adopted a Flaubertian 'aesthetic poignancy' that drew on nineteenth-century French literature and aesthetics (*SFA* 45). Clark's early experiences of living briefly with the Scottish psychedelic folk group The Incredible String Band in the late 1960s and his exposure to Finlay's poetry made a significant impression on him and has influenced his longstanding interests in botanical folklore, early Celtic poetry and the *Carmina Gadelica*, vernacular place names, and traditional fiddle music.

Avant-Folk

As well as music, 'folk,' in the wider context of *Avant-Folk*, is also understood in terms of local dialect, vernacular language, found speech, and regional colloquialisms—aspects of which can also be found in Leonard and Morgan. As chapter one argues, Niedecker's incorporations of folk-speech in her poetry not only offers a tacit challenge to the discourses constructing America's folkways at that time, but it is her 'folkbase,' as she would later describe it, that provoked her correspondence with Finlay (cited in Niedecker, 'Letters' 54). As chapter two reveals, the mutual folk sensibilities of Niedecker and Finlay, particularly in their use of folk-speech, brought them into fruitful dialogue through the channels of small press networks. Michael Gardiner claims that there is a tendency 'among even radical American poets' such as Niedecker to 'see [Finlay's] dialects as quaint and earthy' (132). This is not strictly the case, however, as chapter two will show. Niedecker in fact conceived her own poetry in similar terms and sought an 'earthy' idiom for her poetry that she derived from 'everyday speech' (*NCZ* 147). Where Finlay's 'folkbase' does differ from Niedecker's is in his method of using demotic natural speech to deliberately enhance the artifice of his poetic forms. In doing so, as chapter two argues, Finlay's folk idioms and motifs of his early poetry represent an important phase in his move 'away from Syntax towards "the Pure"' in his concrete poetry of the mid-1960s (cited in 'Ian Hamilton Finlay,' *The Tate Gallery* 92).

Chapter three demonstrates how Jonathan Williams's own penchant for 'earthy' language draws on the examples of Niedecker, Finlay, and William Carlos Williams, all of whom provide him useful models for exploring the language and the cultural traditions of his Southern roots. According to Eric Mottram, 'Williams is one of the rare poets whose ear and sense of measure can record the folk without patronizing and without the chill of research' ('Jonathan Williams' 103). Williams finds a summary of his own 'folkbase' in John Clare's poem 'Sighing for Retirement'—'I found the poems in the fields / And only wrote them down'—but, in Williams's case, his fields of discovery are not just rural ones but also the less salubrious corners of his Southern environment (Clare 19). 'I like to get my ear right to the ground and listen to this Nation talk its trash,' Williams writes: 'In certain styles the South is impossible to beat: the billboard, graffito; e.g., like from nature' (*MB* 166).

Whether Niedecker in Blackhawk Island, Finlay in Orkney, or Williams in Appalachia and Cumbria, the dialect poetry of all three poets foregrounds local, place-specific character that reaffirms Donald Davidson's suggestion that regional literature expresses a 'constant tendency to decentralize rather than to centralize; or to correct over-centralization by conscious decentralization' (232). However, while all three poets are geographically situated on the margins of the main urban literary centres of production, it is only Williams who chose to exile himself from the metropolis. 'By 1966 I became Agoraphobic,' he has claimed: 'The agora in Greek is either open space or the market place—it's the latter I fled from' (cited in Annwn, Interview 52). Rural locations such as Highlands in North Carolina and Dentdale in Cumbria offered Williams alternative places for writing, publishing, living, and socializing. Major cities such as London, he believed, were too 'congested, too expensive, too full of coteries and venal ambitions' (cited in Annwn, Interview 51). Thus, as Williams tells David Annwn, from 'a certain remove seems to be the way I operate best' (Interview 54). As chapter three argues, Williams's tendency towards the *eccentric* and the peripheral also manifests in his self-distancing from Black Mountain College (where he studied in the early 1950s) and the 'school' of poetry that he helped foster in the late

1950s. As Schlesinger notes, despite his close associations with the college, Williams was 'pretty much done publishing the Black Mountain poets (as such) by the mid-sixties' and turned his attention to a much more diverse range of poets that included Niedecker and Finlay, and later Clark and Cutts (para 5).

Williams's ambivalent relationship with the so-called Black Mountain poets, particularly his early mentor Charles Olson, as we shall see, shows how his reservations about Black Mountain are indicative of a wider unease about poetic labels and coteries. Chapter three shows how Williams tempered his Black Mountain connections, particularly Olson's overbearing influence, with a number of 'heretical' models that include the poetry of Dame Edith Sitwell and an English visionary tradition with William Blake as its source. By cultivating this eccentric English lineage, it is possible to see Williams expanding his earlier interests in the folkways and folk-speech of his native Appalachia, finding the origins of that mountain-speech in the various regional dialects of England, Wales, and Scotland. As importantly, Williams's increasing interest in the artistic traditions and vernacular folkways of the British Isles would eventually put him in contact with a number of British poets, publishers, and artists who would influence his post-Black Mountain poetics and the publishing activities of Jargon.

Taking this Scottish and English poetry milieu as the main subject, the final three chapters of *Avant-Folk* move away from the more explicit folk themes of revivalism and vernacular language in order to consider the ways in which other familiar folk tropes—craft and cottage industry—have contributed to and informed Jargon's expanded 'society.'

Despite the synonymous links that artisanal crafts such as carpentry, weaving, and printing maintain with folk tradition, such practices from the Arts and Crafts movement onwards have also revealed subtle links with modernism. As Jerome McGann notes, William Morris's Kelmscott Press, as well as being 'part of an effort to return to an earlier, craft-based method of book production' also, as an instigator of the nineteenth century's 'Renaissance of Printing,' pioneered 'conventions of printing and publishing' that 'were taken up and extended by the modernists' (20). Presses like Kelmscott 'encouraged writers to explore the expressive possibilities of language's necessary material conditions,' McGann suggests, and 'supplied artists with a new horizon of bibliographical and institutional possibilities, and [...] many linguistic innovations as well' (20). Furthermore, according to McGann, Jargon has followed the example of Kelmscott by 'disconnect[ing] itself from highly capitalized means and modes of production' (113). By making their authors more involved with the 'material features' of their writing and its 'audience distribution,' modern independent presses such as Jargon, McGann argues, align closely with the social vision of Morris's Kelmscott Press where 'writing is necessarily imagined as part of a social event of persons' and 'forced […] to confront its material, its economic, its social relations' (113).

Tacit connections between traditional craft practice and modernism are also discernible in one of Jonathan Williams's essays on Southern Appalachians handicrafts in which he quotes Harold Rosenberg's speech for the First World Congress of Craftsmen in 1964: 'What defines art as craft is placing the emphasis on the object to the exclusion of the personality of the artist, his uniqueness, his dilemmas' (*MB* 168–169). This emphasis on the impersonality of craft finds a pertinent corollary in earlier modernist modes, particularly the Objectivists' idea of 'the poem as an object' and its concern 'for what is objectively perfect' (Zukofsky, *Prepositions* 15).

Rosenberg's suggestion also recalls Finlay's idea of poetry as an impersonal and autonomous 'model of order' which later influences Stuart Mills's and Simon Cutts's similar concerns for objective form (*AMO* 22). Chapter four delineates Mills's and Cutts's development of 'an objective aesthetic for literature' by examining the growth of their little magazine *Tarasque* and its eponymous press, both of which functioned out of 'a belief in craft and a high degree of resource' (*SFA* 50; 'The Weather House' n. pag). By promoting a formally objective poetics, as chapter four argues, *Tarasque* also established an incisive critical response to the mimeo revolution of the 1960s. This period witnessed a boom in cottage-industry style small press publishing when, as Geraldine Monk recalls, a 'flurry of indecipherable mimeo magazines became an avalanche' (189). A consequence of this 'avalanche' was the amount of poorly produced magazines that indiscriminately printed questionable writing. Mills sums up the situation accurately while reflecting on the positive qualities of small press publishing which, he believes, were scant by comparison:

> It seems to me that this consistent difference, which marks the more interesting publications, is one component which makes the whole activity viable. In the Sixties there was not enough of it (at least one could not easily find it), but then the Sixties, as David Briars says, was the 'great boom time' for small magazines and, as in most gold rushes, there was more dust than gold being kicked up. ('From Tarasque to Aggie Weston's' 141)

The formal objectivity that *Tarasque* promoted as an alternative to the excessive 'dust' of the mimeo revolution has, as chapters five and six propose, extended significantly to encompass the very format, the edited space, that the poem takes. Indeed, an emphatic aim of *Avant-Folk* is to stress the importance that a more disciplined and modest approach to small-scale, small press publishing has assumed within Jargon's society, both in terms of a formal poetics and as a social medium and facilitator.

The small press publishers examined in *Avant-Folk*—namely, Finlay's Wild Hawthorn Press, Mills's and Cutts's Tarasque Press, Thomas A. and Laurie Clark's Moschatel Press, and Cutts's Coracle Press—have, to various extents, operated from domestic spaces and utilized small, manageable printing technologies such as table-top Adanas and inkjet printers. These relatively modest printing technologies have been instrumental in formulating these presses' respective poetics. 'The confines of doing such work domestically were many,' Kay Roberts (artist and co-founder with Cutts of Coracle) recalls: 'size was determined mainly by our interest in the domestic scale but limits of time and space kept down the edition numbers and quantity of finished books' (10). However, economic frugality and the limited availability of material has not hindered such publishing activities but actually enhanced them. 'The potentiality of publication as form is inexhaustible,' Cutts proposes, and who continues 'to elevate the idea of its availability beyond the mere pragmatism of economics, warehousing and distribution': 'Having built such means, by economic frugality, by persistence, by the way you live, it is possible for the small publisher to move deftly for each new publication,' he reasons (*SFA* 11).

Many of these qualities are shared by the Clarks' Moschatel Press (named after the woodland flower *Adoxa moschatellina*) which they established in 1973 in Nailsworth, Gloucestershire. The Clarks' choice of name saliently reflects their emphasis on the small scale. 'In the language of flowers,' Alan Tucker suggests, Moschatel 'is the symbol [...] of scintillating modesty, a scintilla being a small quantity, an atom, a spark' (142). That refined but potent 'modesty' is extended in what Cutts considers the Clarks' 'sublime austerity of means and format within and without the dictates of their table-top printing press' and, more recently, the inkjet printer (*SFA* 73). According to Thomas A. Clark such frugal 'self-publishing can constitute not a vanity but a freedom':

> Instead of being dependent on a weighty external agency, an industry, the poet can take the whole thing into his own hands. The means become creative. Everything can be exact but also light, since production is a way of life, an activity rather than an occasion. ('An Inconspicuous Green Flower' 144)

This idea of 'production as a way of life' suggested by both Clark and Cutts re-asserts self-publishing as a cottage industry in which these activities are not ancillary to everyday life but an integral part of it.

Emphasizing domestic economies and practices, Cutts proposes that 'through gardening, cooking, and making books there [is] an entire directive as the course of education, encompassing mathematics, the natural and physical sciences, poetry, literature, visual art and design, and construction' (*SFA* 11). Indeed, Coracle is a pertinent example of how integrated work and home can be. Recalling Coracle's first location—'a milliner's shop in a Georgian terrace in South London, perfectly suited for a gallery'—the former Coracle partner, writer, and poet John Bevis has noted how 'the integration, or rather reintegration of the living and working, visual and written, decorative and functional' modalities of the operation, 'allowed the playing out of a very direct conceptual exchange: gallery walls as pages, and the book as a pocket exhibition' ('A Star-gazey Pie' 37). Indeed, in its function as both press and gallery, much of the work that Coracle has published or exhibited has often been prompted by or responsive to the unique properties of a particular environment, region, or building.

In 1988 the American artist and writer Erica Van Horn joined Cutts as co-director of Coracle. Despite the centrality of the book in their own work, as well as for Coracle more generally, Cutts and Van Horn 'are not so much concerned with craft-traditions of limitedness of edition, hand-made papers and elaborate binding, as [they are] with the plain-ness of the simple case-bound book and sewn paperback, and their availability' (Cutts and Van Horn, 'Coracle' n. pag). This printing ethos, however, stretches back to the earlier phases of Coracle when it was based in London and Norfolk and their use of local small family printing firms such as Edward Wells & Sons in Camberwell and Crome & Akers in Kings Lynn, Norfolk. 'They both had letterpress and offset printing,' Cutts recalls, 'and both produced in the main vernacular jobs for the locality—raffle and club tickets, cattle-market posters, and all manner of stationary for weddings and funerals' ('The Norfolk Years' 15). However, working with such 'vernacular' trades firms and other print manufac-turers—'box-makers, block-makers, paper merchants and engravers, makers of cutters, creasers, and die-formes that could be stamped in the press'—provided Coracle a creative impetus that expanded, rather than diminished, the innovations of its own in-house printing ('The Norfolk Years' 15). 'The ideal was never *belle livres*,' Kay Roberts insists with regard to the early years of the press: 'the commercial printer a few doors down the road provided real possibilities' (10).

As the title of Roberts's essay 'House as Format' suggests, the space and economies of domestic living have been an integral factor of Coracle's poetics which have brought notions of warmth, intimacy, dwelling, and social company into the arena of contemporary art as an alternative to the cold, indifferent space of the traditional gallery. This domestic context is extended considerably in the work of Van Horn that often constructs narratives 'around the incidental parts' of her life (Van Horn cited in Kuhl, *The Book Remembers Everything* 7). As Nancy Kuhl notes, Van Horn 'regularly draws the subject of her work directly from the fabric of her daily life, the domestic and artistic work, the simple household objects at hand, the day-to-day aspects of familiar relationships' (10). Such attention to 'significant but often unnoticed habits and customs of family and friendship, the exquisite qualities of home, the work of making art' are keenly felt in Van Horn's documented experiences of living in Tipperary (Kuhl 10). These writings and visual works cover a range of everyday subjects that include the customs and etiquette of serving tea, local sayings, idiosyncratic road signs, bus timetables, and recipes for elderflower cordial. As Susan Howe remarks in her forward to *Living Locally*, a selection of entries from Van Horn's diary, 'Erica Van Horn has produced a meticulous field guide of what it means to be an American discovering the embedded, entangled mysteries of being Irish' ('Foreword' 5). Close in spirit to Niedecker's writing, particularly her homemade gift-books such as *A Cooking Book*, Van Horn's observations often occur within unassuming everyday domestic contexts that subtly and modestly reassert the home as a site of interpersonal and creative significance and a vital source of art and making. As Bevis points out, Coracle has practiced a 'non-ironic engagement in artisan arts, crafts, cooking, etc., which,' he believes, 'recalls some of the deep south interventions of Jargon Society' ('A Star-gazey Pie' 76). Perhaps Bevis has in mind Jargon's bestselling book, Ernest Matthew Mickler's *White Trash Cooking* (1986), another compelling document of late-twentieth century American vernacular culture that, as its title suggests, offers an unsentimental yet sympathetic representation of its rural southern subject.

The domestic values underpinning Coracle's activities are also implicit in the partnerships that structure many of the small presses examined in *Avant-Folk*: Ian Hamilton and Sue Finlay (Wild Hawthorn); Thomas A. and Laurie Clark (Moschatel); Jonathan Williams and Thomas Meyer (Jargon); and Simon Cutts and Erica Van Horn (Coracle). Such partnerships recall Zukofsky's comments in his writings for the New Deal Arts project, the *Index of American Design*, regarding how, in the milieu of pre-twentieth-century craft work, male artisans 'were likely to be found working on something at home, and for their homes, side by side with their wives'—a situation not too dissimilar to the Zukofskys' own (*A Useful Art* 101).

This domestic situation is expanded considerably in Cutts's poem 'A Smell of Printing,' which conflates home cooking with home printing:

> a smell of printing
> in the kitchen from
>
> packets of unfolded
> paper wrapped in

ribbed manila:
uncollated pages

gathered in sections
& sewn after dinner (*A Smell of Printing* 11)

As well as conflating familiar kitchen activities with printing—cooking aromas replaced by the smell of printing, and packets of ingredients substituted for packets of paper—Cutts's poem also draws attention to the subversive potential of domestic printing. The poem alludes to a photograph, used for the cover of Cutts's book, *A Smell of Printing*, of 'Madame Desvignes in her kitchen stitching the first volumes from *Les Editions de Minuit*' (Cutts, *A Smell of Printing*, front flap). As Edward Wright explains, Desvignes was part of the French Resistance's '*Imprimeries Clandestines*, the clandestine press in Paris, in Lyon, in Toulouse [which comprised a] team of writers, printers, bookbinders and their friends who then undertook the dangerous task of distribution, usually by bicycle' (86). Jean Bruller's novel *Le Silence de la mer* (*The Silence of the Sea*) was the first of the Paris-based *Editions de Minuit*. Written during the summer of 1941 and published in early 1942 under the pseudonym Vecors, the book's story of French resistance against German occupation made it a subversive book in occupied France that put the lives of its author, publishers, and distributors at considerable risk. 'The printer Claude Oudeville hand set, printed, and redistributed the type for each page during the two-hour break in his workshop,' Wright explains, whereas 'the sheets were folded and stitched in the kitchen of the Desvignes' apartment' (86). Cutts's poem therefore offers a pertinent reminder that the domestic space is not divorced from the larger political forces outside of it; a point that Niedecker's poetry, as chapter one argues, also repeatedly asserts.

The social possibilities of small-scale, domestic-based publishing are examined in chapter five in the context of an informal series of pastoral-themed poems, cards, and booklets that Finlay, Clark, and Cutts have produced intermittently over the past four decades. Infrequently misconstrued, simplified, or disparaged as a naive and idealistic form that nostalgically romanticizes a lost rural world of retreat and simplicity, pastoral can easily be seen as a precursor to revivalist folk nostalgia. However, conscious of pastoral's complex artifice, many of the poets working within the extended milieu of Jargon's society have knowingly exploited the fictive veracity of the tradition and its familiar tropes in order to facilitate and reaffirm notions of kinship, filiation, and collaboration. If, in the course of the twentieth-century's folk revivals, the 'structural necessity' of folk culture was its 'threatened presence,' which, Boyes argues, 'had to be revived through reperformance,' then for the subjects of chapter five the *imagined* landscape of Arcadia and its *imagined* possibilities provide an equivalent site for the re-evocation, reiteration, and renewal of specific social values (Boyes 18). For this reason, the placeless landscape of Arcadia provides a pertinent analogy for Moeglin-Delcroix's 'utopic' interspaces of the small press publication. Furthermore, it is possible to see in Williams's and subsequently Finlay's, Clarks's, Cutts's seemingly playful allusions to the Victorian landscape painter Samuel Palmer, the suggestion of a visionary pastoral tradition, centred around the figure of William Blake, that Ralph Vaughan Williams had already rediscovered in the British folk revival of the nineteenth and early twentieth centuries. 'The composer, an admirer of and successor to Palmer and Blake,' Wilfrid Mellers suggests, 'lived at a time when the dire as well as beneficial effects of industrialization foreseen by Blake as bard and prophet, seemed inescapable' (141). Yet, as Mellers emphasizes, 'Vaughan Williams did not advocate escape; he rather showed how, in a world changing with bewildering rapidity, hope may reanimate tradition, while tradition succours hope' (141).

Chapter six shifts attention away from the imagined landscapes of Arcadia to examine instead the lived and embodied landscapes that Coracle has engaged with over the last four decades. As this chapter argues, Coracle's longstanding interest in marginal topographies and their representation can be read as critical response to traditional literary and visual representations of landscape. 'Landscape—the art world's code for nature—has become an awkward term for us,' David Reason suggests in the Coracle book *The Unpainted Landscape* (25). This important book in the Coracle narrative, which includes contributions from Jonathan Williams and Thomas A. Clark, provides the thematic backdrop to chapter six as 'a measure of the force of the ethical imperatives which are inescapable in considering landscape art today' (Reason, 'A Hard Singing of Country' 25). Expanding on the ideas set out in *The Unpainted Landscape*, chapter six examines how the work of various individuals who have worked closely with Coracle—Cutts, Van Horn, Colin Sackett, Stephen Duncalf, and Richard Long—have responded to the 'ethical imperatives' of landscape representation via the 'alternative spaces' of small press publishing and how they have critically revised traditional literary and artistic representations of landscape. Chapter six endeavours to show how marginal and vernacular spaces— particularly the interfacial spaces and landscapes of suburbia—have been reinvested as culturally significant spaces via the modest means of the small press publication, the material conditions of the printed page, and site-specific installations.

Williams has claimed with regard to his Appalachian environs that, 'the society I live in is a non-Quaker society of friends' comprising 'some several thousand persons and some few landscapes' (*MB* 164). That society and its landscapes, as the book's coda concludes, have expanded considerably under the auspices of Jargon's wider transatlantic small press network that *Avant-Folk* attempts to map and explicate. Indeed, Williams's tacit suggestion of a social landscape in his 'non-Quaker society of friends' returns to the theme of 'folk.' Only this time, the word connotes friendship and an informal collective or 'tribe' of kindred spirits and sensibilities, and recalls how, as Alison Dundes Renteln notes, the 'folk [is] any group of people whatsoever who share a common linking factor,' whether it be nationality, religion, ethnicity, occupation, locality, or family (1–2).

The main common linking factor for the 'avant-folk' of the present book is the mutual publishing ethos that values the importance of the small scale and its ability to overcome spatial and temporal distance. Indeed, it is the *little* magazine and the *small* press publication that have most effectively overcome the considerable distances that encompass Jargon's transatlantic society, both geographically and stylistically, and, to recall Niedecker's metaphor, connected otherwise isolated dots on the page. Out of that society, as Dale Smith suggests, it is Jargon itself which most formatively 'established a model for how to build a community of writers from the ground up' and highlighted the 'numerous possibilities available to other artists intent on keeping alive the various folkways and urbane intelligences that commingle in the local attention of the artist' (para 1). As we shall now see, all of the little magazines and printed platforms examined in *Avant-Folk*, following Jargon's example, have established their own 'utopic' landscapes and 'elsewhere communities' without losing sight (or compromising the sites) of their immediate locales and social topographies.

Chapter One

The Avant-Folkways of Lorine Niedecker

Old songs, old stories, old sayings, old beliefs, customs, and practices—the mindskills and handskills that have been handed down so long that they seem to have a life of their own, a life that cannot be destroyed by print but that constantly has to get back to the spoken word to be renewed; patterned by common experience; varied by individual repetition; inventive or forgetful; and cherished because somehow characteristic or expressive: all this, for want of a better word, is folklore.

—B. A. Botkin, *The American People: In Their Stories, Legends, Tall Tales, Traditions, Ballads and Songs*

In her 1944 essay, 'Popular and Unpopular Poetry in America,' the poet Louise Bogan bemoans how 'folk' has become 'genteelized and sentimentalized so that at present it bears little relation to the rough, living stuff it once was' (90). There is, Bogan claims, 'a real desire to return to our more primitive art' because of 'a definite suspicion, in the minds and hearts of many Americans, that something we once had—something we once were—has disappeared' (89). However, as Bogan notes, this desire to retrieve what was 'once had' has prompted vain attempts 'to get back to simplicity by *playing* at simplicity' and 'by imitating the surface manners of the folk tradition' (87). This play-acting never really works because 'it results in some charming "pastoral" decoration, but in no profound art' (87).

According to Bogan, two modernist poets who 'succeeded in getting back to a folk tradition in their respective countries' were W. B. Yeats, who 'went back to the peasant songs and stories' of Ireland, and Federico García Lorca, who 'went back to the flamenco tradition' (88). Bogan believes that Yeats and Lorca were successful in going 'back' to their respective folk traditions because 'both poets were dealing with cultures that had escaped, in large measure, any true industrial development' (88). However, Bogan's claims regarding Yeats's and Lorca's appropriations of folk tradition are as revealing, if not more so, of her own problematic assessment of the term 'folk.' Emphasizing how both poets 'went *back*' to their folk traditions, Bogan reinforces the common stereotype of folk as a primitive and anachronistic cultural phenomenon that has been compromised and diminished by technological progress and 'industrial development.' 'Is it not true that most of our primitive folk art has been pretty thoroughly absorbed into our middle-class mores, our bourgeois tradition?' Bogan asks (89). The repeated use of the word 'primitive' in Bogan's essay to extol the virtues of folk—its 'vigor' and its 'rough gaiety'—does in fact reiterate the distorted perceptions and appropriations of folk that she seeks to redress (89):

> Our rural and primitive past, with all its richness of song and history and tall tale and picaresque narrative—it is so near to us, and yet it is difficult to conjure up, to tie in with our mechanized and urban present. It is so difficult to make it the basis of our creative work. (88)

Thus, in 'Popular and Unpopular Poetry in America,' Bogan represents folk as the cultural expression of a bygone preindustrial era; a simple, crude, rural existence, that contrasts markedly with the knowing, urbane bourgeoisie of modern industrialist society. Bogan may note how 'during certain uncreative periods, the taste and the need for folk expression becomes so strong that people begin not only to *play-act* "folk," but to *manufacture* it artificially,' but her own perception of folk is, ultimately, also a projection and a construction (88).

'*Folk* and *tradition* are,' the historian Jane S. Becker argues, 'ideological categories that are culturally and socially constructed, their meanings and uses fluid and vulnerable to manipulation' (39). In the late nineteenth and early twentieth centuries, Becker explains, folk was constructed 'as a critical response to America's industrialist–capitalist society and its culture of consumption':

> Those in search of the nation's folk often sought out people who, they imagined, lived in tightly knit societies, close to the soil, where life more closely resembled a preindustrial and precapitalist ideal. Folkways, these same individuals thought, flourished in simple societies not dominated by industrial organization and production; in such worlds, communications were presumably personal and informal, the community took care of its members, human and spiritual values reigned, and beauty and value lay in carefully crafting from raw goods the material necessities of everyday domestic life. (3–4)

There is a certain irony that this grass-roots alternative to consumerism would itself become a lucrative commodity during the 1930s and 1940s when interest in America's folkways peaked:

> This was the decade of—to name only a few examples—the National Folk Festival, photographs of Walker Evans, Russell Lee, and Dorothea Lange documenting the everyday life and customs of America's common people, songs of labor and life by Woody Guthrie and Aunt Molly Jackson, Thomas Hart Benton's vivid paintings of the nation's vernacular culture set in localized landscapes, and Zora Neal Hurston's renderings of African American folktales, the *Grand Ol' Opry*, the description and celebration of the nation's regions and communities in the Federal Writers' Project's American Guide Series, and the enshrinement of American decorative arts in the images compiled for the Index of American Design. (Becker 12)

This was also the decade when 'Americans could comfortably purchase their traditions (and thereby the spirit of their nation) in the form of goods and entertainments rendered familiar enough to be comfortable—handcrafted blankets and woven coverlets from the Appalachian mountains or the rural southern music broadcast on popular radio shows—yet steeped in an "authenticity" that placed them presumably outside of the commercial world' (Becker 38). This celebration and consumption of the nation's folkways are further instances of Bogan's assertion that many Americans in the 1930s and 1940s were trying to reclaim an imagined way of life that was 'once had' and now fast 'disappearing' in the shadows of the Great Depression. It is not surprising, therefore, that the perceived rural, primitive innocence of America's folkways offered a reassuring and attractive alternative to a modern world blighted by economic disaster, failing industrialist and capitalist systems, and ambiguous technological advancement.

However, as Becker notes, it was not so much a pristine past that Americans were returning to, but rather an established 'ideological construction' that had initially emerged in the late-nineteenth century (21). This construction equated '"traditional" with "backward" and "modern" with "advanced" or "wealthy" or "rational"' and had its roots in a 'pastoralism' that was 'formed by the illusory conception of the transition from rural to industrial society as a fall from innocence into disorder and the assumption that we must look back to the past to find an organic society' (Becker 21). 'The remembered past,' as Becker stresses, 'must lack specificity' and 'many of the facts of country life must be denied or ignored,' including 'the historical role played by capitalism and the complex economic and social forces and conflicts that it generated in both rural and urban environments' (21). It was this 'pastoralism' that 'shaped the thinking of intellectuals and popularizers of the folk in the 1930s,' and made 'primitivism,' 'nostalgia,' and 'isolation' ubiquitous tropes in the construction of America's folk and their folkways during this period (Becker 21, 24).

The poetry that Jenny Penberthy describes as Lorine Niedecker's 'folk period,' approximately between 1936 and 1945, not only corresponds with this period of folk revivalism, but also tacitly questions the ideological constructions that underscore it (*CW* 372). As the present chapter will show, Niedecker's poetry offers one possible answer to the question with which Bogan opens 'Popular and Unpopular Poetry in America': 'What has happened to what was once called "folk song" or "folk poetry"? Into what has it been transformed, if it no longer appears to us in the colors it once wore, in the situation it once held?' (84). Niedecker's writing also questions the validity of the concept of 'folk poetry,' at least in respect of the terms proposed by Bogan (84). As Peter Middleton suggests, 'by the definitions of the folklorists,' Niedecker evades the category of 'folk poet':

> She kept her poetry secret from the local community, she avoided the clichés and the stereotyped forms that folk poets tend to use, and she was published in the most prestigious avant-garde journals. ('Lorine Niedecker's "Folk Base"' 181)

Niedecker's poetry also undermines the dichotomies that underpin the pervasive ideological construction of American folk in the twentieth century—notions of the regional versus the cosmopolitan and the modern versus the traditional—as well as Bogan's distinctions regarding 'formal' or 'classic' folk poetry versus more 'popular' variants (84). The vanguard spirit of Niedecker's folk sensibilities can be seen as significantly revising folk as a modern, outward-looking phenomenon that is critically aware of, and responsive to, contemporary issues and, as we shall see, international affairs. Furthermore, such 'avant-folkways,' as they might be termed, are very much integral to the cosmopolitan and socially encompassing scope of Niedecker's poetics. These societal implications become especially evident in the 1960s when Niedecker's folk sensibilities played a defining role in her own 'renaissance' across the Atlantic—more specifically, in England and Scotland—via the channels of small press networks and the mutual folk sensibilities that motivated them.

Niedecker and the Federal Writers' Project

It was during her 'folk period' that Niedecker wrote the poems that would comprise her first collection *New Goose*, which the Press of James A. Decker published in 1946. In many of these poems Niedecker incorporates the idioms of the 'local speech habits' and the 'local history' of her own Fort Atkinson and Blackhawk Island communities (*CW* 372). Recalling the folk-figure of 'Mother Goose' and the fairytales and nursery rhymes attributed to that character by Charles Perrault and other writers, the title *New Goose* tacitly acknowledges Niedecker's use of certain vernacular and folk sources in her poems. In particular, as Michael Davidson notes, many of the poems 'self-consciously deploy folk idioms and ballad meters' ('Life by Water' 8). However, as Peter Middleton suggests, Niedecker's 'active interest in folklore [also] creates a radically innovative form of poetry' with its roots firmly set in American modernist modes ('Lorine Niedecker's "Folk Base"' 170). Writing in 1966 to Kenneth Cox 20 years after the publication of *New Goose*, Niedecker recalls how she 'literally went to school to William Carlos Williams and Louis Zukofsky' and explains how 'my first book ... is based on the folk—and a desire to get down direct speech (Williams influence) and here was my mother, daughter of the rhyming happy grandfather [...] speaking whole chunks of down-to-earth (o very earthy) magic, descendent for sure of Mother Goose' ('Extracts' 36). Thus, *New Goose*, as the 'new' in the title indicates, shows Niedecker renewing a vernacular folk tradition that was very much in her blood. Although, as Jenny Penberthy suggests, Niedecker's 'poetry based on transcribed vernacular led her back to her own biological folk,' it is also important to remember that it did so via the lessons she acquired from her modernist models (*NCZ* 41). In particular, Niedecker's ear for the 'irregular sounds of living speech' places her in the kindred company of her older contemporary William Carlos Williams and his 'slantwise relationship to the linguistic world around him' (*NCZ* 43; North 15). As we shall see, *New Goose* is a prime example of how, as Penberthy claims, Niedecker's poetry 'offer[s] a rich subtle study of folk habits made by a poet with twin allegiances to a rural backwater and a metropolitan avant-garde' (*CW* 6).

According to Penberthy, the folk strategies of *New Goose* were influenced considerably by Niedecker's employment with the Federal Writers' Project (FWP), which lasted from 1938 to 1941 (*CW* 372). Specific information on Niedecker's employment with the FWP in Madison is scant (Peters 60). Michael Davidson believes that many of Niedecker's *New Goose* poems 'were written concurrently with [her] work for the Federal Writers' Project in its American Guide Series for which Niedecker contributed to *Wisconsin: A Guide to the Badger State*' ('Life by Water' 8). However, according to Niedecker's biographer Margot Peters, 'Lorine didn't contribute to the *Wisconsin Guide* but fourteen signed check sheets for biographies of state leaders like Steven Faville (dairy pioneer), Jason Downer (Downer Seminary and College) and Increase Lapham (naturalist) survive,' the latter of which comprises the subject of Niedecker's poem, 'Asa Gray wrote Increase Lapham' (Peters 63; *CW* 105).

Despite Peters's suggestion, it is still likely that Niedecker was, in some capacity, involved with the publication of the *Wisconsin* guide in 1941. This likelihood is enhanced considerably by the fact that the book is a collective and anonymously authored project that does not acknowledge any of the researchers or writers involved in its production. If Niedecker was part of this collective effort, then this involvement presents a further instance of what Rachel Blau DuPlessis describes as Niedecker's strategies of 'anonymity': 'This is both an advantage and a fate,' DuPlessis reasons, believing that Niedecker used this condition 'to turn the non-elite, non-hegemonic literary career (anonymity, erasure, loss) to an accepted fate' by ultimately 'disappear[ing] into the folk from whom she came' ('Lorine Niedecker' 118). This strategic 'fate' pertinently recalls the anonymity of the folk ballad and the creative commons of the oral culture of folklore and literature as defined by Botkin. According to the folklorist B. A. Botkin, 'what makes a thing folklore, is not only that you have heard it before yet want to hear it again, because it is different, but also that you want to tell it again in your own way, because it is anybody's property' (*The American People* 11).

This idea also encompasses what Botkin calls 'folk literature': 'a species of living literature which has no fixed form [...] and which is constantly shifting back and forth between written and unwritten tradition' (*The American People* 12). Niedecker's 'tactics' of anonymity, as DuPlessis understands them, draw a number of pertinent parallels with such folk literature ('Lorine Niedecker,' 119). In particular, Niedecker's methods of 'presenting [poems] repeatedly in different contexts, not always seeking newness, but multiple tellings,' and her occasional tendencies to publish 'different versions of some poems,' as DuPlessis notes, 'are similar to multiple transmissions of an oral tradition, but play havoc with the print institution of copy text and the authorial ego-frame of "final intentions"' ('Lorine Niedecker' 119). Niedecker's poetry may not share the same aversion to print that Botkin lists as one of his defining traits of folklore in *The American People*, but, by Niedecker's own admission, her writing also expresses a need 'to get back to the spoken word to be renewed' (xxiii–xxiv). As she once reflected in a letter to Zukofsky:

> I don't know how the old time poets did it—the poetic vein was the soft spoken, hushed, sweet-worded kind of thing, almost artificial, but maybe in their own time it was earthy enough for poetry ... now I find when one hasn't been writing for a while, you start off in something like that soft vein, but as soon as you get used to writing again, you pick up everything for poetry, get into everyday speech etc. (*NCZ* 147)

As we shall see, it is this character of Niedecker's poetry, her incisive use of everyday speech—her attention to vernacularisms and colloquialisms, idiosyncratic turns of phrase, dialect, and the homophonic ambiguity of the oral—that, while resisting the kinds of closure and finality that

Botkin associates with printed text, also ensures her poetry does not stagnate in tired, sentimentalized, or paternalistic clichés of 'the folk' and their speech habits.

In addition to focusing her attention on her own local environs and reaffirming her poetic anonymity, Niedecker's work for the FWP may very well have influenced her progressive attitudes regarding American folkways. As one of five projects collectively known as 'Federal One' that was commissioned by the Work Projects Administration, the FWP was a New Deal programme that 'provided jobs for unemployed professional and white-collar workers' during the Depression (Peters 60). As Jerrold Hirsch explains, 'formulated in the context of national depression, New Deal recovery programs, and the growing crisis in international relations,' the FWP was concerned primarily with 'celebrating the idea of a people's demotic culture' by creating 'a history of America that paid attention to the great majority of people, particularly those on the lowest social rungs: the workers, the poor, and the ethnic and racial minorities' (*Portrait* 18, 23, 12). According to Hirsch, the FWP made 'the democratic assumption that the source of society's creative expressions' were to be found in its 'ordinary citizens, not in it genteel classes—in the folk culture, not in refinement' (*Portrait* 22). While this may seem to recall Bogan's misgivings about a 'genteelized and sentimentalized' art and literature and her endorsement of 'folk vigor,' what sets the FWP apart from these broader ideologies of the folk revival of the 1930s is the liberal vision that its officials such as Botkin, Sterling A. Brown, and Morton Royse promoted (Bogan 90). Hirsch describes these officials as being 'romantic nationalist, cultural pluralist, and cosmopolitan [in their] orientation,' quick 'to treat a pluralistic culture as a positive aspect of modernity,' and to recognize 'cultural diversity, as a fact and (in their view) as a positive value' (*Portrait* 23, 4):

> As romantic nationalists FWP officials assumed that the study of the experience of ordinary Americans would contribute to a revitalized national culture; as pluralists they believed all groups had to be taken into account, and as cosmopolitans they hoped the various diverse groups that constituted America could benefit from learning about fellow citizens who were different from themselves. (*Portrait* 22)

Botkin, for example, according to Hirsch, 'thought that listening to the voice of the people such as former slaves could not only change the way Americans understood the past but also help create a better future' (*Portrait* 12). 'Botkin did not look at folk traditions for evidence of what culture was like in some pristine age before it was attested by outside forces,' Hirsch suggests, but saw in them the means for addressing and 'understanding how cultures respond to urbanization and industrialization' ('Folklore in the Making' 3). It was in this spirit that the FWP not only attempted to 'rediscover America' but also 'redefine it' by embracing and learning from the diversity of its vernacular cultures (*Portrait* 18). Thus, by documenting and understanding the diversity of America's vernacular history in this way, the FWP significantly reassessed American folk as a cultural phenomenon that faced the future while acknowledging the past.

'Homely and Honest'

Like many commentators of Niedecker's work, Elizabeth Willis has noted how Niedecker's reception has been coloured by the 'pastoral inclination[s]' of many of her readers who liked to think of her as 'an anomalous rural savant' ('Introduction,' xiii). This inclination to portray Niedecker as a literary equivalent of the popular folk-artist Grandma Moses has also been noted by the writer Gilbert Sorrentino. The subjects of Niedecker's poems, he notes, are frequently depicted as 'a self situated within a projected—and poetic—rural or semirural landscape, for the most part. Her poems live there, or gaze back at this landscape as a reference point' (288). However, as Sorrentino notes, the 'urge to sentimentalize these invariable bucolics is overwhelming' (288). Equally problematic, however, is the urge to sentimentalize Niedecker's difficult life, so that 'the floor-scrubbing, flood-awaiting figure of the poet can be construed as a suffering mandarin' (Sorrentino 289). These sentimentalized images of the suffering poet have had a negative influence on the way that Niedecker's poems have been read and valued. Thus, the more 'Niedecker's poems are recognized as exquisite,' Sorrentino notes, 'the more are they presented as transcending the wretchedness of their genesis' (289).

Such bucolic projections of the 'homely and honest Lorine' recall those of 'the mythical mountain artisan' that became popular in the folk and crafts revival of the 1930s when Appalachia became 'a crucible of the nation's past' (Sorrentino 287; J. S. Becker xi, 42). This is especially apparent, to take one example, in Allen H. Eaton's idealized depiction of the Southern Highlander in his popular book *Handicrafts of the Southern Highlands* (1937). Eaton articulates a rhetoric of dignified hardship similar to the more paternalistic accounts of Niedecker's difficult and isolated life:

> The Southern Highlander and his family are probably as nearly self-sustaining as any group of our population. This is far from saying that his economic standard of living is to be compared with that in other parts of our country; it does indicate, however, that he gets along with a minimum of outside help and that his wants are few and simple. That this is so is due to the fact that many things, which most of

us think, we should have, mean little to him, partly because his point of view, often religious, makes him feel that material possessions are an encumbrance to the soul, and mainly, perhaps, because there is really nothing much that can be done about it. These men and women have literally wrung their living from the soil, and usually it is scant soil and low of fertility. (30–31)

Despite these hardships facing the 'simple,' honest, hardworking Highlander, Eaton still provides his urban reader (subtly demarcated in Eaton's use of the pronoun 'us'), with an appealing image of a 'primitive,' yet bucolic, life—

> where plowing is done with oxen, where the family water supply comes from the old spring, with the old gourd dipper always in reach, where carding and spinning are done by hand and weaving on looms of ancient type, where herbs are gathered for medicine, and barks, roots, and flowers for dyeing yarn, where honey is stored in beegums made by hollowing out a log, where planting is done according to the light or dark of the moon and where grain is cut with the cradle. (31)

According to Rayna Green, Eaton's romanticizing of the Highlanders can be explained partly because his book 'belongs to the post-Depression period, a period when rural nostalgia and attention to the "little man" was at its peak' (xvi). Such a bucolic picture is a prime example of how, as Becker suggests, traditional practices were considered 'restorative, uniting body and soul, nourishing the soul, encouraging self-reliance, and upholding the family' at a time when the national economic recession had created high unemployment, exacerbated poverty, and kindled considerable doubt over the possibility of future prosperity (5).

The spectre of the Depression is discernible in much of Niedecker's 'folk' poetry, particularly in its treatment of domestic, economic, and materialist themes. Penberthy's suggestion that Niedecker's 'domestic poems take pleasure in the quotidian' are reiterated by John Harkey, who describes this pleasure as Niedecker's 'everyday metaphysics' which, he maintains, 'holds firmly to the scales and pleasures and materials of a domestic economy' (*NZC* 82; Harkey 9). Niedecker's poem 'Hand Crocheted Rug' from *New Goose* is a salient example of such 'everyday metaphysics,' although her rendering of traditional manual craftwork is far more ambivalent than that of Eaton:

> Gather all the old, rip and sew
> the skirt I've saved so long,
> Sally's valance, the twins' first calico

> and the rest I worked to dye.
> Red, green, black, hook,
> hitch, nevermind, cramped
> around back not yet the turn
> of the century ... Grandpa forward
> from the shop, 'Ought to have a machine.' (*CW* 102)

The resourceful thrift of 'Hand Crocheted Rug' pertinently reflects Pound's modernist injunction to 'make it new,' as the 'old' material—the crumb blocks and the familial memories and social associations they contain—are reworked into a new configuration (*Cantos* 265). Niedecker's poem is, in this respect, a prime example of what Willis describes as her '"folk" method of reprocessing pre-owned material' ('Possessing Possession' 104). However, Niedecker refuses to romanticize or idealize this particular instance of folk craft. The phrase 'the rest I worked to dye,' not only suggests that this work is done in the speaker's spare 'leisure' time—the time normally allocated for 'rest'—but the homophonic suggestion of death in 'dye' ('die') also implies that this is unforgiving and exhausting work.

The physical demands of manual work are also conveyed in the poem's allusions to ripping, sewing, hitching, hooking, and dying as well as in the descriptions of the physical effects of such intensive, prolonged activities: 'cramped / around the back.' Furthermore, 'cramped' also suggests 'stitches' in the physical, painful sense of 'side stitches' and, perhaps, menstruation. In a similar vein, 'hitch' in addition to sewing also connotes marriage, something that appears to be briefly entertained, and then quickly dismissed, in the word 'nevermind.' The implicit suggestion that Sally has acquired a marriage bed (because she no longer requires her valance) and because 'the twins' first calico' is being recycled for a new purpose, highlights what the poem's speaker does not appear to have. Single and childless, she is a *spinster*, it seems, in both senses of the word.

It is also notable that 'Hand Crocheted Rug' ambiguously records a transitional moment: 'not yet the turn / of the century.' As well as implying an anticipated 'turn' of events for the speaker (marriage, perhaps) and a possible reflection on the outmoded style of skirt that has been 'saved so long,' this enigmatic phrase also raises important questions about certain values. With the crocheting work of the poem occurring on what might be seen as the cusp of a new century, the poem prompts a consideration of whether it is a *dyeing* craft that is being affirmed or a *dying* tradition that is being lamented. Perhaps the introduction of a 'machine' will kill this tradition. Then again, it may also make this uncomfortable work more tolerable and less physically demanding.

In whatever way Grandpa's utterance is finally interpreted, because it comes 'from the shop' (whether from his own or one that sells sewing machines), his suggestion is situated firmly within the context of commodity and commerce, and not a domestic folk economy. It is also significant that it is Grandpa who makes this comment. One would assume that this elderly figure represents an older generation and a way of life that is fast disappearing due to modern technology, capitalism, and industrialism. However, far from preserving the old ways, this elderly figure appears to embrace the prospective (*forward-looking*) benefits of modern technology. In this respect, the ambivalence of Grandpa's comment reaffirms the impossibility of the folk revivalists' claims for a pure folk past that is immune from 'the discomforts of real history nor the pains of the modern industrial present' (Becker 70). Thus, far from disappearing with industrial progress or lamenting an obsolescent past, the folkways that inform 'Hand Crocheted Rug' stand at the intersection of tradition and modernity, remaining responsive to modern and contemporary conditions.

New Goose

The preface to *Wisconsin: A Guide to the Badger State* describes its third section—'a series of selected tours' of the State—as presenting its subject 'in mosaic; isolated bits—chips of description, of history, or legend, of geographic or economic situation—are pieced together to make a variegated but single picture of Wisconsin' (xi). As well as recalling the 'variegated' fabric comprising the 'Hand Crocheted Rug' of Niedecker's poem, this method of composition in *Wisconsin: A Guide to the Badger State* also reflects the broader 'cosmopolitan' vision of the FWP which, as Hirsch claims, considered it 'necessary to transcend all parochialisms in order to be able to draw on the experience of a multiplicity of groups and to achieve a fuller human experience and translate it into national terms' (*Portrait* 23). 'Cultural differences would remain,' Hirsch explains with regard to the FWP's cosmopolitan vision, 'but parochial outlooks were to be transcended in order to achieve a richer, more satisfying national experience' (*Portrait* 23).

Niedecker adopts a similar approach to the question of the parochial and the cosmopolitan in *New Goose* by juxtaposing her locally sourced folk poems with others that, as Eleni Sikelianos notes, are 'rife with references to war, death, dismemberment, Nazism, and the bombing of London during the Blitz' (32). Sikelianos also believes that Niedecker's 'uses of local speech and lore alongside poems of more public concerns might suggest that the uses of local speech were not a geographically limited study but one in a total view of the world scene in an ongoing practice of reportage' (33). This is evident, for example, when the gathering, ripping and sewing of 'Hand Crocheted Rug' are juxtaposed with the 'dismemberment' and 'disjunction' of a poem such as 'They came at a pace' (Sikelianos, 33, 34; *CW* 102). In the latter poem, Sikelianos notes, Niedecker 'is attentive to what bombs do to a body—tear it to shreds'

(33). While this action of tearing is adumbrated in 'Hand Crocheted Rug,' Niedecker also implies that *re-membering* what has been torn apart can, potentially, be healing. Thus, as much as the local or parochial is, to recall the FWP, 'transcended in order to achieve a richer, more satisfying national [human] experience,' it is also possible to see the local inversely as the means of 'bringing home' those experiences and making them relevant. Indeed, according to Harkey, in Niedecker's poetry the domestic is 'a base from which to attend, vigilantly and crucially, to events, gestures, disturbances, names, and possibilities, in the world,' rather than a place to hide or shelter from them (8).

Allison Carruth makes a similar claim in relation to the poems by Niedecker 'that [have] positioned Wisconsin in relation to international geopolitics' by way of Fort Atkinson's local dairy industry (53–54). Fort Atkinson was the national centre of dairy production around the time of Second World War, a fact which Niedecker's work of the forties and fifties reflects. Essentially, according to Carruth, Niedecker achieves this by 'upset[ting] her reader's associations of agricultural life with stillness and simplicity to offer a complex picture of rural work, folk culture, and poetic craft' (53). Local details, such as the domestic and working lives of the women employed by the trade publication *Hoard's Dairyman* (alluded to in Niedecker's poem 'In the great snowfall before the bomb') or the differing 'trade[s]' of the dairy worker and the poet (contemplated in another poem, 'Poet's work') draw considerable attention to the 'significance of wartime factory work and agricultural production for rural communities like those of Fort Atkinson,' Carruth proposes (59). However, they do so by 'radiating outward from that locale to show the international scope and effects of food rationing' and the national consequence of regional food politics during that period (59).

The broader implications of local and domestic affairs are also evident in 'Grampa's got his old age pension,' another of the poems in *New Goose* that uses 'overheard local speech' to significant, albeit subtle, effect (*NCZ* 43):

> Grampa's got his old age pension,
> $15 a month
> his own food and place.
>
> But here he comes,
> fiddle and spitbox ...
>
> Tho't I'd stop with you a little,
> Harriut,
> you kin have all I got. (*CW* 100)

The folk inflections of 'Grampa's got his old age pension' incisively illustrate what Peter Middleton describes as 'the complexity of [Niedecker's] poetic style' which, he suggests, 'can appear to dissolve meaning into a limpid clarity' and leave the reader with 'nothing to interpret' ('Lorine Niedecker's "Folk Base"' 160). Gilbert Sorrentino makes a similar claim in his suggestion that, 'Niedecker's poems seem notably simple, but they make sudden and absolute demands' (289). Echoing these observations, Peter Quartermain maintains that 'Niedecker's poems are so extremely difficult to talk about not simply because paraphrase seems impossible, but because there seems to be no *need* for any' (220, original emphasis).

In this respect, the matter-of-fact style that seems to characterize Niedecker's poetry may seem initially to align it both aesthetically and historically with the 'the explosion of descriptive journalism, documentary photography and films, and social literature' that, according to Becker, 'offered "authentic" reportage of the rich details of daily existence in various areas of the United States' during the 1930s and 1940s folk revival (14). However, the apparent simplicity of 'Grampa's got his old age pension' belies what is in fact a complex exploration of family dynamics that frustrates any straightforward reportage of everyday events. Indeed, the poem's complex ambiguity rests on Niedecker's deft handling of the poem's 'authentic' details in the form of Grampa's demotic language. In doing so, Niedecker convincingly highlights what Peter Middleton calls the 'relational networks' that often go unnoticed when the idiosyncrasies of 'folk speech' are simply exhibited in poems as the 'memorials of different cultures' ('Lorine Niedecker's "Folk Base"' 177).

Clearly, Grampa is well looked after. He has a pension, food, and his own place. He also has some modest pleasures in the form of tobacco (suggested by the spitbox) and the fiddle. However, Grampa's closing remark, 'you kin have all I got,' resists final closure. Zukofsky, according to Penberthy, had suggested to Niedecker that she change the final line of the poem to 'You can have everything I got' (*NCZ* 47). Had Niedecker heeded his suggestion, however, a pivotal pun would have been lost. Where Zukofsky appears to read 'kin' as a more vernacular pronunciation of 'can,' Niedecker seems to have in mind the noun 'kin' and its familial connotations. Thus, any understanding of the poem changes significantly depending on how one reads, or hears, this otherwise inconspicuous word. Have Grampa's 'kin,' his family, taken all he owns? Or, does Grampa mean that his family is the only valuable thing in his life? Or, as Zukofsky would seem to read it, does Grampa simply mean that Harriut *can* have all of his material possessions? Thus Grampa may very well have a 'place'—financially and emotionally—in this family dynamic but, as the poem insinuates, the status of that place in relation to his 'kin' remains equivocal.

Indeed, Niedecker's poem raises further questions about the values—financial and emotional—that inform and complicate familial relationships. It also prompts us to consider just who the exploiter and the exploited are in the poem. Is Grampa a miser or a victim? Perhaps Grampa knows how to 'fiddle' his family, both emotionally and financially. Further questions are raised in the seemingly innocuous word 'little': just how long is 'a little' period of time? There are quantitative and qualitative values implicit in this word that must vary considerably for the retired Grampa and, one assumes, the harried and working Harriut. Niedecker may very well have preserved the 'rough-edged idiom' and the 'elderly, halting manner' of Grampa's speech, as Penberthy suggests, but this folk speech, far from being ossified as an anachronistic curio, instead sustains an ongoing, open dialogue (the 'relational networks' noted by Middleton), with the community from which it comes (*NCZ* 47). Thus, as in 'Hand Crocheted Rug,' it is perversely the older generation of the community that complicates any assumptions regarding traditional folkways as offering reassurance or escape from the complexities, anxieties, and ambiguities of the present.

'Grampa's got his old age pension' also reiterates broader themes of property and ownership that occur throughout *New Goose*. 'Du Bay,' for example, concerns the nineteenth-century Wisconsin fur trader John B. Du Bay, who 'shot a man for claiming his land' (*CW* 97). 'Ash woods, willow, close to shore,' a poem 'in memory of [Niedecker's] grandfather Gottfried Kunz,' concerns the death of a landowner, his will, and the unscrupulous and destructive scavenging of its beneficiaries: 'Heirs rush in—lay one tree bare / claiming a birdbox' (Peters 58; *CW* 93).

These pieces of local and family history adumbrate the shameless opportunism that motivates another folk-inflected poem, 'That woman!—eyeing houses,' which presents a further example of Niedecker's ear for local colloquialisms and, in this particular instance, local gossip:

> That woman!—eyeing houses.
> She's moved in on my poor guy.
> She held his hand and told him where to sign. (*CW* 101)

Like another poem in *New Goose*, 'What a Woman!—hooks men like rugs,' this poem may very well be based on Gertrude Runke, a neighbour of the Niedeckers' who had an affair with Niedecker's father, Henry (*CW* 198). According to Margot Peters, Runke, who was 21 years younger than Niedecker's father, 'hog-tied her lover with demands. Frontage by frontage foot, lot by lot, Henry signed over his ownings on Blackhawk Island to Gertrude's husband, Otto, in exchange for his wife' (18). Whether or not Runke is the subject of 'That woman!—eyeing houses,' Niedecker's poem is, nevertheless, concerned with similar themes of financial swindle and emotional manipulation. The woman's

48

act of 'eyeing,' or sizing-up houses is reaffirmed in the pun, 'moved in on,' which simultaneously suggests strategic offence—the moving in on her target or prey ('my poor guy')—and the physical act of moving into his property. Likewise, 'my poor guy' emphasizes the man's increasing poverty, his naivety, and his status as victim. In addition, the duplicitous nature of the poem's female subject—'That woman!'—is articulated in the line: 'She held his hand and told him where to sign.' Thus, what initially appears to be an act of affection and support (holding her partner's hands) also, more malignly, implies manipulation and coercion.

Niedecker explores similar themes of ownership rights, property, and custody in another poem from *New Goose* that deals with local history:

> Black Hawk held: In reason
> land cannot be sold,
> only things to be carried away,
> and I am old.
>
> Young Lincoln's general moved,
> pawpaw in bloom,
> and to this day, Black Hawk,
> reason has small room. (*CW* 99)

'Place is a special kind of object,' Yi-Fu Tuan writes: 'It is a concretion of value, though not a valued thing that can be handled or carried about easily; it is an object in which one can dwell' (*Space and Place* 12). Niedecker's poem makes a similar claim in the context of the Sauk leader Black Hawk who, in 1832, in response to issues regarding land settlement, led a band of Sauk and Fox people against settlers in Illinois and Wisconsin. As the poem's second stanza acknowledges, the young Abraham Lincoln served (but never saw action) in the militia against Black Hawk, which subsequently forced the Sauk leader into retreat at Blackhawk Island, the final gathering place for Black Hawk and his people. According to *Wisconsin: A Guide to the Badger State*, this event marks a pivotal moment in the broader history of Wisconsin. Following on from the arrival of 'French explorers, hunters, and missionaries' in the middle of the seventeenth century, a 'second wave of settlement, bringing Yankee farmers into the southeastern counties of Wisconsin, began after Black Hawk had been defeated in the summer of 1832' (46–47).

Read in the context of the *New Goose* poems, the Black Hawk War adumbrates the similar issues of property and deceit that occur in the collection's more domestic, folk-inflected poems. These themes of property and ownership are particularly apparent in the extract from Black Hawk's own autobiography that Niedecker condenses into the poem's first three lines:

My reason teaches me that *land cannot be sold*. The Great Spirit
gave it to his children to live upon, and cultivate as far as is
necessary for their subsidence; and so long as they occupy
and cultivate it, they have the right to the soil—but if they
voluntarily leave it, then any other people might have a right
to settle upon it. Nothing can be sold but such things as can
be carried away. (107, original emphasis)

In her allusion to 'pawpaw' (*Asimina triloba*), also known as 'Indian's
Banana' (a native fruit-bearing tree that was first documented in 1541
after its discovery east of the Mississippi River), Niedecker returns to
the question of occupation and cultivation initially raised in Black
Hawk's autobiography. Cultivated for its fruit, pawpaw spread as far
north as Nebraska, a fact that is reflected in the diverse range of local
names it has acquired.[9] Thus, in contrast to the legal contract that
divested the Sauk and Fox people of their land, pawpaw proposes a
different kind of contract that is mutually beneficial to both parties, the
human occupiers and the land's flora that they have cultivated. In this
respect, the poem foresees the botanical dissemination that concerns
Niedecker in her later poem, 'Consider,' as previously discussed in the
introduction. Furthermore, by being invoked in conjunction with the
retreating figure of Black Hawk, the pawpaw poignantly conveys the
contrasting movements of contraction and expansion, loss and gain,
with which the poem deals. Noting a similar dynamic of expansion,
Jonathan Skinner has pointed out that the 'bloom' of the pawpaw,
'occurring in late spring, would indeed have coincided with the militia's
journey north in pursuit of Black Hawk and his warriors' (52).

The 'contraction of room' that occurs in Niedecker's poem also
signals additional themes (Skinner 52). For example, the line 'Black
Hawk *held*' (emphasis added) can be read in several ways: as Black
Hawk's observance of his reasoned beliefs regarding land rights; as his
authoritative opinion; as his opposition or resistance; as his occupation
(in the sense of refusing to leave a specific place); and as his detainment
or incarceration—his being *held* in prison (52). Niedecker reiterates this
theme of incarceration in the poem's concluding line, 'reason has small
room,' which again implies imprisonment and, as Skinner suggests,
puns on the poem's own stanzas (rooms) (53). Niedecker may also be
implicitly punning on the notion of 'contract,' in the legal sense of the
government *contract*, the 1804 treaty that precipitated the Black Hawk
War. Indeed, these themes of contracts, contraction, and incarceration
are implicit in the prosodic limits that the poem sets itself. For example,

9   These include 'Indian's Banana,' 'Prairie Banana', 'Indiana (Hoosier)
Banana,' 'West Virginia Banana,' 'Kansas Banana,' 'Kentucky
Banana,' 'Michigan Banana,' 'Missouri Banana,' Poor Man's Banana,'
and 'Ozark Banana.'

in truncated lines such as 'reason has small room' which suggests, but ultimately withholds, the familiar colloquialism, 'room to move.' Any sense of expansion in the poem is also curtailed by Niedecker's use of abbreviation, such as in the use of the colon in the first line, 'Black Hawk held: In reason,' which replaces a more discursive and verbally extensive clause such as 'Black Hawk held *that*, in reason … '. These strategies, along with the use of terse rhymes (which are particularly apparent in 'sold' and 'old'), achieve what DuPlessis describes as an eschewal of 'fullness, plenitude, plethora, and glut' that characterizes Niedecker's poetry more generally ('Lorine Niedecker' 129). In 'Black Hawk held,' however, such brevity has the more chilling effect of coldly reflecting the themes of broken contracts, incarceration, imposition, and encroachment that shadow the poem.

A poem as terse as 'Black Hawk held' contrasts significantly with the 'warm tones of folk-speech' that Eleni Sikelianos attributes to many of the *New Goose* poems (32). However, as Sikelianos notes, and as the discussion of the preceding poems has shown, Niedecker's folk poems and their 'deep explorations of local speech habits' do in fact 'take on new tones' when read in the context of the collection's other poems that 'are haunted by themes of aggression, loss, or folly' (32, 33). Thus, for all of their warm, earthy, vernacular tones, poems such as 'Grampa's got his old age pension' or 'That woman!—eyeing houses' are not reassuring, homely 'folk' poems, but in fact incisively representative of what Sikelianos considers Niedecker's wider 'worldview' and pertinent 'testament to a mind keenly interested in the relational and in particular, the political, environmental, and social aspects of the world' (32). Far from further quarantining Niedecker and her poetry in an idyllic folk community, the financial deceit and emotional manipulations witnessed in the context of family relations, small-town community gossip, and local history, actually serve to illustrate at the micro level the perennial power dynamics and materialistic concerns that have motivated national and international history.

Niedecker's poetry, however, does not simply reject the contemporary regionalist perspectives that recognize 'the region or local community [as] the central locus for the "folk culture,"' and the provider of 'antidotes to the dislocating forces of mass society in a rapidly modernizing America' (Becker 27). Reiterating Carruth's and Sikelianos's assessments, Michael Davidson, employing the Bakhtinian metaphor of the chronotope, proposes that Niedecker deftly negotiates regional and global positions by 'self-consciously us[ing] the upper Midwest region as a chronotope through which to understand national and global politics from the end of the Progressive era to the Cold War' ('Life by Water' 7). Consequently, when Niedecker remarks in her letter to Gail Roub that, 'I am what I am because of all this—I am what is around me,' she is not writing simply as a 'bumpkin savant' but as a cosmopolitan poet deeply aware of her 'Home/World' (Roub 86; Sorrentino 289; *CW* 462). Indeed, Niedecker's avant-folkways are pivotal in affirming 'the dynamic, global situation' of her poetry, and not simply a means of sequestering it within the regional or provincial environs of a fallacious American folk tradition (Roy 479).

Everyday Aesthetics

An additional way in which Niedecker's poetry revises and subverts popular assumptions regarding American folk is through its close links with traditional handicraft practices. 'As a work ideology, an aesthetic, and a form of work organization,' Howard S. Becker suggests, 'craft can and does exist independent of art worlds, their practitioners, and their definitions' (864). According to Howard S. Becker, it is 'practical utility'—'the ability to perform in a useful way'—that is the predominant principle differentiating craft from art (887, 864). Thus, he proposes, 'in the pure folk tradition a craft consists of a body of knowledge and skill which can be used to produce useful objects' (864). It is the nature of this 'knowledge' and the way it is shared and passed on that, according to Jane S. Becker, makes craft a 'hallmark of folk culture' (62). Unlike mass industrially produced items, the knowledge and skill that artisanal craftwork presupposes is 'evidence of traditions passed down through generations' (Jane S. Becker 62). Niedecker's own experience of vernacular handicraft tradition is evident in her poem 'Hand Crocheted Rug,' with its make-do-and-mend ethos recalling how handicraft is borne out of 'the material necessities of everyday domestic life' and integral to the modest economies and thrift of the home (Jane S. Becker 4).

Niedecker's familiarity with artisanal practices increased through her correspondence with Zukofsky, who from approximately 1936 to 1940 was employed as a researcher on the *Index of American Design*, 'a program of the FAP [Federal Art Project],' as editor Kenneth Sherwood notes, that 'aimed to recover and diffuse information about U.S. culture at a time when interest in handicrafts had just begun to emerge' (*A Useful Art* 3). With both poets working on WPA projects, it is not surprising that Zukofsky and Niedecker exchanged notes on their respective research (*NCZ* 8). It is, therefore, very possible that Zukofsky's writings on a wide range of American crafts such as ironwork, chalk ware, tin ware, kitchenware, cotton prints, friendship quilts, and carpentry for the *Index* could have informed and influenced Niedecker's own poetics.

The influence of Zukofsky's work for the *Index* on his own poetry has been noted by a number of critics. Ira B. Nadel, for example, claims that, among other things, the *Index* 'clarified Zukofsky's emerging social and political thought,' 'immersed him in American history,' and 'confirmed the method initiated by the Objectivist "movement"' (115). Ruth Jennison has elaborated on these ideas and noted how 'Zukofsky's

Marxist account of history and aesthetics mediates his appropriation of precapitalist poetic forms' (176). Similarly, Barry Ahearn proposes that Zukofsky's 'work exemplified the virtues of American handicrafts,' particularly so in his major long poem '*A*' (which, according to Ahearn, is itself 'an American handicraft') and its 'concern with the labor process and with beauty' ('Zukofsky' 90, 83). A prime example of this concern can be seen in Zukofsky's claim in '*A*'-8 that the linen table napkin of the sharecropper's grandmother, 'Is as good to us as Breughel's *Harvesters*' due to its combination of practical utility, aesthetic appeal, skilled craftsmanship, and its value and worth outside of a capitalist economy (66).

Just how Niedecker's poetry might have drawn on Zukofsky's work for the *Index* is not as immediately apparent. It is, however, likely that what Harkey calls Niedecker's 'everyday metaphysics' derives in part from, or finds reaffirmation in, Zukofsky's view of American handicrafts (9). According to Harkey, Niedecker repeatedly 'subverts expectations about small craftworks yet holds firmly to the scales and pleasures and materials of a domestic economy' that has traditionally been identified with such practices (9). In *The Index*, Zukofsky's emphasis on the importance of the domestic as the site of meaningful production—'when men were likely to be found working on something at home, and for their homes'—largely reiterates older assessments of handcraft aesthetics (*A Useful Art* 101).

For example, the American artist Douglas Volk, in his article 'The Human Element in Arts and Crafts,' published in the American arts and crafts magazine *Brush and Pencil* in 1903, considers the home as consolidating the qualities of 'variety,' 'differentiation,' and 'spontaneity' that give value to 'wool and metal work, clay modeling, leather work, [and] everything done by hand' (443):

> A home is a living place with the idea of permanency as its foundation. It is a spot hallowed by associations, to which one is attached by the joys and griefs that have gone into its upbuilding, and the articles with which it is filled ought not to be mere things, but should be animate and cherished memories, or expressions of the tastes, convictions, and condition of the possessor. (444)

The 'everyday metaphysics' of Niedecker's poems which focus attention on the most unassuming of domestic objects and activities such as sewing, manual domestic work, plumbing, and cooking show a similar regard for the modest 'joys and griefs' of the home. However, to reiterate Harkey's claim, Niedecker's poetry expresses more ambivalence toward such 'joys' by both affirming and subverting these familiar domestic tropes in equal measure. Furthermore, and in contrast to Volk and Zukofsky, her 'everyday metaphysics' is also embracing enough to encompass modern mechanical objects that have been produced on larger, industrial scales.

In 'To my pres- / sure pump,' for example, Niedecker elevates the mechanical pressure pump to the stature of Keats's nightingale or Horace's lyre; if not as an object of celebration, then at least, as Jeffrey Peterson suggests, in a spirit of 'affectional identification' (270). Considering the benefit that this new plumbing appliance had on Niedecker and her home, this is perhaps not surprising. Niedecker writes to Zukofsky that 'my little pressure pump is a darling, jet, hums like a fan,' and explains how her 'water comes from a 275 ft. deep flowing well way distant from my house' (*NCZ* 320). 'Well, no more carrying pails of water a half a block,' she remarks optimistically (*NCZ* 320). However, as Niedecker quips, this newfound convenience also brought with it certain inconveniences:

> [P]ressure pump wouldn't start, turned out it was wired wrong—brand new pump, mind you—(it's the rule these days, whatever you buy you have to take back to have it done over—'a slight adjustment') [...] My yard is the worst, cut up badly, but they'll level it out and bring crushed stone for my driveway and I'll be all new before long. The inconvenience of conveniences—it's been tough. (*NCZ* 320)

'The inconvenience of conveniences' accurately captures the ambivalence that characterizes Niedecker's engagement with, to recall Harkey's phrase, the 'materials of [her] domestic economy.' Niedecker's misgivings about the inconveniences of modern conveniences do, to a degree, recall Volk's similar criticisms regarding modern 'mechanical designs' (444). Although Volk acknowledges that such objects have been 'invented to make travel, household arrangements and modes of locomotion more conducive to ease and luxury,' they have done so, he believes, at the price of what he calls 'genuineness and simplicity' (444):

> To foster genuineness and simplicity in our lives and surroundings, it may be well not to avail ourselves of every convenient device for producing meretricious results, but rather to impose upon ourselves healthful limitations under which production and character are strengthened. (444)

Niedecker invokes a similar sentiment in the opening lines of 'To my pres- / sure pump' when she writes, 'I've been free / with less' (*CW* 201). The use of the past tense implies that such freedom is a thing of the past now that the speaker is 'bound' by her new appliance. Indeed, ownership comes with its own 'pressures,' not least the financial responsibility of maintaining and 'servic[ing]' the pump (*CW* 201). Thus, despite the possessive pronoun ('my') of the title, the poem may be read as expressing a similar aversion to material property that occurs in other Niedecker poems such as 'I am sick with the Time's buying sickness,' 'Property is poverty,' *Paean to Place* ('Do not save love / for things / Throw *things* / to the flood'), and 'Black Hawk held' (*CW* 157, 194–95, 268). 'To my pres- / sure pump' also expresses anxiety over the responsibilities caused by ownership and property. The 'service / cost' of the pump might therefore be seen as adumbrating the social responsibilities facing the speaker in 'My friend tree' who has to sacrifice her arboreal 'friend' for the greater good of her 'older friend,' the sun (*CW* 186).

The ambivalence that Niedecker's poem shows for the convenience of the pump is further emphasized in her use of puns. For example, the speaker's remark that 'I plumbed for principles' denotes both the installation of the pump and a former exploration of deep ('subconscious,' Peterson suggests) 'principles' that the 'hygienic control' of the pump has sanitized (*CW* 201; Peterson 269). By contrast, Niedecker's phrase 'jet-bound' which, in addition to conveying the pump's effective water pressure and the speaker's dependent *bind* to the amenities it makes possible, also suggests more positive responses to this appliance (*CW* 201). Perhaps with an echo of the then-modish colloquial phrase 'jet-set,' 'jet-bound' suggests a fast-paced and vibrant modern life of luxury that shifts the meaning of 'bound' from notions of restriction to more positive ideas of destination, futurity, and potential. Indeed, noting the recurrence of the word in Niedecker's poems and letters, Peterson claims that 'jet' functions as 'an image of the work's emergence, a trope of natural compression as much as technological "constriction"' (266). In this respect, constriction and limitation can be seen as generative, rather than restrictive, conditions. This is also implicit in the way Niedecker hyphenates the word 'pressure' in the title of her poem, breaking it across two lines. In doing so, the title serves as a visual reminder of the compressive, condensing forces that motivate and express the flow—the 'deep / trickle'—of her poetry (*CW* 195).

Although DuPlessis believes that in 'To my pres- / sure pump' Niedecker ultimately 'succumbs to modernizing,' DuPlessis's choice of the word 'succumb' insinuates, perhaps too emphatically, a failure or resignation on Niedecker's part ('Lorine Niedecker' 128). In recognizing a more ambivalent assessment of modern convenience that resists such unequivocal judgement, it is perhaps more revealing to read Niedecker's poem from the perspective of what Yuriko Saito calls 'everyday aesthetics.' 'Everyday aesthetics,' Saito proposes, 'should not be exclusively concerned with discounting ordinary and seemingly pragmatically directed actions, such as cleaning, throwing away, purchasing, and preserving,' but, rather, can be recognized as promoting more 'positive aesthetic experiences from unlikely objects and phenomena from our daily life' (245). According to Saito, 'even the seemingly trivial, insignificant everyday attitudes and judgements often wield surprising power that can determine the quality of life, the state of the world or social and cultural ethos in the most literal manner' (243). Niedecker promotes a similar aesthetic experience to that suggested by Saito by including among a list of utilitarian pump parts—'faucet,' 'valve,' and 'ring seal'—the positive comforts that these parts, as a working collective, make possible: 'shower' and 'heater' (*CW* 201).

Furthermore, if, as DuPlessis suggests, the image of the 'little / humming / water / bird' that ends Niedecker's poem refers to 'the spirit of her poetry,' as well as her pump, it is therefore possible to see 'To my pres- / sure pump' as a subtle recasting of William Carlos Williams's 'bold' statement that a poem is a machine made of words (*CW* 201):

> To make two bold statements: There's nothing sentimental about a machine, and: A poem is a small (or large) machine made out of words. When I say there's nothing sentimental about a poem, I mean that there can be no part that is redundant. (*Selected Essays* 256)

In the spirit of the pump it addresses, Niedecker's poem, like Williams's machine, is 'pruned to a perfect economy' with no part unnecessary, superfluous, or 'redundant' in its humming perfection (*Selected Essays* 256). However, the ambivalent sentiments that Niedecker expresses toward the pump wryly subverts Williams's claim that there is 'nothing sentimental about a machine.' Indeed, as Peterson notes, 'for Niedecker the technological is understood on particularly intimate grounds,' and 'the machinery of hygiene is at least playfully, but perhaps more "deeply," identified with her expressive strategies' (276).

As well as offering tacit revisions of Williams's notion of the poem as a machine made of words, Niedecker's 'pump' poems also complicate common distinctions made between handcrafted and machine-made objects, as well as the inherent values informing those distinctions. 'The effort to make a useful object pleasing to the eye or touch,' Eaton writes in his study of Southern Highland handicrafts, 'gives the craftsman an understanding of the age-long struggle to bestow on objects of daily use that quality that renders their ownership one of life's little events' (26). Zukofsky reiterates Eaton's emphasis on an everyday practicability that does not forsake aesthetic character in his essay 'American Kitchenware 1608–ca. 1875' when he praises Shaker furniture for its 'usefulness combined with extreme simplicity of design' (*A Useful Art* 108). Zukofsky here echoes William Morris's famous dictum to 'have nothing in your house that you do not know to be useful, or believe to be beautiful' (*Hopes and Fears for Art* 108). It is a quote that Niedecker may have been well familiar with when she was researching her late poem on Morris, 'His Carpets Flowered' (*CW* 292–294). In identifying similar qualities of usefulness and aesthetic design in an electric pump, and by tacitly acknowledging it as 'one of life's little events,' Niedecker affords this modern convenience the same attention she bestows on more traditionally 'homely' and intimate objects such as granite pails, spitboxes, scythes, and pendulums. In this respect, 'To my pres- / sure pump' might be considered as a prime example of Niedecker's 'awareness of the shifting status of things' which, depending on one's perspective, modulates 'between product, artefact, and work of art' (Willis, 'The Poetics of Affinity' 229–230). Willis's observation finds a pertinent instance in Niedecker's remark to Zukofsky, in a letter from 1964: 'Objects carry such profound implications!' (cited in Peters 190). Yet, as 'To my pres- / sure pump' demonstrates, it is not simply how, or the purpose for which the object is made that gives it value or meaning, and neither is its monetary value, but rather how its owner values and perceives it.

Handmade/Homemade Poetry
Niedecker included 'To my pres- / sure pump' in several small books of her poetry that she made as gifts for friends in 1964. These include *Homemade Poems*, comprising 30 poems for Cid Corman and two editions of *Handmade Poems*—comprising 25 poems each—which she made as Christmas gifts for Zukofsky and Jonathan Williams. With just some minor variations between the three, the contents of these gift-books are predominantly the same and each includes a watercolour painting by Niedecker of her Blackhawk Island home. As their titles suggest, Niedecker's books reflect, and embody, many of the qualities commonly attributed to handicraft tradition; particularly the manufacture by hand of utilitarian objects with limited means. Indeed, Niedecker's holographic method in *Handmade Poems* and *Homemade Poems* and other books—such as *Paean to Place*, made by Niedecker for her friend Florence Dollase in 1969, and *A Cooking Book*, the witty, playful book on cooking that Niedecker gave her friend Maude Hartel as a Christmas gift in 1964—gives these books the 'human element' and the quality of 'human touch' that Volk, and Zukofksy, endorse so emphatically in handicraft practices (443, 444).[10]

---

10 *A Cooking Book*, in particular, continues *New Goose*'s subversions of stereotypical domestic relations and its reassessment of American folkways. 'The fact that I don't know much about the subject of cooking should entitle me to write a book about it,' Niedecker claims: 'Away from the table: I eat / books' (17, 21). Niedecker playfully subverts the traditional role of the woman as housekeeper and cook. Indeed, it is her husband Al who 'ate close to the soil' and is not only the authority on cooking, but also knowledgeable about

Furthermore, like folk handicrafts, Niedecker's homemade books bypass the marketplace and embody labour processes and exchanges motivated by values other than profit. In this respect, these singular books contrast markedly with the artists' books that were being produced around the same time by contemporary artists such as Ed Ruscha. As Johanna Drucker explains, these artists' books earned themselves the name 'democratic multiples' because of their apparent status as affordable, mass-produced and ordinary (as opposed to rarefied) objects that 'conformed to the then prevailing minimalist idea of a fabricated, industrial product which offered an alternative to the fine art traditions of the hand-crafted object' (*Figuring* 175–176). Unlike the 'democratic multiple' both *Handmade Poems* and *Homemade Poems* utilize a domestic economy of the '*home*made'—reaffirmed considerably by the inclusion of Niedecker's paintings of her Blackhawk Island home—to advance a poetics that affiliates itself with the broader avant-garde milieu of Zukofsky, Corman, and Williams.

However, Niedecker's gift-books also inhabit an unusual position within the broader mimeo revolution that, around the same time during the 1960s, was accelerating the dissemination and exchange of new poetry on both sides of the Atlantic. Niedecker was a participant in this 'revolution' due to her inclusion in important little magazines such as *Origin* and *Black Mountain Review*, yet her gift-books circulate outside these larger networks and unlike the multiple copies and comparatively larger print runs of small press productions are made for one exclusive recipient. As well as making reproduction impossible, the handmade, handwritten nature of Niedecker's gift-books also sets them apart from the more mechanical methods of the mimeograph machine which made industrial production possible on a smaller, domestic scale.

The homemade–handmade nature of Niedecker's gift-books might therefore be seen as reaffirming Willis's claims regarding Niedecker's affinities with 'art-work' as conceived by John Ruskin and then promoted in the Arts and Crafts movement in the late nineteenth century ('The Poetics of Affinity' 228). According to Willis, within this milieu '"art-work" signified a direct confluence of art and labor' with 'decorative and domestic crafts' such as embroidery, weaving, and

those things traditionally associated with housewives: family recipes, thrifty tips for using the leftovers and by-products of dishes, the medicinal properties of food, and the meanings behind the names of certain dishes (21). And, as in *New Goose*, such domestic concerns intersect with references to local, national, and international history that include the seventeenth-century English writer Izaak Walton (author of *The Complete Angler*) and the first century Stoic philosopher Epictetus, whose quotation concludes *A Cooking Book*: '"Preach not to others what / they should eat but eat / as becomes you, and / be silent"' (62).

interior design bridging 'a fundamental gap between art and labor, wage work and parlor craft, women's work and manufacturing' ('The Poetics of Affinity' 228–229). In a similar vein, she argues, Niedecker's poems 'insist that art and labor are inseparably bound; her subjects perform their identities, their ideological affinities, and their labors within a literary context that likewise considers itself as knowledge, as work, as relational system, as a product whose consumption demands even future labor' ('The Poetics of Affinity' 223).

According to Jane S. Becker, 'the resurrection of tradition epitomized by the folk revival of the 1930s shared some ideological foundations with the Arts and Crafts movement' that preceded it (16). 'Both,' she maintains, 'looked back with some nostalgia to an idealized preindustrial and precapitalist past as the basis for a healthful national order' and 'advocated an implicitly antimodernist position' that perceived 'the machine and its accompanying reorganization of work' as degrading labor (16). To recall Jerome McGann's claims regarding Morris's Kelmscott press previously cited in the Introduction, it is in fact possible to see the Arts and Crafts Movement's attitude toward modern industrialism from a more forgiving perspective. Indeed, a late advocate of the Arts and Crafts Movement, the typographer, printmaker, and sculptor Eric Gill, in his book *An Essay on Typography* (1931), offers a more nuanced assessment of traditional craft in relation to contemporary machine production. 'It is not a question,' Gill reasons, 'whether machine work be better or worse than hand work—both have their proper goodness—it is simply a matter of difference' (98). Such reasoning—that 'not all things made by machinery are bad things, or that the handicraftsman is the only kind of man that merits salvation'—finds an equivalent in the very format of Niedecker's *Handmade Poems* and *Homemade Poems* (Gill 99). Niedecker may very well have handwritten her poems, but she did so in mass-produced, store-bought, autograph books. These handmade gift-books, therefore, both confirm and subvert Volk's idea of the 'healthful limitation under which production and character are strengthened' in traditional handicraft practices by exercising a similar resourcefulness with commercially produced material considered largely anathema to traditional handicraft values.

According to Antje Petty, the phenomena of the autograph book can be traced back to a centuries-old German tradition and 'the *Album Amicorum* [book of friends], also called *Stammbuch* or, more recently, *Poesiealbum*' which, in the eighteenth and nineteenth centuries, became a profitable commodity for book manufacturers (n. pag). Appearing for the first time in the sixteenth and seventeenth centuries, in German and Dutch-speaking areas of Europe, the *Stammbuch* developed out of the custom for graduating university students to have their bibles signed by classmates and teachers. 'Soon inscriptions went beyond simple signatures to include reminiscences of common experiences,' Petty explains, 'good wishes for the future, or a favorite passage from literature or poetry. Publishers foreseeing a lucrative market printed bibles with empty pages and soon also turned out small decorated books with only empty pages' (n. pag). The intimate, personal nature of Niedecker's gift-books certainly recalls this tradition, but instead of following the custom of filling other people's books with personal inscriptions and literary quotes that express 'the writer's—and by extension the bearer's—social and intellectual standing,' Niedecker reproduces her own poems in a book designed for one specific recipient (Petty n. pag).

Niedecker works with commercial, mass-produced means in what is perhaps her earliest handmade/homemade book, 'Next Year or I Fly My Rounds, Tempestuous,' which she made as a Christmas gift for Zukofsky in 1934 as a tacit celebration of their first year of friendship. According to Penberthy, Niedecker handwrote her poem 'on small pieces of paper pasted over the printed text of a bi-weekly calendar with the original calendar text,' comprised of platitudinous homilies still vaguely discernible through Niedecker's additions (*CW* 371). The idiosyncratic, found format of 'Next Year or I Fly My Rounds, Tempestuous,' however, is far from ancillary to its content. As Penberthy notes, 'the aleatoric nature of the palimpsest exudes parody' due to the way the poem plays with and against the found text and calendar format that hosts it ('Next Year' 42). Niedecker 'teases the mnemonic device' of the pocket calendar, Penberthy suggests, 'by linking her non-sequitur and baffling lines to the predictable chronology of a calendar' ('Next Year' 42). Niedecker further teases the calendar's format by covering the original trite homilies (which, Penberthy observes, are 'just legible when held to the light') with her own poem which works against the flow of the calendar's linear temporality: 'Wade all life / backwards to its source,' Niedecker writes, 'which / runs too far / ahead' (*CW* 41).

As well as being 'an experiment in form,' however, the cut-and-paste method of Niedecker's poem and its use of a mass-produced, pre-made calendar format also recalls the vernacular form of the scrapbook. Niedecker utilized this medium on several occasions, including two comprised mainly of postcards acquired during her travels to South Dakota in 1965 and Lake Superior, Michigan, Canada, North Dakota, and Minnesota between 1967 and 1968. The scrapbook format is also used in a collection of recipes that Niedecker culled from newspapers, magazines, and food packaging.[11] As 'a material manifestation of memory—the memory of the compiler and the memory of the cultural moment in which they were made,' the scrapbook is, like 'Next Year or I Fly My Rounds, Tempestuous,' another form of 'intimate mnemonics' (Tucker, Ott, and Buckler 2; Penberthy, 'Next Year' 42). The scrapbook burgeoned in the nineteenth century as a personal, autobiographical

---

11   These and other scrapbooks of Niedecker's are reproduced online and available for viewing at the University of Wisconsin's *The State of Wisconsin Collection*.

form that used commercially available texts and images for constructing 'individual and group identity in cultures increasingly dependent on reading, visual literacy, and [the] consumption of mass-produced objects' (Tucker, Ott, and Buckler 3). Thus, due to the scrapbook's manner of displaying 'artifacts and ephemera that track the migration of ideas and commodities up and down the cultural hierarchy of capitalism,' this domestic craft practice exemplifies a vernacular form that has developed out of, rather than reacted against, mass-produced commercial objects (Tucker, Ott, and Buckler 2).

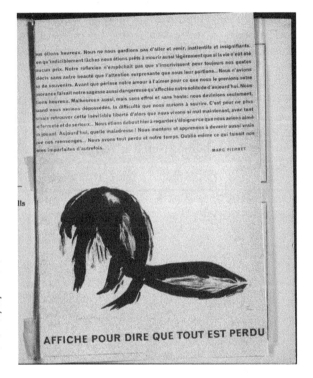

Figure 1. From 'Lorine's home-made book for Æneas,' 1956. Courtesy of The University of Wisconsin Digital Collections Center.

The scrapbook format and its precursor, the commonplace book, are also recalled in the gift-book that Niedecker made for her neighbour and close friend Æneas McAllister in the late 1950s. Reproduced online by the University of Wisconsin's Digital Collection, 'Lorine's home-made book for Æneas' is made primarily out of the sixth issue of the *Black Mountain Review* which included four poems by Niedecker.[12]

---

12 The four poems by Niedecker are 'She now lay deaf to death,' 'In Europe they grow a new bean,' 'He built four houses,' and 'As I shook the dust.' Niedecker includes all of these in the *For Paul and Other Poems* manuscript and amends 'She now lay deaf to death' with the title 'Dead' (*CW* 150, 155–156, 160).

Niedecker assembles her book by retaining only a selection of material from the magazine. In addition to Niedecker's four poems, these include collages by Jess, Zukofsky's extensive poetry and prose contributions, and a drawing by Fielding Dawson. Other contributions to the issue, such as Robert Duncan's essay 'Notes on Poetics: Regarding Olson's "Maximus,"' and poems by Jonathan Williams, Denise Levertov, and Joel Oppenheimer, are omitted. Niedecker supplements her retained material with additional texts on pages taped into the remaining pages of the original magazine. These additions consist of a reproduction of an abstract lithograph image by the French artist and translator of Pound, René Laubiès (Figure 1), which accompanies a text by Marc Pierret and appears to be taken from the page of an unidentified magazine, possibly an earlier number of the *Black Mountain Review* in which he was published.[13]

Beneath Laubiès's image is the legend, in capitals: 'AFFICHE POUR DIRE QUE TOUT EST PERDU' ('poster to say that all is lost'). Immediately following this, at the end of the book, Niedecker has appended the typescript of a poem by Li Po, accompanied by David Gordon's translation, which is illustrated with images of plum blossom (Figure 2).

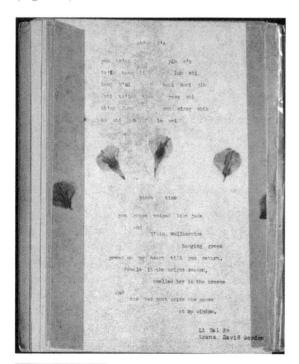

Figure 2. From 'Lorine's home-made book for Æneas,' 1956. Courtesy of The University of Wisconsin Digital Collections Center.

---

13   Laubiès also designed the cover for Robert Creeley's *The Whip* (Jargon 26), which Jargon co-published in 1957 with Migrant and Contact.

The style and content of Niedecker's 'home-made book for Æneas' make it another salient example of her Janus-faced avant-folkways. While Niedecker's gift-book suggests an extended modern collage of found material, executed in the same spirit as much of the poetry and art included in the *Black Mountain Review*, it also recalls traditional mnemonic folk and vernacular forms, including the 'curious fashion for memorial wreaths,' specific to Wisconsin, that, according to *Wisconsin: A Guide to the Badger State*, 'were traditionally made of human hair, wax, feathers, yarn, seeds, or skeletonized leaves' (151–152). In both instances, assemblage and collage practices become quite literally an act of *re-membering* something intimate and personal, which in Niedecker's case is her close friendship with Æneas.

In this respect, Niedecker's book for Æneas might be seen as another pertinent example of her '"folk" method of reprocessing pre-owned material' (Willis, 'Possessing Possession' 104). Furthermore, as in 'Next Year or I Fly My Rounds, Tempestuous,' Niedecker's method of reprocessing pre-owned material in her book for Æneas is carefully considered. For example, the Li Po poem and the images of plum blossoms included by Niedecker adumbrate Laubiès's abstract lithograph and its suggestion of Chinese calligraphy. This in turn recalls the non-figurative abstract expressionist images by Philip Guston, which Niedecker retains in her copy of the *Black Mountain Review*. Similarly, Fielding Dawson's black and white abstract drawing (Figure 3), which Niedecker also retains, visually rhymes with the musical score by Celia Thaew Zukofsky for her opera based on Shakespeare's play *Pericles, Prince of Tyre* which accompanies a substantial extract from Zukofsky's prose work *Bottom: On Shakespeare*.

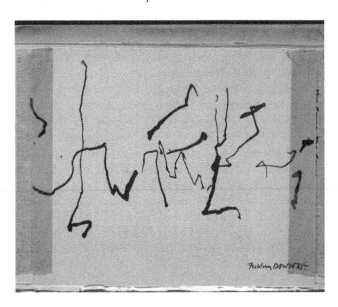

Figure 3. From 'Lorine's home-made book for Æneas,' 1956. Courtesy of The University of Wisconsin Digital Collections Center.

It is possible to see Niedecker tacitly cross-referencing this salvaged material in order to create a personal narrative that is specific and relevant to Æneas. For example, the local detail of Niedecker's 'Four Poems' included in the *Black Mountain Review*—including 'As I shook the dust' which alludes to 'young Aeneas / on the shore'—is echoed in Paul Goodman's short story, 'Noah's Vineyard' (*CW* 160). Niedecker only keeps the first page of Goodman's story, but phrases from the text—'After a flood everything looks both dirty and washed' and 'Everything, after the flood was dirty with silt and new-washed with water'—speak pertinently of the 'life by water' that she and Æneas knew only too well ('Lorine's home-made book for Aeneas' 26).[14] The damaging effects of flooding are also tacitly suggested in the aforementioned text accompanying Laubiès's image—'AFFICHE POUR DIRE QUE TOUT EST PERDU' ('poster to say that that all is lost')—which might suggest the loss of material objects and personal items, or indeed the loss of hope, when faced with the daunting consequences of such natural disasters. The trope of flooding is further echoed in Jess's collage that juxtaposes the photograph of a woman's coat—displayed on what appears to be a sewing mannequin in the pose of a classical statue—against a photograph of a riverside cottage, which suggests another instance of 'life by water.' Within the large open collar of the coat, an oversized eye peers ominously out from where the wearer's chest (and heart) would be, tacitly adumbrating Zukofsky's claim in *Bottom: On Shakespeare* that 'Love sees' and 'needs no tongue of reason if love and the eyes are 1' ('Lorine's home-made book for Aeneas' 131, 132).

These methods of Niedecker's show considerable affinity with Patricia Buckler's, Susan Tucker's and Katherine Ott's suggestion that 'scrapbooks are not transparently autobiographical' but instead 'function as supplements to individual identity' via the 'mass assembling of individual examples [that] will reveal the whole' (2, 3, 2). Adopting a similar methodology in her homemade book for Æneas, Niedecker makes a personal gift out of a heterogeneous selection of texts that through their editing express her friendship with Æneas. Indeed, Louis Dienes's poem 'Strangers to Each Other' which Niedecker retains from her copy of the *Black Mountain Review* speaks eloquently for the tacit narrative of her gift-book. 'I can speak to you now only through / The most obscure formulae,' the female subject of Dienes's poem states: 'The most pure and rare solutions, / And through stories about people like me' ('Lorine's home-made book for Aeneas' 194).

The intimate nature of Niedecker's homemade books might initially seem to simply re-inscribe the romanticized view of the 'personal and informal' communications associated with America's disappearing folkways (Jane S. Becker, 3). However, in terms of their recipients and

---

14 Page numbers refer to those in the original issue of *Black Mountain Review* that Niedecker retains.

their content, Niedecker's gift-books are very much in tune with, and responsive to, a broader cosmopolitan world, but they are so strictly on Niedecker's own terms as part of what DuPlessis calls Niedecker's 'poetics of gift exchange' ('Lorine Niedecker' 129). According to DuPlessis, Niedecker's work functions both as 'gifts [exchanged] on a small personal scale' and as a 'formal answer to Bigness' ('Lorine Niedecker' 129). These qualities can also be attributed to Niedecker's homemade gift-books which, despite their smallness of scale, carry considerable impact in terms of their ability to 'imaginatively create a community [...] where none exists nearby' and partake in 'a familial economy of sharing which rejects the feedback loop of impersonal publication, prize-winning poetry and fame' ('Lorine Niedecker' 129, 130). As we shall see over the course of the following chapters, far from simply being the local circumscriptions of a remote small-town rural life, Niedecker's avant-folkways would go on to play a pivotal role in furthering her 'familial' relations and in ensuring her place within a growing transatlantic company of poets whose poetics and publishing methods, like Niedecker's, show an incisive regard for the empowering economics, and social possibilities, of the small scale and of the creative pragmatics of independent, small press publishing.

Chapter Two

Ian Hamilton Finlay: Scottish Futurist

> I feel that I have come—at least for the moment—to the end
> of poems that are *about*, and want to do poems that just are.
>
> —Ian Hamilton Finlay to Gael
> Turnbull, 29 April 1963

Peter Middleton has suggested that Lorine Niedecker's 'commitment
to what she called the "folk,"' and her 'active interest in folklore,'
resulted in 'a radically innovative form of poetry' that distinguished
her from contemporaries such as Zukofsky and George Oppen ('Lorine
Niedecker's "Folk Base"' 170). Niedecker would later refer to the folk
elements of her poetry as her 'folk base,' which, in a letter written to
Jonathan Williams she believed 'might actually be my only claim to any
difference between most poets and meself' ('Letters' 54 '"Most poets,"'
Middleton suggests 'are presumably the poets she read in magazines
like *Origin*' ('Lorine Niedecker's "Folk Base"' 173). This is not, however,
necessarily the case. Ian Hamilton Finlay, whose poetry appeared in the
sixth issue of the second series of *Origin* in 1962, also shared Niedecker's
interest in 'folk.' Furthermore, Niedecker also claims Williams's poetry
as 'folk too but [with] an intellect beyond it also' ('Letters' 54). Indeed,
as chapter three argues, Williams's 'folk base' owes a considerable debt
to Niedecker's model.

Niedecker may have influenced Williams, but her affinities with
Ian Hamilton Finlay were entirely fortuitous, as Finlay's letter to Gael
Turnbull, written in the June of 1961, emphasizes:

> The more I see of American poems, etc., the more I feel they
> have arrived at much the same conceptions as I have, in my
> own wee way, rather home-made, and AGAINST everything
> I was taught to do by other Scotch writers. I think Lorine

> Niedecker's poems are superb. I am fair touched. (Cited in
> G. Turnbull 35)

Finlay's 'timely affirmation of [Niedecker's] folk aesthetic' was reciprocated by Niedecker who, after receiving a copy from Gael Turnbull, expressed similar enthusiasm for the folk poems in *The Dancers Inherit the Party* (Penberthy, 'A Posse of Two' 18).[15] Writing to Cid Corman in early January 1961, Niedecker explains how a number of the poems in *The Dancers Inherit the Party* seemed to reflect the sensibilities of *New Goose*:

> I thank whatever gods there be that someone's good hand
> (could it have been yours) sent me these poems. Nothing in a
> long while has reached my particular kind of home like they
> have. Certainly one-third of them have simply set me free.
> Could he have seen New Goose? (*BYHM* 26)

'Folk, wild witty things' is how Niedecker describes Finlay's poems to Zukofsky, and claims that they 'will liberate poems in me, half a dozen of his will,' although others, she confesses, are 'a trifle too weird for me' (*NCZ* 272).[16]

Finlay and McGuffie were so 'touched' by Niedecker's poetry that by the end of 1961 they had published Niedecker's second collection of poems *My Friend Tree*. This small collection of 16 poems is comprised largely of a selection taken from *New Goose* along with a scattering of poems that had more recently been published in several little magazines including *Origin* and *The Black Mountain Review*. Measuring approximately 8 × 5 inches, the format of *My Friend Tree*, like *New Goose* before it, is small and modest. Walter Miller designed the book and provided the 'abstract [...] quasi-glyphic' linocuts accompanying the poems (Middleton, 'The British Niedecker' 251). Along with her later book *North Central*, published by Fulcrum in 1968, *My Friend Tree* is,

---

15 Turnbull sent Niedecker a copy of *The Dancers* following Zukofsky's suggestion. Writing to Turnbull, he described Finlay as 'A Scots LORINE NIEDECKER who [...] would, I think, like his work very much' (cited in G. Turnbull, *More Words* 34).

16 In another letter to Zukofsky, Niedecker writes: 'Had fun, Harold [Hein] and I, last night reading aloud the Finlay poems. He didn't approve of most of them but when he got to the two longish ones that feature F's fishing shack home he said "Now that's nice, that shows you where he lives." He was so disgusted with the four-line Christmas one called Bi-Lingual, he got what the umbrella meant and by the time [he] got to the "peedie Mary" poems we were in a gay mood. Peedie will probably always stay in our vocabulary and could lead anywhere' (*NCZ* 272).

as Middleton notes, 'self-consciously crafted with an eye to dominant pictorial values' ('The British Niedecker' 249).

That conscious crafting, however, was not of Niedecker's choosing, as a letter to Zukofsky reveals:

> I must inform you of my disappointment—they are leaving out Ash woods and I rose from marsh mud and three tiny ones [sic]. I told them they can't do this as I wanted to think of this book as a Selected even though it would not say so on it. It seems the artist failed to draw for these and besides it brings expense down to omit. I said I'd send $25 if they'd include Ash woods—after all if this poem doesn't belong with folk, where does it? Or $50 if they'd put both in—and do it without pictures! They answer this book is too near ready to do any of this and that it is enchanting and they know I'll like it and what they want is to go easy in this one, introduce me to Scotland in little poems first. O Lordy, I know that this nobody is going to get me in on art work again, certainly not in *this* country. What do poems need an artist for? (*NCZ* 296)

'Visual adornment of Niedecker's work has,' Middleton suggests, 'been a recurrent temptation for publishers and equally often a goad to reviewers' ('The British Niedecker' 265). W. A. S. Keir, for example, reviewing several recent poetry books (including *My Friend Tree* and *The Dancers Inherit the Party*) in the *New Saltire* magazine disparages 'the gimmicky publishing tricks, the typographical eccentricities, [and] the illustrations' in *My Friend Tree* which, he claims, 'look like Rohrsbach [sic] ink-blots perpetuated by absent minded lab. boys' (82). Keir also bemoans 'the general mess of minimal amateur versifying' which he considers to be 'at its very worst' in Niedecker's book (82). However, the design and reception of *My Friend Tree* reveals as much about Finlay and McGuffie's publishing vision as it does Niedecker's poetry. It also reflects Finlay's own avant-folkways and the 'formative period of a new poetry' concerned with 'a visual as opposed to narrative syntax' (Cutts, 'The Aesthetic of Ian Hamilton Finlay' 32).

Finlay's folk sensibilities are particularly apparent in the early poetry (the principal subject of this chapter) that Finlay wrote in the late 1950s and early 1960s. In *The Dancers Inherit the Party*, Finlay exercises a discerning use of demotic language and vernacular idioms to portray a variety of rural and maritime landscapes (many of which have Orkney as their setting) and their cultures. Developing the demotic and vernacular in the slim booklet that follows *The Dancers Inherit the Party*, *Glasgow Beasts, an a Burd Haw, an Inseks, an, aw, a Fush* (published in 1961 by Wild Hawthorn's sister imprint, Wild Flounder Press), Finlay exploits the phonetic richness of the Glaswegian dialect in a series of related poems that bring a modern avant-garde twist to Ovidian themes of metamorphosis and the supernatural phenomenon of shape-shifting common to folklore and fairytale.

These early publications mark an important period in Finlay's work and show him tentatively moving toward the concrete poetry that would occupy him throughout the 1960s. As this chapter argues, the 'whole range of typographical, kinetic, standing and opening poems' that Finlay pioneered in the concrete phase of his poetry—where 'words have escaped the bounds of sentences' to possess instead 'an iconic presence'—develops significantly out of the folk poetry that precedes it (Black 37). In turn, Finlay's concrete innovations would play an integral part in the garden (later known as Little Sparta) that he began creating with his wife, Sue Finlay, at their Stonypath home in the mid-1960s. Referring to this 'avant-gardening' in 1966, Finlay claims that, it 'is not a whim, but the logical development of earlier concrete poetry—from the poem as an object on the page to the poem as an object properly realised in sandblasted glass, stone, or indeed concrete' (*Selections* xxi). If Finlay's later work is the 'logical development' of his concrete poetry, then his concrete poetry, and what Simon Cutts describes as Finlay's increasing concern for 'a visual as opposed to narrative syntax,' can be seen as the logical development of his earlier avant-folk poetics ('The Aesthetic of Ian Hamilton Finlay' 32).

The Scottish Renaissance

Wild Hawthorn's promotion of contemporary non-Scottish poets such as Niedecker is symptomatic of the disaffection and frustrations that Finlay and McGuffie were feeling in the late 1950s and early 1960s about Scottish literary culture. 'They are just not open to anything,' Finlay complains, referring to the Scottish literary establishment in a letter to Robert Creeley written in the December of 1961: 'And everything is all dreary and second-rate' (*AMO* 12). Writing to Niedecker earlier in the same year, Finlay offers an explanation for this narrow-mindedness when he remarks how 'all the Scotch poets say, you MUST write like THIS and THAT, if you don't you are *washed* and we shan't speak to you—and I knew what they were writing was wrong (for me) and wrong for life (as I saw it) and very wrong for poetry as it *historically* was' (*AMO* 10–11).

For many younger Scottish poets, the cause of this malaise was the domineering influence of the Scottish Renaissance and its figurehead Hugh MacDiarmid. As Eleanor Bell notes, there had been 'a growing impatience' with MacDiarmid's Renaissance project amongst a younger generation of writers who felt the 'need to openly critique forms of national insularity' that had become 'characteristic of the early 1960s Scottish literary context' (240). In early collections such as *Sangschaw* (1925), *Penny Wheep* (1926) and his long poem, *A Drunk Man Looks at the*

Thistle (1926), MacDiarmid innovated what Maurice Lindsay describes as a 'strategy of wringing new music and new imagery out of the enfeebled Scots tongue' (62). Lindsay is referring to MacDiarmid's 'synthetic Scots' (also known as 'Lallans') which, according to Matthew Hart, 'recreates the Scots poetic tradition via the contingencies of the dictionary, mixing contemporary idioms with obsolete and rare specimens from various regions of Scotland' (10). MacDiarmid makes a strong case for the Scottish vernacular in a series of editorials he wrote for the magazine *Chapman* in 1923:

> The Vernacular is a vast utilized mass of lapsed observation made by minds whose attitudes to experience and whose speculative and imaginative tendencies were quite different from any possible to Englishmen and Anglicized Scots today. It is an inchoate Marcel Proust—a Dostoeveskian debris of ideas—an inexhaustible quarry of subtle and significant sound. (*Selected Prose* 22–23)

According to MacDiarmid, the Scottish vernacular is a unique resource for writers because of its marked difference from standardized English or Anglicized Scots. Nevertheless, as his allusions to Dostoevsky and Proust suggest, MacDiarmid saw the Scottish vernacular as entering into a modern, international dialogue and offering 'a vast storehouse of just the very peculiar and subtle effects which modern European literature in general is assiduously seeking' (*Selected Prose* 22). Edwin Morgan emphasizes MacDiarmid's confidence over the eventual 'resumption of the Scots Vernacular into the mainstream of European letters' in his essay 'The Beatnik in the Kailyaird' (MacDiarmid, *Selected Prose* 22). Acknowledging the importance of these liberal aspirations for the burgeoning Scottish Renaissance, Morgan stresses how MacDiarmid, as its spiritual leader, 'wanted the movement to be *modern* in the sense that it would risk dealing with contemporary subjects and would experiment with new forms, but he also wanted it be unmistakably *Scottish*, if possible by a revival and an extension of the Scots vocabulary' (*Essays* 172).

Echoing Morgan's observations, Matthew Hart suggests that it is the 'unresolved tension' of synthetic vernacular poems of MacDiarmid's such as *Sangschaw* and *A Drunk Man Looks at the Thistle* that most effectively facilitate this motivation to be modern without compromising national identity (14). Synthetic vernacular poems such as *A Drunk Man Looks at the Thistle* possess a 'doubleness which is the condition of their existence,' Hart explains, and are 'half-obsessed with folk identity [and] half drunk on the refined spirits of global modernity' (14). The success of a synthetic vernacular poem is that it 'never reconcile[s] popular culture with *l'art pour l'art*,' Hart suggests: 'Such reconciliation would not only be difficult; it would suck the very energy out of a poetry that thrives on the tension between values like oral vs. written, idiolect vs. sociolect, and province vs. metropolis' (14).

However, for many younger Scottish poets, Morgan included, the tensions of the synthetic vernacular had in fact become 'resolved' and 'reconciled' in the increasing cultural myopia of the Scottish Renaissance. Thus, Morgan claims:

> Despite the efforts of Hugh MacDiarmid to deal with the nameably real in contemporary experience, this aspect of his work has been least taken up and developed by others. Too many heads are attracted by the sand. There is a new provincialism—in a movement which in MacDiarmid at least stretched out internationally and fought the Philistines. (*Essays* 174)

The 'new provincialism' had become particularly contentious with the publication of Norman MacCaig's anthology *Honour'd Shade* (1959). Many younger Scottish poets regarded the anthology as 'showing a bias towards the "Rose Street" poets that included MacCaig himself and Sydney Goodsir Smith, whose mentor was Hugh MacDiarmid' (Glen 27). They also saw this selection as reaffirming 'a literary establishment that seven young poets [Finlay, W. Price Turner, Tom Wright, Stewart Conn, Shaun Fitzsimon, Anne Turner, and Tom Buchanan] saw as obstructing their recognition as new voices on the Scottish scene' (Glen 27). Debate over the anthology prompted a public 'flyting' between the two factions which set a precedent for further flytings—'surely a folk art in itself,' as Thomas Crawford wryly noted in one of these flytings— that occurred in various publications such the *Scotsman*, *New Saltire*, and MacDiarmid's incendiary pamphlet, *The Ugly Birds Without Wings* (cited in Henderson, *The Armstrong Nose* 99).

Just how much Finlay and McGuffie were embroiled in these flytings is apparent in the editorial to the same issue of *New Saltire* that published Keir's review of *My Friend Tree*:

> The weird and wonderful Wild Hawthorn Press issues a monthly poetry sheet, *Poor. Old. Tired. Horse.*, which would be much better received if the publishers let it speak for itself and did not rush around Edinburgh taking flying kicks at anyone not prepared to proclaim the merits of 'POTH' in the columns of daily newspapers. (n. pag)

In the same issue of *New Saltire*, Finlay expresses his own opinions about the Scottish Renaissance when he reviews a new edition of John Speirs's book *The Scots Literary Tradition: An Essay in Criticism*, the first edition of which was published in 1940. 'I suppose I am an angry 36-year-old man,' Finlay writes: 'For anger, as well as good poetry, is what has been left to some of my generation by Hugh MacDiarmid and the Scottish Renaissance' (*'The Scots Literary Tradition'* 79). Speirs's compulsion to claim that the Scottish writer 'need not be insular' or 'exclude from himself the best that is thought and said outside Scotland,' according to Finlay, is symptomatic of the very insularity and parochialism that the Renaissance fostered (*'The Scots Literary Tradition'* 79):

> After thirty years (or whatever it is) of Renaissance, this is what requires to be said (perhaps). Isn't this a wonderfully unconscious criticism of the sort of set-up the Renaissance has *actually* created for us? I don't have to quarantine myself from the rest of the world just because I am a Scots, Scottish, or Scotch writer. The astonishing thing is that writers in most other countries, unliberated by Hugh MacDiarmid have been able to take for granted the freedom here cautiously announced by Mr. Speirs. (*'The Scots Literary Tradition'* 79)

The extent to which Finlay had not quarantined himself from the rest of the world is made apparent by his invocation of non-Scottish poets in his review—Paul Éluard, William Carlos Williams, and Louis Zukofsky—all of whom, he claims, are 'contemporary' in a way that MacDiarmid is not (*'The Scots Literary Tradition'* 80). Finlay also questions Speirs's tendency to view the 'traditional' North East fishing communities in George Bruce's poems in a manner that recalls the sentimentalized and nostalgic projections of folk revivalism:

> He says of Mr. Bruce's volume *Sea Talk*: 'Partly, the poignancy of these poems comes from the sense that this recollected world the world of the North East fishing community with its traditional way of life, has vanished with childhood and boyhood; partly, that it existed not only on the bleak edge of the northern sea but on the edge of the modern world ...' Well, I have stayed in Orkney, and I have never felt—except when talking to the local Grand Intellectual—that the modern world was somewhere else, that the island I was on was not part of it. And I wonder if the folk of the north east *really* feel that their community has vanished? In what sense, vanished? Is George Bruce's North East less real than Charles Olson's Gloucester, Mass.? (*'The Scots Literary Tradition'* 80)

As well as reaffirming his own position in relation to the Scottish Renaissance and its parochial attitude to the rest of the world—'When will someone write about the Scotland and its literature, not as The Great Exception, but as a part of the world?' he asks—Finlay's comments also shed light on the concerns and motivations of his own poetry during this period in the early 1960s ('*The Scots Literary Tradition*' 80). For example, by invoking Olson in the context of a relatively conventional poet such as Bruce, Finlay also affirms what Simon Cutts describes as 'Finlay's aesthetic of all art, which is something beyond and before the compulsive modernism of the avant-garde often propagated by the small press' (*SFA* 78). Indeed, Finlay's claim in his review of *The Scots Literary Tradition* that 'the American poet Zukofsky is infinitely closer to being Back—or Forward—To Dunbar than MacDiarmid the poet has ever been' is prescient of a later claim, made in 1966, regarding his distinctions between tradition, experiment, and the avant-garde: 'I am not interested in 'experiment' but in avant-garde work which can take the creative step backwards to join with the past' ('*The Scots Literary Tradition*' 80; *Selections* xx).

Orkney
It was while living and working, intermittently, in Orkney between 1955 and 1959 (more specifically, on the small hilly island, Rousay, situated north of Orkney's Mainland) that Finlay made an important breakthrough with his poetry. Writing to Cid Corman enthusiastically in 1962 about American poets such as Niedecker and Zukofsky and 'the same relation to the world' that they appeared to share with him, Finlay explains how he 'was writing on [his] own up in Orkney, never knowing all this stuff existed':

> I just went by intuition; I felt—FELT—that what was being done was being done here [in Scotland] was all wrong and not traditional or modern either, because real tradition consists in feeling how poetry was, and out of that, how it should be now, etc.—not, that is, just parodying tradition. (Cited in *Selections* 18)

It is notable, therefore, that in his defence of George Bruce's evocations of the North East fishing communities Finlay should draw upon his own experiences of Orkney. Indeed, Orkney might be to Finlay's poetry what Blackhawk Island is to Niedecker's, or Gloucester is to Olson's. According to Alistair Peebles, 'it is not only possible, but essential, in thinking about Finlay's work as a whole (and in thinking about Orkney), to acknowledge the force of that mythic or personal, pastoral or Arcadian vision of the islands, which he himself both created as an ideal and also allowed to take hold as history' (10). It was, Finlay explains in a letter to Ernst Jandl, a place 'where everything was simple and classical, as in an early legend' (*AMO* 34).

Finlay's fascination with Orkney is evident in a number of the poems included in *The Dancers Inherit the Party*. 'Poet,' an addition to the later editions of *The Dancers*, succinctly captures Finlay's affection for Orkney, and above all, Rousay:

> At night, when I cannot sleep,
> I count the islands
> And I sigh when I come to Rousay
> —My dear black sheep. (*D* 213)

Finlay's allusion to the nursery rhyme 'Baa, Baa, Black Sheep' recalls Niedecker's similar use of traditional children's poems and songs in *New Goose*. And, like Niedecker, a subtle, wry humour (as well as implicit sexual undertones) keeps the poem from lapsing into mawkish sentimentality. In this respect, 'Poet' is a prime example of what David M. Black describes as Finlay's 'love of the dangerous edge of whimsy and sentimentality' (36). The metaphor of Rousay as a 'black sheep' implies that this island is more enigmatic, darker, and stimulating—perhaps, sexually, as the 'sigh' implies—than its more ingenuous neighbours. Furthermore, whereas the monotony of counting white sheep traditionally sends the insomniac off to sleep, the black sheep of *Rous*ay in Finlay's poem stirs and a*rouses* the sleeper.

Finlay has claimed that the metaphor of the black sheep also reflects the island's distinctive flora. 'Most of the Orkney isles are low and green,' he notes, 'but Rousay has beautiful hills, covered with heather, which is soot-black through much of the year—a soft black such as one finds in the paintings of Emil Nolde' (*Selections* 282). As well as reiterating the mysterious, enigmatic nature of Rousay, Finlay's allusion to Nolde—a German–Danish painter and one of the first Expressionists—is also an early indication of Finlay's increasing concern for a visual rather than a narrative-based syntax which began while living in Orkney. 'I went to Orkney, where I started to write poetry,' Finlay explains, 'and experienced a problem,' namely, 'how to put words together—essentially a problem of syntax (*Selections* xx). This problem persisted as Gael Turnbull's account of Finlay, written in 1963, indicates:

> 'Too many wurrrds.' In fact, the fewer words in anything, the better he likes it. Especially hates syntax. Has been wrestling several weeks trying to write a brief introduction for an exhibition of paintings by a local painter he admires. 'I get stuck when I have to write a whole sentence. It gets all too complicated.' And how he seeks a poetry that will be 'pure' ('pyoor'). (157)

It is in relation to this problem of syntax that Finlay's poetics align most markedly with Niedecker's 'folk base.' Penberthy suggests that Finlay's poetry closely resembles Niedecker's because it shares 'the same playful manner of many of Niedecker's folk portraits, the same teasing regularity of rhyme working against the less predictable patterns of speech, [and] the same idiosyncratic quality of voice' ('A Posse of Two' 17). These similarities are evident in the 'Orkney Lyrics' included in *The Dancers*, such as 'Folk Song for Poor Peedie Mary' which, in recounting how 'Peedie Mary / Bought a Posh / Big machine / To do her wash,' draws parallels with Niedecker, particularly her use of local speech idioms ('peedie,' Finlay explains, 'is the Orkney word for "wee"'), ballad rhymes, and domestic subjects (*Selections* 112).

'Folk Song for Poor Peedie Mary' also recalls Niedecker's negotiations of preindustrial versus modern technology, as previously witnessed in her poems 'Hand Crocheted Rug' and 'To my pres- / sure pump.' In Finlay's poem, Mary tries unsuccessfully to apply the traditional method of fuelling a fire with peat in order to heat the water of her 'posh' modern machine:

> Peedie Mary
> Stands and greets
> Where dost thoo
> Put in the peats? (*D* 206)

The poem's ambivalence about the ultimate benefits (and quality) of this 'posh' technology also echoes sentiments previously witnessed in Niedecker's poetry about the inconveniences of modern conveniences:

> Peedie Mary
> Greets the more,
> What did the posh paint
> Come off for? (*D* 206)

'Greets' is the Scots word for 'weeps' or 'cries.'[17] Thus, Mary, cries all the more about the poor quality of her modern appliance.

In contrast to the natural, earthy 'folkbase' of Niedecker's poems, the folk speech in 'Folk Song for Poor Peedie Mary' assumes—at least within the structure of the poem—more artificial or incongruous qualities. For example, a more grammatically correct way of phrasing the poem's concluding couplet would be: 'Why' (or 'How') 'did the posh paint / come off?' Instead, Finlay abbreviates the more formal phrase, 'For what reason did the paint come off?' Using this demotic idiom, Finlay reiterates the poem's suggestion of 'folk song' and sustains the poem's accentual meter. The effect is almost childlike in the way that Finlay sacrifices correct grammar and syntax in order to achieve a doggerel

---

17   I am indebted to Alistair Peebles for pointing out the Scots meaning of 'greets.'

that inverts the regular four/three beat pattern familiar to traditional nursery rhymes.

Working the 'teasing regularity of rhyme [...] against the less predictable patterns of speech,' Finlay's doggerel achieves a deliberate 'idiosyncratic quality of voice' that markedly foregrounds the artifice of his poems (Penberthy, 'A Posse of Two' 17). As Finlay explains, '*ORKNEY LYRICS* [...] are about Orkney but perhaps what they are really about is POETRY—poetry which is not DEEP TRIVIAL *thoughts* but a search—not always successful—for GRACE and HARMONY and ORDER' (cited in 'DG' 107). This concern for grace, harmony, and order foresees Finlay's later developments in concrete poetry and his conception of 'a model, of order, even if set in a space which is full of doubt' (*AMO* 22). However, as Cutts notes, the faux-naivety and idiosyncrasies of Finlay's early poetry, and the crisis of syntax that he underwent while writing them, all derive from a 'folk element' that appears to invert or flout the very possibility of grace, harmony, and order:

> There is something ironic in his inversion of language for poetic ends, the incorporation into the verse scheme of the occasional colloquialism, in fact the seeming ease and casualness in making this handful of near-perfect poetry which, by its underlying redundancy, questions the future of poetry with the syntax of speech, the old lyric notion of song. This irony is enforced by the suggestion of a folk element as the axis of the book's arrangement, Orkney folksongs. ('The Aesthetic of Ian Hamilton Finlay' 32)

Folk Possibilities

The 'folk element' of Finlay's poetry is particularly important in terms of its cultural currency within the context of the Scottish anti-Renaissance of the late 1950s and early 1960s. 'The new Scottish poetry,' as Alec Finlay notes, 'was tied up with the ongoing Folk-Song Revival, and an alliance grew between "folkies" and the younger poets' such as Finlay who were dissatisfied with the Renaissance ('DG' 104). The Scottish folksong collector and friend of Finlay, Hamish Henderson, sums up this alliance in his suggestion that 'we are again in a period when folksong and art-poetry can interact fruitfully, and that it is in and through the present movement that this will come about' (*The Armstrong Nose* 125). The folksong revival 'has much to offer Scots writers,' Henderson suggests, because 'it sheds light on the language question, and suggests a way out of the Lallans impasse' of MacDiarmid and his Renaissance peers (*The Armstrong Nose* 96).

MacDiarmid's position on the folksong revival is evident in his flyting with Henderson in 1959 over the *Honor'd Shade* anthology:

> Mr Henderson [...] seems to find his ideal man in the 'muckle sumph,' and to wish to scrap learning and all literature as hitherto defined in favour of the boring doggerel of analphabetic and uneducable farm-labourers, tinkers, and the like. He is presumably at home among beatniks and beatchicks. Personally, I continue to think Dante, for example, or Goethe greater poets—and more credible specimens of homosapiens—than McGonagall or the authors of any—and all—of the 'folksongs' Mr Henderson and his colleagues so assiduously collect. (Cited in *The Armstrong Nose* 97)

MacDiarmid's high-handed dismissal of 'beatniks and beatchicks' may very well be a tacit allusion to Finlay and McGuffie because, although Finlay would later distance himself from such associations, in the early 1960s he found that positioning himself as a Beat 'was a useful way of placing his poems within a new popular movement and separating himself from the curmudgeonly Renaissance' ('DG' 100). Finlay's sympathies with the folksong revival, and his esteem for the aforementioned nineteenth-century Dundee poet William McGonagall, proved to be equally useful for dealing with the dour sensibilities of MacDiarmid and the Renaissance. As Alec Finlay notes, a number of Scottish writers, including Henderson, Morgan, and Finlay, 'used the spectre of McGonagall to tease or goad MacDiarmid' ('DG' 104).

Finlay's own ideas about folk and its interactions with 'art-poetry,' particularly avant-garde poetry, are made explicit in a letter he wrote to Henderson in the February of 1964 which was prompted by his reading of 'a wee report' in the *Scotsman* of Henderson's talk on MacDiarmid and McGonagall:

> Do you have any interest (it seems to me it would be nice if people did have) in the *possibilities* of folk ... i.e. you talk about the long folk line, of the concertina sort, with rhyme-ending, and it's true the earlier Mac is very inventive with this. Do you know my poem, 'Angles of Stamps,' in *The Dancers Inherit the Party*? I tried to use the folk-long-line there, with a kind *ironical sophistication*, and it seems to me that this *use* of folk—i.e., a deliberate use of it, putting it to use, has a lot of possibilities. (Cited in *The Armstrong Nose* 116)

Henderson's talk forms the basis of his subsequent essay, 'McGonagall the What' (1965) in which Henderson celebrates Dundee's 'unchallenged prince of bad verse writers' (*Alias MacAlias*, 274). Henderson argues in his essay that McGonagall's verse 'can teach us a great deal about the nature of folk poetry' (*Alias MacAlias* 274):

Completely devoid of the lyrical knack which would have set his productions on the road to becoming folk-songs, he had the compensating ability—or compulsion—to use *nothing but* the hobbling and broken-backed rhythms and verbiage of pedestrian folk-poetry, and to use these so consistently from end to end of poem after poem that in effect he created a new style. (*Alias MacAlias* 276)

The 'broken-backed rhythms and verbiage of pedestrian folk-poetry' that Henderson singles out in McGonagall's poetry are evident in his poem 'The Famous Tay Whale' which recounts the story of the humpback whale that swam into the Tay Estuary in the November of 1883, was killed, and then subsequently purchased by the showman-entrepreneur John Woods. Recalling a traditional broadside, Finlay published the poem, accompanied by a non-figurative linocut by Alexander McNeish, as an insert to the fifth number of *Poor. Old. Tired. Horse.*:

So Mr John Wood [sic] has bought it for two hundred and twenty-six pound
And has brought it to Dundee all safe and all sound;
Which measures 40 feet in length from the snout to the tail,
So I advise the people far and near to see it without fail.
Then hurrah! for the mighty monster whale,
Which has got 17 feet 4 inches from tip to tip of a tail!
Which can be seen for a sixpence or a shilling,
That is to say, if the people all are willing. (n. pag)

According to Henderson, McGonagall's style 'was formed out of the debris and detritus of folk-song—out of all the things which song, composed in "the idiom of the people," sheds in the process of *becoming* folk song' (*Alias MacAlias* 276). This 'debris' of folk-song, as Henderson describes it, is evident in the poem's crude ballad form, its use of quatrains, its plain and simple language, and its narrative style. The 'blown-up or attenuated' folk-motifs of McGonagall's poetry, as Henderson describes them, are discernible in the poem's doggerel and McGonagall's use of an AABB rhyme scheme, which departs from the more conventional ABAB or ABCB patterns of the ballad (*Alias MacAlias* 272). These crude, unrefined 'folk' elements, Henderson believes, have the positive effect of illuminating 'a wide stretch of the debatable land between art-poetry and folksong' and show how 'the folk process is not only a matter of unconscious modification' but 'also a matter at many different levels, of *conscious creation*' (*Alias MacAlias* 290, 291).

Many of Finlay's poems, including 'Folk Song for Poor Peedie Mary' in *The Dancers*, deploy a faux-naivety that recalls McGonagall's poetry.

For example, Finlay describes his poem 'Black Tomintoul' as having 'an ironic deadpan quality' that, 'like the comedians Laurel and Hardy, is always sophisticatedly and warmly ironic, always delightedly parodying itself' (cited in 'DG' 107). Finlay conveys these qualities by deliberately mispronouncing 'Tomintoul' ('TominTOWEL') as 'TominTOOL' (cited in 'DG' 107). Another poem, 'Archie the Lyrical Lamplighter,' is described by Finlay in his primer to *The Dancers* as 'carefully awful,' whereas 'The Island Beasts Wait for the Boat' is 'the KIND of poem that seems unsophisticated to naive people' (cited in 'DG' 107).

A further instance of Finlay's faux-naif poetics occurs in 'Frank the Bear Writes His Deb Friend.' In this poem, as David M. Black notes, a deliberate 'uncertainty about the use of the comma plays havoc with expectable rhythms and liberates feelings that would have been smothered by "correct" punctuation' (36). Indeed, the poem is very much about being 'frank' and writing as 'frankly' as possible (*D* 183). From such candidness, however, syntactic and grammatical errors abound. 'Only around the comma / There lingers an aroma,' the poem's speaker, Frank the Bear, remarks: 'Whose principle I option is / When writing such a letter / The more you have of them the better' (*D* 183). The poem concludes:

> Myself I must stop, there
> Hoping that this finds, you
> As it leaves, me your old and true,
> Friend Frank, the, Bear,,, (*D* 183)

It is perhaps not surprising, as Finlay explains in a letter to Niedecker, that, 'except for a few people who saw them, all the poets thought' that the poems in *The Dancers* were 'naïve, etc, and technically bad' (*AMO* 11). Writing in *New Saltire*, for example, Keir dismisses Finlay's efforts as 'typically eccentric doodles in the margins of a misdirected talent' (85). Finlay's talent, however, is anything but misdirected. The fey irony and whimsy of Finlay's poems are meant as a deliberate affront to the intellectual pretensions—the 'DEEP TRIVIAL *thoughts*'—of the Scottish Renaissance. Indeed, in the Orkney Lyric, 'Mansie Considers the Sea in the Manner of Hugh MacDiarmid,' Finlay wryly parodies the older poet's manner of conveying deep trivial thought:

> The sea, I think, is lazy,
> It just obeys the moon
> —All the same I remember what Engels said:
> 'Freedom is the consciousness of necessity.' (*D* 206)

Writing to Hugh Kenner in 1978, Finlay remarks that, 'we [...] *have* in Scotland a much-admired poet who talks habitually of the poetry of "thought" (pronounced endearingly as "thot"), as the very highest thing' (40). In Finlay's poem the Engels quote, derived from Hegel, gives a kind of intellectual gravitas to Mansie's observation about the sea's passivity and its subjugation to other, lunar, laws. Furthermore, the manner in which this quote is appended to Mansie's words recalls the prose borrowings that characterize much of MacDiarmid's poetry. As Finlay explains in a letter to Ronald Johnson, MacDiarmid 'simply sticks in VAST undigested chunks of prose (with no indication that they are STOLEN), and to make them look like "poems" he breaks the line every four or five words' (Letter to Ronald Johnson, c. 1966). Finlay offers an incisive parody of this method via the abrupt termination of the lilting lyricism of 'Mansie Considers the Sea,' brought about so emphatically by a ponderous quote from Engels.

A more subtle subversion of Renaissance 'thot' occurs in Finlay's poem 'Castle.' Not only does the poem address another sentimental subject—this time the childhood game of building castles out of haystacks—but it also undermines MacDiarmid's characteristic Lallans. Like many of Finlay's poems from this period, 'Castle' makes effective use of 'a spoken rather than synthetic or literary Scots' that, in addition to contrasting markedly with MacDiarmid's Lallans, also emphasizes its own artificiality (Cockburn, 'Dancing Visions' 9).

'One man is chosen king of every castle,' Finlay writes:

> The others have to stay below the castle.
> Like servants or like slaves they never say
> It's their turn to be kings. Can they not wrestle?
> They should have shots at each, alternately. (D 199)

In his commentary on the poem, Finlay notes the juxtaposition of the colloquial 'shots' and the more formal word 'alternately.' As well as suggesting the action of shooting, 'shots' according to Finlay, 'is a proly word from my childhood' which means to assert one's choice or opinion, whereas '"ALTERNATELY"—which has to be stretched out and sounded in all its syllables—is a posh word reminiscent of Auden' (cited in 'DG' 108). However, as Finlay explains, the relation is more dialectical than dichotomous, because 'the two words together are something else, neither POSH nor PROLY, but NATURAL—natural that is, in the POEM, which is, of course, a created and not a natural thing' (cited in 'DG' 108).

Questions of speech and syntax also concern the poem that Finlay mentions in his letter to Henderson: 'Angles of Stamps.' This poem takes as its subject a popular practice in the late nineteenth and early twentieth century known as 'the language of stamps,' which encoded secret messages via the strategic positioning of stamps on envelopes.

> Stick a stamp at an angle on a letter
> It means a kiss, yes, but what sort, is it a torn
> Kiss, sweet kiss, anguished cool as water
> Rowan burning kiss or kiss as pure as hawthorn? (*D* 176)

Typists (especially in the context of dictation and transcription) and stamps are both suggestive of bureaucratic systems or procedures that are impersonal rather than intimate, and public rather than private. Nevertheless, the poem's speaker looks to this depersonalized system of signification to find a solution to his own problems regarding the communication of personal affairs. In this respect, 'Angles of Stamps' saliently reflects the problems of syntax that Finlay was experiencing in the late 1950s and early 1960s and the similar questions of semiotic versus semantic communication that his poetry was seeking to resolve.

The crux of Finlay's poem seems to rest on the word 'denote' which, as well as punning on the suggestion of a lover's *note*, also indicates how the speaker cannot find the accurate means for communicating his love. Indeed, the poem's allusions to telling, saying and letters, the confusion of repeated words such as 'love' and 'true,' and the advice sought from the speaker's *typist*, all serve to expose the limits of conventional syntax. Kissing, which, like speech, is another way of communicating by way of the mouth is equally problematic. Thus, the poem seems to suggest that language and speech, far from ensuring order and clarity—of communicating 'truly'—actually obfuscates pure intentions. How, then, either via words or visual marks, does one effectively convey a 'sweet kiss, anguished cool as water / Rowan burning kiss or kiss as pure as hawthorn'? Whether 'a stamp [can] say what a kiss cannot'—that is, whether the semiotics of stamps can communicate more effectively than words—remains inconclusive (*D* 176). The typist's remark—'But whether you love your true love as true as you say / only time will tell'—not only highlights the platitudinous nature of a word such as 'true' but it also emphasizes the gulf that exists between words and the things that they are assumed to *correspond* with (*D* 176).

The semiotic potential of the language of stamps that Finlay's poem questions pertinently foresees his later reading of E. H. Gombrich's essay 'Icones Symbolicae: The Visual Image in Neo-Platonic Thought' (1948), which would influence Finlay's ideas regarding 'the being of language' (Finlay, 'Letter to Hugh Kenner' 40). Finlay was particularly responsive to the distinctions that Gombrich makes between the 'didactic' image and 'discursive' speech. The former, according to Gombrich, can be seen 'as a substitute for and supplement of the written word' (184). Gombrich places considerable emphasis 'on the autonomy of this form of symbolism,' and differentiates it from what he calls 'discursive speech' (184). 'Discursive speech is a relatively poor instrument for representing complex relationships,' Gombrich proposes, whereas 'vision allows us to see "all at once" what the word can only impart successively' (171–172, fn.3). Thus, for Neo-Platonists such as Marsilio Ficino the aim was to 'know truth directly, without the crutches of discursive reasoning. What to us is only understandable analytically is revealed to them, as it were, in a flash, as a whole' (171). Writing to Kenner, Finlay explains that Gombrich's 'distinction between "didactic" and "free-floating"—he in fact says "discursive"—corresponds exactly to a distinction I had arrived at on my own (in a quite innocent way)' ('Letter to Hugh Kenner' 40). According to Finlay, Gombrich 'fails to see that other people might discover the same things by *experience*,' rather than through 'academic research' ('Letter to Hugh Kenner' 41). 'Angles of Stamps' is a pertinent example of Finlay's 'innocent' discovery of this distinction. Not only is an unresolved tension between the didactic and the discursive evident in the poem's semiotic language of crooked stamps and little crosses, as well as in the 'free-floating' discursive speech of the poem's speaker, but the '*ironical sophistication*' of the poem also moves it significantly toward achieving its own 'didactic' autonomy.

The faux-naif quality of Finlay's early poems and his 'deliberate' use of folk establish an aesthetic distance that foregrounds his poems as artificial, constructed objects. It was a similar quality of artifice that Finlay valued in Creeley's poetry, as his letter to Creeley, written in late 1961, indicates:

> About movement, I didn't mean anything so posh as historical movement; I meant the way your poems move, what some people would call tempo. There is this idea that you use natural rhythms, American, etc., but I would say that what is remarkable in your poems is their artificiality, that is, the way they exist surrounded by a clear space, a pure style in a pure space. That is, they are beautiful. And there is a great fineness in their actual substance. (*AMO* 12–13)

The beautiful artificiality that Finlay identifies in Creeley's poetry is a consequence of what John Vernon describes as its struggle with 'the difficulties of speech' (313). For example, Creeley's poem 'The Pattern,' according to Vernon, '*enacts* [...] the hesitations, the broken, discontinuous quality, the frantic enjambments and short lines that carry the energy of the poem in jagged spurts, like someone continually catching his breath' (313). By enacting these speech acts, Creeley conveys 'the act of speech struggling upstream against the language it is wading in' (313). Thus, Creeley foregrounds the poem as 'the fact of its own activity':

> I think I first felt a poem to be what might exist in words as primarily the fact of its own activity. Later, of course, I did

see that poems might comment on many things, and reveal many attitudes and qualifications. Still, it was never what they said about things that interested me. I wanted the poem itself to exist and that could never be possible as long as some subject significantly elsewhere was involved. There had to be an independence derived from the very fact that words are things too. Poems gave me access to this fact more than any other possibility in language. (*Collected Essays* 490)

The 'movement' that Finlay esteems in Creeley's work, particularly its role in facilitating what Creeley describes as the poem's 'independence,' also illuminates Finlay's own similar concerns for a pure poetry. It also indicates why, unlike many of the other so-called Black Mountain poets of the period, Creeley's work met with sustained enthusiasm from Finlay.

Finlay's own repeated claims that many of his poems in *The Dancers* are primarily about poetry might initially seem to align with Eliots's claims in his essay 'From Poet to Valery' concerning '*la poésie pure*' and his idea that the subject of a poem is first and foremost the means to its own autotelic end: 'The subject exists for the poem, not the poem for the subject' (339). However, despite Finlay's own aspirations for realizing a 'pure' poetry, his poems do not attempt to hypostatize or sublimate their language in the manner of the Symbolists. Rather, as we have seen, Finlay uses a speech-based prosody that draws attention to the poem's artifice.[18]

As Ken Cockburn notes, rather than being concerned primarily with description, Finlay's early poems 'put the subject matter in the background and foreground instead the movement of thought, conveyed by formal means, principally rhythm and rhyme' ('Introduction' xxii). Finlay's poetry, therefore, might more accurately be compared to Zukofsky's analogy of cabinet-making and the 'certain joints' that the craftsman uses as 'fine evidence' of his skilful construction (*Prepositions* 212). In Finlay's case, the imperfect, accentual meter of 'Folk Song for Poor Peedie Mary'—which takes precedence not so much over the poem's subject as it does its syntax—is an effective equivalent of the craftsman's 'fine evidence,' exposing the 'certain joints' of his poem's construction.

Yves Abrioux compares these 'deliberate stylistic gesture[s]' in *The Dancers* to the 'rhetorical discomfiture' that Wordsworth creates with his use of demotic language in *The Lyric Ballads* (189). According to Abrioux, the 'prose rhythms and persona of Finlay's rhyming poems deliberately heighten this phenomenon,' which 'pits poetry against

---

18   Finlay was, however, an admirer of the Symbolist-inspired poetry of Wallace Stevens. 'Oddly enough,' he tells Stephen Bann, 'the place where his poetry was most relevant to me was Orkney' (*Midway* 293).

rhetoric' and 'provoked the hostility of his Scottish contemporaries—and the admiration of American poets,' including Creeley (189). In this respect, Finlay's use of rhythm and rhyme might be better understood in the context of Barrett Watten's notion of a reflexive 'constructivist aesthetics' which, Watten proposes, refers to 'the imperative in radical literature and art to foreground their formal construction' (xv). Indeed, the examples from 'modernist and postmodernist literature and art' that Watten cites—from 'the Russian constructivists and post-Soviet poets and artists, and American avant-gardes, from Gertrude Stein and Louis Zukofsky to the Language School'—are not that far removed from Finlay's own 'constructivist' sensibilities (xv). In addition to publishing Zukofsky and referencing Stein in some of his later works, the Russian constructivists, and the avant-garde milieu out of which they emerged offered Finlay important models for his move away from writing poems about things to instead make poems that simply *are*.[19]

A Visual Syntax

Finlay's own constructivist sensibility—his desire to 'lay bare the device of [his poems'] construction'—found a useful model in the imperfect poetry of McGonagall (Watten xxiii). It is especially revealing that Finlay also associates the naive constructivism of McGonagall's poetry with the Cubists: 'William McGonagall used RHYME much as the cubists painters used the RIGHT-ANGLE, as an important element of construction and as a way of separating ART from LIFE' (cited in 'DG' 108). Finlay's comment recalls Stein's remark in *Picasso* that 'the basis of cubism' is that 'the work of man is not in harmony with the landscape, it opposes it' (23). However, considering the formative influence that the book had on his work, it is also likely that Finlay is alluding to Daniel-Henry Kahnweiler in *The Rise of Cubism* (1949). Kahnweiler suggests that the Cubists' rejection 'of the more or less verisimilar optic image which describes the object from a single viewpoint' for a 'new method made it possible to "represent" the form of objects and their position in space instead of attempting to imitate them through illusionistic means' (12). 'With the representation of solid objects,' Kahnweiler claims, 'this could be effected by a process of representation that has a certain resemblance to geometrical drawing' (11).[20]

---

19   Gertrude Stein is invoked in a watering can installed in Little Sparta that bears Stein's famous legend 'Rose is a rose is a rose.' The material context of the watering can, however, also suggests the British garden designer, horticulturalist, and author of *Roses for English Gardens* (1903), Gertrude Jekyll. The repetition of the word 'rose' also refers to the rose of the watering can on which the text is inscribed (see Sheeler 117).

20   According to Stephen Scobie, Kahnweiler was a formative influence on Finlay and his interest in Cubism (ix, xii).

Finlay's conflation of McGonagall's folk with Cubism is indicative of his own avant-folkways and a further instance of the role that folk plays in his move away from a traditional 'narrative syntax' toward a visual, constructivist one. Indeed, as Alan Young notes, Finlay 'developed his individual language by finding kinship with pioneers of experimental modernism from whom there is an unbroken tradition of exploration into new possibilities of shaping expression' (212). Young, who alludes to Finlay in the broad context of Dada, uses the terms 'modernism' and 'avant-garde' interchangeably in his book.

One branch of 'experimental modernism' or, rather, avant-garde innovation, that was particularly important for Finlay's work in the early 1960s was the Russian Futurist poets and artists who burgeoned in the decade leading up to the revolution of 1917. The deliberate imperfections of Finlay's poems in *The Dancers*, as well as recalling McGonagall, also share affinities with the poet Velimir Khlebnikov, whose 'combination of naïveté and of a special kind of freshness with technical clumsiness' occurs within 'a highly involved lexical and metrical background where many kinds of irregularities are used in a virtuoso way' (Markov 37). Indeed, faux-naivety plays an important role within the wider history of the Russian avant-garde. According to Christina Lodder, 'it is their complete liberation from recognizable subject-matter that provides a common thread linking the very different styles that were created under the labels of Rayism, Suprematism, and Constructivism' (11). A crucial first stage of this 'liberation', however, 'was a movement which has been known since 1913 as Neoprimitivism' and which Finlay alludes to in his letter to Henderson (Lodder 11).

Noting how many of the Russian avant-garde poets and artists were influenced by folk art and tradition, Finlay explains his own avant-folkways in relation to the Russian avant-garde:

> Do you know any of the Russian poets of the time of the painters Larionov, Goncharova, etc.? They used street-folk-speech (such as I horrified local folk by doing in *Glasgow Beasts*), and the painters, too, were crazy on folk-art and *used* it in their work. [...] I'm sick of folk as a *dead* thing, and they never treated it as such ... Do you know Zoschenko's angry words about the people who resented his using gutter-folk-idioms to make his stories from? Of course the thing is, to use—not to duplicate from outside, but to make from, by understanding. We are surely very narrow if we understand only one culture. (Cited in Henderson, *The Armstrong Nose* 116)

The Neoprimitivism of Natalia Goncharova and Mikhail Larionov to which Finlay refers is an important model for his poetry at this time, particularly in relation to what Jared Ash describes as the

Neoprimitivists' concern with an 'art or an art style that reveals a primacy and purity of expression' and which arises from 'a synthesis of the principles found in primitive art forms and post-Impressionist paintings' (33, 34). Ash's suggestions reiterate those of Aleksander Shevchenko who, writing in his 1913 essay 'Neoprimitivism: Its Theory, Its Potentials, Its Achievements,' claims:

> There are no ideas that are born, only ones that are regenerated and everything normal, of course, is successive and develops from preceding forms.
> Such is our school—taking its genesis from the primitive but developing within contemporaneity. (48)

According to Shevchenko, Eastern art assumes an important role in this synthesis because of its shaping influence on traditional Russian folk aesthetics:

> Generally speaking, the word *primitive* is applied not only to the simplification and unskillfulness of the ancients, but also to peasant art—for which we have a specific name, the *lubok*. The word primitive points directly to its Eastern derivation, because today we understand it by a whole pleiad of Eastern arts—Japanese art, Chinese, Korean, Indo-Persian, etc. (48)

Shevchenko is keen to stress that primitivism 'points to the character of the painting (not the subject), to the means of execution, and to the employment of painterly traditions of the East' (48). It was Larionov and Goncharova, along with Olga Rozanova and Kazimir Malevich, Ash argues, who most forcefully 'espoused the fundamental aesthetic principles and theories, set the priorities, and developed the courage to abandon naturalism in art in favor of free creation, pure expression, and ultimately abstraction' (34).

This resurgence of interest in so-called primitive art reflects how, in the first two decades of the twentieth century, many Russian artists were rediscovering the importance of the East as a part of their reclaiming of their own national identity and heritage. 'Russia and the East have been indissolubly linked from as early as the Tatar invasions,' Shevchenko proposes, 'and the spirit of the Tartars, of the East has become so rooted in our life that at times it is difficult to distinguish where a national feature ends and where an Eastern influence begins' (48). 'Primitive,' therefore, is not used pejoratively, but as a way of distinguishing a Russian tradition. Indeed, for many Russian artists, the artistic values and sensibilities of Western art—particularly its emphasis on verisimilitude, representation, and mimesis—had led to an impasse in Russian artistic innovation. The extent to which Russian artists were left disillusioned and dissatisfied by Western models can be seen in Goncharova's spirited claims for Russian art. 'At the beginning of my development I learned most of all from my French contemporaries,' she explains: 'Now I shake the dust from my feet and leave the West, considering its vulgarizing significance trivial and insignificant—my path is toward the source of all arts, the East' (55).

For artists such as Goncharova and Larionov, the aesthetic legacies of the East endured in vernacular Russian art forms, particularly folk art. These forms helped them develop a style that Camilla Gray describes as the 'free use of a Fauve-derived boldness of line and colour' that functions 'as expressive entities in their own right' (97). Increasingly disillusioned with the Western art establishment, and having exhausted the possibilities that the nascent French avant-garde had offered them—particularly Cézanne, Gaugin, and the Fauves—many Russian artists in the first two decades of the twentieth century began 'turning to national folk-art traditions for that directness and simplicity which Gauguin and Cézanne had taught them to appreciate' (Gray, 97). 'Embroidery from Siberia, traditional pastry forms and toys, and the "lubok"—peasant woodcuts—were,' Gray claims, 'the sources from which Larionov and Goncharova drew their inspiration in this new primitive style' (97). Dating 'from the seventeenth century in Russia,' the *lubki* are 'similar to the English Chapbooks' being a demotic 'means of circulating songs and dances to peasants' (Gray 97). The 'unsophisticated beauty' of the *lubki*, as Shevchenko suggests, assume considerable significance in the Russian avant-garde and can be seen as one of the 'password[s]' for the new style:

> The simple, unsophisticated beauty of the *lubok*, the severity of the primitive, the mechanical precision of construction, nobility of style, and good color brought together by the creative hand of the artist-writer—that is our password and slogan. (45)

The influence of *lubki* is also evident in the small, handcrafted books that, as Nina Gurianova suggests, 'served as a creative laboratory for the avant-garde' and, according to Vladimir Markov, provides 'the classic form of a Russian futurist publication' (Gurianova 25; Markov 44). Not too dissimilar from Niedecker's own homemade/handmade books, these Russian books frequently used cheap paper made of wood pulp (and, like Niedecker, even wallpaper) upon which text would be handwritten, drawn, stamped, as well as printed. However, unlike Niedecker's holographic books, these Russian avant-garde books were printed lithographically in relatively larger numbers.

Rubber-stamping and potato or lino-printing were additional methods of printing that derived from the *lubok*. According to Ash, these avant-garde books 'became another means by which artists and poets reclaimed art and literature from their esteemed positions and blurred the lines between "high" and "low" by re-interpreting, and expanding upon the iconography and aesthetics principles of popular, indigenous art forms' (38). As Markov notes, the illustrations for these publications tended to be 'either primitivist in the manner of folk art, or imitative of children's drawings, but some of them could be termed nonobjective' (41).

Furthermore, these publications 'returned artists to the book by placing them in the same footing as authors and making them not intermediaries, or just illustrators, but literally co-authors and co-creators' (Gurianova 25). The legacy of this collaborative spirit can be seen in the Wild Hawthorn Press publications, including Niedecker's *My Friend Tree*, and many issues of *Poor. Old. Tired. Horse.* (including the combination of Alexander McNeish's linocut with McGonagall's 'The Famous Tay Whale' in the fifth issue), which share a number of *lubki* traits: 'the inseparability and arrangement of text and image on the page; flattened or inverse perspective and non-scientific proportion; an economy of means defined by simplicity of drawing, flowing lines, and a lack of superfluous detail; and a bold non-naturalistic, unbounded use of color' (Ash 35). Many of these qualities are evident in the two woodcuts that Zelko Kujundzic provided for *The Dancers*. The suggestion of Russian Neoprimitivism and *lubki* aesthetics in these woodcuts significantly reaffirm the knowing faux-naif sophistication and the conscious, self-reflexive, avant-folkways of the book's poems. Furthermore, just as Neoprimitivism marked an initial step of the Russian avant-garde away from traditional representation to non-figurative painting, Kujundzic's woodcuts pertinently prefigure Finlay's similar move toward a 'pure' non-objective poetics.

Glasgow Beasts

The influence of the Russian avant-garde is also evident in Finlay's second poetry booklet, *Glasgow Beasts, an a Burd Haw, an Inseks, an, aw, a Fush* (1961) which, according to Alec Finlay, 'playfully fuse[s] the Folk tradition and the modern avant-garde' ('DG' 108). There are clear echoes of the *lubok* aesthetic in the book's series of playful black and white papercut illustrations by Peter McGinn and John Picking that perfectly capture the witty tone of Finlay's poems. J. Derek McClure describes these poems as a series of 'minimalist sketches' that explore the theme of reincarnation via a 'consistent laconic Glaswegian spoken by *something* which has in successive incarnations appeared as a fox, a mouse, a bed-bug and much besides' (167). Finlay's poems in *Glasgow Beasts*, McClure suggests, are representative of a 'transformation of Glasgow patois into a poetic medium' (167). This theme of transformation is also suggested in the full title of the booklet—*Glasgow Beasts, an a Burd Haw, an Inseks, an, aw, a Fush*—which, McClure believes, 'startles the reader by switching from English to a phonetically-spelt rendition of the [Glasgow] dialect' (167).

The merging of conventional English with phonetically spelt dialect, (reminiscent of Mary Campbell Smith's in her popular poem 'The Boy in the Train') also occurs within the poems themselves, such as in the story of the giraffe who gets his neck caught ('sneckit') in a tree:

> so ah says
> haw Sara
> an she says whit
> way ur ye staunin
> aa bandy-leggit?
> bandy-leggit
> ah says
> so help me
> get
> yir
> giraffe
> free (*D* 232)

Not only do standard conventional words—for example, 'laugh,' 'giraffe,' 'neck,' 'tree,' 'says,' 'help,' and 'me'—commingle with more unfamiliar ones such as 'sneckit' (caught) and 'staunin' (standing), but familiar words also undergo phonetic transformations. 'Goat,' for example, actually means 'got' and 'whit / way,' which might initially seem to suggest 'which way' is in fact the Scots for 'why.'[21]

Although, as McClure suggests, 'the absence of punctuation, fragmentary lines and atomistic grammar' in the 11 poems of *Glasgow Beasts* 'convey an immediate impression of incoherence,' the sharp realistic tones of 'the Glasgow voice' do in fact give the poem a more implicit sense of cohesion (167). As Cockburn notes, Finlay's use of Glasgow dialect bridges the individual poems by conveying a unifying and cosmopolitan theme of transformation:

> At one level, the content of the individual poems is less important than the quick leaps from one type of animal to another—large and small, from different continents and of different species—but which are linked by the Glaswegian demotic in which they speak. ('Introduction' xxiv)

According to Alec Finlay, the series of animal incarnations that the poems present makes *Glasgow Beasts* 'a short essay in metamorphosis' which gives a 'nod to Ovid and Apuleius' ('DG' 110). Finlay's

---

21 Again, I am grateful to Alistair Peebles for pointing out the correct meaning of 'whit / way.'

transformations also recall the Scottish border ballad 'Tam Lin' and the broader folk tradition of dark supernatural shape-shifting narratives and tales of transformation.[22] As a soft, gentle mouse—'a moose / a richt wee douce / chap'—the poem's speaker acknowledges the darker implications of such mutability when he notes his mother's warning: 'hint / it / awful / it's / aa / a / trap' (D 32).

Mutability also recalls the Eastern notion of Saṃsāra and the attainment of *moksha* which ultimately breaks this cycle of reincarnation. As Cockburn notes, there is 'a playful Buddhist element to the changes' that the poems in *Glasgow Beasts* perform as well as 'the transitory nature of the "lives" being described' ('Introduction' xxiv). This Buddhist element is emphasized by Finlay's dedication to the Japanese poet Shimpei Kusano (1903–1988)—'tae Shimpei Kusano / whae writ / a hail buik o poems / aboot puddocks / "The Hundredth Class"'—whose poetry, according to his translator Cid Corman, 'is like a sort of modern folklore' (D 219; Kusano vii). *The Hundredth Class (Daihyaku Kaikyu)* was a collection of Kusano's poems, published in 1928, which take frogs ('puddocks') as their principle theme. In his claim that Kusano's frogs 'are the voices of proportion, muting wisdom even as they suffer it,' Corman also recalls the 'sense of scale' that Finlay conveys in the similarly timeless poems of *Glasgow Beasts* (vii):

> They are the voices of nature—in its largest sense—and of absolute innocence. They sing in the face of every moment's doom. They live beyond any idea of PROGRESS. They are gaiety and spontaneity and love and rootedness of fear in man. They mock our pretensions, but share them too—gently. They are a society whose limits are prehistoric and posthistoric. They live beyond abuse within the nature of man's spirit. (vii)

Finlay's affirmation of 'the wee' and 'the douce' in *Glasgow Beasts* achieves a similar effect. As well as being modest and playful—for example, the highland cow that enjoys scaring hikers with his 'herr-do' or the zebra 'heh heh / crossin'—the poems' use of the past-tense imparts a poignant sense of melancholy and mutability (D 229, 227). With its echo of Reynard, the archetypal peasant-hero of folklore, this melancholy is pronounced markedly in the fox's nostalgia: 'nae kiddin / ah wis pretty good / had a whole damn wood / in them days / hen' (D 223). With the concluding word 'hen,' Finlay succinctly conveys the fox's former sexual prowess because, in addition to denoting the traditional prey of foxes, 'hen' is also a common, colloquial Scottish term of

---

22 'Tam Lin' relates the fate of the eponymous hero who, as a captive of the fairies, is finally rescued by his true love after she has successfully held onto him while he metamorphoses, Proteus-like, into various animals.

endearment directed at women and girls. That 'hen' also sounds similar to 'then' ('them days then') only reinforces the sense of past glories that the fox can now only nostalgically recall.

Like Kusano's frogs, many of the beasts that the poems' speaker assumes have also suffered some form of abuse or hardship in their lives. For example, there is the caught minnow, lonely in its 'wee jaur' (D 226). Recalling Finlay and McGuffie's magazine, there is also the poor, old, tired horse who suffers the indignity and frustration of having his lunch 'hung / roon [his] / ear' for most of the day (D 233).[23] Life as a horsefly ('cleg') which, no doubt, would make the life of the horse (or the highland cow) even more intolerable, is also recollected with little fondness: 'honess / pals / like / no been born / a cleg / s e bess' (D 231). Such suffering, however, is endured stoically because nothing is permanent and everything, in what Corman referring to Kusano's poetry calls 'the geography of time,' is subject to change and metamorphosis rather than 'progress' (vii). Nevertheless, Glasgow Beasts advises its reader to 'mind yir back' (D 221). As well as indicating the lively spirit of poems that follow, this advice offered in the book's epigraph—'that's us // noo read on // an mind yir back'—also suggests the theme of reincarnation and counsels the reader to be aware that one's past deeds may determine one's present well-being.

The playful yet poignant manner in which Finlay treats these ontological concerns is a further example of how his poetry challenges the values and principles, particularly the profound 'thot,' of the Scottish literary establishment. Glasgow Beasts met with similar criticism from the old guard of the Renaissance just as The Dancers did shortly before it. Maurice Lindsay, for example, writing in his essay 'The Anti-Renaissance Burd Inseks an Haw,' dismisses Glasgow Beasts as trivial and slight compared to the 'deep and sustained seriousness of purpose' that he believes epitomizes 'the best Renaissance poetry' (64). 'Does Glasgow Beasts suggest high seriousness of purpose?' Lindsay asks before promptly answering his own question: 'I think not' (66). Perhaps most barbed of all, however, are MacDiarmid's criticisms of Glasgow Beasts in his pamphlet 'The Ugly Birds Without Wings' (1962). Finlay's use of 'street-folk speech' instead of Lallans seems to have caused particular offence to the older poet who, adopting the words of Edward Crankshaw, accused Finlay of 'using the language of the gutter' (Albyn 318, 331). According to Finlay, however, 'the whole point of my "Glasgow Beasts" wee book was, that it was *not* in Lallans, which is an

---

23   Finlay's horse also brings to mind Vladimir Mayakovsky's 1918 poem, 'Concern For Horses' and the 'fellow animal pain,' that the speaker feels in response to seeing a horse slip on a Moscow street: 'Horse, listen, / why should you think you are any worse? / Darling, / we / are all / essentially horses, / each and every one of us is something of a horse' (59, 57, 59).

artificial language built of dialects living and dead where GB was in the live un-noticed dialect of Glasgow' (*Midway* 110).

Finlay's decision to use a live speech, as opposed to the synthetic Lallans, draws further parallels with the Russian futurists, particularly Khlebnikov and Aleksei Kruchenykh who, as Markov explains, 'were preoccupied with certain kinds of Russian folklore':

> It is, however, not the 'respectable' imitation of, or use of motifs from, folk epics, lyrical songs, and fairy tales which is so widespread in Russian literature. It is, instead, an interest in the naïve and the 'illiterate' imitation and distortion of literature, especially of romantic poetry, in numerous songs, ballads, and poems which seldom attracted the attention of scholars, who to this day tend to dismiss them as having no artistic merit. (36)

The 'primitive' quality of the avant-garde books that modelled themselves on the *lubki* such as *Sadok sudei* (*A Trap for Judges*, 1910), offered a further affront to the 'respectable' mores of the Russian literary establishment. As Markov notes, the title of this '"almanac" (as Russians call nonperiodic literary miscellanies)' was Khleblikov's invention and deliberately ambiguous (8). The title, Markov explains, can be translated to mean that 'traditional critics are sure to misjudge the appearance of new literature, lacking criteria by which to evaluate it; but another translation "A Hatchery of Judges" is also possible, and then the book becomes a cradle containing new judges of Russian literature, the judges being the participants themselves in this instance' (8). That the texts and images that are included in *Sadok sudei* (by Khlebnikov, David and Nikolai Burliuk, Elena Guro, Vasilii Kamenskii, Velimir Sergei Miasoedov, and Ekaterina Nizen) were printed on the reverse of cheap wallpaper leaves was certainly a goad, if not 'a trap,' for the establishment judges of literature at the time. Indeed, Kruchenykh remarks of the significance of wallpaper in these futurist publications: 'With the wrapping and wallpaper of our first anthologies, books and declarations, we launched an attack on the extravagant tastelessness of the bourgeois[ie's] *verges* and gilded bindings, stuffed with the diseased pearls and drunken lilies of gentle little boys' (cited in Ash 38).

POTH 1964

The tacit affinities that Finlay shows for the Russian avant-garde in *The Dancers* and *Glasgow Beasts* are made more explicit in the special Russian issue of *Poor. Old. Tired. Horse.* (Number 8), published in 1964 in honour of Natalia Goncharova, Mikhail Larionov, El Lissitzky, Kasimir Malevich, Alexander Rodchenko, Vladimir Tatlin, Varvara Stepanova, Olga Rosanova, Liubov Poponova, and David Burliuk (Figure 4). Finlay mentions this issue of his magazine in his letter to Henderson, requesting from him a 'trans. of the folk-jazzy poetry' of the futurists for the issue (cited in *The Armstrong Nose* 116). It would appear that Henderson did not contribute any translations, nevertheless the magazine's four pages jostle with an eclectic selection of work very much in the spirit of the early Russian avant-garde almanacs. Line drawings by Mayakovsky and a typographical design by Lissitzky appear alongside Edwin Morgan's translations of poems by Khlebnikov and Yury Pankratov as well as Anselm Hollo's translation of a poem by Andrei Voznesensky, and J. F. Hendry's translations of poems by Alexander Tvardovskii and A. Khlebnikov. Furthermore, two of Spike Hawkins's 'Pig Poems' (inspired by Larionov's 'Provincial Life' paintings) are included in addition to Jonathan Williams's visual poem 'The Inevitable Form of an Early Flying Machine,' which takes Tatlin's famous glider as its subject. The issue concludes with Mary Ellen Solt's homage to Goncharov, a visual poem suggestive of Apollinaire's calligrammes, called 'White Rose.' The international scope of the magazine (comprising Russian, American, Scottish, and Finnish contributions), makes a defiant stand against the provincial quarantine of the Scottish Renaissance.

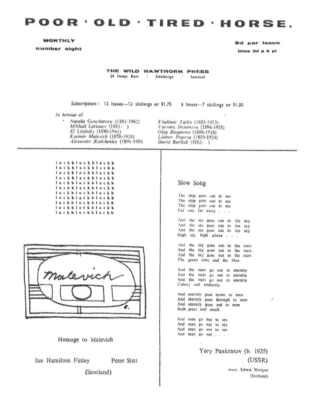

Figure 4. Cover of *Poor. Old. Tired. Horse.* 8 (1964).

Perhaps of most significance in the special Russian issue of *Poor. Old. Tired. Horse.* is the inclusion of a tiny concrete poem by Finlay that shares the magazine's front page with a black and white non-figurative drawing by Peter Stitt. Both items are titled at the foot of the page as 'Homage to Malevich.' This early example of Finlay's concrete poetry—originally published without Stitt's drawing in his first collection of concrete poems, *Rapel: 10 Fauve and Suprematist Poems* by the Wild Hawthorn Press in 1963—signals another breakthrough in Finlay's poetry.[24] The crisis of syntax in Finlay's earlier poems finds a resolution of sorts in this concrete poem that, in its homage to Malevich's iconic painting *Black Square* (1915), permutes two words 'black' and 'block' within a single 'block' of text.

As Stephen Scobie notes, 'the relationship between these two meanings ['black' and 'block'] are suggested not by syntactic means but by visual ones' (183). In this respect, 'Homage to Malevich' builds upon rather than breaks from the more traditional poetic forms that *The Dancers* had previously subverted. The questioning of discursive language in 'Angles of Stamps,' for example, finds an answer of sorts in 'Homage to Malevich' which, to recall Gombrich, substitutes the discursive speech of the earlier poem for a 'didactic' and iconic image constructed out of words.

Again, the trajectory of Finlay's developing poetics saliently parallels that of Russian avant-garde that he celebrates in *POTH*. As John E. Bowlt notes with regard to the Russian Neoprimitivists, the 'disproportionate concentration on such specific artistic concepts as inverted perspective, flat rendition of figures, distinct vulgarization of form, outline by color rather than line, and consequently the shift in visual priorities began a process of reduction that one is tempted to relate ultimately to Malevich's *White on White* (1918)' (*Russian Art of the Avant-Garde* xxvii). Marjorie Perloff identifies a similar shift in the iconic 'cutout flower shape' that Goncharova provides for the cover of the collaborative book *Mirskosta* (*Worldbackwards*, 1912) which presents a 'fusion of the primitivism of the *lubok* or peasant woodcut on the one hand and the movement towards nonobjective (*bespredmetnoe*) art on the other' (*The Futurist Moment* 136). This fusion of folk and non-representational modes extends further still into the constructivism of El Lissitzky who, Bowlt argues, despite being frequently 'presented as the constructivists' constructivist' due to the 'precision and detachment' of his industrial designs in fact 'remained indebted

---

24 *Rapel*, however, does not mark a complete break from Finlay's earlier poetry. By transcribing the first line of the popular Irish song 'The Rose of Tralee'—'The pale moon was rising above the green mountain'—into Glasgow dialect—'the' as *ra* and 'pale,' *pel*—Finlay's first book of concrete poems continues the demotic dialect of *Glasgow Beasts*.

to [...] craft tradition' ('Manipulating Metaphors' 129). According to Bowlt, 'the hand was the beginning and the end of the creative search' for Lissitzky ('Manipulating Metaphors' 130). Nowhere is this more evident than in Lissitzky's famous lithographic collage, *Self-Portrait: The Constructor* (1924) whose superimposition of the artist's eye in the centre of his palm 'symbolize[s] the more abstract concepts that intrigued Lissitzky throughout his life—vision versus touch, space versus surface, composition versus construction' as well as 'the visual artist and the manual artisan' ('Manipulating Metaphors' 133). Thus, to recall B. A. Botkin's salient phrase, in the constructivism of *The Constructor* it is possible to see an extension, rather than rejection, of the 'mindskills and handskills' of an abiding Russian folk tradition (*The American People* 11).

According to Stephen Bann, Finlay's 'Homage to Malevich' marks an important moment in his career because it 'expresses a tension which will prove crucial to his farther development as an artist: that of form and non-form, language and non-language, being set not merely in opposition, but *in a dialectical relationship*' ('Ian Hamilton Finlay' 60). This dialectical relationship can be discerned in the way the poem sets up opposing notions of permanence ('block' and 'lock') and impermanence ('lack'). Considering these tensions in further detail, Susan Howe notes:

> The black (figure) and block (ground) balances with lock (stability) against lack (instability). Something open versus something closed. Are lack and black one and the same image, or exactly opposite? Are block and lock alike? All this is exactly what the title or subject suggested—Malevich's search for formal invention. ('The End of Art' 7)

Finlay's own 'search for formal invention' in the poetry of *The Dancers* and *Glasgow Beasts*, as well as in his early concrete poetry, results in an equally fruitful dialectical relationship between folk and avant-garde sensibilities. That relationship is perhaps most effectively realized in the way that Finlay, according to Howe, has, in 'Homage to Malevich,' produced 'an exact arrangement with complete economy' (6).

A Model of Order

Exactness and economy are qualities that also inform Finlay's notion of concrete poetry as a 'model of order.' Finlay introduced this often-quoted phrase in a letter to the French poet Pierre Garnier in 1963 and remains a defining statement for his poetics. Once again, Finlay turns to the historical avant-garde to frame his ideas, invoking the Belgian sculptor, painter, and De Stijl associate George Vantongerloo alongside Cubism, and, most significantly, Malevich:

> I approve of Malevich's statement, 'Man distinguished himself
> as a thinking being and removed himself from the perfection
> of God's creation. Having left the non-thinking state, he strives
> by means of his perfected objects, to be again embodied in
> the perfections of the absolute, non-thinking life ...' That is,
> it seems to me, to describe, approximately, my own need to
> make poems ... (*AMO* 22)

The emphasis that Finlay places on the autonomy of the poem as an
object is emphasized by his allusions to Malevich and the geometrical
abstractions of the Russian's 'suprematist' paintings, particularly *Black
Square*. In 1915, in an 'attempt to free art from the ballast of objectivity,'
Malevich explains, he 'took refuge in the square form and exhibited
a picture which consisted of nothing more than a black square on a
white field' (342). Malevich coined the term 'Suprematism' to describe
this non-representational art which expresses an emphasis on geometric
forms that 'ignores the familiar appearance of objects for the rediscovery
of pure art' and stands apart from the environment in which it occurs
(342). According to Malevich, for a work to be 'pure' it must exist
independently of the artist. Finlay echoes this idea in his suggestion
that, 'though the objects might "make it," possibly, into a state of
perfection, the poet and painter will not' (*AMO* 22). Like Malevich's
'pure' Suprematist paintings, the 'suprematist' concrete poem aspires
for a formal objectivity and a 'perfection' that exists independently of
its maker.

'I call my poems "fauve" or "suprematist,"' Finlay explains to Garnier,
in order 'to indicate their relation to "reality" ...' (*AMO* 21–22). The
former refers to the label given to the works of Henri Matisse, André
Derain, and Maurice de Vlaminck when, circa 1904, they began 'us[ing]
colour with an unprecedented freedom, intensity and arbitrariness' and
inadvertently 'play[ed] a brief but important role in the evolution of
cubism' and the art of the Russian avant-garde (Fry 12). Despite its
influence on these movements, as Edward F. Fry remarks, 'fauvism did
not mark a decisive advance beyond the innovations of late nineteenth-
century painting,' but rather 'was a recapitulation and intensification
of such previous developments as the modified pointillism of Signac,
the brilliant colouristic achievements and expressive brushwork of Van
Gogh, and Gauguin's decorative colour patterns' (12). Thus, unlike
the formal objectivity of Malevich's Suprematism, Fauvism retains a
tentative reference to the world beyond the canvas.

Writing to Louis Zukofsky in 1963, Finlay explains that some of his
concrete poems 'are like the Apollinaire kind and I call them "fauve,"
as that seems accurate of the kind of feeling involved (its relation
to reality, its kind of SPACE); the other kind more formal, I call

"Suprematist" (after Malevich's movement)' (*AMO* 19). Finlay expands on these definitions in a letter written to Mike Weaver in 1964:

> I say 'fauve' of some poems to mean a certain relation to 'reality'—that those poems refer to the world ... but are not 'realistic' ... , i.e., I mean they are like early Derain, etc. ... constructions arising from life, but not pretending to BE life ... And 'suprematist' I say when I mean that the form is the central thing in the poem ... that it is a 'pure' work ... (or meant to be...). (Cited in Weaver 13)

Thus a 'pure' suprematist poem such as 'Homage to Malevich,' as Anne Moeglin-Delcroix suggests, 'is also an object, of language and a play with letters; an object of language in that it eliminates discursivity, relations between words, and "syntax"' ('Poet or Artist?' 34). As a play with letters, Finlay's language-object, Moeglin-Delcroix suggests, 'is determined by the mechanism of construction and whose closure upon itself guarantees [a] "purity"' that recalls that of Malevich ('Poet or Artist?' 34).

In contrast, Finlay's 'fauve' mode is evident in his poem 'Scene,' which he included in later editions of *The Dancers*. Rather than using the word 'landscape,' the poem's title, 'Scene,' makes an important but subtle pun on 'seen,' emphasizing how the poem is more about seeing, rather than realistically depicting, a landscape. In this respect, Finlay's poem recalls Cézanne's 'realism of the psychological process of perception' and his advice to 'deal with nature by means of the cylinder, the sphere and the cone' (Fry 14; Cézanne, cited in Friedenthal 180). The psychological process of perception is further conveyed in 'Scene' by juxtaposing emotive words with geometrical terms, as in the poem's concluding couplet:

> The rain is Slant. Soaked fishers sup
> Sad Ellipses from a cup. (*D* 212)

'Sad Ellipses' gives to an otherwise impersonal shape a melancholy mood. Indeed, how can a shape be 'sad'? Or, for that matter, how can tea be 'strong, and brown, and Square' (*D* 212)? Yet visual mimetic detail remains implicit in these 'Ellipses' that, one can imagine, might be caused by the slant rain falling in the fishers' cups or, perhaps, the gentle ripples caused by their 'sups.'

Furthermore, like Niedecker, Finlay takes advantage of words that function simultaneously as nouns and verbs:

> The fir tree stands quite still and angles
> On the hill, for green Triangles. (*D* 212)

As a noun, 'angles' denotes geometric angles, but as a verb it adumbrates the 'fishers' (anglers) in the poem. These details, along with specific references to trees, cups, and fishers, prevent the poem from becoming non-figurative or 'suprematist' in the manner of 'Homage to Malevich' and instead still, albeit obliquely, evoke a world beyond itself.

In addition to Fauvism, De Stijl, Cubism, and Suprematism, Finlay, in his 1963 letter to Garnier, also invokes more contemporary avant-garde currents in the form of the concrete poetry manifesto of the Brazilian Noigandres group, 'Pilot Plan for Concrete Poetry,' co-written by Augusto de Campos, Decio Pignatari, and Haroldo de Campos in 1958:

> I think any pilot-plan should distinguish, in its optimism, between what man can construct and what he actually is. I mean, new thought does not make a new man; in any photograph of an aircrash one can see how terribly far man stretches—from angel to animal; and one does not want a glittering perfection which forgets that the world is, after all, also to be made by man into his home. I should say—however hard I would find it to justify this in theory—that 'concrete' by its very limitations offers a tangible image of goodness and sanity; it is very far from the now-fashionable poetry of anguish and self. ... It is a model, of order, even if set in a space which is full of doubt. (*AMO* 22)

In their 'Pilot-Plan,' the de Campos brothers and Pignatari assert that the 'Concrete poem communicates its own structure: structure-content' and, ultimately, 'is an object in and by itself, not an interpreter of exterior objects and/or more or less subjective feelings' (cited in Solt 72). These claims adumbrate Malevich's earlier assertion that 'the visual phenomena of the objective world are, in themselves, meaningless; the significant thing is feeling, as such, quite apart from the environment in which it is called forth' (341). The Noigandres Group and Malevich's emphasis on the autonomous object set apart from its immediate environment is reiterated in Finlay's 'model of order' that, 'set in a space which is full of doubt,' exists independently of its environment. In a similar spirit to the 'structure-content' of the Noigandres' ideal poem, Finlay's 'model of order' is conceived as a construction rather than the expression of a subjective feeling that occupies its environment as an object.

Finlay's notions of a 'pure' and, in particular, 'suprematist' model of poetry, recall the formalism of Roger Fry's 1909 'Essay in Aesthetics' which stresses what Johanna Drucker describes as 'aesthetic purity and aesthetic autonomy' and the 'absolute faith in the object status of the pictorial image; its unity as the basis of its completeness' (*Theorizing* 71, 74). Fry's reading of Cézanne, Drucker suggests, delineates 'a formalism in which visual referents are ignored as surely as linguistic or literary ones—in the name of what is set up as visual autonomy':

> The muted viewer is exhorted to experience the order and variety of visual images according to the terms of a formalist aesthetic. This aesthetic is fundamentally ant-mimetic at the same time that it is essentialist and truth-bound in its search for absolutes. For Cézanne the validation of visual truth lay in the forms of nature; for Fry they approach the domain of universal forms which transcend experiential visuality. Any relation to an external model of visual form is insignificant in his formalist aesthetics and its insistence on the unity and completeness of the image. (*Theorizing* 74)

A poem such as 'Homage to Malevich' certainly gestures toward such 'self-sufficient autonomy' and 'Scene' pertinently recalls Fry's belief that Cézanne sought an 'equivalence, not a likeness, of nature' (cited in Drucker, *Theorizing* 71). Nevertheless, as both poems imply, Finlay's models of order—whether 'suprematist' or 'fauve'—never fully achieve such autonomous completeness because, to recall Bann's point, the linguistic or visual referent retains a dialectical function, drawing attention to the space 'full of doubt' in which the poem is set. 'For language is itself presence and absence,' Bann notes, and 'in terms of Saussure's distinction it comprises both *signifier* and *signified*' ('Ian Hamilton Finlay' 60). Furthermore, as Thomas A. Clark suggests:

> To write a poem is not just to make an object which will take its place among other objects, but to introduce a structure which will reorder and revalue the existing physical and psychic facts. Whether the space beyond a poem, or around it, is hospitable or inhospitable, remote or contiguous, it is everywhere packed with energy. ('Poetry and the Space Beyond' 45)

Finlay tacitly reiterates the dialectical relationship of 'Homage to Malevich' in his booklet *Hints and Tips for Boat Modellers* (1999) when he writes: 'Model yachts are not propelled by model winds' (n. pag). This tension between the constructed 'model' and the natural world beyond it epitomizes the 'semiotic turn' that Perloff identifies in Finlay's work, particularly in his homages to the non-figurative tradition of the avant-garde ('From "Suprematism"' 91). As Perloff suggests, 'the natural world, banished from the suprematist universe' of Malevich— and which is also banished from Fry's formalism—tenaciously 'reasserts itself' in Finlay's work ('From "Suprematism"' 91). Any 'model of order,' therefore, like the 'whimsy' of *The Dancers*, as Hugh Kenner describes it, is invested with a 'bleak and casual panic, as though on the edge of the world' (cited in Finlay, *Domestic Pensées* dust jacket).

In tracing the trajectory of Finlay's poetry from *The Dancers* to *Rapel*, it is possible to see how the folk-inflected whimsy of his early poems prepares and facilitates 'the "violence" done upon discursive language' in his concrete poetry (Bann, 'Ian Hamilton Finlay' 60). What Bann identifies as the dialectical tension—'the equivocal status of the edge, the bordering limit' informing 'Homage to Malevich'—and which 'guarantee[s] that concrete poetry will not, for Finlay, become a barren, formalistic practice,' is tacitly present in *The Dancers* and the tensions that underpin its faux-naif lyric poems ('Ian Hamilton Finlay' 60). Thus, the 'principle of conflict' that not only 'animates the formal structure' of 'Homage to Malevich,' as Bann notes, but occurs throughout Finlay's entire oeuvre as 'a force that will break open the framework of syntax's new shelter on the printed page, [and make] Finlay's career a continual transcendence of medium,' has its germ in the faux-naif folk of Finlay's earliest poetry ('Ian Hamilton Finlay' 61).

Chapter Three

Jonathan Williams: Beyond Black Mountain

> What do you think of when confronted by the term 'Black Mountain.' Is it;
>
> a. A place
> b. A brand of shoe paste
> c. A dance
> d. None of the above
>
> —*Tarasque*, Number 10

Jonathan Williams was born in Asheville, Buncombe County, North Carolina, to Thomas Benjamin and Georgette Williams who, Ronald Johnson explains, 'were straight from the gracious strictures of Southern Semi-aristocracy (yet stubborn mountain folk to the bone)' ('Jonathan Williams' 406). Although he spent most of his youth in Washington D.C., Williams's Southern roots form a significant part of his poetry, particularly his interest in Appalachia's folk cultures and natural history. Williams's links with North Carolina also figure prominently in his associations with the liberal arts college Black Mountain College where he enrolled as a student in the autumn of 1951. Williams's experiences at Black Mountain, as this chapter argues, played a formative role in his development as a poet, photographer, and publisher.

Prior to Black Mountain College, Williams briefly 'studied art history at Princeton, painting with Karl Knaths at the Phillips Memorial Gallery in Washington, etching and engraving with Stanley William Hayter [a British printmaker and artist, closely connected with Surrealism and American Abstract Expressionism] at Atelier 17 in New York, and the whole range of arts at Chicago's Institute of Design,' including photography and typography (Johnson, 'Jonathan Williams' 406). The Institute of Design, formerly The School of Design in Chicago, was established by the Hungarian constructivist and former Bauhaus instructor László Moholy-Nagy in 1944 and, according to Williams, 'was one of those schools rather like Black Mountain' where 'the arts were the basis of the curriculum' (Alpert 56).

The origins of Jargon are traceable to this period immediately predating his time at Black Mountain. 'The first Jargon was done in San Francisco while I was there in June,' Williams tells Barry Alpert: 'Just a very small little folded sheet that with a copper engraving by a man who had worked with Hayter, David Ruff, and a poem of mine,' printed in an edition of 50 copies (Alpert 59). Although Williams dismisses this early poem, titled 'Garbage Litters the Iron Face of the Sun's Child,' as 'an awful Patchenesque poem,' the Neo-Romantic etching by Ruff (a painter, etcher, and printer based in San Francisco) with its suggestion of John Craxton emphasizes the visionary, Blakean sensibilities that Williams would subsequently develop in books such as *In England's Green & (A Garland and a Clyster)* (1962), *The Lucidities: Sixteen in Visionary Company* (1967), and *Mahler* (1969) (Dana 203). This abiding Romantic strain in Williams's work would also complicate the tenacious perception of Jargon as simply a Black Mountain press and would be a contributing factor in Williams's subsequent estrangement from that particular label. Indeed, as this chapter will argue, one of the defining characteristics of Jargon is its refusal to commit exclusively to one single school or style of poetry and its willingness to publish poets 'antagonistic' to one another, such as Charles Olson and Kenneth Patchen (Dana 192).

Williams's non-partisan approach to publishing has, over the decades, as Richard Owens and Jeffery Beam note, formed 'a constellation of cultural figures and objects that brings together in a single orbit the utterly unpolished and the cosmopolitan, the eccentric and the carefully measured, the odd and the familiar' (para 6). The 'cursory but by no means exhaustive index of figures,' that Beam and Owens offer by way of an example, include:

> American authors James Broughton, Robert Creeley, Guy Davenport, Robert Duncan, Russell Edson, Buckminster Fuller, Ronald Johnson, Denise Levertov, Paul Metcalf, Lorine Niedecker, Charles Olson, Joel Oppenheimer and Louis Zukofsky; photographers Lyle Bongé, Elizabeth Matheson, John Menapace, Mark Steinmetz and Doris Ullman; British poets Basil Bunting, Thomas A. Clark, Simon Cutts, Ian Hamilton Finlay and Mina Loy; outsider artists Georgia Blizzard, St. EOM (Eddie Owens Martin), Howard Finster, James Harold Jennings and Clarence Schmidt; bookmakers Jonathan Greene, Doyle Moore and Keith Smith. (Owens and Beam para 6)

To this list can also be added a number of artists that have worked closely with Jargon such as R. B. Kitaj, Sandra Fisher, Paul Sinodhinos, John Furnival, Karl Torok, and Ian Gardner.

The name 'Jargon' may seem to contradict the all-inclusive nature of this constellation. However, as Williams explains, the name was, in part, intended ironically. 'I liked the irony of the word,' he tells Dana, which was suggested to Williams by the painter Paul Ellsworth, a fellow student at the Institute of Design in Chicago:

> He would throw words around, and he kept talking about jargon. 'Life's jargon. Jargon.' I said, 'What do you mean?' and he'd say—he did have it right, in a way—he said, 'I mean in my own speech. My language, as opposed to the tribe's language.' (Dana 203)

The singularity implied by Ellsworth, his emphasis on one's own speech and language, reflects Jargon's ethos and the deliberate peripheral position it would establish in relation to the more uniform languages of 'the tribe' associated with the various prominent poetry schools and movements. Williams claims that he has 'always been wary and sensitive to the "exclusive"' and 'yearn[s] for more accommodation, more generosity, more passion on the part of writers who take it upon themselves to publish others':

> I don't think poetry in the hands of little groups helps very much. It seems to me that there'll be a tremendous useless battle between ... you know there'll be Bly's people, so to speak, or Frank O'Hara's people, or Mr. Creeley's people; or there'll be this that and the other bunch, you know. (Alpert 59–60)

As Kenneth Irby notes, the word 'elite' 'derives from a Latin verb meaning to pick out, to choose, from an Indo-European root *leg-*, to collect' (308). In this sense, Williams's 'elitism' is evident in the way that he has published a broad spectrum of poets who, under the name of Jargon and The Jargon Society, have appeared in contexts entirely different to their 'little groups'; for example, publishing Olson in the same company as Patchen or Bob Brown. Jargon's elitism is, therefore, not so much exclusionary as it is discerning and keen to cultivate what is exceptional regardless of party line or faction. This is evident in the way that Williams, by publishing (and photographing) many of the poets closely associated with Black Mountain, put the writing of a 'group of people, rather embattled and rather isolated' into broader circulation before it formed into another 'little group' within the broader dynamics of 'the tribe' (Alpert 59).

Williams and Black Mountain

Despite his aversions about Black Mountain, Williams readily acknowledges the benefits of attending the college. 'Black mountain has come to be a "way," and a group of people,' he tells Alpert:

> And I, frankly, while I certainly derived a tremendous amount from it, at the time, I want no more to do with it. Obviously, at the time it was a place where I knew some very important people to me. It did a lot of things for me. I published some books for them and they did some things for me, but that's been over with now since about 1956. (Alpert 59)

One of the most positive things about Black Mountain for Williams was his introduction to Olson and his poetry. However, Williams's initial decision to attend Black Mountain was motivated by another influential teacher, the photographer Harry Callahan who had previously taught Williams at the Institute of Design in Chicago:

> It never occurred to me to want to go there particularly. But Harry Callahan the photographer whom I wanted to study with, said one afternoon, 'I'm going to be down in North Carolina this summer. Why don't you sign up at Black Mountain College.' 'Well,' I said, 'I just heard about Black Mountain yesterday.' 'There's a terrific guy named Aaron Siskind, friend of mine from New York, who's going to come down too.' So it sounded perfect. And I didn't know who Charles Olson was. (Dana 201–202)

When Williams did eventually encounter Olson, his first impression was of 'a huge myopic man' (*MB* 83). Although, according to Duberman, 'it was more a case of antagonism than love at first sight between Williams and Olson,' the college rector still managed to influence not only Williams's 'poetic vision' but also his 'whole vision of life' (382):

> The most persuasive teacher I ever had was Olson ... I really didn't have knowledge of or interest in the Carlos Williams/ Pound line of descent. Olson opened that up for me. I found him an extremely enkindling sort of man, marvelously quick and responsive. You got a lot from him at all times. His human condition was very attractive to me. And the conversations were endless, as I say. Night after night, day after day. He changed my whole poetic vision—and my whole vision of life too ... I'm not particularly interested in a lot of Olson's more ponderous material. But his process is something else. (Cited in Duberman 383)

Williams's lack of interest in 'Olson's more ponderous material'—Williams is probably referring to essays such as 'Proprioception,' or the series of lectures from the early 1960s collected in *Muthologos*—may explain why, unlike other younger poets, he never became an avid disciple of Olson in the way that Charles Boer, for example, did. Indeed, the advice and encouragement that Olson would give Williams about publishing would prove to be far more influential than the 'ponderous material' of his later poetics. Although Williams had already established Jargon with the publication of 'Garbage Litters the Iron Face of the Sun's Child,' it was Olson who gave Williams the spur to continue publishing. 'The reason, really, why Jargon started,' Williams tells Dana, 'was to publish Olson':

> Golden Goose published Robert Creeley's first book and were going to publish an Olson book, but then they went bust. And so [...] there was nobody, as far as we could determine, who was going to publish any Olson. Being new to the cause, as well as full of adolescent fervour, I decided I was going to do it. (Dana 192)

Williams's decision was encouraged by the fact that, as Millicent Bell notes, poetry and publishing 'went together all the time in Olson's class' at Black Mountain, 'for students often brought in poetry for classroom discussion already printed in broadsides and illustrated pamphlets at the college printshop where poets Joel Oppenheimer, Edward Dorn, and Nicola Cernovich manned a Kluge job-press' (2). 'At Black Mountain we had people there who could teach us how to use a small press,' Williams recalls in an interview with David Annwn: 'Joel Oppenheimer had had some training in printing so we learned a little about printing. We learned a little about book binding from Johanna Yalovetz who had lived in Vienna' (Annwn 48). As well as anticipating (if not precipitating) the mimeo revolution that began to burgeon in the late 1950s, this print-it-yourself ethos practiced at Black Mountain would play a pivotal role in distributing the poetry being produced there beyond the campus:

> Olson's point was that why the hell should you expect New York publishers, or anybody, to have any particular interest in what people who were student age had to say. If you felt that strongly about it, go to the press. Print it yourself. Print your work and your friend's work for the community that you lived in, or for the better community which I have always hoped was there, and I guess sometimes is: the world of letters which exists courtesy of the post office. (Dana 204)

This 'better community,' as Williams points out, exists beyond the geographical proximities of Black Mountain College. 'I don't live in a community in reality,' Williams tells Alpert: 'I live always outside of it. I have ever since Black Mountain' (65). In this respect, Williams's perspective not only recalls his own claims regarding Ian Hamilton Finlay as a 'man of letters,' but it also reaffirms the 'utopic potential' that Anne Moeglin-Delcroix identifies as a major component of small press publishing.

Nevertheless, Black Mountain's role within this 'world of letters,' and the small press networks that followed it, is considerable. Of particular significance is how Olson actively encouraged Williams to care about his publications and take pride in the high standards of design and production that would come to characterize Jargon's publications. In one particularly illuminating letter to Williams, Olson advises:

> FIND OUT YOUR OWN CONSERVATISM. Don't at
> all be uncomfortable in quietness. For it is now a most
> telling virtue (after all radicalism, and bohemianism—and
> false conservatism—have shown themselves to offer nobody
> anything ...
>
> No, Jonathan:
> sure I steer you right to urge you back to yr own inherited,
> & possessed, quietness
> (yr desire for fine paper, & for fine
> type, is damned healthy
> And you mustn't, beyond that point, lose the
> same distinction (by craving too much change, &
> excitement—drama—in how paper, color, type is used
>
> It should be
> worn like any virtue, not on the sleeve of itself. (*MB* 10)

Olson's aversion towards 'too much change, & excitement— drama— / in how paper, color, type is used' and his assessment of Williams's 'own inherited, & possessed, / quietness' are particularly salient comments in so far as they contrast markedly with the drama and excitement of campus life which Williams had to contend with and which often carried over into the poetry being produced there.

Heeding Olson's advice, Jargon would also go on to publish books of considerable 'beauty and ingenuity' which, in their exacting standards and use of fine paper, type and colour sets them apart as particularly accomplished 'specimens of book-design' (Bell 1). It is perhaps apposite that one of Jargon's most celebrated titles should be Olson's *Maximus / 1–10*, the typography of which Williams considers as 'the best thing

Jargon has given us to date' (*Uncle Gus* 5). *Maximus / 1–10* was published 'in a generously handsome format' in 1953 by Dr. Walter Cantz, 'one of the best printers in Germany' who Williams encountered while serving in the US Army Medical Corps in Stuttgart (Bell 3; Dana 208).

Cantz was also responsible for printing Louis Zukofsky's *Some Time*, which Jargon published in 1956. Recalling Olson's advice that fine publishing 'should be / worn like any virtue, not on the sleeve of itself,' Williams's use of high-quality material and his discerning choice of printers repeatedly demonstrates the 'quietness' and 'conservatism' (as opposed to 'excitement' and 'drama') that Olson recognized and encouraged in the young publisher. Far from simply being an opportunity for ostentation, extravagance, or novelty, the high quality of Jargon's books are, ultimately, put in service of the writer as a 'spiritual ally and outlet' for the specific demands of that particular work (Williams, *Uncle Gus* 12). Herbert Leibowitz describes this as Jargon's 'generative caring' which, be believes, 'is evident in the format and decoration, the choice of paper and typefaces which make each edition an exquisite piece of bookmaking, the meticulous collaboration of poet, painter, and printmaker' ('*Blues & Roots*' 56). 'But,' Leibowitz adds, 'however attractive the books are to look at, and they are justly collector's items, the chief pleasure they afford is the intellectual shock of recognizing an original voice ignored by sanctioned critical opinion' ('*Blues & Roots*' 56).

A telling claim made by Williams in the context of Zukofsky's *Some Time* is that: 'Good design must disappear before the text, just as the writer' (*Uncle Gus* 10). Thus, in order to achieve this and appropriately 'embody Old Zuk's high mandarin/Manhattan lyricism,' *Some Time* was conceived by Williams as 'an essay in Chinese book-making' (*Uncle Gus* 10). Likening it to 'a flowering plum tree,' Williams explains that 'the weight and feel and "flop" of the flexible binding all do their part' (*Uncle Gus* 10). Charles Tomlinson indicates just how integral, and subtle, the book design of *Some Time* is when he confesses to a naïve decision to cut the pages of his 'unread' library copy:

> I was surprised to discover that every time I turned the page two blank pages appeared [...] it was quite some minutes before I realized that what I had carved apart was Jonathan Williams's beautiful intentions, and that the immaculate candour of these backs of pages printed only on one side had never been intended to be read. (*American Essays* 145)

Williams's 'beautiful intentions' with *Some Time* reveal an approach to book design that recalls Mallarmé's belief that the book is 'not simply an exquisitely rendered container or precious relic but a catalyst for redefining the relationship between the book and its reader' (Anar 2).

Furthermore, like Mallarmé, many of the Jargon books achieve this by utilizing both the fine production qualities of the *livre de peintre* and the more radical innovations of the *livre d'avant-garde*.

If not strictly artists' books as such, Jargon's considerable investment in format, design, type, and image as a part of the work itself aligns it with the broader sensibilities of poet-publishers such as Finlay who similarly believes that 'the unit is the book itself rather than the individual poem or page. The aim is unity, expressed through type, paper, texture, colour, and whatever other means' (cited in Cutts and Sackett, *Repetivity*, 37). Such standards, however, could come at a cost. For example, reviewing Finlay's booklet *Telegrams from My Windmill*— the title of which alludes to Alphonse Daudet's *Letters from My Windmill* (*Lettres de mon Moulin*, 1869)—Aram Saroyan draws attention to the expense that such standards entail. Noting how 'the poems are done in red ink on good, very white stock,' Saroyam remarks: 'It isn't anything to be carried around for a day. It's 75¢. The minute I got it I wanted to go home, wash my hands, and find out what was going on' (161). Thus, such a publication contrasts markedly with the more affordable, functional publications such as City Lights's Pocket Poets Series that, as the series title indicates, are intended to fit in the pocket and be carried around. Yet, the affordability of the Pocket Poets books, or the formulaic production and editing of Black Sparrow Press's titles—in which, Williams believes, 'there is no design whatsoever'—compromises the singular qualities of each Jargon title (Alpert 62).

Olson's Boys

It is difficult to overstate just how instrumental Jargon was in promoting the work and reputation of the burgeoning Black Mountain poets in the 1950s. In addition to *Maximus / 1–10,* Jargon published *The Maximus Poems / 11–22* in 1956 and four years later, in collaboration with Corinth Books, published both volumes in a single edition. In addition to Olson, other Black Mountaineers published by Jargon include Joel Oppenheimer's *The Dancer* in 1951 and Victor Kalos's *The Double-Backed Beast* in 1952. Both publications follow the simple format of Jargon 1 and both use drawings by contemporary Black Mountain artists: Robert Rauschenberg and Dan Rice, respectively.[25] Between 1953 and 1959 Williams also published four titles by Robert Creeley: *The Immoral Proposition* and *All That Is Lovely In Men*, with drawings by Dan Rice, in 1953; *The Whip* in 1957; and, in 1959 in collaboration with Corinth Books, *A Form of Women*. Robert Duncan's *Letters: Poems 1953–1956* as well as Denise Levertov's *Overland to the Islands*

---

25   Oppenheimer is something of an exception, as he is the only Black Mountain poet that Williams consistently published: following *The Dancer* in 1951 and *The Dutiful Son* in 1957, in the 1980s Jargon also published *Just Friends / Friends and Lovers: Poems 1959–1962* and *Names & Local Habitations: Selected Earlier Poems, 1951–1972.*

were both published in 1958. Along with Larry Eigner, whose book *On My Eyes* Jargon published with photos by Callahan in 1960, Levertov was another poet closely associated with Black Mountain despite never having attended or visited the college. Together, this roster presents a comprehensive cross-section of what has become generally known as the Black Mountain School of poetry.

With the exception of Kalos, all of these poets, including Williams, were included in Donald Allen's landmark anthology *The New American Poetry* (1960) as representatives of Black Mountain poetry. In his introduction, Allen offers two defining characteristics of Black Mountain poets:

> The first group includes those poets who were originally closely identified with the two important magazines of the period, *Origin* and *Black Mountain Review*, which first published their mature work. Charles Olson, Robert Duncan, and Robert Creeley were on the staff of Black Mountain College in the early fifties, and Edward Dorn, Joel Oppenheimer, and Jonathan Williams studied there. Paul Blackburn, Paul Carroll, Larry Eigner, and Denise Levertov published work in both magazines but had no connection with the college. (Allen xii)

Allen's summary, Duberman notes, introduced 'three measuring rods that categorizers have used to admit or deny a place in the school to given individuals' and which continue to shape the perception of 'Black Mountain as a place, a review and a section in a history-making anthology' (388). However, as diverse as these measurements are, 'they seem downright uniform when set against the actual work of the individuals in question—for the differences in their styles are vast' (Duberman 388). This perhaps explains why Williams, despite his close and largely amicable links with the Black Mountain poets, and his keen promotion of their work, remained ambivalent about being associated with the college and the school of poetry it inadvertently sponsored. Williams's interests and his own sensibilities, while owing a considerable debt to Black Mountain, are, as we shall see, far more diverse than, and at times anathema to, that particular poetry label. When Williams's experiences of Black Mountain are examined in closer detail it becomes apparent that what Olson recognized and encouraged in Williams, namely his 'conservatism' and his 'inherited, & possessed, quietness' is also what, ultimately, distanced Williams from both Black Mountain and Olson.

Williams has claimed that, 'I am as little interested in coterie as I can possibly be,' believing that 'Princeton was one club, and Black Mountain was another. I made distance from each as quickly as possible' (*BD* 119). Broaching the same topic in an interview with Jim Cory, Williams reiterates this sentiment: 'I don't like labels. I don't like being called a

Black Mountain poet. I don't feel comfortable with that. BMC is a place I studied at 40 years ago' (Cory 3).

Whereas Williams saw Black Mountain College as a place where he studied, Michael Davidson considers Black Mountain to be 'both a place and an ideology, a community and a set of legitimating practices and forms' (*Guys Like Us* 40). These 'legitimating practices' might best be seen in Olson's reputation and influence among the mainly male students that fell under his influence at Black Mountain. According to Duberman, Olson 'was impossible to ignore—not simply because of his mountainous size, but because of his largeness of manner, the way he disposed himself' which provoked responses ranging 'from intense dislike to blind adulation' (369). Generally, however, student responses to Olson tended to 'cluster strongly on the side of admiration,' according to Duberman (370). Tom Clark reiterates this largely positive reception and notes how 'his evident personal involvement with his ideas, the experiential intensity with which his thoughts were being shaped even as he uttered them, the quality of challenge and adventure in the conjectural gamble he proposed, won from most of his listeners a trust that included considerable suspension of disbelief' (143). Such trust, in turn, meant that Olson could be 'overprotective of his *boys* and overly reliant on their adoration' (Duberman 376).

Olson's Black Mountain was thus predominantly a male affair that was, according to Davidson, 'organized around a masculine heteronormative model,' and cemented via 'fraternal bonds' that sidelined the college's female minority (18, 16). Williams has reiterated this point by noting how 'Black Mountain's major disservice to many persons was a *machismo* thing that revolved around Olson's stance: that men were shakers and makers, and women cooked the cornbread and made children and kept quiet' ('Colonel Colporteur's' 77). 'Female students,' Davidson suggests, 'who attended Black Mountain were not exactly kept out of Olson's classes, but they had a difficult time learning under his autocratic pedagogy' (36). This was partly due to what Clark calls 'the standard Black Mountain "straight" male view of women as alluring but largely vacuous creatures' (210). With 'many more unmarried men than women in the community during its last years,' as Duberman suggests, 'sexual tension and rivalry could be fierce,' exacerbating 'the decided *machismo* feel to the community' which, under Olson's influence, 'measured masculinity against the specific qualities found in the males at the head of the pecking order: Olson, Creeley and Dan Rice' (397, 398). According to Duberman, this pecking order established 'a hierarchy based on talent, toughness, intelligence and honesty' which 'could be as rigidly exclusive, as impassable to the uninitiated—and *more* male chauvinist—than anything found on a traditional university campus' (407).

Williams had experienced a more 'traditional university campus' as an undergraduate at Princeton. Disillusioned with the 'arrogant, boring' and 'anti-intellectual' students there, Williams left after three semesters: 'There were a tremendous number of people who were sleeping their way through four years, including the faculty' (Dana 199). The highly charged masculine climate of Black Mountain, however, fostered similar indiscretions. 'There were sexual thugs by the dozen on campus,' he tells Ronald Johnson, describing his fellow students as 'he-men flaunting their hemi-demi-semi barbaric yawps in the sylvan air of Black Mountain' ('Nearly Twenty Questions' 229).

Williams's allusion to Whitman's 'Song of Myself'—'I too am not a bit tamed—I too am untranslatable / I sound my barbaric yawp over the roofs of the world'—raises notable questions regarding the deeper impulses and implications of Black Mountain's chauvinism and sexual thuggery (87). As a poet who, according to Robert K. Martin, 'still continues to challenge our assessment of our sexuality and the ways we organize it,' and who 'refuses the tyranny of the family and compulsory heterosexuality,' Williams's allusion to Whitman subtly queers the heteronormative model of Black Mountain by identifying homoerotic dynamics and tensions simmering under the surface of such intensely straight male bonds (xxi). Thus, Whitman's 'barbaric yawps' might also effectively highlight what Rachel Blau DuPlessis considers a distinct 'compact of hetero- and homosexual men in the formation of 1950s poetic manhood, no matter the possible homophobia of the straight men, or the exclusionary campiness of the gay men' ('Manhood' para 82). Whitman's language and imagery anticipates this ambiguous compact of 'manly' virtues and relationships by speaking plausibly for both homoerotic and homosexual relationships while also anticipating the 'accelerated exchange[s] of emotionally complex manhoods' that Williams witnessed at Black Mountain ('Manhood' para 82). That a Whitman poem can 'slip ambiguously between celebrations of same-sex and opposite-sex love' would therefore seem to imply that notions of manliness, and 'manly' relations, do not so much reassert and reaffirm distinct notions of gender and sexuality but, rather, highlight their ambiguity (Erkkila 144).

By exaggerating Whitman's 'barbaric yawps,' Williams not only undermines the 'straight' manhood at Black Mountain, but he also wryly mocks the hyper-masculinized expressions of self that occurred there. Olson, Duberman notes, 'was dealing with a group of mostly late teen-agers / early adults, and in a highly charged, isolated community setting. Which meant, inevitably, a lot of noise' (371). These self-expressive 'barbaric yawps' were, to use Davidson's term, 'legitimated' by Olson's pedagogic model which encouraged noise and expression 'in the hope that something that might count would come out of it; although, Duberman remarks, there was ultimately 'a great deal more "self-expression" at Black Mountain than selves to express' (371–372).

An Unholy Marriage

Just as the quality of Jargon publications contrast significantly with the more impulsive missives of the mimeo revolution, the 'inherited, & possessed, quietness' that Olson encouraged in Williams is at significant odds with the 'barbaric yawps' and 'self-expressions' attributed to many of his peers at Black Mountain. It is then perhaps ironic that by heeding Olson's advice and developing these qualities—as well as the experiences and lessons he learnt at Black Mountain from Olson about poetry—Williams found ways to resist Olson's overbearing influence and the 'embattled and rather isolated' mentality of the college campus.

In his essay 'Am-O,' Williams describes the 'marginal comments made scrupulously and magnanimously by Olson on piles of fledgling JW poems' as 'a useful guide for any of us, now' (*MB* 8). This guidance, however, came with its own costs as Williams has explained:

> The only problem was, Olson is almost enough to wipe you out ... It took me a long time to get out from under Leviathan J. Olson. Of course some poets said that I would be stuck there. They didn't like him. Zukofsky thought I was being victimized. Rexroth thought so. Dahlberg still thinks so. He asks baleful questions like 'Why do you imitate Olson? and Pound?' [Dahlberg has elsewhere referred to Olson as the Stuffed Cyclops of Gloucester.] *I* don't think I do, but I would say it took me ten years to achieve whatever the thing is they call 'my own voice.' (Cited in Duberman 383–384)

Williams eventually found his 'own voice' by assimilating Olson's with those of other instructive models. 'Well, one of the first poems that seemed to me really did the job was a poem about Stan Musial, from 1958,' Williams tells Cory, referring to his poem 'O For A Muse of Fire!' from his 1959 collection, *The Empire Finals at Verona* (Cory 1). Despite the title's allusion to Shakespeare's *Henry V,* 'O For A Muse of Fire!' is concerned with baseball, one of the most popular sports at Black Mountain. Remembering Olson's enthusiasm for the game, which Williams shared, Williams quotes from a letter by Olson in 'Am-O':

> But we played a ball game against the town American
> Legion Juniors last night. And I, for one, missed yr style!
> The way you play baseball is the way ...
> It was wild
>
> how
> badly we played. The baubles! And these quiet kids made
> us look
> like
> dumbheads! ... (*MB* 10)

Black Mountain's macho discourse, according to Duberman, was ingrained in the sport:

> There was, in fact, a decided *machismo* feel to the community in these years—like the costume parties where people came dressed as gangsters and acted as tough as they could; or the drunken binges (men only) where the palm went to those who could swig the home brew straight—*and* hold it down; or the 'wild thrill' from defeating the championship local baseball team; or the fascination with—even the occasional appearance of—motorcycles (George Fick got fifteen stitches in the face after one crash). (398)

On first reading 'O For A Muse of Fire!' the poem seems to be complicit with this machismo culture in its celebration of a legendary moment in baseball history, when one of its most celebrated hitters, Stan Musial, on 13 May 1958 reached his 3,000-hit milestone. 'Only six major-league players in baseball history had hit safely 3000 times prior to this occasion,' Williams adds in a footnote to the poem (*JT*, 259). Williams also replicates the sport's idiomatic punditry and slang, including Musial's nickname, 'Stan the Man':

> The Muse muscles up; Stan the Man stands ... and
> O, Hosanna, Hosanna, Ozanna's boy, Moe Drabowsky
> comes
>
> 2 and 2
> 'a curve ball, outside corner, higher
> than intended—
> I figured he'd hit it in the ground'
>
> (*'it felt fine!'*)
>
> a line shot to left, down the line,
> rolling deep for a double ...
>
> (*'it felt fine!'*)
>
> Say, Stan, baby, how's it feel to hit 3000?
>
> 'Ugh, it feels fine' (*JT* 259–260)

Rather than reiterating the straight macho discourse of the college campus or sporting jargon, however, 'O For A Muse of Fire!' wryly subverts it. The erectile implications of the line, 'The Muse muscles up; Stan the Man stands' along with the refrain '*it felt fine!*'—and the allusion to the Polish-American player Moe Drabowsky who 'comes'— gives a homoerotic undertone to this straight, masculine, blue collar sport. Sexualizing the 'manly' discourse in this way, Williams might also be tacitly undermining the hyper-masculine culture of Black Mountain that asserted itself in such sports.

'O For A Muse of Fire!' also undermines Black Mountain machismo in more nuanced ways. 'If you look at that poem,' Williams explains to Cory, 'it's kind of a peculiar marriage of Edith Sitwell and Charles Olson. Which is an unholy marriage! Neither of course could possibly, would possibly, countenance the other' (Cory 1). Sitwell, a flamboyant English aristocratic, as Clark notes, was introduced by Robert Duncan onto the curriculum at Black Mountain as part of his 'casual heretical recommendations of "Indexed" works and authors (*Finnegans Wake*, Eliot, Stein, Zukofsky, H.D., even Edith Sitwell)' which were antagonistic to Olson's canon of Melville, Lawrence, and Pound (255).

Just how much of a rebuke Sitwell is of Black Mountain machismo can be grasped in Duncan's claim that, 'It's easier to announce that you are a homosexual than to say you read Edith Sitwell' (113). For gay poets such as Duncan, Williams and Ronald Johnson, a substantial part of Sitwell's appeal seems to rest on her tacit challenge to straight machismo. This is particularly evident in Williams's comment to Johnson regarding the 'hemi-demi-semi barbaric yawps' made by Olson's boys at Black Mountain:

> Let's face it, Dame Edith Sitwell was too much, too much indeed, for all those he-men flaunting their hemi-demi-semi barbaric yawps in the sylvan air of Black Mountain. There were sexual thugs by the dozen on campus. A titled English woman like ES would be allowed to cut no ice. ('Nearly Twenty Questions' 229)

The fact that Sitwell was 'titled,' as Williams points out, and that she cultivated an air of eccentricity might have exacerbated the negative reactions she provoked in people. Williams, in advocating this eccentric aristocrat, recalls his own semi-aristocratic southern background— which Olson may very well allude to in his letter to Williams regarding the younger poet's 'inherited' and 'possessed' conservatism—which contrasts markedly with Olson's working-class background. Indeed, according to Williams, as their friendship began to break down he and Olson 'started playing Lazy Southerner and Imperious Yankee,' which brought the simmering social tensions in their relationship very much to the fore (*MB* 6–7).

However, as Williams explains to Johnson, it is as much Sitwell's poetry as her character that he finds appealing and instructive: 'Anyone stupid enough to say he or she hasn't much to learn from Edith Sitwell deserves to be a life-time captive of the Soi-Disant Language Poets or the cult of Ally-Oopists on the West Coast. Her notebooks are wonderful' ('Nearly Twenty Questions' 229). The notebooks that Williams is referring to are *A Poet's Notebook* (1943) and, perhaps, Sitwell's essay to her *Complete Poems* (1957), 'Some Notes on My Own Poetry' (1957). In *A Poet's Notebook*, Sitwell explains the 'texture' and the 'varying uses of consonants, vowels, labials, and sibilants' for determining 'rhythm and [...] variations in speed of the poem' (18). These ideas are developed further in 'Some Notes on My Own Poetry' in which Sitwell proposes how 'assonances and dissonances put at different places within the lines and intermingled with equally skillfully placed internal rhymes have an immense effect upon rhythm and speed' (xvi). 'For me,' Ronald Johnson claims, 'and poets like Jonathan Williams and Robert Duncan, her theories of words' rhythm and texture in the treatise *Some Notes on My Own Poetry* [...] were a text to shove alongside Charles Olson's *Projective Verse* and Louis Zukofsky's anthology, *A Test of Poetry*' ('Six, Alas!' 27).

According to Williams, Sitwell had a 'kind of dexterity' and her poetry 'moves quicker and with more speed than almost anyone else, because she imitated musical patterns' (Alpert, 70–71). It was for similar reasons of dexterous prosody and music that Williams, as he explains to Cory, 'married' Sitwell and Olson:

> I was able to do something with Olson and with Edith Sitwell that became something new. Sitwell ... because she's so interested in so many aspects of *words*. What color they are. If they leave shadows. How much they weigh. And Olson ... what he really is is *symphonic*. There's a big, big symphonic expanse there, particularly in *The Maximus Poems*. (Cory 1)

Like a symphony, 'O For a Muse of Fire!' develops its themes over an expanse of time and space and attempts to come 'very close to the events, to the physical action of the [baseball] game' that it describes (Alpert 71). Olson's characteristic manner of pacing the poem—his use of parentheses and his juxtapositions of short lines with larger blocks of text—are employed by Williams to convey Musial's hit and the velocity and reach of the ball's trajectory. Furthermore, the Olsonian 'facts, to be dealt with' concerning this sporting event that introduce Williams's poem—*'Date,' 'Place,' 'Time,' 'Attendance,' 'Situation,'* and *'Public Address'*—both emphasize the momentousness of the occasion and approximate the tension and anticipation felt by Musial and his spectators (*Maximus* 5; *JT* 259).

In alliterative phrases such as 'The Muse muscles up; Stan the Man stands,' and the densely compacted, strong rhyming assonances of the poem, Williams also invokes the sonic flamboyance that characterizes Sitwell's poems such 'Waltz' from *Façade*:

> Our élégantes favouring bonnets of blond,
> The stars in their apiaries,
> Sylphs in their aviaries,
> Seeing them, spangle these, and the sylphs fond
> From their aviaries fanned
> With each long fluid hand
> The manteaux espagnols,
> Mimic the waterfalls
> Over the long and light summer land. (*Collected Poems* 145)

According to Sitwell, the poem's 'movement' is achieved via 'softening' and 'trembling' assonances that are set against a 'ground rhythm' based on the alliteration of 'm,' 'p,' and 'b' sounds (xx).

Taking these aspects of Sitwell's poetry and marrying them with Olson's poetics in 'O For A Muse of Fire!,' Williams undermines an otherwise straight-talking, straight-hitting 'heroic' sporting moment and turns a bastion sport of Black Mountain machismo into something more sexually suggestive and ambiguous. Indeed, the poem is a prime example of 'the revelatory power of the rhythms & music of everyday speech & the omnipresent unifying energy of eroticism' that, according to Kevin Power, constitutes the major themes and 'emerging forces' of Williams's work (n. pag). These 'forces,' Power suggests, are explored 'with the flexible concepts of "open field" & "collage," allowing things to collect, interact, & cohere' (n. pag). In 'O For A Muse of Fire!,' however, Olson's 'open field' becomes the site of sport where notions of pitch, speed, and energy reflect as much the dynamics of the baseball game as they do the kinesis of Olson's Projective Verse.

Dialect

Williams also alludes to Olson and Sitwell in 'Found Poem Number One,' a poem that dates back to 1952/1953 when Williams's studies at Black Mountain were interrupted by the draft. 'As a conscientious objector,' Tom Patterson explains, Williams 'was exempted from combat training and service, and assigned to non-combatant work for the U.S. Army Medical Corps in Stuttgart, Germany' (9). Williams was assigned duties in the locked ward of the Fifth General Hospital in Stuttgart, 'working as a "neuro-psychiatric technician," subduing and pacifying malingerers and psychopaths and really mean folks' (Dana 209). It is one of these patients that provides the subject and language of 'Found Poem Number One':

FOUND POEM NUMBER ONE:
(Fifth General Hospital, Bad Canstatt/ Stuttgart, 1953:
the speaker, a bop spade from Cleveland in a fugue state,
making the world's first marriage of the poetics of Charles
Olson and Dame Edith Sitwell—and you are there!)

man,
i come from
the 544
       motherfuckin'
              double-clutchin'
                     cocksuckin'
                           truckin' company!

    U CALL—
    WE HAUL
    U ALL ...

we got
2 plys
    4 plys
        6 plys
            8 plys, semi's—

and them BIG motherfuckers
go

CHEW!
CHEW! (*JT* 207)

Williams's poem presents the semi-conscious ramblings of a soldier suffering a fugue state of mind. As the concluding phrase 'CHEW! CHEW!' suggests, this found poem is about verbal trains of thought that create their own kind of musical fugues. An initial allusion to the soldier's military 'company,' expressed in a 'bop,' hipster idiom, morphs into the commercial jingo of a logistics company ('U CALL— / WE HAUL') and what appears to be timber supply ('ply'). The trucks these companies use ('them BIG motherfuckers') transform into trains that go 'CHEW! CHEW!' In fact, when the meaning of the word 'fugue' is recalled, this poem is very much about *loco* (mad, insane) *motion*. In psychiatric terms a 'fugue' denotes the flight from one's own identity and often involves mental travel to some unconsciously desired locality. This is a point that Williams implies in part of the poem's lengthy subtitle: 'and you are there!'

Despite its provenance in Stuttgart, 'Found Poem Number One' is very much a product of Black Mountain. As well as drawing upon two different poetic models that Williams encountered there—either in person (Olson) or through Duncan's curriculum (Sitwell)—the poem also demonstrates Williams's attentive ear for dialect. This defining aspect of Williams's poetry also emerged during his time at Black Mountain which rekindled his interest in his birthplace in nearby Asheville, Buncombe County: 'Most of my connection with Buncombe County, after getting born there, was coming back to go to Black Mountain College' (Dana 188).

In studying at Black Mountain, Williams was not only exposed to the progressive, avant-garde ideas of the college but, in reconnecting with the wider cultural environs of his birthplace, Williams also reassessed the tradition of Southern dialect literature that he grew up with. 'It must have had its effect,' he tells Dana, 'because, in my own way, I finally turned back and became very acutely interested in what southern mountain speech was all about' (189).

Dialect literature remains a contentious subject. As Joan Wylie Hall stresses, the Southern dialect literature, which became widely popular after the American Civil War, has been accused of reaffirming 'the comforting mythology of the plantation South as a lost Eden whose kind and well-spoken masters and illiterate but loyal slaves nurtured each other in a pastoral landscape' (206). Indeed, adumbrating the romanticized primitivism of the folk revivals, both of the white Southern writers that Williams enjoyed as a child—John Charles McNeill, who wrote *Lyrics From Cotton Land* (1906) and Joel Chandler Harris, author of *Uncle Remus: His Songs and His Sayings* (1880)—appropriated African-American dialect in idealized plantation settings. It is reasonable to see both writers' work as pertinent examples of what Gavin Roger Jones considers 'a highbrow convention which employed exaggerated, humorous speech to camouflage a patronizing sentimentality and satire' (8). While the avuncular sentiments of Harris's *Uncle Remus* certainly supports these assessments, Jones also suggests that 'Ethnic dialect could provide writers with a voice for social commentary and political satire' and articulate a 'cultural and aesthetic politics of difference' that could 'over turn linguistic hegemony' (5, 2). B. A. Botkin makes a similar claim in his suggestion that the 'colloquial and illiterate usage' of 'rustic speech' and dialect, what he calls 'its "plasticity," or flexibility, allow[s] words, phrases, and sentences to flow as they will, unrestrained by artificial standards of correctness and propriety' ('"Folk-Say" and Folkore' 266).

It is partly for similar reasons of flexibility that urbane modernists such as Eliot and Pound were drawn to Harris's *Uncle Remus* stories. The black dialect of those stories, Michael North notes, offered 'a prototype of the literature that would break the hold of the iambic pentameter' and provide an incipient 'example of visceral freedom triumphing over dead convention' with 'black speech seem[ing] to Pound the most prominent challenge to the dominance of received linguistic forms' (78). According to North, *Uncle Remus* offered 'a cultural program [...] that would demolish the authority of the European languages and even the Roman alphabet' (99). 'Pound would carry the social and cultural dislocations of the modern period,' North suggests, 'dislocations of which he felt himself to be the deracinated product, to their logical conclusions in a new language' (99). However, Williams's appropriation of a black vernacular in 'Found Poem Number One' seems, uncomfortably so, to corroborate Matthew Hart's suggestion, via Michael North, that 'the Anglo-American avant-garde conducted its formal experiments "over a third figure, a black one,"' which Williams describes problematically as 'a bop spade' (27).

In its use of a third black figure, the demotic idiom of 'Found Poem Number One' also calls to mind William Carlos Williams's Poem XVII, otherwise known as 'Shoot It Jimmy!' from *Spring and All*. 'Our orchestra / is the cat's nuts—,' Williams's speaker brags:

> Man
> gimme the key
>
> and lemme loose—
> I make 'em crazy
>
> with my harmonies—
> Shoot it Jimmy
>
> Nobody
> Nobody else
>
> but me—
> They can't copy it. (*Spring and All* 63–64)

As 'Found Poem Number One' would do subsequently, the older Williams's poem takes the vernacular music of jazz and its idiomatic slang as its principal subjects. Indeed, anticipating Gwendolyn Brooks's 'We Real Cool' or Harryette Mullen's *Muse & Drudge*, 'Shoot It Jimmy!' plays upon the sexual connotations of the word 'jazz' addressing, as Barry Ahearn notes, themes of 'musical and sexual performance' by way of a sexually-suggestive idiom implicit in phrases such as 'soothe / the savage beast,' 'shoot it Jimmy,' and 'I make 'em crazy' (*William Carlos Williams* 72; *Spring and All* 63–64).

However, 'Shoot It Jimmy!' also reasserts its own claims for the spontaneity and unrestraint of a non-standardized, spoken vernacular by way of the jazz musician's disdain for written music—'That sheet stuff / 's a lot a cheese'—which threatens to homogenize and restrict the otherwise free and uninhibited music of the orchestra (*Spring and All* 64). The extent to which standardized sheet music is seen as incarcerating the creative and expressive impulse is made particularly apparent in the pun on incarceration and musical jargon: 'gimme the key // and let me loose.'

According to Ahearn, 'Williams's use of slang in ['Shoot It Jimmy!'] and his faithful reproduction of the spoken word' not only shows him 'attuned to the value of the vernacular' but it also shows him 'giv[ing] up his role as mere observer of the "social class"' to become instead 'its amanuensis' (*William Carlos Williams* 72). This emphasis on recording and transcribing speech contrasts significantly with Eliot and Pound's pastiche and 'mimicry' of what, in the *Uncle Remus* stories, was a white writer's own rendition of an inaccurate rendition of African-American dialect (North 81).

The younger Williams recalls his older namesake by adopting a similar position of amanuensis in his dialect poetry. However, in contrast to the African-American dialect of 'Found Poem Number One,' in his later poems Williams would draw increasingly on the language of his own Appalachian culture. 'I like to catch people speaking "poems" who have never heard of the word *poet*,' he writes in his book *Blues and Roots, Rue and Bluets: A Garland for the Southern Appalachians* (1971), the title of which, incidentally, alludes to jazz musician and composer Charles Mingus's album *Blues and Roots* (1960) which revisits the formative vernacular music forms of his childhood—'a barrage of soul music: churchy, blues, swinging, earthy' (*Blues & Roots* n. pag; Mingus, *Blues & Roots* liner notes).[26] Williams also alludes to the composer Charles Ives and the bluegrass legend Earl Scruggs in his introduction, dovetailing these modern appropriations and practices of vernacular music with vernacular speech: 'It has been my business along with many of my superiors (W. C. Williams, Louis Zukofsky, Lorine Niedecker, A. R. Ammons), to try to raise "the common" to grace, to pay very close attention to the earthy, for one thing' (n. pag). Following the example of these older poets, Williams has defined himself as 'an autochthonous mindless recording mechanism established ecologically within a mountain region' (*MB* 164). Although, according to Herb Leibowitz, 'Williams is not the amanuensis of these mountain folk' but a fellow 'resident' who 'discriminates details of color, scale, motion, and flavor,'

---

26 Duke University Press published a revised edition of *Blues & Roots* in 1985 without Dean's photos. 'Twelve texts have been pared; and thirty-three have been added—eight of which are printed for the first time,' Williams explains in the note to the Duke edition: 'This much alteration made it impossible to conceive of using photographs' (n. pag).

Leibowitz nevertheless identifies similar qualities to those apparent in the poetry of the older Williams as well as Niedecker (n. pag). 'As a chronicler,' he suggests, 'Williams knows when to duck out of sight and merely listen to the confiding talk and gossip (sometimes spiked with wormwood) about weather, work, marriage, church, deathbed vigils, and local characters' (n. pag).

This 'uncondescending demonstration of commonality heard,' as Eric Mottram describes it, is particularly evident in the poems that comprise the section of *Blues & Roots* titled 'Common Words in Uncommon Orders' which plays on Coleridge's famous definition of poetry as 'the best words in their best order' ('Jonathan Williams' 103; Coleridge 45). This tacit allusion to Coleridge also recalls how, in the *Lyrical Ballads*, Coleridge and Wordsworth experimented with 'the language of conversation in the middle and lower classes of society' and 'adapted [it] to the purposes of poetic pleasure' (3). In many of the poems in *Blues & Roots* Williams does express 'poetic pleasure' in the dialect of his Appalachian neighbours which, like Wordsworth and Coleridge, he adapts.

'I listened to mountain people for over a thousand miles and I really heard some amazing stuff,' Williams explains in an interview with Jeffery Beam:

> And I left it pretty much as I heard it. I didn't have to do anything but organize a little bit, crystallize it, you know. That's the thing I love about found material, you wake it up, you 'make' it into something. ('Jonathan Williams's Nation Of Has, For Those Who Haven't' n. pag)

Williams's use of such found material is particularly evident in his use of the speech of his Highlands neighbour 'who lived across the road,' Uncle Iv Owens ('Jonathan Williams's Nation Of Has, For Those Who Haven't' n. pag). Williams has described how listening to Uncle Iv 'is like picking up amethyst crystals in the path. The ear can find them perfectly formed' (*MB* 163):

> I'd run home to write'm down as fast as I could so I could get them down pretty well accurate. I loved his language. He had some of the best language of anybody I've ever heard, and he didn't know how to read or write. He sure knew how to talk—that's the one thing he could do! ('Jonathan Williams's Nation Of Has, For Those Who Haven't' n. pag).

Uncle Iv's crystal-like idioms provide the raw material of the poem 'Uncle Iv Surveys His Domain From the Rocker of a Sunday Afternoon As Aunt Dory Starts to Chop The Kindlin':

> Mister Williams
> lets youn me move
> tother side the house
>
>
> the woman
> choppin woods
> mite nigh the awkerdist thing
> I seen (*JT* 136)

One might initially assume that Uncle Iv's comments simply reiterate staid assumptions regarding parochial, small-town chauvinism. However, the title that Williams gives to this example of found speech subtly subverts such prejudices by drawing attention to Uncle Iv's 'domain.' With his back to the house, Uncle Iv's domain—his place of authority and rule—would seem to be his yard or sharecropper's plot. Aunt Dory, therefore, appears to be doing—and not very well, judging by Uncle Iv's response—man's work. If this is the case, then Aunt Dory's actions prompt some questions. Why is she doing this work? And has this work emasculated Uncle Iv? Indeed, a reversal of traditional gender roles seems to take place as Uncle Iv and 'Mister Williams' move to the *other* side of the house when Aunt Dory starts chopping wood, displacing the men from their traditional positions. As a relatively impartial amanuensis ('a mindless recording mechanism') in a manner that recalls the older Williams, or Niedecker, Williams records this instance of folk speech in such a manner that the poem's intent remains ambiguous. Perhaps the poem is gently mocking parochial values about gender identity—the commonplace roles and domains, public and private, of men and women—but nobody in the poem, it seems, is the target of ridicule or critique. Williams depicts the scene in a matter-of-fact way, without explicit judgement or comment, and appears to simply present what he has heard. Williams 'locates himself between reality and the poem,' as Davenport remarks of 'Uncle Iv Surveys His Domain,' 'and trains himself to be the medium through which reality flows into the poem' (*Geography* 183).

Davenport also believes that this particular poem 'defines a culture' (*Geography* 183). But what culture? And why should Williams feel the need to represent it in this manner? Williams provides one possible answer in an essay on Southern Appalachian craftwork. Referring to Uncle Iv, Williams writes:

> He sprouts poems like a dahlia bush puts out blooms—and he calls it a 'dally' bush, not being concerned with the Germanic botanist Professor Dahl. I am constantly humbled and delighted by this vernal, verbal gift of his. He is, in the root sense, a cultivated man—he is at home in his world,

meager though it may be by modern, televised standards. God knows what a government can do with a citizen like Uncle Iv. He is long surplus. Nobody needs his little sharecropper's farm and his handful of cabbage. But the Appalachians need him and others like him. He has husbanded his acres, respected his land and his neighbors. Few can say as much. (*MB* 172)

Thus, according to Williams, Uncle Iv demonstrates a modest integrity—in speech and lifestyle—that is anathema to the 'televised standards' of a commoditized and materialistic world. However, Uncle Iv's existence is also threatened by that world. As Stephen L. Fisher notes, since the advent of industrialization, Appalachia has suffered acute oppressive social and economic conditions in the form of 'single-industry economies; the control of land and resources by large absentee companies [and] high levels of poverty and unemployment' as well as 'strip mining, the broad form deed, the disappearance of small farms, the flooding of people's homes, and the pollution of the region's rivers, creeks, and groundwater systems' (3, 317). One way that its citizens and communities have resisted these conditions, Fisher explains, is by 'drawing upon and defending their own particular traditions, folkways, and culture' which take on various forms, modes, and activities including 'gossip, backtalk, holding on to one's dialect, moonshining, open violation of game and fencing laws, and migration' (317, 3–4).

It is perhaps not surprising, therefore, that a number of these resistant 'folkways' are taken up by Williams in *Blues & Roots* in order to convey 'a special biota of people and places and work' (*MB* 179). In doing so, Williams avoids stereotyping his Appalachian subjects 'as backward, unintelligent, fatalistic, and quiescent people who are complicit in their own oppression'; neither does he cast them as 'the most vicious and violent people in the United States' (Fisher 3–4). But, like Niedecker before him, neither does Williams assume a populist stance and simply romanticize or idealize Appalachia's communities and traditions. For, with populism comes the danger, Fisher points out, that 'the cultural homogeneity, progressive nature, and good will of "the people" are taken for granted' and 'the ethnic, racial, gender, class, and cultural differences that so often divide "the people"' simply overlooked (322). Indeed, like Niedecker, in his regard for 'the folk from whom all poetry flows / and dreadfully much else,' Williams, does acknowledge these kinds of differences (*CW* 142). He also expresses awareness that community 'entails exclusion as well as inclusion' as he himself encountered at Black Mountain and intuited as a resident of Macon County (Fisher 332). 'It amuses me to read members of the Urban Wolf Pack rejoicing on the liberality of the American character,' he wryly notes referring to his sexuality: 'If people in Macon County,

N.C., read any number of my poems, my house would be mysteriously burnt down' (*MB* 147).

English Jargon

'It's not of course, the regional quaintness that interests Williams but the underpinning of a commitment to place that lines these voices,' Kevin Power suggests with regard to the dialect poems of *Blues & Roots* (n. pag). However, this 'commitment to place'— more specifically, to the Southern States—meant that Williams would travel, both physically and mentally, to the United Kingdom in order to better understand 'Appalachia, the linguistic horizon that [he] has never cared to stray very far from' (Davenport, *Geography* 187). 'These folk are the vestige of an Anglo-Saxon, Gaelic, and Celtic tradition,' Williams suggests, 'and hence about the most narrow people in the Western world, and among the most interesting' (*MB* 171). Williams says this as someone who shares the same bloodlines. 'What Jonathan Williams found in England, Wales, and Scotland,' as Davenport proposes, 'was not a second heritage (as it might seem to a casual glance) but the heritage in which he was raised from the beginning': 'When, for instance, he met the Scots poet Ian Hamilton Finlay [...] he was, as perhaps only a citizen of Appalachia can know, solidly within his heritage' (*Geography* 187).

Williams's interest in this heritage also compounds his longstanding fascination with a British literary and artistic tradition that would contribute significantly to his distancing from Black Mountain. This is, in part, due to that tradition's traceability, via the figure of William Blake, back to Williams's early interest in the poetry of Kenneth Patchen which was at odds with Olson's.[27] Furthermore, Williams's absorption in this British tradition would, eventually, connect him with a range of contemporary British poets, artists, and publishers from the mid 1960s onwards that operated largely outside of the then-dominant American influences of Black Mountain and the broader current of New American poetry.

As Eric Mottram suggests, Williams's interest in the British arts was more regionally specific than broadly national. Thus, according to Mottram, 'one significant way [that Williams] avoids the parochial in speech, measure and material (and there is a sense in which Gloucester simply cannot radiate far enough) is to have extended out from the national scene into Wales and the Wye Valley, the Lake District and Sussex' before settling in Dentdale ('Jonathan Williams' 105). However, with regard to Wales and the Wye Valley, the Lake District and Sussex, Williams had, before setting foot on their soil, already visited these places in his imagination. In his collection *In England's Green &: A Garland and a Clyster*, published by David Haslewood's Auerhahn Press in San

---

27   Jargon published three books by Patchen: *Fables & Other Little Tales* (1953), *Poem-Scapes* (Jargon 11, 1958), and *Hurrah for Anything* (1957).

Francisco in 1962, Williams includes several poems '"about" England, as it existed in the imagination of a poet who had not been there yet in person' (*An Ear* n. pag). Referring to these poems in his foreword to another of Williams's English-themed books, *Lines About Hills Above Lakes* (1964), John Wain comments:

> The fact they are (in a sense) 'about' England and by a poet who had never been to England will seem comic only to those who know nothing of the ways of the imagination. Poets dream creatively of Provence or Sligo, as boys in London live imaginatively in the American west, jazz-lovers in New Orleans *circa* 1905 and Sinologues in a vanished Peking of blossoms and imagist poems. Art communicates across space and time. (5–6)

Williams's imaginative transport, Wain explains, derives from his reading 'certain English writers and painters—Blake, back to Arthur Golding the translator, forward to Lawrence and J. R. R. Tolkien' (5). As Wain intimates, William Blake is the nodal point of this company. The importance of Blake in *England's Green &* is clearly evident in the title which derives from Blake's preface to *Milton*: 'I will not cease from Mental Fight, / Nor shall my Sword sleep in my hand: / Till we have built Jerusalem, / In England's green & pleasant Land' (95–96). Williams also invokes Blake's *Milton* and *The Marriage of Heaven and Hell* in another poem from *In England's Green &*—'Beside the Fount Above the Lark's Nest in Golgonooza'—which uses two books preoccupied with Blake: Ruthven Todd's *Tracks in the Snow* (1947) and Denis Saurat's *Gods of the People* (1947).

Perhaps more significantly in the context of this Blake tradition is another poem included in *England's Green &* titled 'Two Pastorals for Samuel Palmer at Shoreham, Kent,' which celebrates the work of the Victorian painter, Samuel Palmer. Palmer's early paintings and drawings follow firmly in the tradition of Blake, whom the younger artist befriended in 1824. For Palmer, with 'his mind shaped by scripture, Bunyan, and Milton,' Davenport suggests, 'it was one of those radiant encounters in which a disciple found his master' (*Geography* 196). Palmer, as Davenport explains, Blake introduced to 'his mystical friend the pagan painter and engraver Edward Calvert, and eventually an enclave of enthusiastic young men who began to call themselves the Ancients—Palmer's cousin John Giles, the Rev. Arthur Tatham and his brother Frederick, the painter George Richmond, Francis Oliver Finch, Henry Walker, and Welby Sherman' (*Geography* 196–197). 'Only Calvert and Palmer survive in history,' Davenport suggests, but 'the others deserve to have their names kept in the list, epic fashion, because they brightened the last days of Blake and because they are the first members of a family that exists today' (*Geography* 197).

According to Gerda S. Norvig, these Ancients dubbed Blake '"the Interpreter"' after the character in Bunyan's *Pilgrim's Progress* 'who taught the hermeneutic skills of allegorical understanding' to Christian (26). 'From Blake's Ancients (Samuel Palmer and Edward Calvert) stems a tradition,' Davenport suggests, elaborating on his intimation of a British 'family,' which forms 'a tangled and untraced path in and out of official literature and art' (*Geography* 188). Because of its marginal position and because of 'artists oriented toward Blake and his circle but going off by centrifugal flight into wildest orbits, men like Fuseli, Calvert, and Mad Martin,' this tradition, Davenport proposes, is also commonly perceived (if somewhat inaccurately) as an eccentric one (*Geography* 187). That eccentricity, Davenport reasons, is threaded throughout Williams's work: 'The poet's admiration for Edith Sitwell will have had something to do with this exploration of English eccentricity, and the poet's Welsh temperament, and, most clearly, William Blake himself' (*Geography* 187).

Williams's negotiations between this English visionary tradition and its links with his Southern heritage, via his own ancestral roots, inform his poem 'Emblems for the Little Dells, and Nooks and Corners of Paradise,' which was printed as a broadside by the British poet Tom Raworth and published by Jargon in 1962. The title derives from Palmer's praise for the woodcuts that Blake designed for Robert Thornton's book *The Pastorals of Virgil* (1821): 'They are visions of little dells, and nooks, and corners of Paradise; models of the exquisitest intense pitch of poetry,' Palmer claims (S. Palmer 109). The Blakean subtext is continued in the poem's epigraph which cites a remark of Blake's reported by Palmer in Alexander Gilchrist's biography *The Life of William Blake* (1907): 'You have only to work up imagination to the state of vision and the thing is done.'[28]

However, the first half of Williams's poem takes Habersham County, Georgia, rather than Albion, as its subject:

> out of the stills of Habersham: occasionally
> potable calvados;
>
> out of the hills of Habersham: sham
> trochees, Ol'Marse Sidney's poses, Poe's
> memories of the Lost Lenore, ah, Last of the Cherokee
> Queens, elas ...

---

28   This epigraph is omitted from the version included in Williams's book *Jubilant Thicket*, but Williams does quote it in a footnote to the poem (*JT* 163).

alas,
no one has *yet* seen the Soqui River in Habersham County,
Georgia
(not far from modern Lake Lanier) on a winter afternoon
between the hills—

no one except its despisers, versifiers, fishers, hunters,
dumpers
of inner tubes, runners of sugar liquor, and errant crackers,
who are
familiar Christian white folks with
red necks and blue
noses,

brown mule and
black hearts ...

it is hard to see the Soqui River in the late red sun
of a December afternoon (I reckon not even
Henry James saw it!)—
it is too hard to attune to, or atone for;   (*JT* 161)

Williams irreverently invokes one of Georgia's most famous 'versifiers,'
Sidney Lanier (1842–1881), parodying the 'sham trochees' of his poem
'Song of the Chattahoochee' which celebrates Georgia's Chattahoochee
River and the valleys of Hall (later to be renamed Lake Lanier in
honour of the poet). Thus, the opening lines of Lanier's poem—'Out
of the Hills of Habersham / Down the valleys of the Hall'—are
parodied by Williams, transforming the falling water from the Hills of
Habersham into illicit alcohol distilleries ('stills') that make moonshine
(Lanier 24). Williams compares this regional drink to the French apple
brandy, Calvados, conflating two prominent themes that run through
the poem: the transfiguring moonlight of Romantic art and literature
(echoed in the tacit allusion to moonshine) and an earthly, Edenic
paradise which, in Williams's poem, is symbolized by the apple.

Evidently, the products of Habersham's folkways (its home-brewed
liquor) are more palatable—easier to swallow and stomach—than
the lauded poetry of its 'versifiers.' These writings, unlike the liquor,
lack the flavour of the places and locations they seek to convey. The
'sham trochees' and affected 'poses' of 'Ol' Marse Sidney's' poem—'a
ubiquitous bit of nineteenth-century fluff,' according to Williams—have
failed to *see*, and therefore convey, the singular qualities of Habersham
(*JT* 163).

Punning on musical terms such as 'tune,' 'tone,' 'chord,' and
'harmony' in another of *England's Green &*'s poems—written in honour

of the composer Delius's centenary and titled 'Reflections from *Appalachia*'—Williams returns to this theme of *seeing*: 'my eyes / so in tune: atonement, at-one-ment is / *atonement*' (*JT* 272). 'Emblems' also raises the question of how one sees, attunes to, and becomes atoned (at one) with their environment. One way, as we have seen in the context of *Blues & Roots*, is to become its amanuensis—its 'mindless recording mechanism'—by paying close attention and becoming committed to the *genius loci* of a place. Indeed, as Thomas Meyer notes, 'what Jonathan Williams notices *becomes* everything. His attention when it focuses centers. There is no background, foreground, or middleground. There is only what is there—a kind of "in-your-face" phenomenology. Pay attention. Close attention. Is his credo' (paras 41, 42). In 'Emblems,' Williams finds an additional answer to this question by looking imaginatively across the Atlantic's 'dark water' to an abiding English visionary tradition:

> it is a stone's throw across that dark water to
> Secure, Literary Yesteryear: Palmer
> speaking of 'that "stinking hole Shoreham" which indeed is now
> highly scented with the buds of spring'
>
> ... everywhere and forever more everything's stinking, but thanks
> for thinking of us, Sam,
> standing there staring into the sun
>
> with the apple trees sizzling and the Valley yelling FIRE,
> for we are not troubled by problems of aerial perspective in the Valley of Vision—
>
> > Zion is in the Sun
> > Of England's
> > Eden
> > on the Darenth,
> > Kent
>
> and we can turn into the moon of Bunyan's Beulah Land
> *and*
> hear the voice of the Bard. (*JT* 162–163)

Williams evokes Palmer's early 'visionary' art and quotes liberally from his letters that date back to a period when he lived in the village of Shoreham in Kent's Darent Valley between 1825 and 1835. Palmer called Shoreham his 'valley of vision' and repeatedly transfigured its landscape into a Christian vision 'of divine fertility, or rather of the wonder of its earthly paradigm' (Palmer 28; Grigson, *Valley of Vision* 7). Palmer's spiritual landscape in 'Emblems' is invoked via Palmer's description of, 'The interchanging twilight / of that peaceful country // where there is no sorrow // and no night' (*JT* 163). Seen with both Palmer's 'optic nerve[s]' and his spiritual eye, Shoreham, bathed in moonlight, manifests a kind of 'Beulah Land' which in John Bunyan's *The Pilgrim's Progress* represents the 'Earthly Paradise, the happy land where the pilgrims live until it is time for them to cross the River of Death' and in Blake's system, denotes 'the source of poetic inspiration and dreams' (*JT* 162; Damon 42).

Just as the stinking Lazarus was raised from the dead by Jesus in John 11:39, Williams, in 'Emblems,' suggests that the attentive artist or poet can '*raise anything*' to a state of grace and vision:

> roll the apple away from the tomb, put
> an apple in the mouth of Stinking Lazarus;
>
> put it in the sky,
> make a moon of it!
>
> *we are willing to raise anything!* (*JT* 163)

The trope of the apple serves to remind us that what 'stinks' also ferments; excites, stirs, and *raises*. Similarly, what is dejected can be redeemed, transfigured, and revived by the poet who *sees* and who *hears*. With such renewal of attention it is possible that Zion or Beulah 'Rises from the slumberous mass' of earthly phenomena, just as it did for Palmer in Shoreham (W. Blake, 18).

Thus, transfiguration and renewal overcomes the sin of separation recounted in Isaiah 59:2: 'But your iniquities have separated between you and your God, and your sins have hid *his* face from you, that he will not hear.' William evokes a similar sin when he concludes his poem by stating: 'sin is / separation' (*JT* 163). Rather than succumbing to the sin of separation, however, Williams's poem celebrates a symbiosis of person and place. 'Getting together means you are in a state of atonement,' Williams writes in his essay 'Colonel Colporteur's Winson-Salem Snake Oil': 'Sin, to a poet, is being separated from the things in the world. At-one-ment' (83). This separation may also include being separated geographically and temporally. By working the thing up to vision, as Blake advised, such separation is overcome and distance collapsed. In the ferment of the poet's vision art, once again, 'communicates across space and time.'

From Community to Society

As Wain notes, Williams, 'having sent his imagination to England, came over himself to see how it was getting on' (6). Thus, with fellow poet Ronald Johnson, Williams made his first trip to the United Kingdom in the autumn of 1962. The visit, which lasted the best part of a year, involved 'pilgrimages' to many of the sites and locations that he had previously encountered in his reading. Thus, in the spring of 1963, the two Americans 'walked from the mouth of the River Wye at Chepstow, up its long, winding valley, to its source high on the flanks of Great Plynlimon':

> We hitched a few rides to allow us to add Kilpeck Church to Francis Kilvert's at Bredwardine along the route. And Strata Florida and the site of Hafod House further into Wales. And more pilgrimages that summer. To Nottinghamshire to Southwell Minster and the amazing foliate heads and plant carvings in the Chapter House. To Gilbert White's Selborne in Hampshire. To Samuel Palmer's Shoreham in Kent. To the Cerne Abbes Giant in Dorset. To Compton in Surrey for the Watts Mortuary Chapel. To Brighton for John Nash's Royal Pavilion. We were looking for all things, as RJ said, 'most rich, most glittering, most strange.' (*BD* 229)

In addition to visiting these *genius loci* of England's 'Literary Yesteryear,' the two poets also socialized with a diverse literati far removed from Black Mountain's orbit, which included, among many others, Barbara Jones, Stevie Smith, Olivia Manning, Kay Dick, Mervyn Peake, Tom Raworth, Jocelyn Brooke, Andrew Young, Rayner Heppenstall, Michael Hamburger, and Christopher Middleton:

> We went up to Ardgay in Easter Ross in the north of Scotland to meet Ian Hamilton Finlay. We saw Hugh MacDiarmid in both Langholm and Biggar. We saw Basil Bunting up the Tyne above Newcastle at Wylam. And Herbert Read at Stonegrave House in the hills north of York. We went to Broad Town under the Wiltshire Downs to see Geoffrey and Jane Grigson. (*BD* 229)

Along with Stevie Smith and Sitwell, it perhaps these English and Scottish writers above all others that would influence the development of Jargon's activities. Finlay, as we shall see in the following chapter, would connect Williams with a number of younger British poets, artists, and publishers that he would collaborate with, publish, or be published by over the subsequent decades. And Bunting, along with the art patron Donald Anderson, would be instrumental in Williams's semi-residency in Northern England from 1969 onwards in the seventeenth-century cottage, Corn Close, in Dentdale, Cumbria:

> Perhaps it was one of my suggestions, though no doubt I told Jonathan that North Tynedale was even lovelier, besides chance—since cottages are not often empty in such a landscape—that fixed him here to the great advantage of Dent and Sedbergh, overlooking the extravagant meanderings of the Dee and patterns of bracken on the fellside opposite, without close neighbours unless you count the natty red weasel that lives at the side of his waterfall or a score or so of monosyllabic sheep. What better neighbours could a laconic poet wish for? (Bunting, 'Comment on Jonathan Williams' n. pag)

It is perhaps no coincidence that Williams, by this period, had moved on from publishing the major Black Mountain poets and was becoming increasingly involved with aspects of British poetry, art, and publishing. However, although Williams may have largely finished with promoting the Black Mountain poets of *The New American Poetry*, Jargon did continue to publish the work of less well-known figures associated with the college. These publications include two titles by the composer Lou Harrison, two books of photography by Williams's former Black Mountain roommate, Lyle Bongé, and six books of collage-fiction by former Black Mountaineer, Paul Metcalf. In addition, the artist and former Black Mountain student Ray Johnson provided drawings for fellow Black Mountain alumni Russell Edson's book *What a Man Can See* (1969). These titles and their authors serve as a subtle reminder that there was another Black Mountain to the one represented in Allen's section in *The New American Poetry*.

It was perhaps, however, Williams's decision to publish R. Buckminster Fuller's *Untitled Epic Poem on the History of Industrialization* in 1962 that most emphatically challenged the notion of a single Black Mountain 'club.' 'The voluble dome guru,' R. Buckminster Fuller, Tom Clark claims, 'provided [Olson's] main competition for students' attention' at Black Mountain and, according to Ralph Maud, a number of antagonisms and conflicts arose between Olson and Fuller concerning the leadership of Black Mountain (Clark 155; Maud 115–117). Although Williams's decision to publish Fuller's long poem could be simply seen as wilful insubordination, it also emphasizes his acknowledgement of the achievements that occurred outside Olson's classroom at Black Mountain. 'Williams's relations with Olson deteriorated, in part because of complications that developed between them over further publication of the *Maximus* poems,' Duberman suggests, but also 'because Olson didn't approve of some of the other people Williams published—like

Patchen, Bob Brown, Mina Loy or Buckminster Fuller (the latter according to Williams, was "anathema" to Olson)' (383).

The estrangement between Williams and Olson was also due to their differing sense of 'community,' Duberman suggests:

> Black Mountain was, as Williams said to me, 'literally a *place*. The associations were very close and very constant. But if you suddenly are not all in one place, and there is no community in fact, then all the separations and distances and divergences seem to enter.' Among the divergences was Olson's occasional tendency to treat Williams like a servant, to patronize his talents as a poet (Olson was more interested in Dorn, John Wieners, and later LeRoi Jones and Ed Sanders than in Williams), and to regard his publisher's 'sins' in printing the likes of Mina Loy et al., betrayal of the 'movement.' (383)

Black Mountain's 'community' was ultimately too exclusive and too prescriptive for Williams because the 'movement' that Olson conceived ran counter to the eclecticism and variety that characterized Jargon's ethos from its inception. 'I didn't really design my press as an axe-grinding operation,' Williams tells Alpert:

> I hope I didn't. I also hope that it wasn't 'calculated' to try to dominate and make a position that was dominant or exclusive. I don't see how it can be so judged if I printed people as bizarrely disconnected as say Alfred Starr Hamilton and Charles Olson. I mean very few of these people have ever had any regard for each other. (Alpert 59)

Considering Williams's thoughts about the community aspect of Black Mountain, it is particularly significant that shortly after the breakdown of Williams's relationship with Olson in the early 1960s, Jargon underwent a minor name change and became The Jargon Society. The new name arose out of practical financial needs. As a society, the press was not only attractive to private sponsors but also eligible for government arts grants and funding from charitable bodies such as the National Endowment for the Arts, the North Carolina Arts Council, and the John and Cara Higgins Foundation. 'It seemed people would not give money unless they had particular tax benefits,' Williams tells Dana: 'Also, to get money out of the National Endowment or any of the foundations, you had to do this' (204).

A letterhead from the mid-1980s lists '*the* JARGON SOCIETY *inc.*,' as a '*Non profit, public corporation devoted to charitable, educational, & literary purposes*' with Williams serving as 'EXECUTIVE DIRECTOR' and

Thomas Meyer as '*assistant director*.'[29] The letterhead also lists a number of '*COHORTS*' situated on both sides of the Atlantic that include Basil Bunting, Guy Davenport, Lou Harrison, Sally Midgette, John Furnival, and Simon Cutts. Significantly, this 'cohort' indicates the press's broader social vision. Indeed, the addition of 'society' to the name, Williams suggests, 'made us become more social, then, than perhaps we had been before' and brought the press's democratic vision much more to the fore (Dana 204). As Kyle Schlesinger notes, 'unlike other publishers who chose to name their companies after themselves (David Godine; Alfred Knopf; Peter Blum, et al.), Williams's "society" modestly diffuses the spotlight, illuminating the network of writers, artists, and artisans involved in every book' (para 10). Thus, with the change from 'Jargon' to 'The Jargon Society,' Williams's claim that the press became 'more social,' reaffirming what had always 'been kind of a group or community aspect of it,' becomes even more pronounced (Dana 204).

Like Moeglin-Delcroix's notion of the small press publication's 'utopic potential' and Kenner's idea of an 'elsewhere community,' Williams's 'better community' of kindred spirits proposes a space or locus that is, ultimately, displaced and 'eccentric' in the broadest sense of the word (Dana 204). Davenport identifies a similar eccentric infrastructure in the postwar milieu of the New American poetry. 'There is no American capital,' he claims, 'there never has been. We have a network instead': 'A French poet may plausibly know all other French poets by living in Paris. The smallest of American towns contain major poets, and all other kinds of artists. In no other country does such a distribution of mind appear' (*Geography* 168). However, from 1969 onwards (shortly after Davenport wrote these words) with Williams's annual semi-residence in Dentdale, Cumbria—and because of his increased involvement with British poetry, art, and publishing—this idea of a utopic, elsewhere, or eccentric community extended well beyond North America's shores, as the following chapters will discuss.

---

29 I would like to thank the poet and former Jargon Society intern Whit Griffin for providing this letterhead, designed by A. Doyle Moore.

Chapter Four

Small is Quite Beautiful: Tarasque Press

For every activity there is a certain appropriate scale ...

—E. F. Schumacher, *Small is Beautiful*

Although Jonathan Williams had parted ways with Black Mountain's rector by the early 1960s, 'the greater grandeur of Olson's reputation' had crossed the Atlantic and started to influence much of the burgeoning new British poetry (Pattison vi). The growing reputation of Olson and the New American poetry more generally was, as this chapter argues, aided considerably by the revolution in small press mimeograph publishing that peaked in the 1960s on both sides of the Atlantic. With this explosion in publishing, however, came more problematic issues of quality, both with regard to the production standards of the publications and the poetry that they published. As we shall see, the British poets Stuart Mills and Simon Cutts responded to these more problematic consequences of the mimeo revolution both in their poetry and in their own little magazine *Tarasque* by adopting a stance that was at considerable odds with the popular American idiom of the time. Thus Mills and Cutts, the present chapter argues, promoted a poetics that valued construction over expression, formal objectivity over subjective emotion, and which, following Finlay's example, deliberately skirted slightness, understatement, and whimsy. While this provocative position would alienate Mills and Cutts from the broader currents of the British Poetry Revival, their trenchant criticisms of the more expressive aspects of the mimeo revolution and the New American Poetry would in fact cement a long and sustaining relationship with one of Black Mountain's earliest ambassadors, and subsequent detractors, Jonathan Williams.

The New American poetry had started to reach British shores as early as the mid-1950s when, as Richard Price explains, W. Price

Turner's Glasgow-based magazine *The Poet* published Black Mountain poets 'alongside modern Scottish and English poets' ('Some Questions' 109). Significantly, Price notes, *The Poet* 'was a close and acknowledged model for *Migrant*,' Gael Turnbull's magazine and subsequent press which he started in 1957 after purchasing stock from Jargon, Origin, and Robert Creeley's Divers Press to distribute in Britain ('Some Questions' 109). Indeed, the first publication by Migrant Books (later renamed Migrant Press) was 'a single mimeographed sheet advertising these publications, which included Charles Olson's *Maximus Poems*' (Clay and Phillips 149).

In the same year, Migrant co-published Robert Creeley's selected poems *The Whip* with Jargon and Contact. Although Creeley's book 'received almost no attention at the time' in Britain, by the early 1960s British interest in the New American poetry had grown due to the success of Donald Allen's landmark anthology *The New American Poetry* published by Grove Press in 1960 (Migrant flyer n. pag). By 1961, Tom Raworth, for example, 'following threads' of people he liked in Allen's anthology had started his own Matrix press, publishing a number of American and British poets including Edward Dorn, Pete Brown, Anselm Hollo, and Piero Heliczer (Spragg n. pag). In addition, Raworth also edited the little magazine *Outburst*. The first issue, published in 1961, featured a number of writers with links to Black Mountain including Olson, Creeley, Denise Levertov, Ed Dorn, and Fielding Dawson as well as British writers such as Turnbull, Brown, and Christopher Logue. According to Jonathan Williams, Raworth and he 'printed 1 or 2 things together and then I introduced him, I think to Barry Hall' (Alpert 70). This introduction would lead Raworth and Hall—a British artist who provided two drawings for Williams's *Line About Hills Above Lakes*—to establish Goliard Press in 1965 which continued the transatlantic spirit and high production standards of Matrix. Goliard published Olson's booklet *West* in 1966 which appeared alongside a number of Raworth's own broadsides as well as publications by, among others, Michael Horowitz, Anselm Hollo, Elaine Feinstein, Ron Padgett, and Aram Saroyan. In this respect, Migrant, Matrix and Goliard were quick to recognize what Neil Pattison describes as the 'overlapping sodalities in Britain and North America in the 1950s and 1960s' and promote a spirit of 'active, open engagement, committed friendship, and keen collaboration' (vii).

The high quality of Goliard's publications set the press apart from more modestly produced magazines of the period such as the *English Intelligencer*, a 'privately circulated poetry worksheet' established by the British poets Andrew Crozier and Peter Riley and which ran from 1966 to 1968 (Pattison i). 'Reproduced by mimeograph machine and distributed by mail,' Pattison writes, 'the *Intelligencer* made a virtue of speed and disposability, conceiving of itself not as a print magazine, but as another kind of cultural domain, one more accommodating of error, deviation, and internal dispute, than was usual in a traditionally curated poetry journal' (i).

Between 1964 and 1965, Crozier had been a graduate assistant on Olson's poetry programme at Buffalo, SUNY. Other contributors to the *Intelligencer* had also had first-hand experience of Olson: John Temple, like Crozier, had been a graduate assistant at Buffalo between 1965 and 1966 and J. H. Prynne had established an important friendship with the American poet, which Alex Latter describes as a 'trans-Atlantic brotherhood' (66). It is perhaps not surprising then that 'the group [of poets] associated with Black Mountain, and particularly its notional figurehead Charles Olson' were the American examples that many of 'the poets involved with the *Intelligencer* directed most attention' (Latter 21). Thus, despite the *Intelligencer*'s initial intention to open up discussion around the question of 'the island and its language,' Olson and Black Mountain remained touchstones (*Certain Prose* 3).

Olson's influence is evident in Peter Riley's 'announcement' in the second series of the *Intelligencer*: 'To put it simply as possible/ abstract it/reduce it to a formula: what we've seen achieved in America recently can be put as—the poem: Physiological Presence and Cosmological Range' (*Certain Prose* 95). Echoes of Olson's rhetoric and style are discernible in Riley's declarative opening sentence while his discussion of 'physiological presence' and 'cosmological range' recalls the terminology of Olson's essays such as 'Human Universe' and 'Proprioception.' Indeed, Riley's cosmological allusions reiterate Miriam Nichols's suggestion that 'the 1950s and '60s represent the last moment in recent cultural history when a serious poet could write the word *cosmos* without irony or quotation marks and expect serious intellectual attention' (12).

Elsewhere in *The English Intelligencer*, Olson's influence is also discernible in the way many of the contributions frequently deploy capitals (for emphasis), typographic symbols (such as the ampersand), and abbreviations: 'yr,' 'shd,' 'thrfr.' According to Guy Davenport, many younger poets who 'write *wd* and *cd* for *would* and *could*,' have done so unaware 'that these standard epistolary abbreviations, used a hundred years ago to conserve paper, were picked up by Pound in quotations from Adams and Jefferson, and then appropriated as a stylistic idiosyncrasy' ('Introduction' 15). Similar idiosyncrasies are evident in John Hall's letter to Peter Riley, dated 1 April 1967:

> So the land is the constant & what you've done is analyse the strata of its topsoil, the consequence of the different wanderings into the land, & that doesn't have much to do with your territory, yr own life, as the history coming up on it, as do the moments of different qualities from wherever it is they

> come. Quality as already there & then destroyed is hope-less
> & anyway so local as not to matter. (*Certain Prose* 103)

Whether such idiosyncrasies are for the sake of expedience and paper or an emulation of Pound and Olson is unclear. What Hall's mannerisms do demonstrate, however, is what Turnbull describes as 'the fashionable American poetic idiom' that, he believed, inflected much of new British poetry during this period (*Certain Prose* 4). As his letter, printed in the third issue of the first series of the *Intelligencer* indicates, Turnbull had grown weary of the Americanisms characterizing much of the recent poetry published in the newssheet. In response to John Temple's recent work, Turnbull writes:

> I just don't see the point of such near parody's [sic] of Olson, as for example the first poem—I mean, I'm interested to see what Temple can do with his 'roots' etc.—but must he swipe the means so obviously from Olson?—I can't believe this is really what Olson intended, anyway—I know, it's easy to carp, and easy to be negative, etc., but the whole thing seems to me to be an easy transcript into what is currently the fashionable American poetic idiom [.] (*Certain Prose* 4)

As Latter notes, Temple utilized 'a distinctive Black Mountain idiom as well as a common ground of ideas,' which for readers such as Turnbull suggested 'a disproportionate influence of the American example' (80).

Turnbull's reservations about 'the fashionable American idiom' also inform his own publishing concerns with Migrant. Despite being 'an important way of opening the doors wider in Britain to experimental American work' which, Richard Price claims, had until then been closed by the 'strong provincial element' of mainstream British poetry, Turnbull was keen 'to counter the sometimes excessively national focus of those Americans whose writing he valued' by 'keeping an English taproot' ('Migrant the Magnificent' 30; Migrant flyer n. pag). Poets who provided this 'tap root' included Roy Fisher, Mathew Mead and Hugh Creighton Hill, all of whom counterbalanced, rather than amplified, the American dimension of the press and its magazine.[30] Migrant further tempered the American influence by publishing Scottish poets such Ian Hamilton Finlay, Edwin Morgan, and Robert Garioch.

Above all, however, Turnbull is more concerned with the singular

---

30 Hill, who was published in Vincent Ferrini's magazine *Four Winds*, receives ambivalent attention in 'Letter 5' of *The Maximus Poems*: 'You see I can't get away from the old measure of care: how your magazine doesn't raise me, / Not even Hugh Hill, whose triangles / are so nicely made but the course he's running / doesn't strike me as good enough' (26).

qualities of a poet then he is their national identity. 'There is no doubt that I was more interested in what might be done with the British end of it,' he writes in his account of Migrant: 'I felt exiled in Ventura and it was a way of keeping something going for myself, in contact with poets in both England and Scotland. I was wanting to create a context that was not narrowly national and in which I felt I might be able to exist as a writer myself' (25). Turnbull reiterates these sentiments in his letter written to and published in the *Intelligencer*:

> I haven't much sense of 'the island and its language'—my only sense is if this individual or that individual, with his or her voice, discrete and each themselves—and I look to a Robert Garioch, or a Jonathan Williams, or a Tom Pickard—each speaks his own tongue, and makes his own poems as best he can—I hope this island doesn't have a language in a sense. (*Certain Prose* 4)

In expressing a hope that 'this island doesn't have a language,' Turnbull draws attention to the English focus of the *Intelligencer* and the implicit assumption that there is *one* homogenous language for the *one* (mainland) 'island.' Thus, Turnbull's allusion to these Scottish, American, and British poets is a subtle reminder that national identity is not simply about sharing the same land mass. By drawing attention to their singular use of local dialect, Turnbull emphasizes the importance of regional, as opposed to national, identity in these poets' work. As we have seen, the language and culture of Appalachia (and also Dentdale, Cumbria) gave Williams's poetry a distinctive 'folk base' which also incorporates lessons learnt from Black Mountain, the Objectivists, and concrete poetry. Likewise, Pickard, who is influenced considerably by Bunting (and to whom Williams first introduced Pickard), rediscovered the potential of Northumbrian dialect and diction, whereas Garioch's 'literary use of Scots' reflected the 'natural development of the linguistic surroundings in which he grew up' in Edinburgh and became integrated into his 'thoroughly modern and European' poetry (Fulton xii, xxxiii). Thus, according to Turnbull, and unlike Temple, these three very different poets found their 'own tongue' by looking and listening to their immediate environments and by revisiting their own cultural roots rather than by imitating the popular American idioms of the time.

Tarasque Press

Turnbull's choice of poets in his letter to *The English Intelligencer* is also revealing because all three were largely peripheral to the *Intelligencer* axis. Therefore, it is possible to read Turnbull's letter as a tacit criticism of the *Intelligencer*'s remit and its neglect of other important areas of Anglo-American poetry that occurred beyond the one 'island and its language.' However, one subscriber to *The English Intelligencer* who did value these poets (particularly Williams and Garioch) is Stuart Mills. Although Mills's presence in *The English Intelligencer* (and in both Pattison's and Latter's histories of the magazine) is largely peripheral, both the little magazine *Tarasque* and the eponymous press that Mills established with Simon Cutts in 1965 assume an important, if controversial, position within the history of the British Poetry Revival.

'Via its activities of publishing poetry books, pamphlets, postcards and prints,' as Hannah Neate explains, 'Tarasque Press effectively worked as an outpost for avant-garde poetry in Nottingham from the mid-1960s until the early 1970s' (44). Later issues of the magazine, however, extended their scope beyond Nottingham to include poetry from other parts of Britain, Europe, and Northern America. As each issue of the magazine reminded its reader, *Tarasque* took its name from the mythical 'animal which lived on the banks of the Rhone, and ravaged the surrounding countryside' (n. pag). The first nine issues of the magazine sported the same image of an Aztec bird design, the colour of which, along with the cover, changed with each number. The series of dots which proceed from the bird's beak, Stephen Bann suggests, depict a 'belching flame' which reasserts the ferocious nature of both the mythical beast and the magazine to which it gives its name ('Stuart Mills Obituary' n. pag). Those dots, however, might also suggest song and thereby serve as a tacit reminder that for all of its 'vigorous criticism, found material and sideswipes at the literary establishment' *Tarasque* also possessed a gentler lyric side that promoted, and not simply ravaged, British poetry (Bevis, 'A Star-gazey Pie' 24). Both the press and the magazine, as Neate explains, expressed a 'distinct bias towards British poets working in a modernist mode,' publishing Turnbull, Finlay, Fisher, Hugh Creighton Hill, Libby Houston, and Spike Hawkins, among others (47). The magazine also included critical essays on contemporary poetry, including the first on Bunting's *Briggflatts* and the first on Fisher's poetry.

Jonathan Williams's connections with Tarasque begin in 1964 when Mills, with Martin Parnell, opened the Trent Bookshop in Nottingham. This venture, Neate writes, prompted 'contact with Andrew Crozier's Ferry Press, Gael Turnbull of Migrant, Ian Hamilton Finlay's Wild Hawthorn Press, and Jonathan Williams's Jargon Society' (36). In the same year, Cutts, who had begun working at the shop, quickly became involved in the events being organized by Mills and Parnell, including the 'Poetry '66' conference in Nottingham which was borne out of dissatisfaction with the 1965 London Royal Albert Hall event. Although Mills, like Finlay, was included in Michael Horovitz's anthology *Children of Albion: Poetry of the Underground in Britain* (1969), which grew from the seeds sewn by the Albert Hall event, his and Parnell's assessment of the event far was less enthusiastic than Horovitz's. 'I think that Stuart and myself ... were quite unsympathetic to the self-centredness of all of them,' Parnell tells Neate, referring to the performances of Horovitz and Ginsberg:

> Particularly Allen Ginsberg, because we weren't great admirers of beat poets, we actually preferred a different sort of poetry, and just to see these people thinking how great they were, it didn't matter basically—it reminds me of the worst way that Brits perform, taking your trousers down and showing your backside—that is the way they performed. (39)

In contrast to Parnell's account, Horovitz in *The Children of Albion* boasts how the Albert Hall gathering 'was claimed by some as the greatest stimulus for poetry this century' as 'poem after poem resonated mind-expanding ripples of empathy' (339, 337). For Horovitz, the event ushered in a 'return of Albion's golden age,' that followed a 'Blakean way' (368, 349). However, unlike the Blake-centred visionary pastoral tradition that Jonathan Williams evokes in his 'English' poetry, Horovitz's Blake was filtered through the prophetic American lens of the Beats, particularly Ginsberg. 'In the light of the Jerusalemic mythology, catalysts like Ferlinghetti, heralds like Corso and a high priest like Ginsberg were indeed called for to revive Albion today' and inspire its British 'children,' Horovitz claims (344):

> Albion's children are strongly in evidence all over the country and—most colourfully & plentifully—all over London, at work and play in their own gardens of love, where only 'Thou Shalt Not' is taboo—in an atmosphere of their awareness, radiating a *sense* of community & a more open, humane and practiced way of life—of which much of this Miscellany is the best symbolic expression. (371)

As a tacit retort to the Albert Hall reading and the unfettered 'sense of community' it encouraged, the Poetry '66 event organized by Mills and Parnell foresees *Tarasque*'s subsequent critiques of the British contemporary poetry scene, particularly the mélange of mimeo publications, 'the new underground exchanges,' indiscriminately celebrated in *The Children of Albion* (Horovitz 365).

Williams attended Mills's and Parnell's two-day conference and compered the opening evening event of Poetry '66, 'A Concert of Poetry and Jazz with New Departures and Leading Poets.' 'Pete Brown was good,' Williams recalls: 'Spike Hawkins was very funny; Adrian Mitchell and Christopher Logue were very intense; and Michael Horovitz simply would not shut up' (cited in Neate 41). Williams's presence at Poetry '66 instigated important and enduring relationships with Mills, Cutts, and the British artist Ian Gardner, who subsequently became involved with

Tarasque in the late 1960s. Williams's relationship with these younger British poets and artist is perhaps not surprising considering their mutual inclination for wry humour, sardonic wit, and incisive whimsy. Writing on the occasion of Williams's sixtieth birthday, David Annwn suggests that his 'wit has become more piercing, acerbic, the art more pronounced, the attention more "lush" in its true Yorkshire sense': 'Like Cider ripening, he has become more better, tarter—more bite' (*Catgut* 7). These qualities—acerbic, biting wit—also describe the general tone of *Tarasque* which, in tune with Williams's similar reservations, was frequently aimed at the dregs of Black Mountain.

Victor Gudgin, a student at the Nottingham College of Art with Cutts, sums up state of affairs in his essay 'Situation' which was printed in the third issue of *Tarasque*:

> POETRY has been lazy since Olson in the U.S. and Eliot (possibly Gascoyne) or even Yeats in this country. POETRY in the States has been hard headed about itself as art—i.e. it has asked for facts. Olson being the last to do this 16 years ago—impetus largely Pound's—his ideas have been done to death and, despite Olson's advice, poets in the U.S. will not shut up and listen. (n. pag)

As a press, and more so as a magazine, Tarasque would counter such lazy ignorance by advocating 'an increasingly formal sense of poetry' that pitched itself against the New American poetry that burgeoned *after* Olson (*SFA* 51). Indeed, it is worth stressing that Olson is not the problem according to Gudgin, but the poets who have tried unsuccessfully to emulate him and 'done to death' his idiom.

Emerging during 'the hey-day of the "Little Magazine" and "Little Press" activity [that was] attempting to cater for the surge of influence from American poetry,' *Tarasque*, as Cutts explains, sought a counter-position and made a 'polemical stance' out of 'concern at the absence of quality' of the poetry being written and published at the time (*SFA* 51). This 'polemical stance' was also an aesthetic one, Cutts explains, because 'quality in this sense of our concern seemed to be inseparable from some increasingly formal sense of poetry, and from some reduction to a more common basis than the banal desire to express oneself' (*SFA* 51). The eschewal of self-expression—what Cutts elsewhere describes as 'the emotional directness that the voice conveys'—is made evident in Mills's and Cutts's editorial, 'some pointers taken at random from notebooks, and other sources,' to the second issue of *Tarasque* that stresses the importance of '"Material" as opposed to the remote idea of "having something to say"' (*SFA* 95; Mills and Cutts, *Tarasque* 2 n. pag).

Comparing Tarasque's stance with that adopted by J. H. Prynne in his letter to the editors of the magazine *Mica* (printed in its fifth issue along with Finlay's poem-sequence 'Five Sapphic Fragments'), it is possible to see how the position taken by Mills and Cutts departs from the American idioms of the time. In his letter, Prynne acknowledges what he considers to be a problematic trend in 'the kind of work' that *Mica* was printing, 'much of which seems to be in the mode prevalent among a section of the more interesting American writers' (2). Like Gudgin, Prynne diagnoses an impasse in innovation:

> Current American writing doesn't seem to have gone much further than the basic Imagist resolution at the beginning of the century—the breakthrough of Pound and Williams. Not only do few writers seem to wish to go any further—or advance in any other direction—but hardly any of the current endeavour at new experiment seems aimed at technical means for a change of attitude or approach. (2)

Prynne also questions the 'implicit anti-intellectualism of the current short lyric,' believing that 'its explicit dogma is the pre-occupation with Zen and derived vatic utterance,' and claims that 'a lot of American poems now being written are opiate, offering substitutes for experience rather than modes of access' (2, 3).

To a degree these concerns concur with those expressed by Mills and Cutts just a few years later in *Tarasque*. For example, Prynne reaches similar conclusions about the 'near-vicious over indulgence' of the new poetry and its preoccupation with 'personal image' (3). He also insists that 'the object [of the poem] should not be the poet's anterior experience (Eliot's fundamental error), but the poem's achieved shape' (3). However, where Prynne differs from the editors of *Tarasque* is in his belief that the 'short lyric' is the cause, rather than the solution, to the problem of indulgence (28). As an alternative, Prynne advocates the 'ordering' of words into their 'grammar of feeling: the movement forward speeded or checked by the adverbs, bent, inverted or split by the conjunctions, maintained always by the constant verb' (28). Prynne's emphasis on speed, movement, and force (on 'bent, inverted, or split' adverbs) recalls Olson's emphasis in 'Projective Verse' on the '*kinetics*' and the '*process*' of the poem, as well as Olson's urge to 'USE USE USE the process at all points, in any given poem always,' and 'MOVE, INSTANTER, ON ANOTHER!' (*Collected Prose* 240). Again, echoing Olson's belief 'that right form, in any given poem, is the only and exclusively possible extension of content under hand,' Prynne writes: 'It is the mind at work directing, directing the convictions or importance to what is in fact important, working every proposition into the final contours of the poem and the shape of its own defining' (Olson, *Collected Prose* 243; Prynne 28). But whereas Prynne was concerned with finding an appropriate form to order words into a 'grammar of feeling,' Mills and Cutts were trying to find the formal means for doing away with emotion altogether.

As Neate notes, 'Cutts and Mills considered themselves 'more "classically modernist"' than many of their Beat and Black Mountain-inspired contemporaries and found instructive 'precedents and ancestry' for what they were trying to do in Wyndham Lewis's *Blast* and poets like Ezra Pound and T.E. Hulme' (46). This 'classically modernist' stance, Cutts explains, was a way of situating himself and Mills 'very much outside the predominant influences and the culture that was going on' in the sixties: 'We were kind of old stooges in a way, opting for a more reductive sort of modernist approach than was going on. We were not entranced by the developments at the time, this kind of free spirit of the time' (*SFA* 29–30). The 'reductive sort of modernist approach,' however, was just one among other ways of resisting the American *zeitgeist*. As Bevis points out, 'the influences on the written work were beyond the stock of the small press clique,' to encompass ninetheenth-century French poetry, Post-Impressionism, Imagism, Vorticism, Joyce, and Debussy, all of which were considered 'milestones at the cusp of symbolism and imagery' ('A Star-gazey Pie' 25).

For Cutts in particular, nineteenth-century French literature—'from Baudelaire to the Symbolists, centering on Mallarmé'—was a formative influence that fed into an initial discovery of Joyce and an abiding interest in modernism and the historical avant-garde (*SFA* 95):

> In the summer of 1963, I had the chance to spend three months reading James Joyce's *Ulysses* and to following through many of its antecedents and influences by way of late nineteenth-century Symbolism and stream-of-consciousness prose workings. Somewhere along the linage of it all, perhaps even away from its intense literariness, I discovered Mallarmé and the prospect of *making* a text on the page, and thereby discovered Apollinaire and visual arrangement. Back home, it was the Imagists and Ezra Pound that allowed me to feel a movement forward, even T. S. Eliot's drafts of *The Waste Land* on an old Olympia typewriter. (*SFA* 12)

Charles Tomlinson, writing in his introduction to Cutts's collection *A New Kind of Tie: Poems 1965–1968* elaborates on these French affinities:

> The source of these early poems is, in part, Verlaine—the Verlaine of Fêtes Galantes and Romance sans paroles, and also Laforgue prior to the Derniers Vers, but Verlaine and Laforgue seen through Mallarmé (On évite le récit) and through the achievement of the literary cubists. I imagine Cutts has read Jacob, Reverdy, and Salmon. (n. pag)

Although these influences are close in spirit to a number of American poets such as Frank O'Hara, John Ashbery, and according to Tomlinson, Kenneth Rexroth and 'the American objectivists, who also learned from the French,' Tomlinson believes that Cutts's French sympathies set him apart from the 'young poets today' who tend to 'go to school to the Americans' (n. pag).

Tomlinson does, however, omit to mention one American that has impressed significantly upon Cutts and his French sensibilities: Edgar Allan Poe. For Cutts, Poe 'was consistent with the whole latter half of the nineteenth century in France' due to his 'workman-like sophistication of the artist effect' which Baudelaire and Mallarmé would incorporate into their own writing (*SFA* 101, 105). It was from Poe and the French writers that responded to his writing, Cutts explains, 'that I was given the reassurance that language is its own artificial system, which can refer less well to anything outside itself than to itself' (*SFA* 95). 'His certainty that there is little beyond language,' Cutts writes of Poe, 'undoubtedly enabled a poet like Verlaine or Mallarmé to assume that he was dealing with language, a material (*'poetry is not made of ideas but words'*)' (*SFA* 107). Such sentiments echo Paul Valéry's similar belief, 'elicited from Poe by Baudelaire,' that 'A poem does not say something—it *is* something' (Eliot 340; Valéry, cited in Eliot 337).

Cutts's concern for the objective quality of the poem—its status as an autonomous object of words rather than a vehicle of subjective expression—is evident in an early untitled poem that provides an epigraph of sorts for *A New Kind of Tie*:

> As for verse, what sort
> of reality does it bear
> in sunlight, after the winter
> of close hills above the river
> and the tight view of pages
> under tungsten lighting
> Is it the same name
> it belongs to? (n. pag)

The poem demonstrates what Cutts describes as an 'Impressionist aesthetic' which is both 'an artistic style [and] a psychological one': 'The Impressionist painting avoided the narrative or descriptive by this concern with the effect that Mallarmé had spoken about; it recreated itself each time it was viewed' (*SFA* 95–96). A similar impressionistic recreation is effected in 'As for verse' by the changing context in which the poem is read—from natural 'sunlight' to the artificial luminescence of 'tungsten lighting'—and its status as a made or constructed object, emphasized by 'the tight view of pages,' that stand apart from the 'reality' beyond it. Rather than representing 'reality,' therefore, Cutts's poem *bears* a relationship to it. Homophonically, it might also be said to expose (*bare*) or disclose that reality, rather than simply represent it. In this respect, Cutts's poem reflects the cubist influence noted by Tomlinson and recalls Pierre Reverdy's similar emphasis on the autonomous, non-mimetic art work:

> We are at a period of artistic creation in which people no longer tell stories more or less agreeably, but create works of art that, in detaching themselves from life, find their way back into it, because they have an existence of their own apart from the evocation or reproduction of the things of life. Because of that, the Art of today is an art of great reality. But by this must be understood artistic reality, and not realism—which is the genre most opposed to us. ('On Cubism' 145)

This idea of 'an art of great reality' is also reiterated by Max Jacob's similar claim that the literary cubism, like its painterly counterpart, uses 'reality merely as a means not as an end' (cited in Breunig 226).

The French avant-garde is also a touchstone for Mills's poetics as his poem 'Neo-Fauve' (first published in *Tarasque* 4, *sans* title) demonstrates:

> Park your bike in the sunshine.
> Remove your yellow trousers
> And hang them up to dry.
>
> On the pier ten men are playing trumpets.
> The bay is full of steamers.
>
> You have come a long way. (*Made in English* 49)

The title that Mills later gave his poem not only suggests Finlay's 'fauve' poems but also the group of French painters—'le fauves' ('the wild beasts')—that lent Finlay that term. 'Les fauves' was a nickname, attributed by a sceptical critic, for describing the paintings of a small group of post-Impressionists that were characterized by their 'briskly applied strokes, patches and dabs of brilliant colour' (Whitfield 9). Mills's poem tacitly evokes the paintings of the key Fauves, Henri Matisse and André Derain, via the use of one single, bold, primary colour: the cyclist's yellow trousers. It is the only colour presented in the poem but, like the unpainted areas of a Matisse canvas, which 'give off as much light as the strokes of colour' and 'radiate the energy of colour while remaining colourless,' 'Neo-Fauve' conveys a vibrant colourful picture (Whitfield 69).

The limpidity of sunlight after a rain shower is tacit in the image of the bike and the trousers drying in the sunshine and the blithe activities of the scene (the bay *full* of steamboats and the pier equally bustling with a large brass band) convey a profusion of colour, light, and energy that recall the vibrant landscapes painted by the Fauves, particularly those of the Southern French fishing village of Collioure that Matisse and Derain painted in the summer of 1905. Mills's seaside scene also recalls the lesser-known Fauves Raoul Dufy and Albert Marquest, whose paintings of the French seaside town of Saint-Adresse and its 'manufactured attractions'—'Tricolours and yachting flags, bathing tents and hoardings covered with posters' along with sailboats, promenades, and piers—all of which provided the painters 'the primary colours which nature did not' (Whitfield 130).

In addition to the Fauves, Bann suggests that 'Neo-Fauve' evokes two French poets with strong links to Cubism: Guillaume Apollinaire and Pierre Albert-Birot ('Tarasque' 134).[31] Exactly how 'Neo-Fauve' alludes to these two poets is not immediately apparent, but one possible answer lies in Mills's enigmatic use of the singular second-person pronoun and the ambiguous nature of his poem's addressee: 'Park *your* bike in the sunshine. / Remove *your* yellow trousers,' '*You* have come a long way.' Apollinaire adopts a similar method of address in 'Zone,' his celebrated 'poèm-promenade' whose central theme is also travel: 'You walk towards Auteuil you want to go home on foot' (cited in Breunig 47, 73). Like Apollinaire's 'Zone,' Mills's didactic apostrophizing and his use of active verbs serve to implicate the reader more emphatically in a landscape that is not so much mimetically represented as it is emotively invoked so that the reader is less an observer of the landscape than a participant in it.

Echoing the concluding line of 'Neo-Fauve,' Albert-Birot also invokes travel—more specifically, mental travel—in the nineteenth of his *31 Pocket Poems* (*Trente et un Poems du poche*) published in 1917:

> What a lot of shapes colours and sounds
> What a long way you can travel in a human head
> THE EIFFEL TOWER IS NO TALLER THAN A
> MAN (21)

Albert-Birot's poem tacitly challenges mimetic convention—particularly perspective—and, like Matisse and Derain before him, betrays 'a

---

31 Bann translated Albert-Biro's poem 'Shopping' for the twenty-third issue of Finlay's *Poor. Old. Tired. Horse.* Other issues of *POTH* included examples of Albert-Birot's poster-poems ('poêmes-affiches') as well as several translations of Apollinaire's poetry including, in *POTH* 13, Apollinaire's tribute to the so-called 'primitive' painter and associate of the Fauves, Henri 'La Douanier' Rousseau. Incidentally, Mills also pays tribute to Rousseau in his poem 'Le Douanier,' first published in *Tarasque* 5, circa 1967.

response to landscape at once spontaneous, uninhibited and innocent' (Whitfield 71). The Fauves' similarly 'innocent' response to landscape is echoed in Albert-Birot's 'blend of the everyday and the imaginary' and his ability to present 'a celebration of every trivial component of life' as if an 'innocent newborn discovering the world for the first time' (Wright, *31 Pocket Poems* vi). The revelations of innocent discovery are particularly apparent in the plethora of 'shapes colours and sounds,' rather than nominalized phenomena, that Albert-Birot's poem delights in.

The 'studied simplicity' of 'Neo-Fauve' stands in a line of avant-garde innovation that has its roots firmly in the 'drastic paring-down' of Fauvist painting and what Matisse called its 'purity of means' (Bann, 'Tarasque' 134; Whitfield 69). That Fauvism should have initiated 'the transition of twentieth-century painting from representation to object,' and an 'effacement of individuality' that the Cubists would develop more rigorously, is especially salient in relation to Mills's and Cutts's similar preoccupations with objective form and the 'area of intersection between visual and literary sensibility' that they, along with Gardner, would increasingly explore (Whitfield 195, 205; Bann, 'Tarasque' 134).

The Wee and Twee
In their pursuit of a 'formal sense of poetry,' Cutts, Mills, and Gardner, eventually 'moved through the ever-compressing, seemingly orthodox poem with its arrangement of line and stanza' to explore what Cutts describes as 'narrative' and 'syntactical' concrete poems which resisted 'the banal desire to express oneself' (*SFA* 51). According to Mills, particular emphasis was placed on 'the small image, the artefact, and (in those days) the so-called Concrete Poem':

> Ian Gardner would paint small watercolours. Simon Cutts could often be seen coaxing a small fretsaw through the intricacies of a piece of work no larger than a florin, and as the poems shrunk in size so did the format of the booklets. ('From Tarasque' 141)

That Tarasque's evolution from 'orthodox' to 'concrete' poetry should recall the similar trajectory that Finlay's poetry took is perhaps not surprising considering the influence of the older poet on Mills, Cutts, and Gardener. Williams has even described all three as 'disciples' of Finlay due to their various collaborative and publishing projects with the older poet (Alpert 62–63).

Notwithstanding Williams's suggestion of partisanship, the relation between Finlay and these younger poets could be strained. Indeed, 'the principle of conflict' that Bann identifies in 'Homage to Malevich' also extends into Finlay's social and professional relations ('Ian Hamilton Finlay' 61). Finlay's flytings with MacDiarmid, as discussed in chapter two, is but one example. A more notorious instance occurs in Finlay's embattled lawsuit with Stuart Montgomery's Fulcrum Press in 1969 over the copyediting and erroneous marketing of a 'new edition' of *The Dancers Inherit the Party*. The battle resulted in many of Finlay's closest friends, including Williams, being drawn acrimoniously into the affair which, perhaps inaccurately, is considered to have caused the ultimate downfall of Fulcrum.[32]

While *Tarasque*'s unforgiving critiques of the contemporary poetry scene may consciously model itself on this incendiary aspect of Finlay's character and poetics, Finlay's influence is also apparent in the way that his concrete poetry significantly expanded the symbolist, modernist, and avant-garde models that Mills and Cutts adopted. As John Bevis suggests, Finlay's model provided Mills and Cutts 'less an aesthetic bath, than a new focus on elements of the poem that had been traditionally taken for granted,' such as the conception of line and space ('A Star-gazey Pie' 27).

Cutts has claimed that a presiding concern of Tarasque was the formulation of 'an objective aesthetic for literature' (*SFA* 50). Concrete poetry offered 'some solution to [this] question of an aesthetic for poetry,' particularly the 'certain objective quality' of Finlay's mode, which reaffirmed what Mills and Cutts had already intuited in relatively 'orthodox' poetic forms (*SFA* 50):

> [T]he embracing of concrete poetry was the alignment of a certain objective quality of working, for instance in the oeuvre of Ian Hamilton Finlay, with an emphasis on structural procedure for poetry in general which had been working itself out over a long period of time in other genres of Tarasque poetry. (*SFA* 50)

---

32   'The energy and money needed to fight and lose the case [with Finlay] is said to have broken Fulcrum—although a flood that affected stock was probably the very end,' Price surmises with regard to the fall of Fulcrum ('Some Questions' 104). Another contributing factor, however, was the campaign that Allen Ginsberg seems to have launched against Montgomery. 'I had a letter from Robert Creeley, which was largely a carbon of a letter to Montgomery, protesting at his treatment of Edward Dorn and John Wieners,' Finlay writes in a letter to Ronald Johnson in the February of 1970: 'I am not sure what he did to them but it appears (from Robert's letter) that A. Ginsberg (you know that one who wrote that famous long poem, I always forget its name) is actually circulating a petition about the Wieners affair. All this gives me a gloomy I-told-you-so sort of satisfaction' (Letter to Ronald Johnson, 11 Feb 1970).

Cutts, therefore, is keen to emphasize that Finlay 'attracted our attention by the firm quality and consistency of his work, irrespective of his being a concrete poet' (*SFA* 51). He also stresses that 'in no sense has Tarasque Press been entirely dedicated to the arena of concrete poetry; because of our firm literary origins, and because of the lateness of our embracing that area, we have always been the "derriere-garde" of such a movement' (*SFA* 51).

Just what Finlay offered younger poets such as Mills and Cutts who were dissatisfied with the solipsism of contemporary British and American poetry is intimated in Jonathan Williams's own acknowledgement of Finlay's influence. Like Sitwell, Finlay is another poet who, for Williams, complemented, as well as challenged, the strictures of Olson:

> I one day realized that when Olson had said by ear was the first and great commandment, by eye was the equally the first and great commandment. Which I got from Finlay. He was a very instructive poet to me. He never worries about these things. As I say, the English think he's whimsical, a lot of people think he's dull or limited. I think he's probably the most interesting poet over there and one of the most interesting poets anywhere. (Alpert 72)

The perceived whimsicality of Finlay's poetry is crucial in understanding the important position he assumes for both Williams and Tarasque Press. Despite being championed by a number of Black Mountain poets, including Creeley and Duncan, Finlay's poetry, appearing on the surface as being 'a bit wee and twee' and 'too whimsical,' is anathema to the more expressive and earnest New American idioms that followed in the wake of Black Mountain (Dana 219). However, as Hugh Kenner notes in his review of *The Dancers Inherit the Party*, 'Finlay invests' any suggestion of whimsy 'with bleak and casual panic, as though on the edge of the world' (Finlay, *Domestic Pensées* dust jacket). Also tempering the assumption that Finlay is too whimsical, Thomas A. Clark suggests that 'the recurring use of affectionate diminutives' in Finlay's poetry such as '"Little," "peedie," [and] "wee,"' is not simply done so for affectation or sentimentality ('Paper and Stone' 66). Rather, Clark proposes, 'such diminutives convey a care for fragile, unprotected things, a redressing of the balance in their favour' which has more to do with 'justice rather than sentimentality' and which Clark considers ultimately as 'a compensation or homage paid to the small or unconsidered' ('Paper and Stone' 66).

The judicial implications of Finlay's 'affectionate diminutives' and his 'wee and twee' sensibilities are evident in the postcard that Finlay, in collaboration with Ron Costley, produced in 1976 called *Small Is Quite*

Beautiful. Costley renders this aphoristic statement in a script suggestive of the Roman square capitals (Capitalis Monumentalis) traditionally used for inscriptions on temples, columns, and monuments. In terms of sentiment and format, this conflation of the monumental with the diminutive in *Small Is Quite Beautiful* is a telling example of what Stephen Scobie describes as Finlay's 'ironic modulation of scale' (177). In this particular instance something as quotidian, cheap, small, easily reproducible and as easily disposable as the postcard is wryly imbued with grand, monumental stature.

Furthermore, in terms of its semantics and its format, *Small Is Quite Beautiful* foregrounds the printed formats that proved pivotal for the development of Finlay's poetry and poetics throughout the 1960s and which Mills and Cutts would continue to innovate through Tarasque: the *small* press, the *little* magazine, the postcard, and other forms of printed ephemera. As Clark explains, the 'standing poem' which Finlay innovated in 1966, is particularly significant in terms of its 'modest format' and its assertive 'self-possession': 'It sits quietly within the situation, making a difference, suggesting another possibility' ('The Standing Poem' n. pag). With the words of a poem or text 'printed on the front of the card, rather than inside,' Clark suggests, 'poetry moves from the private into the public realm': 'Instead of being assigned to a secluded, literary space, it enters the ordinary, everyday world, taking part in the occasion' ('The Standing Poem' n. pag). Consequently, the innovative and modest format of the small press publication possesses an ability to interact with its environment that the more conventional book lacks. In this respect, such publications bear close resemblance to the artist's book which, according to Johanna Drucker, 'one encounters with no introduction and no warning and which suddenly, oddly, uniquely transforms the viewer's expectations by its unexpected innovative originality' (*Figuring* 182). This 'power' that Drucker attributes to the artist's book, its capacity for intervention and its ability 'to function subversively in the most ordinary of surroundings simply by its transformation of the standard form and format' is a quality that it shares with the small press poetry publication, whereby the printed format, working *together* with the poem it accommodates, poses the possibility of intervention, spontaneity, and surprise (*Figuring* 182). As Clark reasons, the card format is particularly suited to such affects:

> Our relation to literary products is usually voluntary; you go to the shelf to find the book to look up the poem. By contrast, a card is available at a glance. You can forget it for days or weeks and then come into a room and discover it again. It takes you by surprise. ('The Standing Poem' n. pag)

Small press publishing is also tacitly suggested in *Small Is Quite Beautiful* via Finlay's allusion to the British economist E. F. Schumacher's popular book, *Small is Beautiful: A Study of Economics As If People Mattered* (1973), which questions the 'idolatry of large size' by promoting 'the convenience, the humanity, and manageability of smallness' (48). 'Today we suffer from an almost universal idolatry of giantism,' Schumacher proposes: 'It is therefore necessary to insist on the virtues of smallness' (49). As a result, Schumacher promotes the virtues of 'appropriate technology' and small-scale enterprise in the face of a Western economic, social, and political system that holds firmly to 'the illusion of unlimited powers' and an unwavering belief in the mantra, 'the bigger the better' (3, 47). Thus, in answer to such 'giantism' Schumacher proposes that:

We need methods and equipment which are

- cheap enough so that they are accessible to virtually everyone;
- suitable for small-scale application; and
- compatible with man's need for creativity. (21)

In many respects, Schumacher's ideas recall the 'healthful limitations' of the artisanal craft production examined in chapter one (Volk, 444). Thus it is perhaps not surprising that Theodore Ropak couches his assessment of *Small Is Beautiful* in terms that derive from the discourses that we have seen underpinning folk revivalism. 'If there is to be a humanly tolerable world on this dark side of the emergent world system,' Ropak suggests, 'it will surely have to flower from the still fragile renaissance of organic husbandry, communal households, and do-it-yourself technics' (cited in Peterson 250, fn. 10).

Another example of 'do-it-yourself technics' can be found in the small press poetry publishing that burgeoned in the late 1950s and mushroomed in the 1960s when affordable and accessible printing technology, particularly portable mimeograph machines and offset lithographic printing, resulted in equally affordable and accessible publications that could be easily disseminated. 'Whereas traditional letterpress printing required the skilled intervention of printers in the setting of type and image,' Beatriz Colomina and Craig Buckley suggest, 'the new technologies made the process of designing print more accessible and more directly manipulable by magazine makers themselves' (9). Furthermore, 'the pasteups to make offset lithographic plates,' Colomina and Buckley note, 'could be produced in more diverse spaces, from drawing boards to kitchen tables' (9). For the first time, these printing technologies put 'the means of production in the hands of the poet,' as Steven Clay and Rodney Phillips explain: 'In a very real sense, almost anyone could become a publisher. For the price of a few reams of paper and a handful of stencils, a poet could produce, by mimeograph, a magazine or booklet in a small edition' over the course of several days' (13–14).

According to Peter Brooker, from the 1950s onwards, particularly in the USA, the 'rapid turnover' of a 'plethora of short-lived publications' helped considerably 'aid the accelerated transmission and absorption of ideas' across networked communities of poets (965). By the 1960s this accelerated transmission had increased considerably, as Ron Loewinsohn recalls:

> But more important than the quality of their contents was the fact of these magazines' abundance & speed. Having them, we could see what we were doing, as it came, hot off the griddle. We could get instant response to what we'd written last week, & we could respond instantly to what the guy across town or across the country had written last month. Further, many poets who didn't stand a Christian's chance against the lions of 'proper' publication in university quarterlies or 'big-time' magazines could get exposure &, more importantly, encouragement &/or criticism. For all its excesses it was a healthy condition. (222)

For Finlay, Mills and Cutts, such 'excess' was proportionate to the accessibility of the new technology which encouraged creativity, innovation, and expression. In the context of the mimeo revolution, Finlay's postcard might, therefore, be read as redressing such 'excess.'

As a grammatical emphasizer, Finlay's inclusion of the additional word 'quite' in Schumacher's original title appears to reaffirm the thesis of *Small is Beautiful*; small is *really* or *truly* beautiful. However, as a moderating adverb, 'quite' also implies that small is *conditionally* beautiful. In other words, small is beautiful, but only to a degree. Beauty is limited or relative. Consequently, *Small Is Quite Beautiful* is not only an assertion of smallness, but also an assertion of the values and sensibilities that make it so: moderation, proportion, and discernment, or, as Clark suggests, 'measurement and judgement' ('Paper and Stone' 66). As Robert Tait noted as early as 1965, pertinently foreseeing Scobie's similar assessment of Finlay's ironic modulations of scale, a Finlay poem is 'a small focusing thing in which the tiniest formal shift seems momentous' (3).

Evidently, Finlay found the qualities of measurement and judgement lacking in much of the 1960s small press poetry. As a letter from Finlay to Stephen Bann written in 1966 reveals, concrete poetry was particularly affected by the excesses of self-publishing:

> I do feel that everyone should have to pass an exam (set by myself) before they're allowed to set up as 'concrete poets' …

> Honestly Stephen, all those ignorant young ones are getting
> out of hand—they are like a blight with their 'Zen' and all
> that nonsense ... They seem to appear like mushrooms now,
> and the first thing they do is, edit an anthology—or start a
> magazine [.] (*Midway* 99)

For Finlay, the mushrooming of little magazines and small presses
in the mid-1960s meant that the pure, 'narrower concrete' of the
movement's 'vigorous and creative [first] phase'—as innovated and
practiced by, among others, Pierre Garnier, Eugen Gomringer, Pedro
Xisto, Ronaldo Azeredo, the Noigandres group, and Gerhard Rühm—
was compromised by the influx of less stringent poets and editors (Bann,
'A Context for Concrete Poetry' 133). It was for similar reasons that
Finlay eventually distanced himself from Dom Sylvester Houédard—an
enthusiastic proponent and practitioner of concrete poetry and an early
champion of Finlay—because, as he explains in a letter to Turnbull,
'People like Sylvester are—alas—turning what was once a *pure* intention
into a frenzied race of 1000 poets to do the *next new thing* ...' (*AMO* 32).

Finlay's position on the new wave of concrete poetry is especially
apparent in his critique of the Polluted Lake Series of concrete poetry
booklets published by d. a. levy's Renegade Press in Cleveland. 'The
important point is that everyone ought now to be able to SEE the clear
divergence between concrete and NEW BANDWAGON GUTTER
CONCRETE,' Finlay remarks in a letter to Stephen Bann in 1966
(*Midway* 118). Finlay describes the Polluted Lake booklets, which
included titles by Edwin Morgan and Dom Sylvester Houédard, as
'incredibly filthy little copies' of his *Canal* and *Ocean Stripe* booklets and
'quite the worst publications one could imagine' (*Midway* 118).[33]

Thus, Finlay's aphoristic slogan, *Small Is Quite Beautiful*, not only
presents a critical assessment of the excesses of the mimeo revolution, but
it also reclaims the word 'small' as a value and a quality that, far from
being simply 'twee' or innocuous, can also be incisive, provocative, and

---

33 Morgan, however, offers a more enthusiastic assessment of these
   booklets in a letter to Houédard, noting that Finlay 'could hardly be
   expected to like the polluted lake school, but it seems to me to be a
   genuine piece of Americana, a sort of do-it-yourself frontier concrete
   kit deliberately rough and non-beautiful. Ian greatly overrates the
   virtues of purity' (*Midnight Letterbox* 148). As Morgan intimates,
   Finlay considered such concrete impure, whereas he, like Houédard,
   welcomed these 'polluted' innovations. Indeed, the 'wider ecumenism'
   that Houédard advanced as a Benedictine monk at Prinknash
   Abbey in Gloucestershire, finds a pertinent parallel in the openness
   and inclusivity of his 'wider' poetic vision, which could happily
   accommodate Finlay and Niedecker, on the one hand, and Bob
   Cobbing and Writers' Forum on the other (Houédard 118).

discriminating. Recalling Rachel Blau DuPlessis's claim for Niedecker's poetry, Finlay's postcard can be read as his own 'formal answer to Bigness' ('Lorine Niedecker' 129).

Tarasque

Finlay, however, was not alone in his reappraisal of the small scale and the small press. As a magazine and as a press, Tarasque's operations occurred predominantly 'on a miniature scale' that incisively reflected both its 'aesthetic focus and [its] polemical stance,' both of which were adopted as a critical response to the state of contemporary small press poetry (Bevis, 'Swings and Roundabouts' 16; Neate 46). 'The middle sixties was the time of the small press,' Ian Gardner reflects in his preface to Mills's *A Far Distant Landscape*, 'all was Xerox at best and duplicated by and large. Tarasque was never this!' (n. pag). 'The first few issues of *Tarasque*,' as John Bevis explains, 'had been run off on the bog-standard mimeograph,' but the means and quality of production not only improved but they also became an integral part of Mills and Cutts's poetics, with a 'new regard for paper, type and assembly [leading] to a promotion of the primacy of the publication' ('A Star-gazey Pie' 29).

As a magazine and as a press, Tarasque's critical response to the ubiquitous 'bog-standard mimeograph' of the period can be traced back to its inception at the Poetry '66 event. As well as a critique of the Albert Hall event of 1965, the event organized by Mills and Parnell, as Neate explains, 'also sought to gain representation for small press publishers, a community that, maybe intentionally, lacked a coherent voice': 'A circular sent to a long list of potential participants set out the intentions of the conference: to "trace the role and development of small magazines and presses in the country since the early fifties"' (39, 40). The 'role and development' of British little magazines and small presses would not only remain a principal concern of the magazine but also, as we have already seen, a prime target of its unforgiving and sardonic humour which, at times, could equal the notorious incendiary spleen vented by Geoffrey Grigson in the pages of *New Verse*.

According to Nicholas Zurbrugg, the 'ordered, impersonal aesthetic' that characterizes Finlay's concrete poetry of the 1960s, 'is perhaps best understood historically as a reaction against the excessively subjective and authorial emphasis of writing and criticism in the sixties' (120). *Tarasque* articulates a similar criticism of 'the excessively subjective' writing of the period and the tenacious image of the *poète maudit* by printing many of its contributions anonymously. In this respect, *Tarasque* followed *Migrant*'s 'rhythm of appearance, its mixture of anonymous extracts from letters, poems, unplaceable prose, and reprinted material,' which was 'not so much an attempt to publish as a means by which other writing might be allowed to happen' and to help define 'a context'

(Migrant flyer n. pag). However, unlike *Migrant*, *Tarasque* was more about provoking responses and adopting critical positions rather than allowing writing to simply 'happen.' Indeed, from the perspective of Mills and Cutts's magazine, the real challenge was to stem, not encourage, writing that simply happened. Far from compounding the fashionable notion of a spontaneous and subjectively expressive writing that 'happens,' *Tarasque* promoted carefully considered writing and equally considered printing standards.

In the fifth issue of the magazine, for example, the editors claim that the 'availability of effective and cheap methods of publishing material has resulted in a mimeograph invasion which has undermined the critical faculty':

> 'Comment' has replaced reasoned criticism and the serious poet is often too swamped by trivia. Small magazine editors are almost as common as bookmakers. 'Magazines received' is now meaningless. This section could well be left out of publication; there are in fact too many 'magazines received' (*Tarasque* 5 n. pag)

In the same issue, Mills and Cutts satirize this popular feature of little magazines:

> I am told the biggest bag of 68 will be made by the newly formed U.C.O. (Underground Cultural Organisation) which is an amalgamation of virtually every small mag in Britain with the notable exception of P.O.T.H. The new magazine which will appear twice yearly bound in pink suede is to be called Scrotum... the magazine you can *feel*. I've got my copy on order now! (n. pag)

The acerbic tone recalls one of Tarasque's touchstones, Wyndham Lewis's little magazine *Blast*. Just as Lewis's magazine would 'curse / with expletive of whirlwind' and *blast* 'all products of [Britannic] phlegmatic cold,' the satirical announcement in *Tarasque* caustically ridicules the vain self-indulgence ('the magazine you can feel') of the mimeo invasion (Lewis 15). Particular targets, in this instance, are the 'garish and purposefully shocking' magazines such as the *International Times* and *Oz* which, Neate explains, were 'at the forefront of the counterculture and linked to the Underground Press Syndicate,' lampooned by Mills and Cutts in their fictitious 'U.C.O.' (45). With its allusions to big bags, scrotums, and pink suede, the announcement implies that these publications are, figuratively speaking, a load of 'bollocks' and, perhaps, masturbatory, in the sense of self-serving, indulgent, and gratifying.

That Finlay's own magazine *Poor. Old. Tired. Horse.* ('P.O.T.H') is exempt from judgement only reaffirms his kindred sensibilities with *Tarasque*. Indeed, the tone of the anonymous editorial of *Tarasque* 9 suggests Finlay as a possible author:

> ... to be honest I don't *like* many little magazines—most of them are so ugly as to make one wonder what sort of people poets are that they can bear to produce more ugliness than there really is. I have recently decided to give up arguing about aesthetics since it's clear that this is only useful where some framework of common values exists, that one can discuss within. It is become very clear to me that much of the so-called 'exchange' that goes on is mere rhetoric which has no genuine concern with establishing points of real contact. I get the feeling that too many people are too uneducated—not in any snob way (I left school at 13 myself) ... but there are libraries; and the past and standards are important. I do feel that many poets of this time show a vulgarity that is much greater than that in advertising copywriters ... (n. pag)

Mills and Cutts draw similar conclusions about the value of 'exchange' within the small press community in the seventh issue of *Tarasque* when they parody the popular trend of little magazines to list recently received publications: 'Nugget, Lilliput, Esquire, Family Doctor, Locospotter, Penthouse, Practical Motorist, "Poetry" Chicago, Meccano Magazine, Exchange and Mart, Health and Efficiency' (n. pag). The deliberately ridiculous list of mainstream magazines, poetry periodicals, pornographic and naturist magazines, enthusiast magazines, and trade publications exaggerates the lack of critical discrimination and purpose—or, as Finlay terms it, a lack of 'framework of common values'—that the 'received' lists of the typical mimeo magazine imply.

Parodying the culture that *Tarasque* itself was part of puts the magazine in an unusual position. As Bann notes, because Mill and Cutts were 'in effect simultaneously attacking the soft internationalism of the "underground" and the hard internationalism' of mainstream establishment poetry' *Tarasque* adopts a controversial position between, on the one hand, establishment '"extremist" poetry critics' (Bann provides the example of A. Alvarez) and, on the other, their contemporaries in the small press poetry 'underground' ('Tarasque' 134). 'Criticism of the *Children of Albion* from dark, satanic quarters was to be expected and even welcomed,' Bann suggests, 'but the assertion of such standards from within the brethren was disconcerting,' if not heretical ('Tarasque' 134).

Even the poets that Mills and Cutts had published under the Tarasque imprint were not immune to the magazine's spleen, as Anselm Hollo discovered when his book *& It Is A Song* (1965) was reviewed by Cutts in the fourth issue of *Tarasque*.[34] As a contributor to Horovitz's *Child of Albion* anthology, a participant of the London Royal Albert Hall reading in 1965, and a European poet who 'seems to come to words through the American Experience,' Hollo was a prime target for criticism (Cutts, 'I'm Singing' n. pag). Considering that Migrant published *& It Is A Song*, Cutts's review might also be read as a judgement on Turnbull and Shayer's critical faculties.

According to Cutts, 'Anselm Hollo is a cosmopolitan figure. In essence his influence should be a healthy one' (n. pag). Cutts here betrays scepticism about the damaging implications of cosmopolitanism on contemporary poetry, implying that Hollo's shortcomings as a poet cannot be compensated for, or justified by, the fact that he is a well-networked, international citizen of the poetry underground. In a subsequent issue of *Tarasque*, this cynicism about cosmopolitanism is accentuated in one of the questions comprising a sardonic exam paper on contemporary poetry: 'Is a poet more likely to deceive himself (and others) as the nature of his talents in (a) a provincial, or (b) a cosmopolitan milieu?' (*Tarasque* 10 n. pag). An answer of sorts can be found in Bann's observation that during the 1960s, the cosmopolitan milieu of the mimeo revolution permitted the kind of 'circumstances where the quiet voice of discrimination was seldom heard' ('Tarasque' 132). From this perspective, Cutts's observation of Hollo's standing within the wider poetry community might also be read as an unforgiving diagnosis of the small press infrastructures that indiscriminately promoted such poetry.

Nevertheless, Hollo's poetry is also made an example of. According to Cutts, far from being a 'healthy' influence, the solipsism that he identifies in Hollo's poetry is the result of a 'crass observation' of everyday experience:

> Hollo attempts to give us a 'flowerpot of reality'; what we sooner end up with is a miss at using the minutiae of life in verse, and the objects, the gas stove, 'reading a play,' are more banal than they actually seemed before our attention was drawn to them. (n. pag)

In this respect, Hollo's approach to experience is essentially subjective. In other words, his poems fail because they are concerned with the effects things have on the speaker rather than the things themselves.

---

34 Mills and Cutts had published *52 Poems*, Hollo's translation of poems by the German artist Rolf Gunter Dienst. With his brother Klaus-Peter Dienst, Dienst also co-edited the little magazine *Rhinozeros* from 1960 to 1965, which promoted many of the new British and American poets, particularly the Beats.

As Mills writes in his poem 'Handy Hint 2': 'You must say what the weather is / doing / Not what the weather is doing / *to you*' (*Made in English* 133). Thus, echoing Finlay's 'model of order,' Cutts reasons:

> Hollo writes the poem but can give it no relevance outside its happening the once. Poetry must surely endow an event with a universality that works outside the particular instant. It must transcend it. In the bad verse, all we can see is rather egotistical desire to say what happened one day in Mr. Hollo's life. ('I'm Singing' n. pag)

Cutts's criticism of Hollo's 'egotistical desire' also extends to the title that he gives his review: 'I'm singing and it is a song.' The additional phrase 'I'm singing' not only turns the title of Hollo's book into a trite truism, but it also implies that the poem has failed to convey its own 'song' or achieve the kind of objective autonomy that *Tarasque* sets as its benchmark.

The problem for Cutts is that in Hollo's poems 'we receive no interknit intellectual/emotional gem' ('I'm Singing' n. pag). Here Cutts saliently recalls Ezra Pound's claims in 'A Retrospect' regarding the poem's 'intellectual and emotional complex in an instant of time' (*Literary Essays* 4). Just how far Hollo is from achieving the 'sudden liberation' invoked by Pound—the 'sense of freedom from time limits and space limits' and 'sense of sudden growth'—is evident, for example, in Hollo's poem 'Song of the Tusk' (*Literary Essays* 4):

> The elephant
>   bogged down
> thousands
>   of years ago
>
> The fragmented tusk
>   now in a glass case
>
> No no these are untrue statements
> it is I
>   who sits in the glass case
>   counting
>   the stubs of museum tickets (*Braided River* 5)

As a poem of 'statements' rather than observations, the poem's speaker, sat in the ticket booth of a museum paralleling the exhibits incarcerated in glass, fails to deliver the kind of 'intellectual/emotional gem' that Cutts seeks. Instead, the poem concludes with the speaker imagining riding the elephant and 'throwing stones at the women on the beach' who, 'Frightened,' 'close the glass case over themselves and their lovers / for thousands of years' (*Braided River* 5). Again, to recall Pound in 'A Retrospect,' Hollo's poem seems to 'mess up the perception of one sense by trying to define it in terms of another' (*Selected Essays* 4).

Indeed, with the exception of the suggestion of libidinal anxiety or emasculation—implied in the image of the encased 'fragmented tusk'—the poem, to use Olson's phrase in 'Projective Verse' (1950), sprawls:

> If [the poet] sprawl, he shall find little to sing but himself, and shall sing, nature has such paradoxical ways, by way of artificial forms outside himself. But if he stays inside himself, if he is contained within his nature as he is participant in the larger force, he will be able to listen, and his hearing through himself will give him secrets objects share. (*Collected Prose* 247)

The formal, objective models of order that Finlay, Cutts, and Mills value do, contrary to Olson, recognize and value 'artificial forms outside' of the poet. Hollo, however, falls short in respect of either of these formal approaches. As well as failing to sufficiently hear 'through himself,' as Olson advises, Hollo also fails to exploit the 'artificial forms outside himself.' According to Cutts, the poems are compromised by 'imprecision,' 'over-familiar comments about virility,' and an excess of subjective emotion ('I'm Singing' n. pag). Cutts describes the latter as 'over-feelings': 'What we often have is a deadweight, crusted with dead sentiment. The emotion often spills itself or just isn't touched' ('I'm Singing,' n. pag). Hollo's poetry, therefore, is too expressive (and excessive) of emotions and self-conscious to such a degree that any 'sentiment" fails to communicate beyond the subjective speculations and experiences of the poet-speaker. Olson may have cautioned in 'Against Wisdom as Such' that the poet 'cannot afford to traffick in any other sign than his "one," his self, the man or woman he is,' but Hollo's poetry in *& It Is A Song* highlights the problems of adopting such a stance when it is not sufficiently disciplined (*Collected Prose* 262–263). Thus, 'Hollo's world,' according to Cutts, 'is one of sensual satisfaction and fullness in satisfaction,' little else ('I'm Singing' n. pag).

The Small Poem
The prosaic verisimilitude and discursive solipsism that Cutts criticizes so vehemently in Hollo's poetry contrasts markedly with the poetics of the small poem that he and Mills promote in the sixth issue of *Tarasque*. Part anthology, part manifesto of sorts, *Tarasque* 6, as Cutts explains in his foreword, was compiled in order 'to suggest a definity of area amongst poets of a diverse and otherwise unconnected nature' (*SFA* 93). Examples range from J. M. Synge, T. E. Hulme, Günter Grass, Georg Trakl, and Bertholt Brecht to contemporary British

poets such as Libby Houston, Hugh Creighton Hill, Spike Hawkins, Pete Brown, and Finlay. American representatives are, by comparison, less prominent. Only small poems by Ezra Pound, Robert Creeley, Eli Siegel, and Jonathan Williams are included alongside the anthology's more generous selection of modern and contemporary British and European poets.

Anticipating the later tacit claim of Finlay's *Small Is Quite Beautiful*, Cutts proposes that the poems included in *Tarasque* 6 are 'small [and] not short,' and is keen to stress that the adjective 'small' is 'a delineation of size' rather than an a measure of importance (*SFA* 93). In this respect, Poe's claim in his essay 'The Philosophy of Composition' that 'brevity must be in direct ratio of the intensity of the intended effect' seems especially relevant to the small poem as conceived by Mills and Cutts (Poe 483). Indeed, Poe is one of three writers that Cutts cites in foreword, appearing in the French company of Stéphane Mallarmé and Théophile Gautier.

Suggesting that as 'a small item of artifact,' the small poem aligns more readily with the plastic arts than with the longer narrative forms of poetry, Cutts quotes from the Gautier's poem 'L'Art,':

> The sense of artifact of entailed in the production of the small poem brings the poet nearer to the plastic artist ...
>
> ... 'Sculpte, lime, cisele
> Que ton rêve flottant
>   Se scelle
> Dans le bloc resistant,'
>
> than the narrative poet. Its effects cannot carry philosophy, the weight of the reasoning mind. (*SFA* 93–94)

In carving, filing, and chiseling ('Sculpte, lime, cisele') the resistant block of material, Gautier's poem suggests that the artist gives form and substance to what is otherwise vague and fleeting. In this respect, Gautier's metaphor of the sculpture adumbrates the 'perfected objects' that Finlay evokes in his letter to Garnier, as well as the 'hard and clear, never blurred nor indefinite' poetry of the Imagists who are represented in the *Tarasque* 6 by Pound (Lowell, vii).

Imagism is also implicit when Mills, in his introduction to the anthology of small poems, 'quotes from one of the poets in the selection':

> The proper subjects for poetry are;
> the Seasons, the Affections, Fishing Boats,
> Inland Waterways, Non-Alcoholic Beverages,
> Certain Flowers, Certain Trees.

> Improper subjects are;
> Sex, Drugs, War and Self.
>
> Adjectives should be used sparsely, if at
> all, and not ever in proportion of more
> than one to every 9 nouns. ('Introduction' n. pag)

Pound, clearly, is not the author of this advice, but there is a discernible echo of Pound's suggestion in 'A Retrospect' to 'Use no superfluous word, no adjective which does not reveal something' (*Literary Essays* 4). One possible author of this advice is Finlay who, as Cutts notes, 'seems to write poetry about certain simplified subjects [as] a concession to the usual idea of poetry' ('The Aesthetic of Ian Hamilton Finlay' 32). Indeed, echoing the 'proper subjects' listed in *Tarasque*, Finlay has claimed with regard to *The Dancers Inherit the Party* that, 'The things I have written about often are WINDMILLS, CANALS, FISHING BOATS, THE SEA, LOBSTERS AND TUGBOATS' (cited in 'DG' 108).

These 'proper subjects' might appear to simply exacerbate the twee, whimsical character of Finlay's poetry, yet, for all their disarming innocence they also presented a challenge to the trends and sensibilities dominating poetry at the time; from the popular idioms of the Beats and the Liverpool Poets to Finlay's Scottish contemporaries. For example, the cover of the 1962 summer issue of *New Saltire* (the same issue that printed Finlay's review of John Speir's book *The Scots Literary Tradition*), announces 'poems about war by David Craig and Ian Crichton-Smith.' The latter's poem-sequence 'Word War I' in particular is a telling example of poetry preoccupied with the 'improper subjects' of war and self:

> I can't cry for these men.
> Their physical wrestling is too strange
> for the purer boil that stirs my pen.
>
> They're like the stones of Stonehenge
>
> staggering about blind fields. (24)

Crichton-Smith's use of hyperbole and pathos illustrates what Finlay would later describe in his defining letter to Garnier as 'the now-fashionable poetry of anguish and self.' Indeed, Crichton-Smith is perhaps one of those poets who, as Finlay wryly remarks to Dom Sylvester Houédard, 'should bear the anguish of not writing anguish poems' (cited in Zurbrugg 121). With dull metaphors and laboured similes—soldiers 'staggering about blind fields' 'like the stones of Stonehenge'—Crichton-Smith commits the errors of adjectival superfluity and abstraction that Pound condemns in 'A Retrospect.' 'Don't use such an expression as "dim lands *of peace*,"' Pound advises: 'It dulls the image' (*Literary Essays* 4). So too, it seems, does 'blind fields.'

Mills's and Cutts's promotion of the small poem in *Tarasque* 6 can be understood as their own critical reply to the improper subjects dominating the poetry of the mimeo revolution in the mid-1960s. As Mills wryly explains in his introduction to *Tarasque* 6, the small poem offers an alternative to the earnest pretensions of 'the near epic' and 'anything dealing with certain emotional experiences, anything stemming from a desire to add to the general bulk of knowledge and anything stemming from a conviction that the poet contains within him seeds that could bring about humanity's wholesale re-assessment of existence' (n. pag). 'The small poem which I have in mind,' Mills proposes, 'does none of these things yet remains vigorous despite claims to the contrary that it borders on whimsy and the banal' (n. pag).

Mills's own 'Neo-Fauve' poem, with its allusions to waterproof trousers, weather, bicycle excursions, and seaside entertainments, is a telling example of a small poem bordering on the banal and whimsy. Yet, as Roy Fisher suggests, it is more accurate to describe Mills's poems as 'brief, elegant, quietly incisive and lightly but very durably constructed' (69). While 'Neo-Fauve' might not share quite the same 'mastered fragility' that Robert Tait attributes to Finlay's early poems, Mills's poems do nevertheless show a similar aversion to what Tait describes as 'the embattled ego' that Finlay so vehemently eschews:

> Roaring, savaging poetry can come to seem to him a betrayal
> of the main value poetry can have; for the embattled ego can
> so easily be content to thrash about, whale like. And poets,
> feeling better for the therapy, can fall into ways of simply
> screwing up their language and perceptions till the right note
> of trouble or whAmbAm is hit, sustained, released—leaving
> spreading sensations of relief. (2)

The small poem is not only Mills and Cutts's corrective to such 'savaging poetry' and a way of keeping language and perception adequately honed and focused, but it is an incipient example of what would become the Tarasque aesthetic: 'a certain delicacy and slightness of key [and] a choice of the poetic everyday as opposed to an assumed or inherited Grand Manner' (Cutts, 'The Weather House' n. pag).

Jonathan Williams's poem 'Silers Bald,' which Mills and Cutts include in *Tarasque* 6, illuminates many of the qualities of the small poem that the magazine extols. 'Silers Bald' is one of the five poems comprising the sequence 'Five Trail-Shelters from the Big Pigeon to the Little Tennessee' which was first published in Williams's book *Elegies and Celebrations* (1962) which is one of the three volumes that documents

Williams's work from 1953 to 1955, the period, incidentally, when he was most involved with Black Mountain:

> just in front of the
> round iron john
> in the beech grove
>
> the fresh bear droppings
> give you
>
> something
> to think about (*JT* 153)

The poem's title and subject refers to the mountain in the western Great Smoky Mountains that straddles the state lines of Tennessee and North Carolina. 'Silers Bald,' however, departs from more traditional representations of mountain landscapes. Any suggestion of heroic wilderness is already undermined by the fact that this poem is not about a mountain but a shelter (the site of temporary human habitation) that has been constructed on it. And, while the indication of a bear's presence in the vicinity is itself a sobering prospect, 'Silers Bald' does not rehearse the familiar tropes of the romantic mountain sublime. 'The still and solemn power of many sights,' that Shelley finds on Mont Blanc, for example, are not concerns that Williams shares in 'Silers Bald' (Shelley 128). And, unlike, for example, the figure in Caspar David Friedrich's iconic painting *Wanderer above the Sea of Fog* (1818), the speaker in Williams's poem assumes a modest, less elevated, position in the landscape. Indeed, as the allusion to the 'iron john' suggests, the speaker is, quite literally, a tentative *squatter* in this mountainous landscape. Far from being a privileged spectator or heroic conqueror of their environment, the poem's speaker is a humble part of it and their intention to defecate saliently parallels, or reiterates, what the bear has already done.

'Silers Bald' also rejects 'the inherited Grand Manner' of mountain landscape representation practicing what Finlay suggests: using adjectives sparsely and relying instead on nouns to do the work. Furthermore, Williams adopts a colloquial style that undercuts any pretension to solemnity. This is evident in Williams's use of the word 'john' to describe the toilet in the beech grove. The introduction of this slang term has the effect of deflating any suggestion of the 'grove' as a romantic or sacred place. Furthermore, the lack of descriptive words in 'Silers Bald' means that the poem's sole adjective, 'fresh,' resonates more alarmingly, much like the bear droppings it describes. The effect of such deliberate economy—or, to use Cutts's term, its 'slightness of key'—means that the reader is given 'something to think about' rather than having the poet's emotions imposed upon them. In this respect, what Gudgin claims in his essay 'Situation' in the context of Mills, Cutts, Spike Hawkins and their 're-evaluation of the poem' is also applicable to 'Silers Bald':

> the poem has been stripped of its flab
> and presented for what it is.
> its result is simplicity—it succeeds
> in existing free of self-consciousness
> that has characterised poetry, U.S.,
> U.K., Continental, for decades. (n. pag)

Williams wrote 'Silers Bald' a good decade before the advent of *Tarasque* and at least five years prior to his discovery of Finlay. Nevertheless, as an example of the small poem, 'Silers Bald' effectively demonstrates how, to recall Poe, 'brevity' can work effectively in 'direct ratio of the intensity of the intended effect' of a poem. In the wider context of Tarasque Press, Williams's poem also reflects a growing concern with landscape and its representation that, as chapter six discusses, would preoccupy much of Mills and Cutts's subsequent work. Indeed, a kindred sensibility between Williams and this particular thread of British poetry would, over the following decades, manifest more consciously through Williams's strong friendships and working relationships with Finlay, Mills, Gardner, and Cutts. 'Simon Cutts could almost be a family member of my tribe,' Williams has remarked: 'I sometimes think, "Gee, is that a Simon Cutts poem? Or is that my poem?"': 'We're very much on the same wave length in terms of what we try to do. Not many other writers are close to me in that way' (Annwn, 'Interview with Jonathan Williams' 57).

Aggie Weston's
Williams also sustained a close relationship with Mills who, after relocating to Belper, Derbyshire, published several publications by Williams under the auspices of his post-Tarasque project, the little magazine *Aggie Weston's* and the eponymous 'editions' he occasionally produced.[35] According to Cutts, by the early 1970s, Tarasque Press had 'given way to a variety of concerns, all in themselves incidentally developing further means of approach to the synthesis of the plastic and literary arts' ('The Weather House' n. pag). Whereas Cutts would go on to explore the possibilities of the book and the edited space of the gallery with Coracle, Mills remained largely committed to the format

---

35   The first *Aggie Weston's* Editions, published in 1977, was Williams's small book of poems *Super-Duper Zuppa Inglese (And Other Trifles from the Land of Stodge)*, which included illustrations by one of Williams's earliest English contacts, the artist Barbara Jones.

of the little magazine and, from 1973 to 1984, published mainly single 'monographic' issues of *Aggie Weston's* dedicated to a specific poet, artist, or photographer (*SFA* 29). Issues included photographs by Jonathan Williams (No. 18, Spring 1982), texts and photographs by Richard Long (No. 16, Winter 1979), the writings of the artist Trevor Winkfield (No. 8, Summer 1975), and the long minimal poem 'Light' by another mainstay of the Wild Hawthorn–Tarasque axis, Robert Lax (No. 21, Winter 1984).[36]

The monographic format frequently adopted by *Aggie Weston's* finds a precursor in *Poor. Old. Tired. Horse.*, which devoted several of its numbers to the work of one individual.[37] Mills's magazine, however, also recalls Lucy Lippard's opinion that, in the context of artists' books, 'the periodical could be the ideal vehicle for art itself rather than merely for reproduction, commentary, and promotion' ('Escape Attempts' xviii). In a similar manner, the only 'commentary' that Mills tends to include in each issue of his magazine is an explanation of its title:

> The name of the magazine comes indirectly from a work by Kurt Schwitters; 'A Small Home for Seamen.' I have been told that it was one Agnes Weston who founded the seamen's homes in this country and I hope that this magazine will likewise provide some sort of refuge.

Conflating a relatively nondescript aspect of maritime culture with the avant-gardism of Kurt Schwitters and his 1926 assemblage *Kleines Seemannsheim*, *Aggie Weston's* can be seen as extending the proper subjects for poetry initially proposed in *Tarasque* 6. However, whereas *Tarasque* had ravaged the landscape of contemporary poetry, *Aggie Weston's*, as the word 'refuge' suggests, took a less antagonistic position in response to the state of contemporary poetry and the cultural establishment more generally. Indeed, by the late 1970s, Mills was himself seeking refuge

---

36   Lax's work was widely promoted over the decades by Finlay, Mills and Cutts, and the Clarks. Finlay included Lax's poetry several issues of *POTH*, including the tenth 'concrete' number in 1964. In 1965 Finlay also dedicated the seventeenth number of the magazine to Lax's poem 'The stone, the sea' with illustrations by Lax's longstanding collaborator Emil Antonucci. Several Lax publications also appeared under through Wild Hawthorn Press, including *Sea Poem* (1966) and *Color Poems* (1976). In 1971 Tarasque published Lax's book *Able Charlie Baker Dance* and the postcard *4 Boats, 3 People*. Thomas A. and Laurie Clark devoted the first issue of their monographic magazine *The Blue Boat* to 'Nine Poems' by Lax in 1983 and Coracle published an edition of Lax's *New Poems 1962–1985* in 1986.

37   For example, Robert Lax (*POTH* 17), Ronald Johnson (*POTH* 19), Edgard Bragaor (*POTH* 21), and Charles Biederman (*POTH* 22).

from the establishment when funding for *Aggie Weston's* was rejected by the East Midlands Arts Association and Coracle took on the production and distribution of the magazine (*SFA* 35).

Rather like many of the contemporaneous 'democratic multiples' that appeared under the moniker of the artist's book, the modest design of *Aggie Weston's*—its use of quality paper stock, its sparing use of text in relation to the A4 format, and the offset reproduction of images and photographs—came at a cost.[38] This cost is made clear in the letter of rejection by Vicky Allen of the East Midlands Arts Association, which Mills had approached for funding, reproduced in issue 14 of the magazine. As the letter indicates, the consistently high quality of *Aggie Weston's* indicates just how much these standards were at odds with the economic climate of the literary marketplace. Included in the magazine, the letter reads as a kind of negative-manifesto for the values of *Aggie Weston's* and other kindred small press publishers.

> The panel were concerned that the production was almost too good, certainly in relation to the print run. They also thought that in the present economic climate it was indefensible to have areas of expensive blank white paper. They were not against very short poems and supporting the epic, but they felt that one short poem on a page was not enough. If you accept that a good poem is a good poem and will stand by itself, it probably makes marginal difference whether it is printed rather badly on newsprint or very beautifully on art paper. They also queried whether the man at the bookstall would consider he'd got 25p worth of text, even if he recognized that it was beautifully produced. (n. pag)

It seems particularly dispiriting to criticize a publication on the grounds of it being 'almost too good' in relation to its scale of operation. Indeed, Allen's comments inadvertently adumbrate the more negative implications of Finlay's motto 'small is *quite* beautiful' by making a judgement of value based not on the publication itself, but on its perceived stature—and monetary worth—within the marketplace. Anything too small and too limited in terms of print run or production, Allen seems to suggest, is not worth the effort, care, or pride that a more commercial and more widely distributed publication merits. This

---

38   Drucker notes the 'sham flat-footedness' of the democratic multiple 'which belied its own privileged status of production': 'Though the democratic multiple was designed to sell cheaply ($5 to $20), in largish unnumbered editions (500 to 5000 copies), it was expensive to produce. The per unit cost might be affordably low, but the upfront capital expenditure was significant ($1000 to $10,000 or more)' (*Figuring* 176, 177).

question of size and scale is also apparent in the way that Allen discounts the qualities previously promoted in *Tarasque* regarding the small poem. Poems are judged on monetary value and words commoditized in an exchange where more words equate better value for money. A small poem, therefore, no matter how good, cannot justify '25p worth of text.' It is simply not worth the paper it is printed on when quantity, rather than quality, is the measure. Thus, the values that Mills and Cutts established in *Tarasque* are at considerable odds with those implied in the East Midlands Arts Association rejection letter: the visual qualities and the poetics of the page; the autonomy of the poem; the status of the printed format as an object in its own right (rather than simply the ancillary vehicle for the poem); and the scrupulous care, attention, and pride for the quality of a publication. All of these qualities, according to the East Midlands funding body, are 'indefensible' standards to adhere to within the 'economic climate.' That *Aggie Weston's* endured as long as it did in such an unforgiving economic climate—and that the final issue comprised Robert Lax's long minimal poem 'Light' which proportionately left *a lot* of blank paper—is testimony to Mills's commitment to the magazine and to the wider community of small publishers who supported it. *Aggie Weston's*, and *Tarasque* before it, remain pertinent testimonies of the network of poets, artists, and publishers who have continued to 'elevate the idea' of the small press publication beyond what Drucker has described as the 'economically advantaged mainstream' (*Figuring* 182).

Chapter Five

Opening the Folds: A Pastoral Vanguard

A World Cup without Scotland
is like a pastoral without sheep.
— Ian Hamilton Finlay

A photograph of Jonathan Williams (Figure 5) taken in the late 1970s by the North Carolinian photographer Elizabeth Matheson gives a good indication of how far Jargon's utopic 'elsewhere' community had extended (geographically and temporally) by the late 1970s.[39] The photo was taken in the locality of Dentdale where, with Thomas Meyer, Williams had been semi-residing since 1969 and where the two Americans played host to a broad spectrum of visitors to their cottage, Corn Close. It was also in this rural part of Cumbria where, as Williams tells David Annwn, he 'learned a little about sheep from the hill farmers. They spare me palaver about art and seem happy enough to tolerate a couple of "odd" Americans' ('Interview' 52). Matheson's photograph is, in this respect, very much a reflection of Williams's embrace of the region's long history of sheep farming and wool manufacture. In particular, the dry-stone walls clearly visible in the photograph, and the shepherd's crook that Williams holds, both reiterate the strong presence of sheep farming in the local landscape.

Further allusions to shepherding in Matheson's photograph evoke a pastoral tradition that extends well beyond the dry-stone walls of Dentdale. This is evident in the phallic road sign that Williams stands behind which was made by the American typographer and designer A. Doyle Moore who also runs the Finial Press in Champaign, Illinois. Moore's manipulated road sign suggests the rustic ithyphallic god Priapus who appears in the foundational pastoral text, Theocritus's *Idylls,* as well as the more familiar pastoral figure of Pan. Indeed,

---

39   The Jargon Society published Matheson's book *Blithe Air: Photographs from England, Wales, and Ireland* in 1995.

the road sign's warning triangle serves as a pertinent reminder that Pan (who is frequently depicted with an erect phallus in the ancient world) is traditionally associated with panic and terror. A further pastoral reference is apparent in the jumper that Williams wears, which reproduces Samuel Palmer's self-portrait, painted sometime between 1824 and 1825. The jumper, which was knitted by the British artist Astrid Furnival, makes a material pun on the very fabric of Palmer's celebrated pastorals, which Geoffrey Grigson describes as 'visual poems on rural and strictly shepherd themes' (*Samuel Palmer* 1).

Figure 5. Jonathan Williams in Dentdale, Cumbria, circa. 1979. Photo by Elizabeth Matheson.

Palmer's pastoral vision is extended into the contemporary milieu of avant-garde poetry and art via Furnival's jumper. With her husband, the artist John Furnival (a frequent collaborator with Williams and Ian Hamilton Finlay), Astrid Furnival was part of the literary and artistic collective known as '"The Gloup"—the (Gloucestershire grouP)' which, as Bob Cobbing explains, was the 'name given by Jonathan Williams to the group of concrete-kinetic poets living in the West of England, mainly in Gloucestershire' from the late 1960s onwards (*GLOUP and WOUP* n. pag). In addition to the Furnivals, individuals associated with the Gloup included Dom Sylvester Houédard, Kenelm Cox, Charles Verey, Thomas A. Clark, and Laurie Clark. 'Not since Grimson and the Barnsleys' (two furniture designers closely associated the Arts and Crafts Movement), Clark suggests, 'had the Cotswolds contributed so much to the art of its time' ('Foreword' n. pag). Thus, in these various respects, Matheson's photo indicates how the English pastoral tradition that Williams had first imaginatively invoked in poems such 'Emblems for the Little Dells, and Nooks and Corners of Paradise' was something that he was engaging with more tangibly as a resident in Britain.

Pastoral may seem to be a mere shibboleth in the extended society of Jargon, but its appeal and relevance in the small press milieu, as this chapter argues, is more extensive. As 'an elusive and largely imaginary space'—'a nowhere place, a utopia'—the fictive Arcadia of traditional pastoral serves as a potent locus, and a fitting analogy, for the imagined communities and social dynamics implicit in small press networks such as Jargon's (Cosgrove, *Geography* 68). To recall Moeglin-Delcroix's observations regarding the 'utopic' small press publication, pastoral's archetypal *locus amoenus*, Arcadia, denotes an equivalent 'autonomous world that is confined, lateral, marginal and far away' and which 'is "without" place because in proposing another organisation of life, it situates itself outside the ordinary functioning of the world' ('Little Books' n. pag). For these reasons, as we shall see, pastoral has become a much maligned term largely synonymous with escapism and sentimental idealism. However, in the literary and artistic milieu of *Avant-Folk*, it is possible to see pastoral being reclaimed as a viable and incisive mode for reflecting on the social dynamics and amity of small press publishing, as well as a means of foregrounding the materiality of the poem and the printed format. Thus, while the world of Arcady might ultimately be a hypothetical one, in the context of Ian Hamilton Finlay and Thomas A. Clark's innovative reassessment of pastoral, it is the *possibility* of this world that motivates the social pragmatics and collaborative spirit of small press publishing.

Arcady

Pastoral, according to Rosanna Warren, 'archetypally situates itself in an idealized and artificial landscape' and establishes 'an elemental poetic space' that puts it at considerable odds with the unforgiving realities and hardships of contemporary life (52). The fictional Arcadia that provides the ambient setting of Virgil's *Eclogues* is the most familiar pastoral 'poetic space' as well as the most misunderstood. As a *locus amoenus*, Virgil's Arcadia embodies what are perhaps the defining principles and motifs of pastoral: a 'nostalgic yearning for the distant in space or time' and an ardent desire for 'a situation of stable perfection, far removed from anything odd or evil, tragic or transitory, a situation impossible to achieve' (Putnam 4).

Such nostalgic and idealist sentiments are at the root of a common consensus that pastoral is a naïve form concerned with little more than escapism, fantasy, or retreat. Samuel Johnson, for example, found that typical pastoral idylls, 'not professing to imitate real life, require no experience, and, exhibiting only the simple repetition of unmingled passions, admit no subtle reasoning or deep enquiry' (421). By the time of Milton, Johnson argues, pastoral had become an 'easy, vulgar and therefore disgusting' form and also an 'exhausted' tradition because 'its inherent improbability always forces dissatisfaction of the mind' (95–96). Such a pejorative view has endured and is implicit in the 'contemporary sense of pastoral' which, Terry Gifford claims, has been compounded by 'the Georgian poets' lasting effect upon English culture' who found in the pastoral motif of retreat a means of 'escapism from complexity and contradiction' (71).

There is, however, a strong counter-argument in support of pastoral's continuing relevance. Indeed, as Gifford suggests, the discourse of 'retreat' in pastoral 'is its strength and its inherent weakness' (46). The pastoral can 'either simply *escape* from the complexities of the city, the court, the present,' Gifford argues, 'or *explore* them. This is the difference between the pejorative and the primary senses of the pastoral' (46). Recent critical reassessments of pastoral have recognized the possibilities that the 'primary senses of the pastoral' might afford contemporary poetry. While 'Arcadian or bucolic traditions' have been frequently 'misunderstood or misrepresented as simply a contraction into conservative nostalgia, especially when seen in the context of post-Romantic culture,' as David James and Phillip Tew have noted, 'in origin and practice the dynamics of pastoral texts are far more adaptable' and capable of 'intersect[ing] with successive phases of literary innovation' (13). According to Iain Twiddy, it is the 'traditional elements' of pastoral which, by being adapted and interpreted 'in a multiplicity of ways,' have ensured its imaginative durability:

> The animal herders and beneficent landscapes of Sicily and Kos, Mantua and Arcadia, and the leisurely life associated with early versions of pastoral and pastoral elegy may have ceded their grip on the poetic imagination; but the psychological processes and social appeals which those figures and locations enabled—emotional simplification, withdrawal from previous attachments, the voicing of aspirations and the establishment of a legacy—are still necessary. (1)

These positive assessments of pastoral are supported by a broad spectrum of twentieth-century poets who have turned their attention to the formal possibilities of pastoral and its longstanding tradition in order to make it new. From the mainstream poetry of Ted Hughes and

Seamus Heaney (two of Twiddy's subjects) to the innovative vanguard of 'the Cambridge pastorale' of Peter Riley, Andrew Crozier, and Veronica Forrest-Thomson, it is possible to see the 'contested term' that is pastoral enduring in various currents of late twentieth-century poetry (Lawson 41; Loughrey 8).

Pastoral is not the dominant mode or concern of either Finlay or Clark, but it is, nevertheless, a significant component of both poets' work. Indeed, Clark's claim that the importance of pastoral should not be overlooked, even if it 'constitutes no more than a glade within the larger work of Ian Hamilton Finlay,' speaks as eloquently for his own relation to the tradition ('Pastorals' 155). However, while both poets have utilized and extended their pastoral sensibilities in collaborative projects and mutual interests, the wider concerns of their work remain distinctly different. In Finlay's case it is possible to see pastoral as an extension of a broader neo-classicism that underpins the major phases of his work, particularly his innovations in concrete poetry, his public works, and his gardens; all of which express the 'order and calm & abiding values' at the heart of his neo-classic sensibilities (I. H Finlay, *Selections*, xxi). However, as Alec Finlay stresses, Finlay's '"model of order" was not [...] a hermetically sealed enclosure' or a retreat, but something that was 'interrogative, accusatory of the age, [and] determined to acknowledge fury, power, and destruction' ('Picking the Last Wild Flower' 47). Pastoral, as we shall see, equipped Finlay with a rich fund of imagery, motifs, and ideas that enabled him to test 'the lyrical, the pure, the heroic, and the tragic, one against the other' and seek 'a conception of wholeness' which, Alec Finlay suggests, is 'both new and ancient' ('Picking the Last Wild Flower' 47).

Although Clark considers Finlay one of the poets he most admires and feels closest to, his concerns differ from Finlay's in a number of ways (Herd 97). Most notably, Clark's poetry expresses both a classical and a romantic vision that refuses to privilege one mode over the other. 'Romanticism for me is caught up with a sense of movement, a sense of kinetics,' he tells Glyn Pursglove in a 1978 interview, 'whereas Classicism is a stasis. One has to get the two together': 'Classicism will always be broken into by a shaft of romanticism' (18). In Clark's poetry, pastoral performs a pivotal role in conciliating these contrasting sensibilities, particularly in what I call Clark's 'phenomenological candour,' which, as I discuss below, utilizes a number of key pastoral motifs.

Despite these differences, both poets share a similar regard for simplicity that informs their respective notions of neo-classical order and phenomenological candour. Whereas Clark describes this as a 'yearning for an impossible simplicity,' Finlay professes an appreciation of the 'simple, plain, [and] wee bit severe' (Herd 101; *AMO* 38). As Clark's allusion to Meliboeus in the *Eclogues* indicates, this emphasis on simplicity is one that dovetails with the familiar sentiments and values of pastoral: 'If we are, like Meliboeus, exiled from simplicity, the poem serves to remind us that it is nevertheless our home' ('Pastorals' 52). In the case of Finlay and Clark, however, the poem does so by means of its form as well as its content. This, as we will see, is particularly apparent in the series of folding cards that Finlay and Clark collaborated on intermittently throughout the 1990s. 'The sheep, the flute, the country love affairs' may be, as Clark suggests, 'emblems of a directness of relations, a more felicitous association between person and person, between humans and animals, between society and the natural world,' but these values are also realized in the simple, laconic forms of their poems and the relations and dialogues those forms establish with, and within, a broader pastoral *continuum* ('Pastorals' 152–153).

Unfolding Pastoral

Being 'historically diversified and transformed' by its contemporary context, pastoral strikes a 'balance between formal and conventional elements, on the one hand, and the various themes, feelings, and attitudes they encode or express' (Alpers 456, 458). As a tradition and as a literary mode, pastoral is continually re-inventing and modifying itself out of response to the historical moment. Therefore, rather like the folk aspects of Niedecker's poetry, it is not an ossified form, but one that is continually evolving. Thus, as John Barrell and John Bull point out, 'What is called "Pastoral" in 1580 is not at first sight much like what is called "Pastoral" in 1770, and yet the reader is left with a firm impression of a shared tradition, of a common body of material being worked over' (7–8).

These ideas of pastoral showing both fidelity to antecedent models *and* a capacity for progressive transformation are shared by Thomas K. Hubbard, who considers pastoral in terms of 'literary filiation' and 'intertextuality' (7). Due to its 'supreme conventionality and formal continuity,' Hubbard argues, pastoral is 'an attractive medium for finding one's place relative to tradition: for each successive poet, the form posed the challenge of how to say something new entirely within the confines of established parameters and formulae that were so old' (6–7). Pastoral is a matter of 'how poets position themselves relative to their precursors and to the literary tradition as a whole,' with citation and appropriation playing key roles in determining an 'author's choice of a specific precursor or precursors with whose work he stands in a special and significant relation' (7, 11). Filiation, however, is not only a case of a poet asserting their 'new and independent voice' against the 'cumulative weight' of a pastoral tradition, but also an instance of *interdependent* voices articulating themselves *within* that tradition (Hubbard 6). 'Filiation,' therefore, suggests a more felicitous continuum of descent, transmission, and relation than it does, as Hubbard argues, simply a Bloomian 'challenge to poetic authority' (5).

Both Hubbard's idea of intertextual filiation and Alpers's emphasis on pastoral's 'generative powers' reflect Finlay and Clark's approach to pastoral (Alpers 442). Clark, for example, recognizes an *unfolding* of tradition in pastoral that counters a simple 'avant-garde notion of disruption and difference.' 'It's only within a continuum of the same, in an understood context, that difference can register,' he has suggested.[40] Finlay expresses similar sentiments in his professed aversion to experimentation: 'I am not interested in "experiment" but in avant-garde work which can take the creative step backwards to join with the past' (*Selections* xx). This is also how Finlay sees his own poetry and the continuum that it participates in. 'I only half-share your delight in ALL manifestations of THE NEW, because, you know I am more classical in NEED,' Finlay writes in a letter to Dom Sylvester Houédard: 'I like to feel where a poem is leading, and if it fits with the one before and the one after' (*AMO* 30). These needs expressed by Finlay and Clark for a sustaining context in which difference can develop finds a corollary in Alpers's suggestion that 'pastoral historically transforms and diversifies itself' by reinterpreting older sources and models (445). Indeed, in the cases of Finlay and Clark, and very much like Alpers's perception of pastoral, there is less emphasis on an avant-garde revolution of form than there is on the evolution and unfolding of antecedent forms.

This notion of a pastoral continuum is particularly evident in Clark's *Pastoral* (2010), a blue enamel plaque inscribed with white text:

> *Loyal Order*
> *Of Ancient Shepherds*
> *Friendly Society*

Recalling his earlier excavations in *Some Particulars*, which are discussed below, Clark's poem is a found-text taken from a sign discovered on a high street in Dundee marking a lodge belonging to the Loyal Order of Ancient Shepherds Friendly Society. One of the numerous Friendly Societies that flourished during the nineteenth century, also known as 'fraternal societies,' these mutual cooperatives provided insurance, pensions, and other financial benefits for their members. The Loyal Order of Ancient Shepherds began in 1826 in Ashton-Under-Lyne as the Ashton Unity, but lodges were subsequently established in other UK cities. Despite its name, and unlike similar societies such as The Order of the Free Gardeners, the Loyal Order of Ancient Shepherds was not an organization devoted to a particular profession, but provided financial and 'pastoral' care for a broad spectrum of workers of different professions (Dennis 124–126).

Pastoral evokes a particular continuum by recalling pastoral's close connections with Epicureanism. Indeed, according to 'biographical

---

40 Thomas A. Clark, email to the author, 9 January 2011.

tradition,' Virgil himself studied with Siro the Epicurean in Naples (Hardie 12). Furthermore, according to Rosenmeyer, pastoral 'is Epicurean by persuasion' and based on similar ideas of companionship (105). For this reason, as E. E. Sikes has noted, Epicureanism has 'not improperly been called an ancient Society of Friends' (59). Epicurean amity is also inscribed more tacitly in the literary filiations that have developed around it. In a similar spirit, Clark's plaque proposes a continuum—a 'loyal order' and a 'society'—of fraternity and affiliation. Considering its provenance (chanced upon on a drab street in Dundee) *Pastoral* also signals the 'utopic' potency of such affiliations. Indeed, Clark's found text reflects his regard for 'the flicker between literal and imaginative space' and his belief that 'our environment can be subject to a nominal transformation' ('An Inconspicuous Green Flower' 144).

The phrase 'Ancient Shepherds' in Clark's *Pastoral* recalls most immediately Samuel Palmer and the Ancients. 'Blake and the "Ancients"!' Raymond Lister writes: 'What deep associations those words induce in the hearts of those of us who are devoted to romanticism in English art and literature' (99). However, it is not just romanticism that the Ancients and Blake 'induce,' but also pastoral which, via the Ancients, encompasses Blake, Milton, Bunyan, and Virgil. It is these 'deep [pastoral] associations' that Clark's *Pastoral* conjures. For example, Clark's 'loyal order' of pastoral also invokes subsequent followers and admirers of Palmer, particularly the etcher F. L. Griggs who, with Martin Hardie and Sir Frank Short, published a *Final Edition* of Palmer's etchings and organized an exhibition of his work at the Victoria and Albert Museum in 1926.[41] Closely connected with Griggs are the younger 'Goldsmiths' etchers' that included Graham Sutherland, Joseph Webb and Robin Tanner—all of whom derived from Palmer 'a shared enthusiasm for life in the countryside and a love of things traditional' (Meyrick 61, 64). The Clarks' own relation to Tanner was, however, more than textual due to their acquaintance with him and his wife, the writer Heather Tanner, while living in Wiltshire in the early 1970s. Considering Robin Tanner's influence on Laurie Clark's work as an artist, it is perhaps not surprising that Robin Tanner's collaborative partnership with Heather Tanner—illustrating a number of her books such as *A Wiltshire Village* (1939)—prefigures the Clarks' own collaborative projects and working style.

Therefore, it is possible to identify a cabal of poets and artists united in their regard for Palmer and the Ancients who, as Davenport has suggested, 'are the first members of a family that exists today' (*Geography*

---

41 With Laurie Clark, Thomas A. Clark organized an exhibition of Griggs's work at the Cheltenham Art and Gallery Museum in 1988. He also wrote the essay for the exhibition catalogue: *Silences of Noons: The Work of F.L. Griggs (1876–1938)*.

197). In addition to the artists previously mentioned, Davenport himself can be added to this 'family.' As well as the author of a collection of short stories called *Eclogues*, and invoking Palmer in his long poem *Flowers & Leaves* (published by Jargon in 1966), Davenport has also, according to Andre Furlani, made 'pastoral conducive to utopian intervention' (xxxiv).

Davenport's good friend Ronald Johnson is another member of this extended family. Sharing similar sources, references, and allusions to those employed by Williams in *In England's Green &* and *Emblems*, Johnson's first collection *A Line of Poetry, A Row of Trees* (published by Jargon in 1964) and more so, as I have elsewhere suggested, his seasonal poem *The Book of the Green Man* (1967) effectively delineate the roots and branches of a British visionary company traceable to Palmer (125). Furthermore, and somewhat ironically, it was Johnson's 'English' seasonal poem—as interpreted through the eyes of this American poet— that first introduced Clark 'to visionary landscape, and the Pastoral' (cited in Hair, *Ronald Johnson* 223).

One final addition to this pastoral continuum worth particular mention are the 'New Arcadians'—the title given to the small press launched in 1981 by Patrick Eyres, Ian Gardner, and Grahame Jones. The press subsequently became the New Arcadian Press which aimed to re-examine 'the traditional association of text and image in English landscape art, despite the vagaries of fashion within an international Post-Modernist Wasteland' (Eyres, *Arcady* n. pag). The New Arcadian Press has also sought to 'acknowledge a continuous classical International Style' via the *New Arcadian Journal* and a diversity of broadsheets, small books, cards, prints, posters and ephemera (Eyres, *Arcady* n. pag). In the *Arcady* issue of the *New Arcadian Journal*, Eyres offers a chronological summary of the New Arcadian's influences in terms of artists and publishers:

> **Ex Libris:** the intention of Cotman and Girtin's 'Brothers' to express their medium as landscape poetry, combined with the activity of Bewick and Blake—authors, illustrators and printers of their own books—encapsulate New Arcadians. Renewed by William Morris, the tradition of the Private Press flourished between the wars: vide activities of [Eric] Ravilious, [Edward] Bawden, [Eric] Gill, the Nash Brothers et seq. (n. pag)

In terms of the latter half of the twentieth century, however, it is Finlay and the Wild Hawthorn Press that is perhaps the most significant of influences for the New Arcadians and their pursuit of a 'continuous classical International Style.' The playful whimsy of Finlay and his tendency toward cultural allusions and referencing of the art world is evident in the small book by Eyres and Gardiner called *Eye Spy Trees*, co-published by 'Eye Spy Arcady Books' and Gardner's Blue Tunnel Publications in 1980. The small booklet is written in 'affectionate memory of the News Chronicle I-SPY TREES' spotters' guides, popular with British children in the 1950s. In that same spirit the book invites its reader to spot the trees painted by several key landscape and pastoral painters, including Lorraine, Poussin, Gainsborough, Constable, and Salvator Rosa. Notably, Samuel Palmer's 'Tree of Heaven' is also included. Described as 'A wide-spreading tree / fresh / from a corner of Paradise,' Eyres recalls Palmer's comments on Blake's Virgil prints regarding the 'dells, and nooks, and corners of paradise' and also alludes to Palmer's remarkable painting *In a Shoreham Garden* (c. 1830) which depicts an apple tree in full blossom in a Kentish garden: 'EYE SPY the fruits / a conspicuous white silky down / like large marbles' (n. pag). Considering his claims for 'Certain Trees' as appropriate subjects for poetry, Finlay's spirit is evident in the way that Eyres and Gardner have heeded his advice with innovative playfulness.

Furthermore, the name of the New Arcadians is intended to compliment Finlay's Little Sparta, as the New Arcadian's website explains: 'Throughout the 1980s, the *New Arcadian Journal* championed Finlay's cause during the Little Spartan and other Wars, and *Broadsheets* and *Cards* were generated as propaganda' ('New Arcadian Press' n. pag). Clark's *Pastoral* with its emphasis on fidelity (suggested by the word 'loyal') and its echo of Finlay's own emphasis on 'order' inadvertently recalls how Finlay, as Williams notes, 'has been a whole Academy for an alert group of poets in the Decadent South'—that is, England (*BD* 73).

Otium and Quiescence
Clark's *Pastoral* also laconically expresses his own pastoral filiations which, as Clive Bush suggests, are an integral component of Clark's 'radically revised romantic discourse' and what David Reason describes as a 'lyricism' arising from Clark's 'commitment to both passion and meditation' (Bush 10; Reason, 'Line' n. pag). This commitment to 'passion and meditation' saliently recalls Clark's negotiations of romantic kinesis and classical stasis as well as his concern with 'the interface between the visionary and the immediate' which finds a potent precursor in Palmer's synthesis of visionary romanticism with classic, Virgilian pastoral (Bush 92).

Indeed, Clark uses Palmer's writings to engage certain 'visionary' concerns in the series of found poems—which Clark calls 'excavations' because, 'like excavating [...] one arrives at something which is real but has been hidden'—included in his book *Some Particulars* that Jargon published in 1971 (cited in Hair, *Ronald Johnson* 135).[42] In this relatively

---

42 Denise Riley adopts a similar method in her 'Letters from Palmer'—included in her Reality Street Editions book, *Selected Poems*

early book, and his first for Jargon, Clark expresses similar concerns to those delineated in *Tarasque*'s anthology of small poems regarding objective form and the subjective voice. As Clark explains in a letter to Jonathan Williams, his method of 'excavation' is a way of getting beyond what Olson famously called the 'lyrical interference of the individual as ego' (*Collected Prose* 247):

> i suppose really it dates back several years right through my involvement with the short poem, the attempt to find those surprises in language. years of working in a short space via haiku wc williams creeley concrete etc. but trouble i always found with such a small tight space was how to distance it from one's own mind, the language became more and more self referant [sic] and 'obscure' in the worst sense. so for a couple of years i've been making poems using texts which were outside my head and treating them in different ways, permutational, fragmentary, etc. (Cited in Hair, *Ronald Johnson* 135)

In his excavations of A. H. Palmer's *The Life and Letters of Samuel Palmer* (1892)—a text also mined by Williams and Johnson in their 'English' poems—Clark's poems foreground Palmer's frequent allusions to light and its illuminating effect on his ocular and oracular vision; what Palmer calls 'the optic nerve' and 'spiritual eye,' respectively (A. H. Palmer 176). Clark's poems frequently emphasize how the 'luminous' and 'amber' forms of his paintings are depicted in the ambience of 'sunrise' and 'twilight': 'I saw the sun / among those / separate huts / cool and discrete' (*Some Particulars* n. pag). Another of Clark's 'excavations' re-presents the content of Palmer's letters to manifest an ouroboros made of light:

> bite it
> beginning to end
> light (*Some Particulars* n. pag)

Here, light (presumably the natural light of the sun and the 'unearthly lustre' of 'the spiritual eye') substitutes the image of the traditional ouroboros, the serpent or dragon frequently depicted in alchemy and Gnosticism, consuming its own tail as a symbol of circularity and renewal (A. H. Palmer 176).

Trevor Winkfield has also picked up on the palpable 'luminous' quality of Palmer's paintings: 'moonlight and sunbeams appear to activate the paper from behind,' he notes, 'as though we were holding the drawings up to light' (*Georges Braque and Others* 54). Frequently cast

---

(2000)—which draw extensively on *The Letters of Samuel Palmer*, edited by Raymond Lister (1974).

in the luminescence of dawn or moonlit dusk, as Winkfield notes, with shepherds and poets depicted in quiet rest and repose, Palmer's paintings and etchings rehearse, and reinvigorate, an intrinsic component of pastoral: namely, *otium*. Meaning leisure, ease, and free time, *otium* is the Latin equivalent of the 'Epicurean notion of *hedone katastematike* (tranquil joy)' that underscores Theocritus's *Idylls* (Rosenmeyer 69). *Otium*, according to Thomas Rosenmeyer, traditionally occurs at noon, 'when the sun becomes too hot for comfort, when the whole nature enters into a state of suspension, and all flux, or almost all, is put to rest' (67). However, in Palmer's pastoral sensibilities this *otium* occurs predominantly at twilight, when the sheep are folded and 'we feel evening silently settle over the world' (Panofsky 301). As Williams's *Emblems* reveal, in Palmer's world, the time of dusk and moonlight 'not only thrill the optic nerve but shed / a mild, / a grateful, / an unearthly lustre / into the inmost spirits' (*JT* 163).

As a 'custodian of quiet,' Clark frequently invokes in his poems a quiescence, a stillness and calm, similar to that conveyed in Palmer's paintings and etchings (*In Defence of Quiet* n. pag). In a letter to Robert Stacey, quoting one of his own poems from *Pauses & Digressions* (1983), Clark proposes that, 'at least one prime purpose in this age, is to make yourself available, to arrive at

> that essential hour
> when things exert
> their legitimate power
> and candour drops
> like a ripe fruit
> into your desultory heart' (Cited in Stacey 29)

A similar sentiment is evident in 'the autumnal ripeness and clarity' that Clark invokes in his and Simon Cutts's collaborative booklet, *Salon d'Automne*, published by Coracle to coincide with an exhibition at London's Serpentine Gallery in the October of 1984, that included work by Richard Long, Andy Goldsworthy, Chris Drury, and Yoko Terauchi (n. pag). Evoking Franz Jourdain's Paris art gallery, the Salon d'Automne (which, as its name suggests, organized its shows in the autumn months of October and November) Clark proposes a 'pastoral role' for an ideal, hypothetical gallery space which has 'grown from several exhibitions at Coracle Press in the last few years' (n. pag). While this pastoral space would provide 'a precinct where a new relation pertains between things, a relation that is almost pastoral or utopian,' Clark's use of the word 'almost' reiterates his emphasis that pastoral is predicated by loss and oriented toward, or conditioned by, a possibility and promise that may not be fulfilled (n. pag). For, according to Clark, pastoral 'flourishes in a late time': 'Whether we go back to Theocritus and Bion or to Virgil and Ovid, the genre conjures a simplicity already lost or on the verge of loss' ('Pastorals' 153). By recognizing what is absent—but also, what is *almost* present—pastoral invokes what is, potentially, recuperable. Likewise, the gallery space creates an ambience that evokes, rather than fulfils, an ideal. In the 'late time' of autumn, Clark proposes, the gallery aims 'to cherish variety, subtlety, fineness, and to bear these with us towards any possible spring' (n. pag). This 'possible spring' is encouraged by the 'sense of ease and belonging' that the Salon promotes which, Clark insists, 'is neither a comfortable retreat from reality nor an act of defiance' (n. pag). Rather, that 'possible spring' is an arrested moment, poised *between* such possibilities.

Returning to the poem from *Pauses & Digressions* that Clark cites in his letter to Stacey, it is possible to see a similar 'sense of ease and belonging' invoked in the 'extended / deliquescent pause' he presents:

> it is afternoon
> that extended
> deliquescent pause
> while the little tune
> of the ripples
> plays about your ankles
>
> that essential hour
> when things exert
> their legitimate power
> and candour drops
> like a ripe fruit
> into your desultory heart (n. pag)

The extended pause of this 'essential hour' echoes the traditional noontime of *otium*, when 'only a limited range of activities is permitted' and otherwise desultory 'motions and passions' are given respite (Rosenmeyer 76–77). Echoing Clark's poem, Rosenmeyer is keen to stress that *otium* 'is *not* the abolition of energy, not withdrawal and curtailment, but a fullness in its own right' (71). Likewise, in Clark's poem it is only in the 'ripe' clarity of the arrested moment—in the 'deliquescent pause'—that 'things exert / their legitimate power.' The power exerted by these 'things' is further emphasized by Clark's use of the word 'candour' which, as well as suggesting 'whiteness,' also evokes notions of 'purity,' 'integrity,' and 'innocence,' as well as 'freedom from mental bias, openness of mind; fairness, impartiality, [and] justice' (*OED*). With the suggestion of all these meanings, the *candour* of Clark's poem conjures a prelapsarian moment of 'fullness,' or plenitude, in which yet-to-be-nominated 'things' exert *their* powers on the attuned and receptive perceiver.

Clark's poem suggests how *pauses*—delay, respite, arrest, *otium*—make it possible to *digress* from the straight path of habitual perception. Such pauses and digressions, Bush suggests, demonstrate how a 'turning aside from the way, an interruption of the path,' is not simply 'a figure of speech but is at the very heart of metaphor, of poetry itself as the practice of knowledge' (56). This idea also finds expression in Clark's notion of 'A Place Apart' in which *'Noise, distraction, disinformation, / are kept outside its parentheses'* (*A Place Apart* 8, original emphasis).

However, a place apart, as Clark's poetry repeatedly demonstrates, can also be a spatial and temporal place: a glade or a fold, the shelter of the shade, or the quiet tranquillity of dusk. *'In the heat of noon,'* for instance, *'the shade of oak leaves restores order among the faculties'* (*Shade at Noon* n. pag, original emphasis). Such 'spaces' are recuperative *'parentheses'* that permit reflection, focus, respite. While this may appear to reiterate the assumption that pastoral promotes escapism and retreat, these set apart places also have social implications that adumbrate the values of Epicurean amity. Thus, Clark suggests in *A Place Apart*: *'At times you will need a place to go'* in order *'to be alone or to seek / the shelter of good company'* (7, original emphasis). *'In the lee of a fold,'* Clark writes in his prose-poem 'Twenty Four Folds,' *'you might find / a hearth, a conversation, some / huddled sheep, accumulated/ debris'* (*Fold* 14, original emphasis). Thus, as this poem suggests, 'company' can take many forms and is capable of encompassing the human and the non-human.

Clark makes this point more explicitly in his brief essay on Finlay's use of pastoral imagery:

> The images remind us of essential ingredients in a civilised life; productive labour leavened by dance and song, gracious social relations, closeness to nature. They teach us that tenderness and joy are not additions to but vital constituents of a fully human condition. ('Pastorals' 153)

It is the *pause* of *otium* that encourages the re-evaluation of these societal relations by setting aside the necessary time and space 'for friendship and gratitude and compassion' to flower, imbuing such arrest with social 'feelings that take the sting of paralysis out of the calm of the bower' (Rosenmeyer 70).

According to John Freeman, Clark's poetry demonstrates an Epicurean 'discipline of idleness' which permits a 'shared and achieved space of leisure' in which 'isolated acts of attention' come to bear 'consequences of pleasure and virtue' (14, 6). A 'discipline of idleness' also underpins the phenomenological candour of Clark's poetry akin to what Nan Shepherd in her book *The Living Mountain* describes as 'living in the clear simplicity of the senses' (93). Like Shepherd, for Clark this 'candour' makes it possible to recognize friendship, gratitude, and compassion in both human and non-human company. Leisure and rest refresh the senses so that, 'once again / for the first time,' the phenomenal world announces itself with candour as the perceiver finds themselves in the *company* and 'order of things' (Clark, *The Hundred Thousand Places* 7).

Clark uses this phrase, 'the order of things,' and expresses a similar sentiment in an earlier poem, one of his *Sixteen Sonnets* (1981):

> as I walked out early
> into the order of things
> the world was up before me (n. pag)

In its suggestion of the English title of Foucault's *Le mots et les choses* (1966), Clark makes implicit parallels between his poetry's phenomenological candour and Foucault's endeavour in *The Order of Things* to examine 'the knowledge of living beings, the knowledge of language, and the knowledge of the economic facts' as well as the philosophical discourses determining them (x). In Clark's poetry, however, the *order of things* evoked arises from candour—a 'nonjudgmental acceptance of the given'—and by 'being thrown, to use Heidegger's term, into a world which you haven't made, which comes to you as a gift' (Herd 102, 100). What David Wheatley calls Clark's 'tentative and oblique angle to the more established modes of pastoral writing' is one way that Clark has acknowledged this grace and discerned in the 'small harmonies which attune our ears to harmony' a larger order of things (Wheatley 14; Herd 101).

Evening Orders

If there is any truth to 'the lingering pastoral myth' that Finlay worked as a shepherd on Orkney, then, undoubtedly, he would have been all too familiar with the hardships of the herding life (Peebles 17). Nevertheless, Finlay's poetry does not present an 'anti-pastoral' corrective to classical pastoral idealism but shows more concern for articulating similar classical notions of harmony and order that might extend his own 'model[s] of order.'[43] 'The sum of my work is tragic,' Finlay has remarked: 'But it is centred on the lyrical; so much of it is pastoral, Virgilian' (cited in Innes 12). Finlay's work, however, does not seek to exclude or evade this tragic strain, but rather holds that possibility in check with 'a fervent idealism' and lyricism that accentuates it (Stewart 116). In this respect, Finlay's work recalls an enduring 'dialectical vision of the pastoral tradition, where paradise is more evident in its loss, violation, or unavailability than in its immanent realization' (Hubbard 2). As Alec Finlay notes, 'we encounter a profound lyricism' in Finlay's

---

43 According to Terry Gifford, 'anti-pastoral' represents a corrective to the fantasy and idealism of traditional pastoral by depicting more accurate images of rural life (116–145).

work that is 'placed implacably alongside images of violence or terror' and which creates 'a radical extension of fragility through a confrontation with death' ('Shadow and Stitch' 128). Thus, rather than seeing these later phases of Finlay's work as a departure from the 'proper subjects' of poetry outlined in *Tarasque*, Finlay finds them as complementary elements within the violence and terror of a broader cultural history. Indeed, Heraclitus's proposition that 'What opposes unites, and the finest attunement stems from things bearing in opposite directions, and all things come about by strife' is particularly useful for encapsulating this aspect of Finlay's work (15). Pastoral also offers another rich source of motifs that articulate and expand these ideas of harmony and contention. Finlay's work therefore appears to confirm what Timothy Saunders considers pastoral's capacity for attuning otherwise 'mutually distinct and mutually distinctive' alterities, 'such as "culture" and "nature" or "poetry" and "politics"' (13).

An interaction of alterities is evident in the text accompanying Finlay's medal (produced in collaboration with Michael Burton) commemorating the First Battle of Little Sparta.[44] The medal depicts a machine gun and is accompanied with the text, 'Flute begin with me Arcadian notes'—a loose translation of a line in Virgil's *Eclogue* VIII: 'incipe Maenalios mecum, mea tibia, uersus,' which Guy Lee translates as: '*With me begin Maenalian verses, flute of mine*' (Virgil 87, original emphasis).[45] Finlay's commentary notes:

> The machine-gun is a visual pun (or play!) on Virgil's flute with the vents in the barrel-sleeve as the finger-stops. But—Et in Arcadia Ego—is the flute to begin or the gun—or is the duet in fact to be a trio: does the singer (if he is to continue the pastoral) need both? (Cited in Abrioux 242)

For Finlay the answer is *yes*: pastoral endures in his work as a confluence of peace *and* strife, harmony *and* contention, concord *and* discord. Indeed,

---

44 Finlay renamed his Stonypath garden 'Little Sparta' in 1983 after ongoing bureaucratic struggles with the Strathclyde council concerning unpaid tax duties. Not recognizing Finlay's claim that his building, the Garden Temple, constituted a religious building exempt from tax duties, the Strathclyde council attempted to seize a number of Finlay's works in lieu of unpaid taxes. With his supporters, Finlay, held a successful resistance and commemorated the event with the medal and a plaque, situated at the entrance to Little Sparta, the site of the 'battle.' The aptness of the pastoral allusion is emphasized considerably by the setting of this plaque and, Stonypath more generally, which is neighboured by several sheep pastures.

45 Virgil's line derives from a refrain in Theocritus's first idyll: '*Begin, my Muses, begin the herdsman's song*' (3, original emphasis).

the tacit implication of Arcadia in Finlay's allusion to Virgil in his commemoration plaque is a poignant reminder that such idyllic environs presuppose their own kinds of 'warfare.' As Mark Scroggins suggests, Finlay's work repeatedly reminds us 'that any experience of nature, Rousseauvian, Romantic, or otherwise, must include a recognition of that violence that makes such peace possible' (n. pag). Thus, building on the 'principle of conflict' that Bann identifies in 'Homage to Malevich,' Finlay's poetry serves as a reminder of how concord presupposes discord and peace, if it is to endure, must precipitate strife ('Ian Hamilton Finlay' 60).

Finlay's awareness of this balance is evident in one of his *Ten Sentences* published by Wild Hawthorn in 1996: 'Arcadia and Sparta share / a common border' (*Selections* 253). Here, as well as referring to the pastoral tensions of his own Little Sparta, Finlay conflates the fictional and idealized *locus amoenus* of Arcadia with the actual geographical location from which it takes its name: the wild, barren mountainous district situated in the central Peloponnesus. This real Arcadia, as Finlay notes, borders Sparta, the ancient Greek state which was renowned for its imposing military culture and its 'Spartan' society; its 'rugged virtue, rustic hospitality [and] low standards of living' (Panofsky 297). The actual and the ideal are therefore not exclusive but mutually co-dependent on, or conditioned by, 'a common border.'

In '*Et in Arcadia Ego*: Poussin and the Elegiac Tradition,' an essay which directly influences Finlay's own pastoral sensibilities, Erwin Panofsky makes a similar observation about Virgil's *Eclogues*, noting how 'in the imagination of Virgil [...] a bleak and chilly district of Greece came to be transformed into an imaginary realm of perfect bliss' (300). Virgil achieved this in his *Eclogues* by emphasizing 'the virtues that the real Arcady had (including the all-pervading sound of song and flutes not mentioned by Ovid)' and by imaginatively attributing 'charms which the real Arcady never possessed: luxuriant vegetation, eternal spring, and inexhaustible leisure for love' (299).

Similar notions of balanced opposition to Virgil's imagined Arcady also inform Finlay's ideas about order which, likewise, draw upon and utilize specific pastoral tropes. For example, the 'Epicurean invocation of calm' bestowed by *otium* is also discernible in Finlay's theories about concrete poetry (Rosenmeyer 70). The broader implications of Finlay's 'model of order,' for instance, are evident in his later neoclassicism and what R. C. Kenedy describes as Finlay's concern with 'static ideas':

> Finlay's work is dedicated to the concept of endurance, timelessness, and equilibrium. Tensions and romantic-seeming, unbalanced forces are excluded from his compositions. They are not without forces, but their vectoral energy is always counterbalanced. Even his predilection for the metaphor's

> rudimentary structure comes from this desire for an absolute
> and static equilibrium. He equates forces in order to still their
> rebelliously separate existence and in order to produce, from
> the suddenly engineered union, a tranquil thought, larger
> than its parts. (41)

Finlay's 'model of order,' in this respect, invites comparison with what
Warren considers a defining paradox of the 'conventionality' of the
pastoral *locus amoenus* which not only 'affords it blessed protection' but
also 'its fragility, its evanescence': 'Its generic purity and artificiality
direct our attention inevitably to all it has excluded' (53).

Similar fragile tensions between static equilibrium and kinetic
disequilibrium are evident in the folding-card Finlay produced in
collaboration with Richard Demarco called *A Calm in a Teacup* (1973)
which establishes its own equivalent *locus amoenus*. Inverting the familiar,
colloquialism 'a storm in teacup,' Demarco's watercolour, which is based
on the children's illustrator Kate Greenaway's 1905 painting of the
same name, depicts the image of a ship calmly sailing on the surface
of a cup of tea. Implicit in this image and text is another 'model of
order' surrounded by a space full of doubt or chaos, with the proverbial
storm no longer in the teacup but *without* it. And for Finlay—who ran
a special 'tea' issue of *Poor. Old. Tired. Horse.*, the *Tpoth* issue)—this card
is also playful testimony to the reassuring effects of this beverage. In
the context of Finlay's pastoral affiliations, however, *A Calm in a Teacup*
reiterates Epicurus's recognition in 'the difficulty of positing *stasis* in
world in which nothing stands still' (Rosenmeyer 69). Indeed, according
to Rosenmeyer, Epicurus's 'use of the word *galēnē* (calm of the storm)
and its derivatives shows his awareness of the marginal swirl, which no
philosophy can throw out entirely' (69).

Finlay's metaphor therefore indicates the importance of establishing
another kind of space or place apart that permits the possibility, but
not necessarily the realization, of order. This also recalls Virgil's
'search for an order' in the *Eclogues*, 'which is rarely attained but is,
nevertheless, a prerequisite for happiness' (Putnam 13). However, as
Virgil demonstrates, such order is always threatened by 'unrequited
love, by death, by some indefinable outside force,' and by 'motives and
passions that engulf *otium*, and never cease to threaten the balance'
(Putnam 13; Rosenmeyer 76–77). As Erwin Panofsky argues, there is
a pastoral tradition beginning with Virgil where 'tragedy no longer
faces us as stark reality but is seen through the soft, colored haze of
sentiment either anticipatory or retrospective' (301). This culminates
most poignantly, Panofsky argues, in Nicolas Poussin's painting, *Et in
Arcadia Ego* or *Les Bergers d'Arcadie* (c. late 1630s), which 'no longer shows
a dramatic encounter with Death but a contemplative absorption in the
idea of mortality' (313).

Yves Abrioux has interpreted Finlay's 'fauve' and 'suprematist' modes in a way that elaborates significantly Finlay's reflections on the pastoral *memento mori*, 'Et in Arcadia Ego.' According to Abrioux, Finlay employs 'the term "fauve" when formal rigour implies the virtue of simple goodness and "suprematist" when the question of power becomes more obvious' (166). These two modes offer equivalents to the different approaches to Death that Panofsky proposes: 'contemplative absorption' on the one hand and 'dramatic encounter' on the other. From Abrioux's understanding of the two terms, Finlay's 'suprematist' mode is evident in his *Footnotes to an Essay* (with Gary Hincks and Stephen Bann, 1977) or *Of Famous Arcady Ye Are* (with Michael Harvey, 1977) in which classical pastoral references and allusions are conflated with martial imagery such as *Panzer* tanks, machine guns, warships, and camouflage. These and other motifs not only demonstrate modern instances of dramatic encounters with Death, they also function as contemporary equivalents of Pan—Arcadia's panic-inducing deity.

Indeed, Finlay's 'suprematist' pastorals are a pertinent reminder that the shepherd's *otium* is a hiatus imposed by Pan. In the first of Theocritus's *Idylls*, which are the germ of the pastoral tradition, it transpires that:

> We're not allowed to pipe at midday, shepherd—not
> allowed.
> It's then that Pan rests, you know, tired from the hunt.
> We're afraid of him; he's tetchy at this hour, and his lip
> Is always curled in sour displeasure. (1)

Otium is therefore determined by the larger powers and forces that Pan embodies. The implications of 'the marginal swirl' in *otium* are further amplified by Rosenmeyer's claim that *otium*, deriving from the word *negotium*, 'is originally a military term, meaning something like the American "liberty," a soldier's leave from duty' (67). Meaning 'vacation, freedom, escape from pressing business, particularly business with overtones of death,' *otium* therefore tacitly adumbrates the classical motif, 'Et in Arcadia ego' (Rosenmeyer 67). As Panofsky explains, this term can be translated as 'Death is even in Arcadia' or 'Even in Arcadia, I Death, hold sway' (296, 310). Considered in the politicized context of Eclogue I, the martial origins of *otium* indicate an irony of sorts when the shepherd Meliboeus laments: 'Some godless veteran will own this fallow tilth, / These cornfields a barbarian' (Virgil 35). As Guy Lee explains, this refers to 'the forcible transfer of land from the possession of its former owners and tenants into the hands of soldiers demobilized by their victorious commanders' following the civil war between Brutus and Cassius (Virgil 22).

Similar martial tensions underscore Finlay's postcard *Found Eclogue*

(1998) in which Finlay reinterprets the word 'eclogue,' from the Latin *ecloga*, meaning, 'choice' or 'selection,' in a modernist context of found poetry and appropriation. The postcard reproduces an advertisement for a 1939 Harbour Ferry from the magazine *Classic Boat*, thereby adopting another of Finlay's proper subjects for poetry: fishing boats. This particular boat served in the allied evacuation of 1940 as a 'Dunkirk Little Ship' and was later renamed Shepherd Lad, evoking archetypal pastoral shepherds such as Tityrus and Meliboeus. These pastoral connotations are continued in the description of the boat's construction, 'Pitch pine on oak,' which denotes the North American pinewood that, along with oak, was commonly used in shipbuilding as well as the 'pine' and 'monumental oak' of Milton's melancholy pastoral, *Il Penseroso* (29). Furthermore, 'pitch pine' also conjures the woods of the Arcadian mountain Maenalus where 'Pines talk' and 'are ever musical' due to the musical pitch of the shepherd's syrinx that resounds through the trees (Virgil 87). Considering that 'pine' also means to yearn for something, this Shepherd Lad may very well be Meliboeus in Virgil's first eclogue who pines for the 'sweet ploughlands of home' given over to demobilized soldiers (35). This seems all the more poignant, perhaps even ironic, when Shepherd Lad's role in assisting the return home of allied troops from Dunkirk in the Second World War is taken into account.

The conjunction of wartime Dunkirk and pastoral lyricism in *Found Eclogue* is another instance of how Panofsky's essay '*Et in Arcadia Ego*: Poussin and the Elegiac Tradition' informs Finlay's pastoral sensibilities. However, it is also worth noting that Panofsky's essay develops ideas first advanced by Bruno Snell in his essay 'Arcadia: The Discovery of a Spiritual Landscape.' In response to the 'intrusion of contemporary events' such as civil wars and political quarrels, Virgil's *Eclogues*, Snell argues, convey an elegiac and lyric 'longing for peace and a home' (291, 292). As a 'nostalgic refugee from sombre realities,' Virgil, Snell writes, 'places his hopes, not upon a just state, but an idyllic peace in which all beings will live together in friendship and fraternity' (293):

> Virgil's sensibility fastens upon the familiar daily activities, the constant traffic with the same routine objects, the peaceful life of the home soil. His love is for the familiar things is a longing rather than a happiness. (291)

Familiarity in this instance breeds reassurance, not contempt. It also creates another kind of continuum. However, such tranquillity and order is something that is to be *pined* for, because, ultimately, it 'is a longing rather than a happiness' that Virgil conveys in the *Eclogues*. According to Snell, this means that 'Virgil's relation to the world is lyric; it impels him to seek out that which is dear to him,' but which, ultimately, is located 'in an area beyond the harsh facts of experience' (295). It is this 'tender emotion' that creates what Panofsky considers to be the poignant 'dissonance' in Virgil's Arcadia (Snell 292):

> In Virgil's ideal Arcady human suffering and superhumanly perfect surroundings create a dissonance. This dissonance, once felt, had to be resolved, and it was resolved in that vespertinal mixture of sadness and tranquillity, which is perhaps Virgil's most personal contribution to poetry. With only slight exaggeration one might say that he 'discovered' the evening. (330)

A similar 'vespertinal mixture of sadness and tranquillity' pervades Finlay's work, especially what he calls his 'evening poems' which, as much as elegiac and melancholy are also playful, light, and lyrical (cited in Abrioux 241). This 'evening' quality is evident in the folding card by Finlay and Ian Gardner called *They Returned Home* (1972). The card comprises two watercolours by Gardner that creates a visual pun in their depictions of a landscape and a waterscape. The first watercolour depicts a path to a distant cottage, wending its way through undulating hills, reminiscent of the Pentland Hills surrounding Stonypath. The second, by substituting a boat for the cottage, transforms the meadows into swelling waves, thereby turning the path into the wake of the boat. Accompanying these two images is Finlay's text: 'They returned home tired / but happy. The End' (n. pag). However, under the card's whimsical surface there is a more melancholy mood of mortality, with home (be it cottage or port) connoting Death. Not only does the boat's *wake* imply this, but a sense of terminus is implicit in the sobering statement, 'The End', spelt ominously with a *capital* E.

Finlay and Gardner's card is a later, poignant example of Hugh Kenner's claim regarding the bleak whimsy and casual panic inflecting the poems in *The Dancers Inherit the Party*. That sense of panic is emphasized considerably in the image of the sea and ocean that pervades so much of Finlay's work. As Prudence Carlson notes, Finlay conceives 'the Ocean as both source and end':

> Finlay has cast the Ocean as a kind of super- or *meta*-trope not only for Nature and Nature's fathomless (destructive/ re-creative) power, but also for the vast reservoir of (re) interpretative acts undertaken to make brute secular nature once again divinely, transparently sing. In either of its guises, the natural or the cultural, the Ocean is finally the soul's home. (n. pag)

Stephen Bann, suggesting that 'the alibi of the Ocean is Death' in Finlay's work, sees the ocean as representing an 'irreducible'—one might say, terminal—"'Other," beyond which no further symbolic conversions are possible' ('Ian Hamilton Finlay' 70). Indeed, as John Dixon Hunt suggests, the sea and the ocean 'is nothing if not cruel and destructive,' in Finlay's work (92). It sounds 'the notes of loss and disaster' and warns us (as Pan does) that 'nature is violent and destructive' (92).

This Oceanic *meta*-trope of loss, disaster, and Death is also evident in Finlay's postcard, *The Homeward Star* (1998), which appropriates lines from Samuel Palmer's translation of Virgil's first eclogue. Finlay transposes the pastoral setting of Palmer's translation to a maritime context in two distiches. Indeed, that term is echoed in the texts' allusions to 'stitching': 'The homeward star / The stitching sail'; 'The homeward sail / The stitching star.' In Finlay's rendering, Palmer's 'homeward star' becomes the star by which homesick seafarers navigate their way home, with 'The stitching star' suggesting a constellation stitched in the night sky. However, 'stitching' further emphasizes homesickness by suggesting the feeling of sharp, sudden pain, which is exacerbated by the reminder or promise of home.

Finlay's screen-print *Evening/Sail* (1970) evokes a similar evening mood via a laconic statement that declares the sewing a blue sail when evening comes. There is a sense of fated inevitability in the poem's claim that 'EVENING / WILL / COME—'; even if the sail has not yet been sewed, it *will* be (n. pag). This fate is as inexorable as evening itself, which casts its own mortal shadow on the events of the day. As Stephen Scobie notes, 'the sewing of sails is something that might be done in an evening, after a day's work; but the association of evening with the end of day suggests also the end of a life, the sewing of a shroud' (192).[46] *Evening/Sail* therefore is a poignant reminder that breath, synonymous with life and spirit, is also the *animating* power of sailing ship—the thing fills its sails—and, so to speak, gives it life.

The mortal *adumbrations* of *Evening/Sail* find an appropriate form in the 'Westward-Facing Sundial' situated in Little Sparta which reproduces the text of *Evening/Sail* in altered lineation. Like a *memento mori*, the sundial looks, as Michael Charlesworth suggests, 'a bit like a grave marker' (78). Due to the unforgiving elements of its environment, this sundial has now sadly all but eroded, making its text practically illegible. Although unintentional, the declining condition of the sundial makes it a striking equivalent to weathered sails in need of mending and sewing. If, as Patrick Eyres suggests, in the sundial 'Shadow and motto conjoin to embark the imagination upon a metaphoric voyage,'

---

46   The poem may also reflect Finlay's pleasure for making model boats with coloured 'hankie' sails. These sewn sails appear in Finlay's *A Mast of Hankies* (1975), which reproduces Dave Paterson's photos of Finlay's crate-wood boats.

then in the 'Westward-Facing Sundial' this 'voyage' is oceanic, solar, and all-too mortal ('On Sundials' 99). The poem's 'delicate elegiac idea [...] that things will not last,' as Charlesworth notes, is accentuated by the physical property of the sundial, with the text of *Evening/Sail* 'enacted by the [deteriorating] body of the work' (78).

Unfolding Palmer
As well as mediating a rich and complex pastoral tradition, Samuel Palmer has been a significant point of reference in additional ways for Finlay, Clark, and Simon Cutts. All three poets have produced a series of folding-cards and poems in response to two Palmer etchings, *Christmas* or *Folding the Last Sheep* (1850) and *Opening the Fold* or *Early Morning* (1880). Although Palmer uses the word 'fold' solely in the context of the sheepfold, Finlay, Clark, and Cutts have exploited the multiple suggestions of this word in order to reflect on the material properties of poetry and publishing. Indeed, by manipulating the material properties of the card and paper that the poem is printed on, all three poets have amplified implicit themes 'folded' into Palmer's pastoral titles.

A notable precursor to these folding cards is John Furnival's Openings Press which, with Dom Sylvester Houédard and Edward Wright, he launched in 1964 with the aim of producing small 'mailable works' by an international range of poets and artists (Furnival 34). The first Openings was Louis Zukofsky's 'Finally A Valentine' which was followed by publications of work by Finlay, Ronald Johnson, Tom Phillips, and Hansjörg Mayer. In this series of 'Openings,' Clark notes, 'the form the publication takes in some way duplicates the content. By experimenting with folds a method is arrived at whereby the reader literally *unfolds* the meaning of the poem as he reads' ('Openings Press,' 6).

A similar 'unfolding' occurs in Clark's folding-poem *Folding the Last Sheep* (1973), which consists of a single sheet of white folded paper, upon which the words 'Folding the last sheep' are printed in blue. Playing with the idea of 'folds' and 'folding' further, Clark's little poem has its own enclosure in the form of an envelope. Thus, the reader of *Folding the Last Sheep* assumes the role of the shepherd in order to read it: taking the poem from its enclosure and, ultimately, returning it to this fold after the activity of reading is over. A playful allusion to Palmer's theme of sheepherding is also apparent in *Folding the Last Sheep*'s function as a standing poem which, when opened and placed on a surface, physically recreates the form of the sheepfold itself.

This small, modest poem initiates a transtextual dialogue that continues in subsequent poems by Clark, Finlay, and Cutts. Like the shepherds in Virgil's *Eclogues* that invoke one another's songs, or Virgil himself who appropriates Theocritus and Gallus in the *Eclogues*, these folding-poems acknowledge a pastoral continuum that unfolds the 'Loyal Order of Ancient Shepherds' intimated in Clark's *Pastoral*. For example,

Cutts's poem 'After Samuel Palmer's version of Virgil's "Eclogues"'—
first published in his book, *Pins: Some Poems* (1980) and reprinted in his
first Jargon collection, *Piano Stool: Footnotes* (1982)—elaborates on Clark's
Folding the Last Sheep:

> folding
> the flock
>
> open-
> ing the
> fold
>
> fold-
> ing the
> last
>
> sheep (n. pag)

A variation of this poem, 'Eclogues 1984–2000: After Samuel
Palmer's Virgil,' makes further connections between the sheepfold and
the verb 'folding' by suggesting both shepherding and the manipulation
of paper:

> open-
> ing the
> fold
>
> open-
> ing the
> first gate - fold
>
> fold-
> ing the
> last
> sheet
>
> close-
> ing the
> last
> gate   - fold   (*If It Is At All* 52–53)

If we recall that the word 'develop' means, 'to unfold more fully' and
'bring out all that is potentially contained,' then Cutts further *develops*
or elaborates the self-reflexive qualities of this folding-poem in *Eclogues:
After Samuel Palmer* (2004). This version reformats 'After Samuel Palmer's

Version of Virgil's "Eclogues"' as a more elaborate letterpress case-bound book with sewn double gate-fold pages. 'Gate-fold' is a term probably most familiar for collectors of vinyl and refers to a publication or, in the case of magazines, an insert larger in dimension than the page or format in which it is folded. Thus, when opened, a gatefold LP is twice the diameter of a standard LP cover. In the case of Cutts's *Eclogues*, the form of the physical book—its gatefold pages—enact the word play and association of the poem, making what Cutts calls 'the possibility of the book as a physical metaphor for its subject' palpable (*SFA* 46).[47]

Clark is also interested in the creative possibilities of small press printing and its creative potential for using format innovatively in conjunction with content. The 8 × 5 Adana press that he and Laurie Clark used to print their Moschatel cards and booklets had a significant influence on Clark's poetry. 'At certain periods our little Adana press was perhaps the main influence on my work,' he tells David Herd: 'I would have a certain size to work with, a particular paper, a favourite typeface, and these would be the beginnings of a poem' (98). This awareness of the physical properties of printing and a poem's format—which is apparent not only in the Clarks' Moschatel publications but also in Furnival's Openings, Finlay's Wild Hawthorn, and Cutts's Coracle publications—inverts Charles Olson's dictum, via Robert Creeley, that 'FORM IS NEVER MORE THAN AN EXTENSION OF CONTENT' (*Collected Prose* 240). For the small press poet-publisher, form *and* content are integral to the very format and the choice of material used to realize the poem.

The folding-cards and poems that Clark, Finlay, and Cutts have made which oscillate between two Palmer etchings—*Opening the Fold* and the aforementioned *Folding the Last Sheep*—comprise a cyclical or diurnal meditation on birth and death, first and last things. In this respect, these folding-cards and folding-poems implicitly recall the title of Robert Duncan's book *The Opening of the Field* and the 'eternal pasture folded in all thought'—the 'place of first permission' and 'everlasting omen of what is'—that Duncan invokes in his book's opening poem, 'Often I Am Permitted to Return to a Meadow' (7). Furthermore, as Geoff Ward notes, in this poem Duncan tacitly puns on the word 'omen,' which derives 'from the Latin *omentum*, "a fold,"' thereby conflating notions of portentousness with the sheepfold (196).

Clark makes similar implications apparent in *Folding the Last Sheep*, which proposes not so much 'first things' as it does 'final things in the midst of frivolities' (Duncan, 7; Clark, *Salon d'Automne* n. pag). The sheepfold, to borrow Duncan's phrase, is a place of protection, providing

---

47   *Eclogue* also includes a bibliography that lists a number of folding-poems, including Clark's *Folding the Last Sheep* and Cutts's 'After Samuel Palmer's Version of Virgil's "Eclogues,"' offering a further unfolding of a distinctive pastoral continuum.

'certain bounds [that] hold against chaos' (7). However, as a place where sheep are folded at the end of the day, these 'bounds' that hold against chaos also constitute more chillingly a place of *closure* and terminus. Clark conveys this impression through the interplay of his standing/ folding poem's text and its material form and format with the enveloping fold of the envelope physically manifesting, or enacting, the closure and finality that the text implies.

Finlay has taken a further step in materializing semantic content by installing a life-size dry-stone sheepfold in Little Sparta. Inscribed on the fold's walls is the title of Palmer's etching and Clark's poem—'FOLDING / THE LAST / SHEEP'—whereas the wooden gate to the enclosure bears the legend 'ECLOGUE' (cited in Sheeler, 113–114). Like the homely sentiments of *They Returned Home*, this sheepfold offers the reassuring presence of shelter (which seems particularly welcome in the harsh weather conditions of Little Sparta) while also, much like the tomb in Poussin's *Et in Arcadia ego*, imposing on the landscape a sobering suggestion of cessation and closure.

Eclogue realizes in stone an earlier proposal called *Hirtenlied* ('Shepherd's Song') that Finlay produced in collaboration with the Clarks and Pia Maria Simig (1999). The card consists of Laurie Clark's drawing of a sheepfold that opens out to reveal the words, 'HIRTENLIED / FOLDING / THE LAST / SHEEP' and the following explanation:[48]

> Intended as a contribution to a Bundesgartenschau established on what was once a military training ground, this recreation of an old-fashioned sheepfold includes as a text the title of an etching (1850) by the English pastoral artist Samuel Palmer. The visitor is invited to open the latched gate and enter the secluded space within the sheepfold which, like the Palmer etching it recalls, stands for the pastoral tradition reaching back to Virgil and Theocritus. (n. pag)

Situated on an old German military training ground, *Hirtenlied* continues Finlay's exploration of martial and pastoral themes as well as Clark's concern for places set apart. The military location of this proposed installation also serves as a poignant *memento mori* for the pastoral tradition that it recalls, particularly the aforementioned martial connotations of the shepherd's *otium*.

---

48 Like Cutts's *Eclogue* (which includes *Hirtenlied* in its bibliography), *Hirtenlied* includes a bibliography that, in addition to folding-poems by Clark and Cutts, also cites E.V. Rieu's translation of Virgil, Raymond Lister's *Samuel Palmer and the Ancients*, and *The Illustrations of William Blake for Thornton's Virgil*. Thus, a pastoral continuum is unfolded—this time with Palmer as its nexus—that connects back to Blake and Virgil and extends up to the modern sensibilities of Finlay, Clark, and Cutts.

The inevitability of death that Finlay entertains in *Evening / Sail*, as well as its conflation of land and sea via the onset of darkness, is also evident in the texts that comprise Finlay's *Pastoral* (1997). On two separate sheets of folded paper, Finlay's presents two texts that follow the present-tense idiom of Clark's *Folding the Last Sheep*:

TRIMMING   STOWING
THE   THE
LAMP   SAIL (n. pag)

To trim a lamp is to make it ready for burning as the Gospel of Matthew recalls in the Parable of the Ten Virgins: 'Then all those virgins arose, and trimmed their lamps' (25:7). However, in Finlay's poem, the trimming of the lamp assumes nautical significance, either suggesting a ship's lamp trimmer or the lamplight that might guide, or greet, a ship home. As with many of Finlay's poems, however, the reassurance and joy of such homecoming is undercut by the suggestion of death. Thus, the ship's sail—stowed at the end of a journey, just as Finlay's two texts are stowed in their envelope—becomes another 'omen' of mortal closure in a manner akin to the sewn sail in *Evening / Sail*. 'Trimming' therefore, might, suggest the putting of things in order in preparation for an impending and inevitable event. Thus a solemn, grave ambience broods over what would otherwise be an occasion for celebration.

In collaboration with the Clarks, Finlay produced another folding-card called *Folding the Last Sail* (1997) that follows the same format as Clark's *Folding The Last Sheep*. However, Finlay's card substitutes the word 'sail' for 'sheep' (n. pag). Finlay incorporates the same text in a later folding card, *After Simon Cutts, After Samuel Palmer* (1999) which, as the title suggests, alludes to Cutts's 'After Samuel Palmer's version of Virgil's "Eclogues"':

    loosing
    the sheets

    open-
    ing the
    hold

    fold-
    ing the
    last

    sail (n. pag)

The poem puns on three interconnected themes. Acknowledging Cutts's poem, Finlay invokes the material book in the form of paper sheets being loosed—perhaps from their binding—and the laying press that *holds* a book in place when it is being worked on. But 'sheets' also suggest the ropes or chains attached to the lower corners of a square sail and establish a nautical context that is developed more explicitly in the allusions to the 'hold' and the 'sail' of a ship. In addition, however, is a pastoral context which is established in the implicit homophones: 'ship'/'sheep' and 'hold'/'fold.' Indeed, the ship's hold presents an equivalent enclosure to the fold that *holds* sheep. Conflating ship and sheep this way, Finlay presents another 'evening' poem that intimates a diurnal pastoral cycle (opening the fold—losing the sheep— folding the sheep) in the routine preparations for a boat's *berth*, a word that homophonically invokes both final things and new beginnings.

Closing the Fold

The folding poem and cards made by the Clarks, Finlay, and Cutts are Spartan in their design and laconic in their execution. Their texts and formats promote sententiousness and concision that does not conjure an impossibly ideal Arcady but rather invoke the qualities associated with that *locus amoensus*: simplicity, amity, contemplation, recreation. In this respect, the pastoral mode that these poet-publishers have unfolded offers a new perspective on William Empson's idea in *Some Versions of Pastoral* of 'the pastoral process of putting the complex into the simple' (22). For all their simplicity, these folding-cards, as we have seen, articulate a number of 'complex' concerns that inform the broader poetics of all three poets; namely, Clark's phenomenological candour, Finlay's neo-classical model of order, and Cutts's ideas regarding the published format as the poem's 'physical metaphor' (*SFA* 12). In their engagement with these concerns, all three poets also recall 'the contrast within Virgilian pastoral' that Raymond Williams in *The Country and the City* suggests exists 'between the pleasures of rural settlement and the threat of loss and eviction' (17). This is nowhere better exemplified in the *otium* enjoyed by Tityrus and the exile suffered by Meliboeus in Virgil's first eclogue. 'The conflict between these two themes,' as E. V. Rieu suggests in his translation of the *Eclogues*, 'makes a beautiful poem of what might have only been a pretty one' and 'sounds the keynote' of Virgil's poems (123–124). As the pastoral-themed poems of Finlay and company gently insist, such dissonance not only accentuates the impossible perfections of Arcadia but they also prevent those perfections from becoming too prettified or, indeed, petrified. There will always be, as Samuel Palmer writes, 'Some little stirring in the fold' which gives definition to the *possible* pleasures and ideals of the Arcadian landscape (133).

What singles Finlay, Clark, and Cutts out from other versions of modern or contemporary pastoral is their *knowing* acceptance of the tradition. (The same can also be said for Jonathan Williams and Ronald Johnson.) Unlike Empson and Raymond Williams, and unlike more recent critics such as Gifford, none of these poets feel it necessary to reconcile or apologize for what most commentators consider pastoral's inherent flaws. Instead, they have consciously used these contested terms—idealism, nostalgia, retreat, leisure, and melancholy—as the means to articulate and address wider concerns by actively engaging with the various instances of 'unrest' and dissonance that 'throw into relief the trappings of pastoral stasis' (Clark, 'Pastorals' 152).

'It is,' Clark claims of pastoral, '*a fiction* to which we look back in order to remind ourselves of what our first freedom was, what we were without the chains of perspicacity and guile' ('Pastorals' 155, emphasis added). Thus, in these contemporary approaches to pastoral, there is a knowing use of the tradition and its most traditional sensibilities to renew the sustaining possibility of 'a world beyond our own jangled nerves, with its own claims and demands and pleasures' (Clark, *Salon d'Automne* n. pag). That world 'beyond our own' might, as in the case of Clark's poetry, be the sensual, more-than-human world lost to habitual perception, but it might also be, to recall Moeglin-Delcroix's apposite trope, the networked utopic world of the publication itself ('Little Books' n. pag). In either case, what may seem initially as the reactive retreat into, or the projection of, a fictional ideal in these poets' work is in fact a discerning understanding of a longstanding pastoral tradition, the lessons and values of which can reorient its reader in the 'late time' of a secular modern world.

Chapter Six

Coracle's Unpainted Landscapes

> As a souvenir or memento of somewhere,
> the typical postcard is insufficient—a place
> is at least as much what may be seen from
> it as what it might look like.
>
> —Colin Sackett, *View*

In his book *Landscape and Western Art*, Malcolm Andrews, argues that an abiding tradition of landscape painting has played a significant part in determining the 'visual prejudices that may never find formal expression in works of art, but that are crucial shaping influences in terms of the way in which we privately respond to both our natural environment and the pictures of that environment' (1). 'A "landscape,"' therefore, Andrews reasons, 'cultivated or wild, is already artifice before it has become the subject of a work of art,' because the 'process of marking off one particular tract of land as aesthetically superior to, or more interesting than, its neighbours' is a discriminatory and complex one comprised of 'visual facts and imaginative construction' (1, 3). Alluding to the title of Kenneth Clark's influential book *Landscape into Art* (1949), Andrews expands on this idea by proposing that the 'mental conversion' involved in creating such artifice is a twofold process: 'land into landscape; landscape into art' (3).

An early one-word poem by Ian Hamilton Finlay titled 'Arcady' makes a similar claim about the mental conversion of land into landscape, and landscape into art. Finlay's poem consists of the 26 letters of the alphabet italicized in capitals in Times New Roman font. In a 1966 version of this poem published by Tarasque, as one of their *Private Tutor* broadsides, Finlay devises a series of questions about the poem that also serve as a tacit commentary. One asks:

'Roam' is a verb we associate with Arcady. Can one roam among the letters of the alphabet? Might it be that the letters of the alphabet can be compared to fields and forests, mosses and springs of an ancient pastoral? If so, why? (*Selections* 147)

Here, Finlay, as Yves Abrioux suggests, brings to the fore 'the suggestion of a mimetic relationship between the alphabet and an idyllic landscape' (Abrioux 198). However, like the folding-poems (discussed in the previous chapter) that proceed 'Arcady,' Finlay's poem does not propose that the letters of the alphabet simply describe or represent a pastoral landscape, but instead implies the possibility that they might constitute an equivalent one. Indeed, rather than simply being slavishly mimetic of the 'real world' beyond them, the letters of the alphabet (and the language that they make) might instead be recognized as constituents of, and participants in, the so-called 'real world.'

Thus, building on the distinctions that he initially made between art and life in *The Dancers Inherit the Party*, Finlay tacitly attributes non-mimetic, objective, and autonomous qualities to language. In this respect, 'Arcady' adumbrates Pierre Reverdy's claim in his 1917 essay 'On Cubism' that cubist paintings, 'in detaching themselves from life, find their way back into it, because they have an existence of their own apart from the evocation or reproduction of the things of life' (145). Reverdy reiterates this sentiment in another essay, 'Some Advantages of Being Alone' (1918) when he claims: 'A work of art cannot content itself with being a *representation*; it must be a *presentation*' (149). 'A representational work of art is *always* false,' Reverdy reasons: 'It never represents except conventionally what it claims to represent. The convention may be of the eyes or of the mind' (149).

From the perspective of Reverdy and Finlay's 'Arcady' language can be seen as occupying a significant place within what the cultural geographer David Matless calls the 'cultures of landscape' (9). 'Culture' in the context of landscape, Matless explains, 'variously indicates ways of life, habits of place, spheres of representation, material objects [and] forms of media' as well as 'the modes through which nature is valued' (9). Matless uses the term 'colloquial' to emphasize such multiplicity and diversity—'the presence of different voices, forms of attention given, and a varied cultural constitution, moving across the academic and the popular, the specialist and the ordinary'—which significantly departs from the fixed, single perspective of traditional landscape painting, its systemized rules, and its prescribed conventions (6). By emphasizing a diversity of active processes, Matless concurs with Andrews's suggestion that we are actively involved in the mental conversion of land into landscape and 'creative producers of landscape images' rather than simply passive 'consumers' (1).

Matless is one of numerous cultural geographers who have sought alternative ways of articulating the ways in which landscape is encountered and conceived. Echoing Reverdy's claim for a presentational art, the geographers John David Dewsbury, Paul Harrison, Mitch Rose, and John Wylie have aspired to 'work on presenting the world, not on representing it, or explaining it' ('Enacting Geographies' 438). According to Wylie, there has been 'a rhetorical and substantive shift, from studies of *representation of* landscape, nature, identity, space, place, the body and so on, to studies instead investigating various performances of these tropes' (163). This 'shift' has tended to be called either 'non-representational' or 'performative' theory due to the emphasis it places on 'common, embodied cultural practices' such as 'walking, looking, driving, cycling, climbing and gardening' (Wylie 166). 'If non-representational theory takes the work of representation seriously,' the co-authors of 'Enacting Geographies' explain, 'what it does not take seriously is representationalism, or, discursive idealism' (438). Instead, importance is placed on 'attentive analyses of, and quite often, direct personal participation in, embodied acts of landscaping' (Wylie 166). Thus, whereas Reverdy promotes a non-representational art that is essentially detached from the world, non-representational theory, as conceived by Dewsbury and his co-authors, is very much embodied in it:

> Our understanding of non-representational theory is that it is characterised by a firm belief in the actuality of represen- tation. It does not approach representations as masks, gazes, reflections, veils, dreams, ideologies, as anything, in short, that is a covering which is laid over the ontic. ('Enacting Geographies' 438)

Rather than foregoing representation altogether, non-representational theory foregrounds 'the act of representing (speaking, painting, writing)' and considers such practices 'to be *in* and *of* the world of embodied practice and performance, rather than taking place outside of that world, or being anterior to, and determinative of, that world' (Wylie 164). In other words, 'representations are apprehended as performative in themselves; as doings' ('Enacting Geographies' 438). In a similar spirit, Hayden Lorimer defines such performative practices as 'more-than-representational' ('Cultural Geography' 83).

Such approaches to landscape contrast markedly with the established academic practice of '"representationalism"—[the] signature theory of cultural geography's landscape school,' which, Lorimer suggests, has, like traditional landscape painting, 'framed, fixed and rendered inert all that ought to be most lively' ('Cultural Geography' 84–85). The longstanding associations of the term 'landscape,' as Tim Creswell argues, are problematic and leave little 'space for temporality, for movement and flux and mundane practice. It is too much about the already accomplished and not enough about the process of everyday life' (269). If, as Creswell proposes, landscape 'encapsulates[s] the notion of fixity—of a text already written—of the production of meaning and the creation of a dominating power,' then non-representational theory offers ways for reassessing these established modes and prescriptions as well as the power relations that they promote (269).

To understand embodied experiences of space and place, Lorimer argues, requires a 'focus [that] falls on how life takes shape and gains expression in shared experiences, everyday routines, fleeting encounters, embodied movements, precognitive triggers, practical skills, affective intensities, enduring urges, unexceptional interactions and sensuous dispositions' ('Cultural Geography' 84). 'Attention to these kinds of expression,' Lorimer suggests, 'offers an escape from the established academic habit of striving to uncover meanings and values that apparently await our discovery, interpretation, judgement and ultimate representation' ('Cultural Geography' 84). The contexts in which 'embodied acts of landscaping' have been studied, Lorimer points out, have frequently been 'manicured, husbanded and domesticated settings' such as the smallholding, the allotment, the private garden, and local parks where '"green space" becomes a practised formation of living: a setting for hard graft, and the artistries and industries of cultivation':

> Here, the hobby farmer, the plotter, the vegetable grower, the artist, the dog-walker, the dog, the human rambler and the fruit harvester are encountered in passionate, intimate and material relationships with the soil, and the grass, plants and trees that take root there. These garden studies set out to make sense of the ecologies of place created by actions and processes, rather than the place portrayed by the end product. ('Cultural Geography' 85)

Nigel Thrift has also noted the importance of 'intimate and material relationships' in non-representational theory by emphasizing the importance of what he calls 'the materiality of thinking' and 'the "performative" working methods and procedures of writings (and, very importantly, other methods of exposition) that emphasize how the whole business of praxis and poiesis is wrapped up in the stubborn plainness of a field of things' (8). According to Thrift, 'methods of exposition' that 'emphasize the materiality of thinking [...] include the study of material culture, the sociology of science, performance studies from dance to poetry, installation and site-based art, elements of architecture,' as well as 'various aspects of archaeology and museum studies' (8). In these and similar fields of material thinking and practice, Thrift, with Stephan Harrison and Steve Pile, have identified fruitful means for understanding 'the entanglements—the invisible hyphens—between nature and culture, human and nonhuman' that 'comprise what we know as landscape' (*Patterned Ground* 10, 9).

As well as reassessing *how* one experiences, practices, or embodies landscape, non-representational theory, as Lorimer notes above, also reassesses the insignificant, disvalued, and mundane spaces in which they occur. Before the advent of non-representationalism in the field of cultural geography, the naturalist Richard Mabey had already acknowledged these kinds of spaces in *The Unofficial Countryside* (1973), a book that Iain Sinclair describes as 'the unacknowledged pivot between the new nature writers and those others, of a grungier dispensation, who are randomly (and misleadingly) herded together as "psychogeographers"' ('Introduction' 11).

Mabey's book documents the ecology of 'habitats that have grown out of human need,' and to which 'the labels "urban" and "rural" by which we normally find our bearings in a landscape, just do not apply' (20). These 'unofficial' habitats, Mabey suggests, include 'the water inside abandoned docks and in artificially created reservoirs; canal towpaths, and the dry banks of railway cuttings; allotments, parks, golf courses, gardens; the sludge of sewage farms and the more elegant mud of watercress beds' (20).

In addition to the so-called new nature writing and psychogeography, Mabey's book is prescient of other recent re-evaluations of overlooked or disparaged landscapes. A one-time collaborator with Finlay, the Swiss sociologist and economist Lucius Burkhardt, for example, in his essay 'What Do Explorers Discover?' (1987), extends Mabey's idea of an 'unofficial countryside' by arguing that in contemporary society nature is longer 'in the countryside,' but 'in the city or at least on the city margins: on gravel pits, construction sites, abandoned industrial plants, disused quarries and slag heaps, between railway sidings, along walls, or in the hands of the Federal Army' (270).[49] This perception of 'nature' is part of what Burckhardt has named 'strollology': 'the science of walking, [and] the aesthetics of space' that aims to reassess 'certain approaches to the preservation of landscape, those namely which at times to preserve the so-called typical landscape' (282). Echoing Andrews's ideas regarding the mental conversion of land into landscape, Burckhardt argues that 'this typical landscape does not exist' but 'is an artistic feat with an ideological dimension' (282, 19). 'For "landscape" is not to be found in the nature of things but in our mind's eye,' Burckhardt proposes, 'it is a construct that serves as a means of perception for any society that no longer lives directly from the land' (19). What is considered worth preserving within an environment, what is deemed appropriate, beautiful, of value, or of use, is therefore a consequence of ideological constructs. 'To espy a landscape in our environment is a creative act brought forth by excluding

49   Wild Hawthorn Press published Finlay's and Burckhardt's folding card, *Capital, n. a Republican Crown*, in 1981.

and filtering certain elements,' Burckhardt insists, 'and, equally, by rhyming together or integrating all we see in a single image, in a manner that is influenced largely by our educational background' (31).

Adumbrating Burckhardt's landscape theories, Marion Shoard in her eponymously titled essay, published in 2002, coins the term 'edgelands' in order to articulate her ideas regarding the cultural and ecological importance of the 'interfacial landscape' (121). According to Shoard, 'unkempt wasteland,' 'rubbish tips and warehouses, superstores and derelict industrial plants, office parks and gypsy encampments, golf courses, allotments and fragmented, scruffy farmland' are invaluable sites of biodiversity that provide 'similar and often greater wildlife benefits than urban wildscape, and on a much more extensive scale' (128). 'For plants and animals being driven out of the countryside by modern agricultural methods,' Shoard proposes, 'interfacial areas provide an obvious first refuge, benefitting not only from their own ecological resources but also from their proximity to that other increasingly wildlife refuge, gardens' (128–129).

The poets Paul Farley and Michael Symmons Roberts have popularized Shoard's term, 'edgelands,' using it as the title of their book *Edgelands: Journeys into England's True Wilderness* (2011). Farley and Roberts 'decided to write the book together in the anonymous tradition' as a means for 'letting' this interfacial terrain of landfills, canals, lofts, and bridges 'speak for itself, rather than framing ourselves within it as intrepid explorers' (9). The book's intentions do, however, appear somewhat conflicted. Despite the authors' desire to let these landscapes speak for themselves, *Edgelands* uses relatively conventional narrative techniques to represent those terrains. The voices of Farley and Roberts may very well blur as one anonymous voice, but that voice, nevertheless, discursively imposes its subjective observations on the book's chosen edgelands via 'a meditative approach' which entails 'pausing to describe, explore, and imagine' those places in order to 'see them afresh' (10). In this respect, the book falls short in providing a sympathetic account of the kinds of geographies that, according to Tim Cresswell 'are lived, embodied, practiced: landscapes which are never finished or complete, nor easily framed or read,' and which 'should be as much about the everyday and unexceptional as they are the grand and distinguished' (Cresswell 280). *Edgelands* frames its unofficial and liminal topographies too comfortably and predictably, even if they are 'everyday and unexceptional' compared to the 'grand and distinguished' subjects of traditional landscape painting and writing. And, in contrast to Matless's suggestions, *Edgelands* omits the colloquy of voices, idioms, accents, and perspectives that might enable more nuanced and attentive engagements with its landscapes.

It is possible to find more apposite approaches to these questions of official and unofficial landscapes in the manifold activities of Coracle,

Simon Cutts's small press and gallery that he established with the artist Kay Roberts in 1975 following the dissolution of Tarasque. Like its predecessor, Coracle's touchstones include avant-garde and modernist art and literature, concrete poetry, and contemporary British and American poetry. Conceptual art is not only an additional influence on Coracle (particularly in the context of British Land Art), but it is also one that contrasts with the longstanding influence of Finlay whose use of traditional forms and references to the Western fine art tradition distances him from the conceptualism of Sol LeWitt, Lawrence Weiner, or Joseph Kosuth. Thus, like another of Coracle's major influences, Jonathan Williams, Cutts has resisted towing one exclusive party line and instead cultivated a diverse roster of poets and artists that, like Coracle itself, cannot be easily categorized.

'*It's very Coracle*. Not Coralesque, or Coraclist, or Coraclean, simply *Coracle*,' John Bevis reflects: 'Aside from the underplayed wit, it's not obvious what the common denominator is' ('A Star-gazey Pie,' 19). It is therefore apposite that Cutts chose the name 'Coracle' because of the 'adaptability' that the word suggested:

> I was hunting for a name and wanted a good noun, a good extant noun for an object in the world, and *coracle* seemed to come up, seemed to be a sort of example for a lot of things, least the one-man-boat that people say. More that the coracle is adaptable and it is a boat you can use for crossing territory, and you can take it on your back and get to the next piece of water and cross that, cross land, take it to the next piece of water and so on. This adaptability is really the issue more than it is *my* boat. (*SFA* 36)

Coracle has never been a one-person operation. 'If,' as Bevis notes, 'the core of Ian Hamilton Finlay's work was collaboration, for Coracle it was co-operation' ('Swings and Roundabouts' 18). Roberts left Coracle in the early 1980s, but over the decades a number of individuals have been involved with the press and gallery, including John Bevis, Colin Sackett, David Bellingham, Clare Rowe, Ian Farr, David Gray, and Erica Van Horn. Furthermore, Coracle's 'shucking off formal partnerships to craft a new, loose organic collective' led to numerous projects that, in addition to poets such as Clark, Finlay, and Williams, has included artists and sculptors as diverse as Andy Golsdworthy, Stephen Willats, and Gustav Metzger, as well as less easily categorized individuals such as Bernard Lassus (whose activities have encompassed visual art, landscape architecture, and town planning) and the aforementioned Lucius Burckhardt (Bevis, 'A Star-gazey Pie' 35). Thus, very much like its namesake, Coracle's activities have been amphibious, treading a singular path through the varied terrains of art, poetry, and landscape theory via the means of unconventional gallery exhibitions, poetry readings, bookshops, and the production of artists' books, ephemera, and constructed objects.

What has remained consistent over the last four decades has been Cutts's regard for the edited format and the edited space. These concerns are evident in Coracle's commitment to small press publishing, its explorations into the creative and critical possibilities of the printed format, as well as in its equally innovative use of physical spaces, such as the former shop in Camberwell that Cutts and Roberts transformed into a gallery, bookshop, reading venue, and print shop. 'The gallery space was seen as an active element of the work,' Bevis notes, 'just as the programme of exhibitions would be seen as an artistic work in its own right' ('A Star-gazey Pie' 40). This regard for the environment and setting of work is part of another consistency in Coracle's extensive portfolio and, according to Cutts, 'one of its most enduring concerns' namely, its 'critical extension to the ways of representing the exterior landscape, or even the interior garden' (*The Presence of Landscape* dust jacket).

Coracle's interest in landscape is perhaps most pronounced in the 1987 touring exhibition *The Unpainted Landscape* (and eponymous book) that exhibited a broad range contemporary artists 'working with landscape' such as Richard Long, Andy Goldsworthy, Hamish Fulton, David Nash, and herman de vries (Cutts, *The Unpainted Landscape* 9). 'As a survey of artists who worked in the landscape with other strategies than that of imitation,' Cutts claims, 'it remains one of the freshest anthologies, and one which still infers a potentially theoretical approach to this area' (*The Presence of Landscape* n. pag). Written contributions to the book by Jonathan Williams, Thomas A. Clark, and Lucius Burckhardt, among others, offer further perspectives on the theoretical approach to landscape and the means of its representation. Artists included in *The Unpainted Landscape* such as Long, Goldsworthy, and Nash, as Mel Gooding notes, show awareness that 'we do not perceive the world around us as a series of pictures, that we do not perceive the space we inhabit as it was imagined and constructed by the great Renaissance theoreticians of mathematical and aerial perspective, as from a fixed viewpoint, as if framed by a window' (10).

With regard to Long, Fulton, and de vries, Anne Moeglin-Delcroix identifies their books (some of which Coracle has published) as the most significant medium for 'rediscover[ing] a more authentic relationship with nature [that] is inseparable from promoting experience at the expense of representation' (*Ambulo* 5–6). Echoing the embodied practices of non-representational theory, Moeglin-Delcroix proposes that 'emphasis has been progressively placed no longer on landscape but on the search for the best means, differing according to the various artists, of rendering an experience in the strongest sense of the word: a lived experience of the world, a personal practice, that is to say, a deliberate way of being *in* the world rather than before it' (6). For Moeglin-Delcroix it is the innovative use of the printed format (such as the use of the accordion fold) as well as the use of text for non-descriptive ends in conjunction with visual images that have provided the most effective 'means' for rendering these 'lived experience[s] of the world' (6).

Cutts makes a similar point in *The Unpainted Landscape*, remarking how the exhibition's artists 'do not try to reproduce the appearance of the landscape by way of painted effects,' but instead 'have established new procedures for an art of landscape, and have chosen to work with wider means at their disposal':

> They have used the recording photograph, the idea of time and sequence to make a journey, the notion of change and substitution in a place. In fact they have re-examined the composition of an art related to landscape. (9)

Land Artists such as Long and Fulton along with many of the other poets and artists who have worked closely with Coracle have expressed similar attitudes towards landscape as Cutts does here, tacitly promoting the idea that 'we are part of the world, not privileged observers of it' (Gooding 16).

Simon Cutts: The Airfields of Lincolnshire

As a press and gallery that has utilized many of the activities noted by Thrift (particularly poetry, installation and site-based art, and museum studies) and because it has tended to opt for 'a certain delicacy and slightness of key [and] a choice of the poetic everyday as opposed to an assumed or inherited Grand Manner,' Coracle's activities saliently adumbrate the non-representational theories outlined above (Cutts, 'The Weather House' n. pag). 'Some constant qualities,' as Bevis notes of Coracle's diverse back-catalogue, 'are suggested by the prevalence of the timeless raw materials of landscape, Englishness, gardens, water, interiors, weather, walking,' all of which he claims are 'tempered by a gut instinct to turn any first notion on its head, to pull the rug from under one's feet rather than settle for the tired, the safe or the unexceptional' ('A Star-gazey Pie' 23).

Trevor Winkfield, recalling Coracle's early shows, also notes a distinctive English sensibility that gallery cultivated in response to the ubiquitous 'American aesthetic' and 'the obnoxious hand of International Modernism' that then dominated the art world (7, 8):

> Those early shows at Coracle were full of stuff that Marinetti and most critics [...] would have hated: allusions to crazy paving, pillbox hats, allotments, meringues, braids, toy

railways, embroidered topiaries, caravan sites, skirting boards, tree bark, wind instruments, the month of February, linoleum, greenhouses, tartan slippers, hedgerow airports, garden implements doubling as musical tools, in fact the whole kit and caboodle of suppressed Englishness. (8)

The legacy of Finlay's proper subjects for poetry—or, for that matter, Mills's earlier 'Neo-Fauve' poem—is discernible in this litany of subjects and themes which might at first come across as twee, fey, or eccentric. Yet, as Bevis suggests, there is incisiveness to this middle-Englishness that, and again like Finlay's 'proper subjects,' critiques certain cultural and aesthetic assumptions:

[W]e find the back alleys and allotments, ditches and verges, no-man's land seen from a passing train, our very literal social margins. In the domestic arena, we are asked to consider the loft, the skirting board, the alcove and the porch. These are equivalents of that mental space where whatever we may take for granted, our assumptions vegetate. ('Swings and Roundabouts' 17)

Coracle's reassessments of 'the poetic everyday' contrast notably with Farley's and Roberts's interest in similarly neglected, marginal, and overlooked landscapes. In contrast to the authors of *Edgelands*, Coracle's work has tended to eschew more traditional framing devices and modes in its exploration of predominantly British interfacial landscapes, implementing more innovative and appropriate ways for embodying landscape practices and allowing those landscapes to speak for themselves. In this respect, the formal objectivity that Mills and Cutts promoted in *Tarasque*—its emphasis on 'Words [that] exist as themselves without implying a sensibility of their creator'—might be recognized as a significant precursor to Coracle's landscape approach (*SFA* 94).

'Description always employs narrative, and therefore the condition of the narrator,' Cutts writes in a 1968 essay: 'To remove this personal factor was a purificational move for me' (*SFA* 95). Many of the Coracle publications would realize this purification through a synthesis, not only of text and image, but also of the physical material and the method of production that the particular publication or object takes, allowing the printed or constructed platform, but especially the book, to become 'the primary form' (Cutts, *Letterpress* 126). In this way, Cutts would realize the view that he initially proposed in *Tarasque* 6: 'The sense of artefact entailed in the production of the small poem brings the poet nearer to the plastic artist' (*SFA* 93).

The germ of such aspirations is implicit in an early poem titled 'Les coquelicots,' which presents another example of Cutts's French affinities.

Sharing its name with Claude Monet's painting of 1873, Cutts's poem shows a regard for the Impressionists while also anticipating his later poem, *A History of the Airfields of Lincolnshire*:

> after the last greenhouse
> the airfield
>
> the vague ness
> of long
>
> poppy-grass (*A New Kind of Tie* n. pag)

In addition to his choice of title, Cutts evokes Monet's painting in the long poppy grass, which recalls the undulating form of Monet's iconic poppy field. This association is made even stronger in Cutts's use of the word 'vague' that suggests both the French word for 'wave' as well as the English word for something indefinite and undefined. In these respects, the word works effectively to convey Monet's impressionist style, the flux and volume of the swaying poppy-grass, and, perhaps, the shimmering effect of the horizon's heat haze.

The larger landscape of Cutts's poem is, however, notably different to Monet's Argenteuil one. Whereas a solitary country house situated behind a copse of trees is the only form of human habitation in Monet's painting, the possibility of a similar rural idyll is undercut in Cutts's poem by the presence of a greenhouse and an airfield. Indeed, the suggestion of plural greenhouses indicate husbandry on a large commercial scale, whereas the airfield—whether military or civilian—represents a relatively large-scale human presence within the landscape.

This notion of a landscape's human history is developed in *A History of the Airfields of Lincolnshire* that Laurie and Thomas A. Clark installed on a single wall of their Cairn Gallery in Nailsworth, Gloucestershire in 1990. This poem derived from an earlier poem—'Airfields,' published in Philip Steadman, Stephen Bann, and Mike Weaver's little magazine, *Form* (Number 7, March 1968)—and would, later, form the basis of two books—*A History of the Airfields of Lincolnshire* and *A History of the Airfields of Lincolnshire II*—as well as a later site-specific installation.

Like the earlier 'Les coquelicots,' these airfield poems acknowledge how human presence has marked the landscape. In this instance, however, the location is the agricultural fields of Lincolnshire. Known as 'Bomber County' because of the strong RAF presence there during World War II, much of Lincolnshire's agricultural land provided military airfields for Bomber Command. Unlike Cutts's earlier poems, however, the printed formats of *A History of the Airfields of Lincolnshire* (published by Coracle in 1990) and *A History of the Airfields of Lincolnshire II* (published by David Bellingham's WAX 366 in 2000) become the primary form of these one-word poems. The physical properties of the page, the placement of text, binding, the colour of type, and the cover material all serve to suggest specific horticultural features of the topographies they evoke: poppies (*Papaver rhoeas*) in the case of *A History of the Airfields of Lincolnshire* and flax (*Linum usitatissimum*) in the case of its sequel.

A History of the Airfields of Lincolnshire repeats in a red courier typeface the word 'poppies.' The word runs as a frieze across the bottom of the booklet's 32 white pages, sewn in sections. The 'heads of the folded pages remain uncut,' Cutts explains, 'leaving them open at the bottom' (*Letterpress* 119). Thus, the impression of an expansive skyline and low-level horizon is enhanced by the materiality of the page. Furthermore, the effect of the typography of these pages effectively recalls the flat and monotonous expanse of Lincolnshire's topography, which exacerbates the profusion of red poppies within it. The booklet's cover is green with the title *A History of the Airfields of Lincolnshire* printed, also in a courier typeface, in a darker green. As well as suggesting a field, the green colours of the cover also evoke camouflage. Combined with a typeface that recalls the kind of strike-on typewriter text found on military memos and telegrams, this colour scheme conflates the martial theme of the poem's title with its agricultural setting.

By evoking the pervasive agricultural weed that was once found in abundance populating Lincolnshire's former airfields, Cutts's poem also recalls Caitlin DeSilvey's notion of 'rewilding,' particularly in the context of what DeSilvey calls 'residual military landscapes' such as the disused World War Two Government Code and Cypher School at Bletchley Park ('Rewilding' 61). The dereliction and abandonment of sites such as these, DeSilvey suggests, have made the sites vulnerable to the 'invasion of relict prewar plants and more recent interlopers' that have reclaimed the land ('Rewilding' 61). However, the rewilding of residual military landscapes also serves, as Gillian Rose explains, 'a sophisticated ideological device that enacts systematic erasures' by exploiting some basic assumptions regarding the values attributed to 'the cultural' and 'the natural' (87). Taking US residual military landscapes such as Hanford Reach National Monument and Rocky Flats National Wildlife Refuge as her examples, DeSilvey argues that 'ecological processes can become cultural agents of attempted historical erasure, [in which] naturalisation risks negation' ('Rewilding' 62). As well as negating the ethical implications of the former military landscape in question, naturalization also neutralizes it and, to adopt Alison Byerly's claims regarding the picturesque, becomes another 'act of appropriation in which [a landscape's] intrinsic qualities are sacrificed to the agenda of its audience' (52).

Recounting his experiences of the capital's marginalized landscapes in *London Orbital*, Iain Sinclair makes a similar assessment about historical erasure in the context of 'the Paradise Park formerly known as the Royal Gunpowder Mills' in Waltham Abbey, East London (127). This 'decommissioned nowhere,' Sinclair claims, comprising 175 acres of land 'thrown open to the public,' has naturalized and erased its less than salubrious history by means of the heritage industry (128, 127):

> Enclose the wildest wood in the parish, cut your own canals, build a city of sheds, blow up houses, rebuild them, stage underwater detonations, and keep it all under wraps. […] One day when the research and development has moved elsewhere, the abandoned colony will be turned over to the heritage industry. Wild nature, thriving in an exclusion zone, will be promoted and paraded. (128)

Such scepticism, however, is not limited to Sinclair's epic 'reconstruction of an edgeland mythology' (Sinclair, 'Introduction' 12). The geographer David Havlick has expressed similar concerns about the implications of rewilding decommissioned land, noting how former military sites that have been reclassified as wildlife refuges (M2W, or military to wildlife conversion sites) and invited 'new conceptions of places developed through an integration of history, science, politics, and environmental discourse' (151–152). However, these 'new geographies that blend environmental and military characteristics,' Havlick reasons, carry with them certain ethical implications. 'By embracing the wildlife and environmental attributes of M2W sites,' Havlick suggests, 'we may implicitly also embrace their companion military activities' (151). Havlick notes, as an example, how the former military base, the Rocky Mountain Arsenal in Colorado, has 'produced wildlife habitat and weapons of mass destruction,' yet 'both of these histories remain present in the landscape that now carries a new name as a wildlife refuge' (153).

A History of the Airfields of Lincolnshire touches implicitly on some of these issues, but it does so by heeding Finlay's earlier advice in *Tarasque*, using adjectives 'sparsely, if at all' because, despite its title, Cutts 'history' of the airfields of Lincolnshire does not give its reader a conventional discursive 'history' of the subject. Rather, the book conveys with minimal intervention a complex conflation of Lincolnshire's agricultural industry, military heritage, and its geography. Furthermore, by eschewing description and narrative, Cutts's poem resists being read simply as an elegiac poem or war memorial. In this respect, *A History of the Airfields of Lincolnshire* reiterates what Jonathan Jones has suggested in the context of the recent Bomber Command Memorial in London's Green Park: 'No amount of stone and bronze can ever end the ethical debate about Britain's bombing strategy during the Second World War' (n. pag). If anything, the presence of the symbolic flower of remembrance, the poppy, in *A History of the Airfields of Lincolnshire* makes an ambiguous statement about the cultural memories inscribed and erased by 'nature.'

Whether Cutts's poem remembers the bomber crews killed in action whilst bombing their European civilian targets, those civilian victims, or even, perhaps, the disappearing airfields themselves, remains equivocal.

These questions are made more explicit in the site-specific installation based on *A History of the Airfields of Lincolnshire* that was constructed in 2002 along a former railway track, converted into a cycle route, near Skellingthorpe in Lincolnshire. The 'poppies' text, cast in anodized aluminium (a lightweight yet durable material used in the construction of airplanes) is supported by seven concrete slabs of runway salvaged from nearby RAF Swinderby. Whether Cutts's installation is acknowledging the erasure of an important, albeit problematic, part of Britain's cultural history or celebrating the way in which nature has reclaimed or 'rewilded' these sites is, again, uncertain. Indeed, perhaps the installation will itself in due course also be reclaimed by its environment. Notwithstanding these questions, *A History of the Airfields of Lincolnshire* is a poignant reminder that the agricultural fields of Lincolnshire are both vibrant green spaces and the former sites of weapons of mass destruction.

Cutts wrote the sequel to *A History of the Airfields of Lincolnshire*, *A History of the Airfields of Lincolnshire II*, in response to the changing flora of Lincolnshire's former airfields. 'In the intervening years since the first *History*,' Cutts explains, 'the predominant vegetation had changed from poppies to flax or linseed with its small blue flowers, the overspill of a change to a useable crop' (*Letterpress* 119). Like its precursor, *A History of the Airfields of Lincolnshire II* achieves its full effect through the synthesis of text, typography, page, and format. Inverting the uncut pages of *A History of the Airfields of Lincolnshire*, Cutts's sequel, as Gilonis explains, 'is made up of accordion-fold sheets printed on both sides but not trimmed at the bottom, so that when the book is opened the pages "gather" at the foot and splay at the top, much after the manner of flax (planted in industrial quantities in the level ground of Lincolnshire)' (120). Thus, like the uncut flowers they evoke, the booklet's pages remain uncut as if ready for reaping.

Gilonis also notes how the binding is in 'flax-blue' and the text—consisting solely of the repeated word 'flax,' which bunches across the top part of each page—is 'leaf-stalk green' (120):

```
    x  f        x  f   x    f         x  f      x
  flax  flax  flax  flaxflax  flaxflax    flaxflax  flax
   flaxflax      flaxflax  flaxflax      flaxflax  flaxflax
    f  x          f  x  f  x              f    x    f
```
                                              (*Letterpress* 74)

Unlike the low, monotonous horizon of the repeated 'poppies' in *A History of the Airfields of Lincolnshire*, the fragmentary bunches of the word 'flax' in *A History of the Airfields of Lincolnshire II* suggest the more irregular sprays of the flax plant. According to Cutts, the fragmented repetitions of 'flax' are also 'evocational of small bursts of explosion in the sky above,' perhaps a reference to the German *Fliegerabwehrkanone* (FlaK) anti-aircraft guns that would have met the RAF bombers on their raids (*Letterpress* 119). Furthermore, like the cover of *A History of the Airfields of Lincolnshire*, the blue cover of Cutts's sequel suggests a field, only this time it is a field of flax in full flower with its fibrous texture also serving as a reminder that flax has been traditionally grown in Lincolnshire for food and for the fibre required for manufacturing linen and paper. Thus, the poem not only achieves a subtle non-referential relationship with the landscape to which it obliquely refers, but, through the materiality of its own format, *A History of the Airfields of Lincolnshire II* also tacitly recalls how it is implicated and materially *bound* in the history of the landscape that it presents.

Erica Van Horn: The Book's Passage
As a primary form, the book also remains a principal interest of the American artist Erica Van Horn who, since 1988, has co-directed Coracle with Cutts. Recalling Niedecker's own domestic economies, Van Horn's work, as Nancy Kuhl notes, is concerned with the way in which the book can 'collect and transform remnants, remembrances, and reminders': 'From fragments that otherwise might be forgotten, the artist makes new meanings in beautiful and unexpected ways' (7). Furthermore, like Niedecker, Van Horn has been committed to 'exploring the daily aspects of her life,' although for Van Horn, Kuhl suggests, this occurs through a fractious yet productive interplay of text and image:

> A creative tension is always present between her interest in language as a practical and physical matter worthy of sustained exploration and her deep interest in visual narrative; textual and imagistic qualities of identity, community, and memory are revealed by contrast and comparison. (7)

A prime example of this 'creative tension' occurs in Van Horn's book *Stiles & The Pennine Way* published by Coracle in 1993 (Figure 6). While Van Horn's book takes walking and landscape as its primary themes, it departs significantly from traditional walking narratives and their depictions of landscape. Indeed, rather than evoking Wordsworth's poetry or Alfred Wainwright's celebrated guidebooks of the region, Van Horn's book shows greater affinity for the 'lived body and bodily practice and performance[s]' that non-representational theory seeks to foreground (Wylie 165). Van Horn's book achieves this by reproducing in offset print the sleeves of the rain jacket she wore during an 11-day walk with Cutts from Belper, Derbyshire to Dent, Cumbria. Walking the Pennines for seven days of that journey, Van Horn repeatedly encountered two things: rain and stiles. 'The stiles were so frequent, and the rain so constant that I got sick of pulling out the notebook and just got out my (waterproof) pen and made the tick on my rain-coat sleeve' (n. pag). Rather like Richard Long's text-work *Wind Line, A Straight Ten Mile Northward Walk on Dartmoor* (1985) which marks the variant wind directions of this walk with a column of arrows, Van Horn records apparently mundane phenomena in a matter-of-fact, nondescript way. The persistent bad weather is tacitly acknowledged by the consistent use of the raincoat that was worn over the duration of the 11 days, and the stiles by the tally marks (which, visually, are not too dissimilar to a stile or gate) scored on its sleeve for each day walking the Pennines. Reproduced in the centre of the book, the image of Van Horn's green coat fabric repeats the function of the stiles and gates she recorded by bridging the book's prose commentary, just as a stile bridges two different boundaries in order to make passage through or over them possible.

Figure 6. Erica Van Horn, *Stiles & the Pennine Way*, Coracle, 1993.

As a place of considerable natural beauty it is perhaps odd that Van Horn should focus on something as banal as the stiles encountered on the Pennine Way. Yet these constructions reveal a lot about the landscapes in which they occur, indicating questions of land ownership, access, and enclosure. In this respect, stiles are subtle, yet significant, markers of the ways in which land is not only composed, but how it is encountered and valued. Following Van Horn's tally marks give an indication of the changing landscape of her journey. The 18th of June is especially notable because, unlike the other days, Van Horn records just one stile. Perhaps the walk led to a stretch of open, non-arable land. Maybe there were missing stiles, or damaged boundary walls, that made them unnecessary. Then again, perhaps on this particular day, less distance was covered. Such speculation encourages a more involved engagement with Van Horn's text as well as an assertive rather than passive engagement with the landscape that it documents.

The minimal means by which Van Horn documents her extensive walk, and, as Nancy Kuhl suggests, the manner in which the visual record of tallies 'interrupts' the more conventional narrative would suggest 'that the marks and the practice of making them, are at least as important as the straightforward description of the journey' (Kuhl 19). Notably, where Van Horn's record differs most significantly from similar text-works such as Long's aforementioned *Wind Line* is her use of a 'straightforward description of the journey' that works reciprocally with the visual tally strikes (Kuhl 19). Indeed, this use of personal narrative closely aligns *Stiles & The Pennine Way* with what Lorimer calls geography's 'small stories' (Lorimer, 'Telling Small Stories' 197). These 'localized multi-sensual biographies' that focus on 'everyday [...] prosaic, sometimes unglamorous' events, Lorimer suggests, emphasize 'the complex interplay between [...] embodied experiences and the formation of geographical knowledge' (203, 202). According to Lorimer, 'interpretation' of these small stories occurs 'as an active and visceral performance,' in which 'geographical learning [takes] place *amidst* the micro-spaces of [the] body *in* the landscape' and any 'analysis of these actions must respect the modest forms and rhythms that experience often takes' (203, 214).

In *Stiles & The Pennine Way* Van Horn presents the process of a body moving through the landscape and its weather patterns. 'I never did have any great thoughts on the eleven day walk,' she writes: 'The emptying of my mind happened very naturally and lent a certain clarity to the days, and to the sense of distance and time. The counting was just one thing' (n. pag). But in that emptying of mind, to quote one of Thomas A. Clark's aphoristic reflections in his prose-poem 'In Praise of Walking,' 'the least emphatic occurrences are registered clearly' (139). 'A dull walk is not without value,' Clark also proposes, while also insisting that, 'Walking is not so much romantic as reasonable' (139, 138). Both of Clark's statements adumbrate the sentiment of *Stiles & The Pennine Way* and its own dispelling of the loftier, heroic associations of walking with hiking, exploration, and 'profound' Wordsworthian thought.

Clark's suggestion that 'Everything we meet is equally important and unimportant' during a walk is a sentiment that Van Horn's book foregrounds (137). Indeed, Van Horn's 'note book, ready to record the ideas, thoughts, and observations' during her walk creates an apposite passage for the non-figurative record of a small story placed at very centre of *Stiles & The Pennine Way* (*Stiles* n. pag).

Colin Sackett: Type and Place

Colin Sackett, a book artist, designer, and printer based in Axminster, Devon who has worked closely with Coracle since the 1980s and runs Uniformbooks, has also taken 'the phenomena of landscape and its classification' as a central theme of his work (Cutts, *Certain Trees* 100). Geography, in particular, informs Sackett's interest in landscape, especially 'human geography,' as Jim Mays notes: 'the places where the interests of man and nature intersect, or conflict, as distinct from physical geography or political causes associated with geography (climate change, population levels, sustainability)' (para 1). Mays also describes Sackett as 'a writer who makes books like poems but not in verse, an artist who works with the materials of book production rather than oil paint and canvas' (para 7). In this respect, Sackett's approach to the subject of landscape departs significantly from what Cutts describes as the 'intrinsic correspondence between the devices of painting and the imposing scene in front of us [...] as in the tradition and effects of watercolour' ('Notes on the Unpainted Landscape' 9). 'Landscape, in an analytical or theoretical sense, rather than depictively,' Sackett claims, 'is what a major part of [my] work is "about," even when the concern is seemingly about listening, or reading, or *direction*, there is often a place or a type of place that is the basis of a particular work' (*Repetivity* 32).

Sackett's interest in landscape in 'an analytical or theoretical sense' is informed considerably by a long-standing interest in geographical maps and texts books, many of which Sackett first encountered at school. One example of Sackett's interest in this topographical literature are the diagrams and drawings by the geographer Geoffrey Hutchings, a selection of which Sackett presents in *The True Line: The Landscape Diagrams of Geoffrey Hutchings* (2009). 'As drawings,' Sackett remarks of such texts, 'they sought to dispense a particular function, acting as an aid to the understanding and "reading" of the landscape, as opposed to depiction for *artistic* purposes—the brevity of these compositions more like transcription than impression' (*Englshpublshing* 90). In *The True Line*, Sackett emphasizes Hutchings's imagist-like 'direct observation and interpretation of landscape' by enlarging map details, tabular summaries, and specimen transect charts, all of which foreground the interactions between Hutching's handwritten text and his line drawings (v). As Stephen Daniels suggests, in the new context of *The True Line*, 'the astonishingly eloquent style' of Hutchings's work is brought to the fore, so that it 'now seems one of the lost arts' as well as 'model for the pursuit of knowledge [and] technical practice' (630).

According to Daniels, Sackett's work shows a strong 'sense of topographical appreciation' (630). This appreciation, however, is also topological. The latter, as Wylie explains, 'is a form of geographical/ mathematical thinking that conceives space and spatial relations primarily in terms of connective properties rather than distance and position' and 'implies that space and time are not geometric and linear' (203). An unattributed epigraph included in Sackett's book *Geeooggrraapphhy* (2009) reiterates this topological appreciation of landscape in its claim that, 'Landscape is made of names and numbers as much as shapes and lines' (n. pag). This approach to landscape is reaffirmed in the paratextual details of Sackett's work, much of which explores and utilizes the peripheral details of print design, publishing, and book production: indexes, bibliographies, abbreviations, codes, map details, annotated marginalia, and typographical specimens. 'Regional geography,' David Matless notes of Sackett's scrupulous appropriations of geography texts, 'makes for contemporary book art, convention sparking experiment' (18). Indeed, as Mays suggests, didactic geographical literature and functional cartography assume a significant place in Sackett's work, providing ample opportunities for his explorations into 'the nature and limits of the book from a typographer's point of view: testing how books function, the codes they assume and the constraints they impose; how some rules can be ignored with impunity and others can be extended to striking effect' (Mays para 1).

The combination of Sackett's interests in landscape, printing, and book design are evident in *Recto/Verso*, the sixth and final case-bound laser printed booklet comprising his *English Handwriting Models* (1998) and later reprinted in his Coracle book *Englshpublshing* (2004). *Recto/ Verso* takes for its subject the prosaic details of watercress labels; more specifically, the information printed on the front and reverse of those labels. Before presenting a series of examples of the printed information on these rectangular cards, Sackett provides a quote from the publication *Watercress, Production of the Cultivated Crop* (London, 1983): 'The brand name, address and Code of Practice number of the producer should be included on a small rectangular card inserted in the bunch' (*Englshpublshing* 48). As well as adopting these basic stipulations, many of the examples that Sackett presents also provide recommendations for storage, details about the conditions of cultivation, and, occasionally, advertisements for recipe books:

> *26.* Vitacress hygienically grown
> in pure spring water | wash
> thoroughly before use, to store,

> wash, shake off surplus water and
> refrigerate in airtight container.
> For our colour recipe and code
> of practice fact booklet send large
> sae to Vitacress Salads Ltd,
> Fobdown, Arlesford, Hampshire,
> SO24 9TD.
> 27. Supreme watercress |
> cultivated in spring water by A.W.
> & R.W. Biggs, Whitchurch, Hants. (*Englshpublshing* 48)

'Each label—Kingfisher, Lustrecress, Sylvasprings—tethered the cress to a particular and identifiable landscape,' Sackett notes: 'a clay and chalk valley with water from a spring or stream, or raised from boreholes, channeled to flow gently across the wide beds of screeded concrete and gravel' ('Collection' 29) The rectangular form of these labels also reiterates 'the rectilinear forms' of the watercress beds that 'impose upon and contrast with the gentle, rolling topography of the ground,' predominantly in the southern counties of Hampshire, Wiltshire, and Dorset where the conditions are conducive for cultivation ('Collection' 29).

In *Recto/Verso* the topographical landscape is replaced by the topological one of the labels—the '"printed landscapes"' that make 'it possible to identify and connect similarity and likeness; the diversity of layouts and colour [...] gathered and fixed to the activity and geography of their time' ('Collection' 29–30). These '"textual depictions" of the landscape particular to each label' not only map a topology of spatial relations and proximities via 'repetitive statements of conditions,' but they also indicate a topography and, to recall Mabey, a disappearing unofficial landscape (*Englshpublshing* 48). As Sackett observes, 'in the last ten years such labels have disappeared, along with the rubber band, as the packaging of watercress has changed almost entirely to sealed plastic bags, chilled and lose, and kept fresh at fridge temperature' ('Collection' 29). These increasingly obsolete labels are commensurate with the changing landscape that they parallel: 'As with much cultivation, larger sites have been developed and many smaller farms have given up or been absorbed, the number of growers declining in response to the exacting demands of the centralised market' ('Collection' 29). Whatever changes may have happened to these unusual landscapes, their textual counterparts remain as a poignant reminder of their former existence.

The use of found texts in *Recto/Verso* obliquely reflects Sackett's early interest in Kurt Schwitters and Dada that, with sound poetry and his subsequent discovery of Finlay in the mid-1970s, has informed Sackett's work. As he explains to Cathy Courtney in an interview for *Art Monthly*:

I didn't have a visual arts background but I'd been interested in Schwitters since I was at school and I'd read a lot about Dada. I didn't think Finlay had anything to do with that although I later found that concrete poetry perhaps had a legacy from Dada. There were catalogues of Finlay's which showed his early 60s work and I began to understand the work I was seeing in the 70s and saw the relation to Schwitters and the sound poetry. ('Bibliopoly' n. pag)

The influence of concrete poetry is especially evident in what Cutts describes as Sackett's sustained 'investigation of print-form and reading, disintegration, continuity and re-formation' (*Certain Trees* 11). The suggestion of concrete poetry is especially evident in *Aggregate* (Figure 7), the superimposed type of which bares certain resemblance to Heinz Gappmayr's 'sind' (1964). Whereas Gappmayr's text repeats, overlays, and distorts the word 'sind' (the 'first and third person plural present indicative of *sein*, to be') in a dense palimpsest of iteration, *Aggregate* superimposes the terms and abbreviations derived 'from the map of a suburban area measuring ten by ten kilometres ("TQ26, Ordnance Survey 1:25000 second series") in the form of a lexical map, index, and commentary' (Gappmayr 112–113; *Englshpublshing* 23).[50]

Figure 7.
Colin Sackett,
Aggregate, London,
1992/1994.

---

50   The original 1992 edition comprised a 120-page photocopied cloth-covered, case-bound, and slip-cased book that reproduced each of the squares of the ten by ten kilometre range on an individual page.

In his interview with Courtney, Sackett explains how he 'took all the language, but none of the topography or roads, and superimposed the 100 territories':

> All the locations remain in their fixed positions within each square, but their particular relationships are lost. In the suburbs one understands the geography of the local area by the inter-relationships between human landmarks like schools and parks rather than topographical features. ('Bibliopoly' n. pag)

Stephen Bann suggests that in the work of the first-generation concrete poets 'the references to nature are never *specific*': the poet 'may draw his imagery from nature' but he 'does not make us aware of the backcloth beyond the poem' ('A Context for Concrete Poetry' 145). *Aggregate*, by comparison, is very much about a specific human landscape and the 'backcloth' of its mapping. So much so, in fact, that *Aggregate* conflates topology, topography, and typography in its mapping of 'a hundred square kilometres that are part of the London Boroughs of Sutton, Merton and Croydon,' where Sackett grew up (*Englshpublshing* 22). 'It includes the schools, parks, libraries, etc., I went to,' Sackett writes, perhaps making a conscious pun with his use of the italic, 'and the *type* of place, with which I was most familiar with during my first twenty years' (*Englshpublshing* 22).

Thus, understood as a noun, *Aggregate* is concerned with how place is constructed by the aggregation of many individual sites into one collective whole that ultimately constitutes 'a particular *mental* geography of the suburbs' (*Englshpublshing* 22, emphasis added). 'There seemed to me to be specific ideas of connectedness,' Sackett explains, 'a psychological understanding of the way one location is related to another' (*Englshpublshing* 22). *Aggregate* might therefore also be read as a verb, with Sackett's lexical map forming its own aggregate of locational terms that, via the superimpositions, truncations, and abbreviations of its text, presents an 'accumulative interference' that isolates 'each locational term from relationships within its own territory' (*Englshpublshing* 22). Abbreviated terms for designating allotments ('Allot Gdns'), schools ('Sch'), hospitals ('Hospl'), and recreation grounds ('Recn Gd') are aggregated and superimposed over industrial estates, golf courses, farms, nurseries, and sewage works. The result is a palimpsest in which certain words and abbreviations are clearly discernible while others are barely legible due to the dense proximities and contiguities of the map's more built-up areas. This ambiguity of proximity is further emphasized by a series of unaccounted for letters and terms in both the index and the map, such as 'K,' 'BP,' 'rts und,' and 'sc,' all of which enhance the topological dimension of *Aggregate* and reiterate the idea that landscape is constructed as much from 'names and numbers' as it is 'shapes and lines.'

Indeed, all of the typographic elements in *Aggregate* are integral to the 'largely hypothetical ideas of orientation in landscape [that] were provoked by being in this place' and which, according to Sackett, has the effect of 'a sort of historical and acoustical "depth" in the place, a pre-electrical *radio* of invisible/inaudible sound' (*Englshpublshing* 22). Thus, despite the strong visual impression of *Aggregate*, its mapping of 'acoustical "depth"' also recalls Sackett's early interest in sound poetry, constructing a mental geography of the suburbs that conflates illegibility and invisibility with inaudibility and silence. This is especially apparent in the way *Aggregate* also maps an *invisible* '"wild" [...] island within the suburban' which is manifested between the type and in the white lacunae of the page (*Englshpublshing* 22):

> One part of this suburban landscape seemed anomalous, its 'identity' could be perceived as an 'inverted wilderness': a large flat area bordering Mitcham, Carshalton, Croydon and Wallington—a square mile or so—of officially private common-type land, gravel pits and ex-sewage workings. There is a network of paths and the whole area is fenced-off unofficial access is available about every few hundred yards). The area is used for riding motorbikes, rabbiting, watching birds, etc.; that is, marginal activities. (*Englshpublshing* 22)

Where, however, in *Aggregate*'s palimpsest of locations and landmarks can this 'inverted wilderness' be located? One assumes in one of the many blank spaces (wild islands) that punctuate the dense typo/topology of Sackett's text. If this is the case, then *Aggregate* adumbrates Shoard's observation that such 'areas are so little acknowledged that they have not even been given distinctive names' and 'in our imaginations, as opposed to our actual lives,' barely exist (117).

Martin Dodge, in his consideration of the 'deeply typographic enterprise' of topographic mapping, believes that 'textual absences' can, inversely, 'render areas silenced on the map, and demonstrate most clearly how cartographic practice is not an instrumental mirror of territorial truth but is actively constitutive in the ongoing creation of geographical imaginaries' (n. pag). Such typographic omissions add a new textual slant to what J. B. Harley describes as the power of cartographic process:

> By this I mean the way maps are compiled and the categories of information selected; the way they are generalized, a set of rules for the abstraction of the landscape; the way the elements in the landscape are formed into hierarchies; and

the way various rhetorical styles that also reproduce power are employed to represent the landscape. To catalogue the world is to appropriate it, so that all these technical processes represent acts of control over its image which extend beyond the professed uses of cartography. The world is disciplined. The world is normalized. (245)

To this catalogue of control and power might be added cartography's propensity to officiate certain landscapes at the neglect of others. The 'inverted wilderness' of *Aggregate* and the 'feeling of detachment and in effect, *invisibility*' that this anomalous suburban no-man's land elicits is perhaps a result of such hierarchical nomination (*Englshpublshing* 22). Indeed, *Aggregate* exemplifies how maps, as Doreen Massey explains, have the potential to 'disrupt the sense of coherence and totality' (rather than 'tame confusion and complexity') of conventional cartography (109). In exposing the 'incoherencies and fragmentations of the spatial'— which, in the case of *Aggregate*, is done so via the illegible/inaudible aggregate of words and letters—and in locating fecund lacunae within such fragmentations, Sackett's text can be read as 'a map (and a space) which leaves openings for something new' (Massey 109).

Stephen Duncalf: Suburban Fauve

The kind of unofficial landscape encountered in Sackett's *Aggregate* is also a primary subject for Stephen Duncalf, an artist originally from Nottingham, who who became acquainted with Cutts while both were students at Nottingham College of Art. Like his Nottingham peers, Duncalf's work has encompassed painting, drawing, constructed objects, poetry and prose. Throughout the 1970s he worked closely with both Coracle and Ian Hamilton Finlay who, John Bevis claims, once 'nominate[d] Duncalf as his favourite artist' ('Stephen Duncalf' 2).

Finlay's endorsement is not surprising considering the affinities they share, particularly their regard for the small scale and their use of the prosaic, mundane, and everyday as the subject matter of their work. Furthermore, Finlay no doubt would have found in Duncalf's abstract wooden constructions such as *Tunnel* (1978) certain echoes of the wooden models and toys that he constructed in the early 1960s during his transitional move to concrete poetry.[51]

---

51 'In the area of poetry,' Finlay explains, 'I felt an absolute need to turn from the rhythmic to the Static, and as I was unable to explain this to myself, and knew no one who could explain it to me, (or who had the faintest inkling of the feeling I was talking about), I had to find such temporary solutions as I could, and turned to making little toys—things of no account in themselves, yet true to my inspiration, which was away from Syntax towards "the Pure"' (cited in 'Ian Hamilton Finlay,' *The Tate Gallery* 92).

'Duncalf's objects lie between their dislocated narrative and the material presence of their construction, and at times occupy the margins of painting itself,' Cutts suggests: 'There were always written pieces to accompany and exist alongside the objects, and books were made at home on his table; the domestic scale of his activities was always conducive to publication' (*Certain Trees* 58). Furthermore, the prosaic subjects of Duncalf's work—which include railways and their scale-model equivalents, allotments, and domestic dwellings—not only extend the 'proper subjects' for poetry advocated in *Tarasque* but 'the domestic scale of his activities' align Duncalf very much with the small press publishing ethos examined in *Avant-Folk*. Indeed, in addition to publishing his own City Gardens Press publications, Duncalf took the DIY ethos to its logical extreme by painting on hardboard salvaged from skips and, in the case of his installation at the Coracle gallery in Camberwell, constructing a mock-up of Edward Hopper's painting *Seven A.M.* (1948) out of hardboard, scrap, and metal. The model-maker's inclination for rendering the smallest of details is evident in Duncalf's faithful replication of Hopper's signature on the gallery's doorstep.

Duncalf's reconstruction of Hopper's *Seven A.M.* is essentially an extension of the 'model railway and battlefield layouts' that he constructed out of the remnants of domestic objects and other found material (Bevis, 'Stephen Duncalf' 3). What might be considered nothing more than a hobby, in Duncalf's work, assumes wider significance, as an untitled prose-poem included in his Coracle booklet *Good Hoofs* (1976) indicates:[52]

> A rusty slab lies upon the landscape,
> whose field is a woodcut with bales of
> black, painted by the sky and threaten-
> ed by its thunder, whose corner of ink
> will turn chalk-grey when the cloud
> moves in. Beneath this manoeuvre, a
> moss track is thrown into a most unu-
> sual but damned nice light, a shaft of
> which has settled upon the points,
> lever and telegraph of a small-gauge
> railway, whose cardboard trucks have
> been made soggy by the closeness of
> the wet hedge which has grown new
> match-heads, unstruck and smart
> against the grubby, burnt ends of
> last winter. In the centre of the
> rusty slab, a small glinting square

---

52 The significance of Duncalf's model-making activities being more than a hobby is compounded by the fact that 'To earn money [Duncalf] painted and finished toy soldiers' (Cutts, *Certain Trees* 58).

> appears, namely, the opening of a
> skylight.   (n. pag)

Like Cutts in 'As for verse,' Duncalf's poem conflates 'reality' and 'artifice' and draws attention to their dialectic relationship. Here a familiar nondescript landscape ambiguously blurs into the domestic milieu of its scaled equivalent, the model railway. The 'real' weather of the outside world, via the attic's skylight window illuminates and animates the model's artificial landscape, throwing the moss-covered track 'into a most unu-/sual but damned nice light' which affects the colour of the woodcut field. Natural phenomena, however, also invert the distinctions that normally demarcate the natural from the artificial. What one assumes is a real 'wet hedge' is, in fact, a model one that has, presumably, been wetted by rainwater from the open skylight window. (Such dampness might perhaps mean that the 'moss track' is also real.) And, despite being an inorganic object, the artificial hedge has nevertheless 'grown' new buds in the form of un-struck match-heads. By evoking the flaming colours of flowers, seasonal mutability is suggested on a domestic scale by way of 'the grubby, burnt ends' of last winter's matches which, like 'real' flowers at the end of their flowering period, are spent and extinguished. Mediating these two realms is the rusty slab, which not only provides part of the model's landscape but, by sitting anomalously *upon* it, is also *reflective* of the world outside. In this respect, Duncalf's poem is an effective example, as Bevis suggests, of how 'his work testifies [to the] possibility of the ideal – or model – synthesis' (*Ducts & Tracts* dust jacket). The scale model, however, is not an exact replication, or representation, of 'real life' but its proportioned equivalent that stands apart from it. And, very much like Finlay's 'Fauve' poems, the material in *Good Hoofs* might be likewise considered as 'constructions arising from life, but not pretending to BE life' (Finlay, cited in Weaver 13).

In 1991 Coracle published *Ducts & Tracts*, a selection of Duncalf's notebooks that offer further insight into his interests and working methods. Just as Finlay's 'proper subjects' counter the 'near-epic' pretensions of contemporary poetry, the subjects of Duncalf's paintings, as *Ducts & Tracts* reveal, oppose the prevailing values, trends, and attitudes of the art world. '*They are looking for an art / which is big and serious,*' Duncalf writes (one assumes approvingly) in one entry, attributing the quote to 'J.M.' (n. pag, original emphasis).

Duncalf's ultimate gesture to the 'big and serious' art world, however, would come in the form of a statement in 1999 that renounced his involvement with 'Art':

> With a view to much needed refreshment and change—next
> year, and for the foreseeable future, I will cease to make work,

or concern myself with Art and all its associations. The time is well nigh to pause, reflect, and to re-assess. (Cited in Bevis, 'Stephen Duncalf' 5)

Unfortunately, Duncalf has remained true to his word and achieved a self-effacing anonymity that surpasses even that of Niedecker.

Before his self-removal from the 'Art' world, however, Duncalf found an alternative to the 'big and serious' in what Bevis describes as the 'blue threads picked from our cultural margins: cabbage patch, branch line, corporation tip. Those no-man's-lands where nature is stalemate with industry' (*Duct & Tracts* jacket note). To a certain extent, Duncalf's fascination with such invisible landscapes recall Sinclair in *London Orbital* who similarly acknowledges the 'mountains of landfill,' 'Overgrown paths, turf islands' and 'Industrial ghosts' of London's no-man's lands (46, 49, 51). However, whereas Sinclair attempts 'an articulation of the specifics of named territories' in *London Orbital* (and usually with at least one travelling companion), the territories encountered in Duncalf's work are nondescript to the point of anonymity and bereft of human presence (Sinclair, 'Introduction' 12).

Indeed, it is difficult to tell from his work that Duncalf, from the late 1970s to the early 1980s, lived in Victoria Rise, Clapham before relocating to Whalley Range in Manchester in the mid-1980s. Names, regions, localities are rarely disclosed, which makes the terrains in question even more enigmatic and uncanny. Recalling the same sorts of territory that Sackett maps in *Aggregate*, Duncalf's work evokes invisible, unofficial spaces, those 'parts of the landscape,' as Bevis notes, 'that have no correspondence, even no identity, reaching out from the hinterland of the allotment, the cabbage patch or railway cutting to unclaimed tracts beyond':

> Looking to the perimeters of some of these, we are aslant to the natural world in a place of almost nothingness, where shape and colour flare unabated. Long before the advent of the Sunday psychogeographer, Duncalf showed us a suburban netherworld of places unclaimed by the glamours of either crowd or wilderness, discounted through the simple agencies of anonymity, oversight, and absence of history. ('Stephen Duncalf' 2–4)

Whereas a writer such as Mabey still adheres to a hierarchy of place—'The habitats I've described in this book are in no way a substitute for the official countryside,' he writes in *The Unofficial Countryside*: 'The last thing I want to do is excuse the dereliction, the shoddiness and the sheer wastefulness of much of our urban landscape'—Duncalf's excursions in such landscapes are made without judgement or recourse to an official standard of value (22).

Considering the vivid colourful 'flare' of Duncalf's paintings, it is perhaps not surprising that Duncalf has been dubbed 'the Suburban Fauvist.' Both Duncalf's watercolours and his oil paintings are characterized by a use of bold primary colours, expressive brushwork, and simplified, abstracted forms, which give a vibrancy to the most mundane subjects (such as caravans and the exposed interior of abandoned houses), recalling Derain or Matisse. However, the juxtaposition of wildness with the tameness of suburbia might make the 'Fauve' tag paradoxical. Nevertheless, 'the thematic ripeness of suburbia' that pervades Duncalf's work does have a tang of the feral to it. In the broader spirit of Coracle, as previously noted by Bevis, this subverts any suggestion of 'suburban complacency.' Indeed, Duncalf's feral environs are far from comforting, as his prose-piece 'Deuteronomy' demonstrates which transposes Moses's wanderings in the wilderness to suburbia's edgelands:

> On a walk, between pond, hedge, and valley, I came upon a region of cess, and was entangled in some rattling old cushion-wire and other household effects discarded in the bracken. Where a waterfall once channelled out the clay, now a murky furrow breathed fog. ('Deuteronomy' n.pag, original emphasis)

The once-green world of pond, hedge, valley, bracken, and waterfall gives way to a polluted midden ('cess') and a wilderness of fly-tipped detritus in which the narrator becomes disoriented amidst a *'tumbled-down chimney stack,'* a *'mossy television,'* and *'an old Ford'* car (n. pag, original emphasis). Although the narrator eventually emerges from this material slough *'to begin a new life, collecting and cutting wood,'* Duncalf would continue to find the raw material of his work in such dereliction and abandonment (n. pag, original emphasis).

Ducts & Tracts, for example, reads as a congeries of sketches, observations, and ideas for projects that stem largely from the forsaken, decaying, discarded leftovers of suburbia. Notes include observations on the *'usual suburbia of the discarded-training shoe and hideous- / cadillac-driven-onto-a-garden'* and 'A TIPS ALPHABET' that begins with *'Ash, Asbestos'* and concludes at W with *'Window Frames, Wire, Wing-mirrors, Wheels'* (n. pag, original emphasis). It is in such lost and marginal no-man's lands that Duncalf finds his alternative to the *'big and serious'* landscapes of more traditional painting.

Another entry records a May walk:

> Yesterday, after the rain, caught in a half-light of thunderous wedgewood [sic] between the library and the post box. I sorted out a new route through suburbia, ending up at a strange   of semi-detached abandon.

I needed the walk, the mileage, the release—charged with blossom, with green. I returned to my work somewhat sadly but after 10 minutes plunged into a particularly potent tract of landscape painting. (n. pag, original emphasis)

'Puns, ambiguities, and other tropes,' as Bevis suggests, are prominent in Duncalf's writing, including this entry in *Ducts & Tracts* ('Stephen Duncalf' 2). Duncalf's use of the word 'tract,' for example, in this particular context utilizes ambiguity to considerable advantage, suggesting either a written work treating of a specific topic (for example, painting a landscape with words) as well as duration of time and a space or an expanse of land. All of these meanings seem equally plausible in Duncalf's sentence. Ambiguity is also evident in the text's anomalous lacuna that subverts the surrounding syntax. It is possible that Duncalf's speaker has arrived at a place of semi-detached abandon (perhaps a derelict semi-detached house). Alternatively, the walk itself might have invoked in the speaker a mood of 'semi-detached abandon,' although whether this emotive 'abandon' is positive or negative remains unclear. Such ambiguity nevertheless reiterates the sense of detachment and disinterest that Duncalf expresses toward his suburban environs in his visual work and in his writing.

Duncalf's journal entry also recalls how distinctions between topographical features, natural phenomena, and manmade objects frequently blur in the landscapes that he presents. This is implicit in the way that Duncalf describes the impression of the meteorological phenomena of a storm's after-effects in the context of the characeristic blue colour of Wedgwood ceramic ware. However, even when 'charged with blossom and green,' the landscapes that catch Duncalf's eyes fuse with, and manifest in, its man-made objects:

But even in the windows of great warehouses there is the occasional landscape. Sometimes the damp on a lintel forms a patch of figurative significance, or between the bars of an old structure, polythene flaps and catches the gleam of winter sunlight. (n. pag, original emphasis)

These '*occasional*' landscapes subvert the 'aestheticization of landscape' that Alison Byerly finds so problematic in the cult of the picturesque because of the way it fixes and idealizes the landscape as 'a legitimate object of artistic consumption' (53). 'An artwork,' according to Byerly, 'remains fixed, presenting the same face of succeeding generations, though interpretation of it may differ, a living ecosystem, however, cannot achieve this stasis' (54). Similarly, Shoard has noted how 'English people like to see diverse but calm landscapes in which various elements are arranged in an orderly manner considered picturesque' (120). By contrast, Shoard reasons, interfacial landscapes embody the 'naked function' of their environments, display 'the detritus of modern life,' and often appear 'raw and rough [...] somber and menacing, flaunting their participation in activities we do not wholly understand' (121). Far from fixing his interfacial environments into static representations, Duncalf depicts them in an ambiguous '*half-light*' that blurs any clear distinction between the human and non-human, the organic and artificial, or the domestic and the world beyond it.

Thus, Duncalf's landscape 'tracts' are properly 'interfacial' in the sense of being the meeting-point or common ground between two or more different phenomena. 'Duncalf's work ethic is perhaps that ambiguity is itself a springboard for imaginative leaps,' Bevis proposes: 'We find it in his finished works, in paintings which might be sculptures, of steamtrains that might be topiary, and flags which might be battle-fields' (*Ducts & Tracts* dust jacket). If landscape is 'an ordering of reality from different angles,' as Yi-Fu Tuan proposes, then Duncalf's work repeatedly dissembles and disorders those angles into unsettling and uncanny reliefs which 'lead into a time, a place, a sensibility' that speaks most eloquently for the imaginative and topographical vibrancy of suburbia's enigmatic edgelands ('Thought and Landscape' 90; Bevis, *Ducts & Tracts* dust jacket).

The Allotment

Of all the 'unofficial' landscapes with which Coracle has engaged, the allotment stands out significantly. Why the allotment should be partic-ularly relevant to the Coracle ethos is partly explained by David Crouch and Colin Ward's assessment of its marginal status, both culturally and topographically, which they claim is a consequence of allotments being frequently 'located in awkward corners, unattractive areas or steep land, or sites vulnerable to flooding' as well as 'roundabouts, along railway lines and in triangles adjacent to factories, on land not earmarked for other uses' (190, 191). DeSilvey reiterates the tacit edgeland status of allotments, describing them as 'interstitial' 'third spaces' in which familiar dichotomies are collapsed:

> Because allotments fail to conform to conventional discourses of municipal recreation and leisure, they often occupy an interstitial space where no one will claim full responsibility for them. Allotments can be thought of as 'third spaces', where static dichotomies—private and public, production and consumption, labour and leisure—break down into tangled contingencies. ('Cultivated Histories' 444)

Thus, the allotment, Crouch and Ward claim, symbolizes an 'unofficial horticulture' that evades and contradicts 'administrative conception[s] of the landscape' which tend to polarize it as either rural or urban

(271). Furthermore, as a communal and functional space, the allotment contrasts with the private garden, 'fail[ing] to conform to the leisure industry's conception of passive leisure and, in the wider landscape, to the ideal of private, individualized space, provided, constructed and clearly demarcated in the form of house-and-garden' (Crouch and Ward 272). Consequently, as Crouch and Ward insist, the allotment signifies 'a different kind of place in which different values prevail' and is 'loaded with assumptions, attitudes and experiences that bring us back to into our own culture, whether or not we are plot holders (272, 5).

It is therefore perhaps not surprising that the 'allotment *idea*,' particularly the stereotypical ideas of its 'culture [which] is seen as odd, a bit funny or eccentric, the last of the summer wine, prize leeks, pigeons, and a messy use of materials that has not caught up with the DIY superstores,' has proven to be a popular subject for Coracle, especially Duncalf (Crouch and Ward 5). As a 'cabbage patch vorticist,' Duncalf has frequently, to quote one of *Blast*'s manifestos, made 'New Living Abstraction[s]' out of the material forms of the allotment and its culture (Bevis, 'A Star-gazey Pie' 60; Lewis 147). Vegetable plots, scarecrows, shed structures, trellises, and wheelbarrows are particularly prominent in Duncalf's booklet of line drawings *Huts By-way Engine Orchard*, published by Coracle in 1977.

Figure 8. Stephen Duncalf, *Huts By-way Engine Orchard*, Coracle, 1977.

In Duncalf's drawing *Orchard* (Figure 8), some of the allotment's most familiar human objects—wheelbarrow, scarecrow, ladder, spade, and shed—commingle with and metamorphose into the plot's organic forms. The geometric lines of a ladder blur with those of a wheelbarrow before both dissolve into the foliage of an apple tree and hedge whose organic shapes are repeated in the scattering of cabbages in the soil below. Duncalf repeats the regular geometric lines of the wheelbarrow and ladder in other man-made forms: a spade sunk into the wavy lines of the soil, the parallel lines of an adjacent path, and the angular profile of a distant building. Situated incongruously between these two poles—the constructed and the organic—is a scarecrow whose clothes repeat the informal shapes of the allotment's foliage but whose posture reiterates the vertical and horizontal forms of the various garden tools.

The formal ambiguities and tensions in Duncalf's drawings reflect the intrinsic no-man's-land qualities of the allotment, which are as much cultural as topographic. Recalling 'the entanglements—the invisible hyphens—between nature and culture, human and nonhuman,' that Harrison, Pile, and Thrift advocate in their non-representational approach to landscape, Crouch and Ward believe that the allotment, as 'an essentially peopled landscape,' sits 'somewhere between the city and the country yet representing neither contemporary projected landscapes' and 'fall[s] between being a public and private landscape in a way that few others do' (209). It is perhaps this *'awkwardness* of the allotment'—that it is not deemed 'desirable or exciting in the consumer city, not part of the mainstream of modern life, not pleasant in its associations with frugality and improvisation'—that aligns it most pertinently with Coracle, whose relationship with the materialism of the contemporary art world expresses an equivalent and deliberate *awkwardness* (Crouch and Ward 4). There is also an echo of Coracle's concern for 'unpainted landscapes' in Crouch's and Ward's suggestion that the allotment 'breaks the rules [and] fails to comply with the accepted image' of the picturesque or aesthetically pleasing landscape (15). According to Cosgrove, landscape traditionally 'distances us from the world in critical ways, defining a particular relationship with nature and those who appear in nature,' and promotes 'an aesthetic entrance not an active engagement with a nature or space that has its own life' ('Prospect' 55). By comparison, the allotment provokes a more intimate, lateral relationship with the land:

> The Allotment is a metaphor itself, about working the land, holding onto the ground, being close to the earth, about caring, about contesting space we cultivate, sharing space with other people, and about ways of making movement through which we construct our knowledge of the world around us. (Crouch and Ward xi)

Therefore, the allotment is both a prime site and a fecund trope for the embodied engagements with landscape that Crouch calls 'grounded performance' and 'a tangle in the mundane' (cited in Wylie 168). These entangled performances are particularly apparent in the do-it-yourself ethos and artistic licence exercised by 'plot-holders [who] create *their* own landscape[s]' (Crouch and Ward 187). The corrugated iron and plastic, reclaimed doors and tyres, and ad-hoc sheds that typically characterize plots make the allotment a kind of *Merzbau* borne out of a resourceful need that, nevertheless, permits creative flair and encourages what Crouch and Ward describe as an 'untamed collective individualism' (193).

Such qualities make the allotment a prime metaphor for Coracle's spirit of cooperation and non-conformity as well as its aesthetic. Ray Garner's description of the allotment aesthetic as one of 'unrestrained simplicity,' 'understatement' and 'design with room to breathe,' certainly strikes a note with Cutts's 'slightness of key' and his regard for 'the poetic every day' (cited in Crouch and Ward 192). Similarly, Crouch and Ward's claim that to have an allotment plot 'is to work with simple objects [whose] significance in the lives of the plotters is often very big,' also reaffirms Coracle's commitment to the small scale (viii). Above all, however, it is perhaps the unconventionality of the allotment that makes it such an appropriate metaphor for the Coracle ethos.

According to Crouch and Ward, the allotment 'does not fit into acceptable categories and the official landscape, nor does it possess the criteria of recognised design and position in culture that would make it respectable' (209). A similar spirit of non-conformity informs Stuart Mills's assessment of Coracle:

> It is not eccentricity that puts Coracle Press apart from, and widely ignored by, the Literary and Art Establishments in the country, for the English always have time for their eccentrics. It is the unconventional that makes them sweat, particularly when someone oversteps the mark in the full knowledge of where the mark is. ('Coracle' 14)

By drawing attention to the contingent 'marks' that circumscribe established categories and criteria, Coracle is not just an idiosyncratic or eccentric enterprise, but also a subversive one that has repeatedly challenged convention. As Mills notes, to 'know that the mark is merely chalk dust' which 'can be blown away,' makes an endeavour such as Coracle not only unrespectable but also a threat ('Coracle' 14). Like the marginal status of the allotment, the subversive Englishness of Coracle gives it a considerable critical edge that prompts incisive reflection on what is culturally and aesthetically centralized and uniform.

Renshaw Hall

The allotment also figures significantly in Coracle's unpainted landscapes due to its 'proletarian' origins as 'a working-class' and 'productive landscape' borne from 'conditions of need and poverty' (Crouch and Ward 15, 190). The 'working-class agitation' of the allotment finds a striking equivalent in 'Allotment' project that Coracle organized in the short-lived Renshaw Hall gallery space in Liverpool in the late 1980s (Crouch and Ward 18). In 1986, feeling increasingly disillusioned with the art world, Coracle sold its original Camberwell base and became even more marginal to the London-centric art establishment. 'It seemed appropriate,' Sackett writes, 'to politicise the project's location and thus to de-centralise from London' ('Allotment' 75). Liverpool was an appealing location because of its 'unique and imbalanced mixture of decay and new development,' and because of the city's orientation, looking 'away from the rest of the country' (Sackett, 'Allotment' 75). This new, outward-facing perspective was also reflected in the name change from Coracle to 'Coracle Atlantic Foundation' that, like Jargon before it, was partly done in order to make it eligible for funding. The new moniker, as Bevis observes, was 'Coracle working on a grand scale and with a grand title' ('A Star-gazey Pie' 57). The grand title was reciprocated in the 'grand' premises of Renshaw Hall, a large warehouse-sized building situated on three streets—Renshaw Street, Benson Street, and Oldham Place—in the centre of the city.

Renshaw Hall had served as a postal sorting office, a dance hall, an army recruitment centre, and, up until 1984, an employment office. The building's history was an important part of its appeal, as Sackett explains:

> The identity of Renshaw Hall in local history is strongly linked to its recent use as the central dole office; most people we met in the city had signed-on at the building, its reputation based on a memory of tragedy and comedy. ('Allotment' 78)

The location of Renshaw Hall was another attractive factor. As well as 'not [being] evident from the street, surrounded as it is by terraced shops and houses,' the locality of Renshaw Hall 'separated [it] geographically, psychologically and economically from the rest of the city,' making it 'already isolated and "special"' ('Allotment' 75).

The name 'Allotment,' Sackett recalls, was prompted by the 'idea of using a system of moveable and adaptive site huts [which] seemed the most appropriate and cost-effective method of locating specific positions on the floor when several activities were occurring simultaneously' ('Allotment' 79). According to Sackett, it was the 'legal term rather than the evocative suburban term' that prompted the name 'Allotment,' as 'the idea of allocating the space or part of the space to an artist or group of artists seemed an exact definition of a future working structure' ('Allotment' 79). The 'cavernous space' of Renshaw Hall, Bevis explains, 'a turbine hall of the north,' also had the 'potential for siting the single, gob-smacking grand oeuvre' which, in 1987, was 'perfectly realized in the first [and last] exhibition': Richard Long's *Stone Field*, a solid rectangular installation measuring 37 × 20 metres and comprising 70 tons of processed white 40 mm limestone chippings, sourced from a quarry in North Wales ('A Star-gazey Pie' 59).

Despite the grand scale of Renshaw Hall (which now serves as a car park) and Long's massive installation, Coracle Atlantic Foundation continued to adhere to the values of scale and 'slightness' that characterized its earlier incarnation. Indeed, in many respects, Allotment brings together a number of prominent themes and ideas that underscore Coracle, particularly in terms of its innovative approach to the concept of the edited space and the related practice of small press publishing.

What is immediately apparent with Allotment is that Renshaw Hall was not simply a convenient site to accommodate a pre-existing piece of art but, rather, an object of aesthetic significance and possibility in its own right. According to Sackett, 'the emptying of the space,' at Renshaw Hall 'was central to the potential that we began to envisage' (78). Thus, the choice of Richard Long as the first exhibitor at Renshaw Hall was based partly on 'his use of visually homogenising materials [that] would highlight the physicality of the building' ('Allotment' 79).[53] 'The last point was important in the inaugural project,' Sackett stresses, 'because the positive activity of emptying the space indicated a level of collaboration with the artist' (79). In this respect, Renshaw Hall exemplifies on a large industrial scale the qualities that Thomas A. Clark attributes to the gallery:

> If the gallery is not just a place to present work (or to exploit it) but is respected as a space with its own discretions and possibilities, then the chances of an innovative use of space are more likely. How light enters a room, for instance, its shifts and moods throughout the day can be of constantly changing interest. ('The Gallery and the Book' 70)

It is not difficult to imagine the effect that the shifting light, cast through Renshaw Hall's series of high windows and skylights, would

---

53 This regard for the unique properties of a specific space was, for Coracle, a concern from the very beginning. What Kay Roberts describes as the unique 'adaptable and accommodating' space of the gallery, bookshop and living quarters at 233 Camberwell New Road, Trevor Winkfield remembers as constituting as 'much an environmental experience as a Schwitters Merzbarn' (Roberts 9; Winkfield 7).

have had, illuminating Long's white rectangular field of limestone, especially when set against the industrial backdrop of its cavernous steel truss roof and girders, its peeling paint, and exposed brickwork. Indeed, the poster designed by Sackett for *Stone Field* goes some way in conveying these interactions of light, space, and installation. 'From a high viewpoint,' Bann remarks of Sackett's poster, 'we look down on the incredible prospect of receding stones, which endows the literal space of the warehouse with a powerfully symbolic character' ('Coracle's Concrete Thinking' 55).

As well as endowing 'symbolic character,' *Stone Field* and the material that comprises it might also be seen as establishing a dialectical relationship with the physical space of Renshaw Hall. In this respect, *Stone Field* reiterates Long's earlier claim (made in 1980) that: 'The creation in my art is not the common forms—circles, lines—I use, but the places I choose to put them in' (19). Clark makes a similar claim for the place that a work occupies in his suggestion that 'the clarity of the work order[s] the space around it'—perhaps as the jar in Wallace Stevens's 'Anecdote of the Jar' orders the wilderness surrounding it ('The Gallery and the Book' 71).

The relationship that *Stone Field* maintains with its environment is something that Ian Hunter noted in his review of the exhibition for *Artspool* in 1987. Hunter considers *Stone Field* to be 'something of a departure' for Long because of the way it blurred the two familiar modes of his work: the landscape works which Long made 'in far-off and usual locations' and which can be 'seen mainly as photographic records in galleries or publications,' and Long's 'gallery-based works [that] while having obvious landscape references, tend to rely upon the architectural structure of the space for some of their structure and meaning' (cited in Sackett, 'Allotment' 81). By comparison, Hunter proposes, *Stone Field* fits neither of these modes:

> *Stone Field* seems to be both: that is, an essentially landscape work, obviously indoors, but functioning both within and outside the architectural context. For example, the perspective and eye-level orientations seem to operate within the kind of phenomenon one associated with the outdoors. One almost senses the curvature of the earth or the earth's influence when looking at it. (Cited in Sackett, 'Allotment' 81)

As a 'landscape work' *Stone Field* negates the kind of perspectives and power dynamics that Creswell and others have found so problematic in traditional representations of landscape. Long's 'landscape,' as Hunter notes, 'can only be experienced by physically moving over or alongside it and over a period of time' (81). As a result, *Stone Field* negates the possibility of adopting a fixed and dominating perspective and instead encourages an embodied act of landscaping that occurs through an interaction and engagement with the unique physical space of Renshaw Hall.

Considering its considerable size and its large-scale material construction, it might seem strange to compare *Stone Field* with Coracle's small malleable booklets. Yet, Cutts considers *Allotment* 'an advanced form of publication': 'As the space of the page is allotted editorially to a writer or artist, so too could the more material, physical space of a building' (Cutts, *The Coracle*, jacket notes). Echoing Cutts's claim, Bann notes that 'the book can be a spatial invention, just as the installation can be a text' ('Coracle's Concrete Thinking' 55). *Stone Field* corroborates the claims made by Cutts and Bann by tacitly reiterating many of the qualities and production methods associated with small press publishing.

As Clark suggests, 'the freshness and idealism, the disinterestedness and tact that we may find applied to the orchestration of space in a gallery, is characteristic of the whole enterprise of artists' books' that Coracle have published, including Long's palm-sized accordion booklet *A Walk Past Standing Stones* (1978), and the simple, unpretentious hardbound books *Twelve Works* (1981), and *Sixteen Works* (1982) ('The Gallery and the Book' 73). The latter two, Clark notes, are 'characteristically restrained and workmanlike,' possessing an 'austerity [in which] there is considerable variety and movement' ('The Gallery and the Book' 72). The workman-like quality noted by Clark finds a pertinent equivalent in the manual labour involved in the renovation of Renshaw Hall and the physical installation of the 70 tons of limestone used to construct for Long's work. Indeed, the practical construction of *Stone Field* parallels the distinction Clark makes between artists' books and the *livre d'artiste*:

> The latter is essentially an aspect of printmaking and bears the same evidence of authenticity as does the original print; edition number, fine paper, expensive price, traces of the artist's hand, etc. in contrast, the artists' book is often cheap, mass-produced, and seldom involves the artist in its printing. ('The Gallery and the Book' 71)

In this respect, the artist's book, as conceived by Clark, pertinently reflects the broader milieu of the conceptual art from which certain forms of artists' books emerged in the late 1960s. Not only are Long's Coracle publications suggestive of the 'simple and readily available form[s]' that Sol LeWitt attributes to conceptualism in his landmark essay 'Paragraphs on Conceptual Art' (1967) but, like the manual construction of *Stone Field*, they also reiterate LeWitt's claim that conceptual art 'is usually free from the dependence on the skill of the artist as a craftsman' (13, 12).

It is possible to see in Allotment the 'alternative space' of the small press book, suggested by Moeglin-Delcroix, coming full circle, finding its extra-textual, extra-typographical equivalent in the allotted space of Renshaw Hall. Unfortunately, the future Allotment projects planned by Coracle Atlantic Foundation ended when Liverpool City Council terminated the building license. 'The list of potential projects being worked on at the time of its closure,' Cutts recalls, 'included a concert by Test Department, installations by Richard Serra and Anthony Gormley, leading to the full rendition of the Allotment Project' ('Allotment 3' 13). This 'full rendition,' Cutts explains, was conceived 'with the idea that a building and the use of its space could be a form of publication, an issuing of new forms within a more physical context' ('Allotment 3'). Thus, 'multiple individual projects would take place simultaneously [...] across the vast interior space of Renshaw Hall, producing a veritable magazine of activity, an anthology of published parts' ('Allotment 3' 13).[54]

With the termination of Renshaw Hall's building license came the dissolution of Coracle Atlantic Foundation and the possibility of 'a national, international and community based art centre' (Cutts, 'Allotment 3' 13). Nevertheless, the outward-looking perspective that the name Coracle Atlantic Foundation suggests—even when working within the quintessentially 'English' context of the allotment—has endured in the subsequent work and projects that have occurred under the original moniker of Coracle. Indeed, to recall the remote situation of Niedecker, it is the printed platform that has abided as the most effective means of sustaining an international community of creative and social activity. When Van Horn joined Coracle in 1988, she made Coracle's trans-Atlantic perspectives even more tangible and, with Cutts, would eventually move a little further out across the Atlantic by moving to Ireland where, in its 'remote form,' Coracle 'continues as printer-publisher, editor of spaces, employing many of the devices and formats of hypothetical publishing inherent in the small press' (Cutts and Van Horn, 'Coracle' n. pag). Here in Tipperary, Roger Conover has noted of the couple's rural dwelling, 'All's well in the secret spaces of modernity and conceptualism, camouflaged by whitewash and thatch' (cited in Cutts and Van Horn, 'Coracle' n. pag).

---

54 Although the plan for simultaneous individual projects was never realized, Cutts's poem 'Civil Defence' was projected for one evening 'on the back wall of Renshaw Hall, beyond the edge of Richard Long's *Stone Field* which occupied the whole of the building at the time.' As 'Allotment 3' this brief intervention was intended 'an interval between proposed future installations' (Cutts, 'Allotment 3' 13).

Coda: Certain Trees

I like the way that our publications fall through the system but yet exist in the world.

—Thomas A. Clark, 'An Inconspicuous
Green Flower'

Johanna Drucker has questioned the appealing myth of the artist's book as a 'democratic multiple' (*Figuring* 176). Books such as Ed Ruscha's *Twentysix Gasoline Stations*, as she explains, were 'meant to circulate freely outside the gallery system, beyond the elite limits of an in-crowd art going audience and patrons':

> While the idea worked fine in the abstract, in reality it depended upon creating a system of distribution and upon finding an interested audience for these works which were at least as esoteric in many cases as the most obscure fine arts objects. (*Figuring* 176)

Thus, as a 'multiple,' the artist's book 'assumes a sophisticated artworld viewer initiated into a play with conventions and their subversion which characterized much of the work of the advanced guard' in the 1960s and 1970s (*Figuring* 176).

The point that Drucker raises regarding a 'sophisticated,' 'esoteric' in-crowd recalls the similar questions of specialism and exclusivity that that name 'Jargon' has provoked. One might accuse the poets, publishers, and artists examined in *Avant-Folk* of fashioning a clique of initiation via the sustained use of certain references such as pastoral, as well as through a network of self-serving friends, publishers, and collaborators. To do so, however, would miss the broader significance of such small press networks. As Simon Cutts has remarked in reference to Coracle's printed ephemera of postcards, exhibition invites, announcements, and statements, the principal concern is circulation and dissemination: 'Sent, given away, left on public transport, sold,' Cutts suggests, 'it's all the same thing, a form of distribution' (*SFA* 113). Writing with Colin Sackett in the context of their exhibition *Repetivity: Platforms and Approaches for Publishing* (2000), which showcases the work of 16 small press publishers, Cutts similarly singles out a 'determined concern with availability' and '*repetition*, in both the production and the distribution of publications' as a shared impetus for a diverse range of publishers that includes Wild Hawthorn Press, Writers Forum, and Folding Landscapes (*Repetivity* 3). In a similar spirit, Alec Finlay—whose press Morning Star was also included in *Repetivity*—has described the infrastructure of small press distribution as 'a great circulatory system' of 'poets, artists, publishers, booksellers and collectors who together form an economy, quite separate from the established book trade' and whose exchange is valued by a 'common currency of friendship' ('"And So Books ..."' 16).

This 'currency,' however, can be seen as a creative act or work in its own right and not simply the ancillary means of dissemination and distribution. Indeed, the 'circulatory' social network examined in the preceding chapters might be described as a *sociopoetic* practice. This is the term that Craig J. Saper employs to describe the 'direct mailings and alternative distribution networks' that 'emerged from, or were influenced by, the underground art scene of the 1960s' and precursor movements such as COBRA, Fluxus, Lettrism, and concrete poetry (129). In particular, Saper identifies the phenomenon of 'assemblings'— 'the periodic mailing of very small editions (fifty to five hundred) containing prints and poems, pamphlets, and small art objects, collected in folios, bound volumes, or boxes'—as a prime example of a 'sociopoetic' practice that posits 'the production, distribution, and use of periodicals *as* artworks and poetry' (129, 151). In such networks and collectives, 'the social situation became a canvas for art and poetic practices' (Saper 151). Thus, Saper argues, these 'production and distribution systems'— the networks, publications, and collective, participatory works defining such activity—were also 'the context and frame of reference' of that activity (151–152). The work becomes increasingly 'about the interactions among distribution systems, a community of participants, and the poetic artisanal works' (Saper 151).

Reading the activities of Jargon's broader 'society' from a similar 'sociopoetic' perspective helps explain the prominence, and important function, of unconventional, non-literary forms and formats within its networks. Adopting Roland Barthes's terminology, Saper, in the context of the 'assembling,' defines such texts (which include 'recipes, scores, instructions, questionnaires, forms, and manifestos') as *receivable*, believing them more capable of establishing 'a more intensely *intimate* relationship' with the recipient (130, 4). The intimacy of the *receivable* text means that it bypasses the 'mercantile constraints associated with the gallery system and mainstream publication' to underpin, instead, 'a network of relationships linked by sending and receiving texts in the mail or as part of a network of participants' (Saper 4, 3, 4). The unique and singular gift-books that Niedecker made for her various friends might be considered *receivable* in this sense. So might Finlay's use of the questionnaire format (as in his poem *Arcady*) as well as Mills's and Cutts's use of this format in later issues of *Tarasque* and its sister broadside sheet *Private Tutor*. The pastoral folding-poems produced by Clark, Finlay, and Cutts are further examples of *receivable* texts. Like the assemblings examined by Saper, all of these relatively small, minor, fugitive publications function on the basis of networks of 'producer participants' that ensure 'intimacy, particularity, and [the] intense impact' of effect and meaning which develops incrementally in dialogue with their 'producer participants' (Saper 4).

While the orbit of such receivable texts might be considered relatively small and limited in the *Avant-Folk* milieu, the creative horizons they have opened continue to expand. What might at first seem self-serving in Jargon's broader society of avant-folk is actually integral for sustaining the very social continuum that Williams's press helped nurture into existence. Far from hermetic or closed-off (as the ubiquitous motif of the pastoral sheepfold might initially suggest), it is a continuum that remains open, inclusive, and aleatory. Thomas A. Clark hints at the latter when he notes how his own Moschatel publications 'get little acclaim but a lot of attention, that they are not given by the culture but are a discovery for each person who comes across them' ('An Inconspicuous Green Flower' 144). Thus, in bypassing the impersonal mercantilism of mainstream publishing, Clark's *receivable* texts benefit from a liberty of distribution—of encounter and attention—not permitted by more traditional channels of distribution.

To conclude *Avant-Folk*, I want to offer one final and relatively recent example of 'sociopoetic' practice whose roots are traceable back to Niedecker and the early efforts of Jargon. In 2006 Cutts and Erica Van Horn organized an exhibition at the Centre des livres d'artistes at St Yrieix-la-Perche and called it *Certain Trees: The Constructed Book, Poem and Object 1964–2006*. The show, which was later exhibited at London's Victoria and Albert Museum in 2007, illustrates what Cutts describes in the exhibition's accompanying book as the 'linked concerns and sensibilities' of a 'loose group of acquaintances' who have continued to explore the possibilities of the small poem, the constructed object, and small press publishing ('Absent Trees' 9). Indeed, as the allusion to Finlay's 'proper subjects' implies, Finlay is something of a mutual reference point for the variety of work featured in the exhibition. This included many of the poets, artists, and publishers encountered in *Avant-Folk*—for example, Thomas A. Clark, Stuart Mills, Stephen Duncalf, and Colin Sackett—in addition to Brian Lane, Robert Lax, Steve Wheatley, Martin Fidler, David Bellingham, and Les Coleman. However, as John Bevis (another participant in the exhibition) notes in his essay for the book, '"Certain Trees" is not the name of a group of artists, and there will never be a PhD, or auction, or late-night review, devoted to Certain Treeism' ('Swings and Roundabouts' 15). Nevertheless, Bevis acknowledges that 'the idea of the group is central to the work' included in the exhibition and stresses the importance that collaboration, little magazines, small press publishing, mail art, and printed ephemera have played in consolidating within this milieu a loose sense of collectivity and affinity ('Swings and Roundabouts' 15–16).

Affinity is especially evident as a theme in the two-page 'epigraph' of the *Certain Trees* book. As well as directly referencing Lorine Niedecker, Stuart Mills, Gael Turnbull, and Roy Fisher, this epigraph also tacitly recalls how the roots of such alliances developed out of The Jargon Society, *Migrant*, and The Wild Hawthorn Press. Indeed, and perhaps punning on the exhibition name, the *Certain Trees* epigraph implicitly suggests a genealogical tree that despite its many and diverse branches has its roots firmly set in a common ground.

Recalling the title of Cutts's and Van Horn's exhibition and one of the proper subjects promoted in *Tarasque*, Roy Fisher's poem 'Epitaph' begins the epigraph to *Certain Trees*:

> certain trees
> came separately from the wood
>
> and with no special
> thought of returning (6)

'Epitaph' is one of the tributes to Niedecker that Williams includes in *Epitaphs for Lorine*. Thus, despite recalling the 'Certain Trees' of *Tarasque Six*, Fisher's reference to 'certain trees' is more likely meant as an allusion to one of Niedecker's most familiar poems, 'My friend tree' (*CW* 186). Tacitly suggesting the felled tree of Niedecker's poem, Fisher establishes a similar theme of sacrifice and renewal.

Niedecker's poem, according to Peter Middleton, represents 'a transformation of everyday observation into metaphors of social relations,' reminding its reader of how 'sometimes precious attachments have to be sacrificed for a greater good' ('The British Niedecker' 254). In Fisher's poem such sacrifice is apparent in the 'certain trees' that are cut down and transported from the woodland in order to supply, presumably, timber or firewood. With this comes a promise of renewal that is implicit in the word 'wood' that suggests both woodland and the material that individual trees provide. The poem also suggests coppicing, the system of woodland management in which new tree growth is nourished by the stools or trunks of older felled trees, thereby allowing new trees to burgeon 'separately from the wood' of their hewn elders. 'Epitaph,' therefore, reiterates a faith in biological laws and renewal that, as we have seen in the example of 'Consider,' informs many of Niedecker's poems. If, as Niedecker writes in 'Wintergreen Ridge,' 'Life is natural / in the evolution / of matter,' then 'Epitaph' and 'My friend tree' remind us that so is death (*CW* 247).

Indeed, the relation between "Epitaph' and 'My friend tree' is accentuated considerably in *Certain Trees* by the reproduction immediately below Fisher's 'Epitaph' of the title page of Niedecker's Wild Hawthorn book *My Friend Tree*. As well as reiterating the tacit social relations that occur between the two poems, this image of the book's title page foregrounds Walter Miller's linocuts rather than Niedecker's poetry, none of which is reproduced.

The tacit alliance of image and text suggested in *My Friend Tree* is also implicit in Stuart Mills's poem 'If we came together, you and I,' which provides the third and final component of the *Certain Trees* 'epigraph.' In the immediate context of *Certain Trees*, Mills's poem, dedicated to Gael Turnbull and first published in the Tarasque Press booklet *The Menagerie Goes for A Walk* (c. 1968), elaborates the social relations and arboreal amity of Fisher's poem:

> If we came together, you and I
> on a walk together,
> the tree you would take
> to put in your garden.
>
> But I would climb up with
> a sharp knife
> to cut out some wood,
> this my joy to take back.
>
> Your tree
>   growing birds
> and the children playing.
>
> My wood
>   shaped and polished
> in a corner to touch.
>
> Shade from your tree
> touch from my wood.
> A wood full of trees
> a tree full of wood. (*Certain Trees* 7)

The poem presents two contrasting sensibilities that nevertheless, to paraphrase Fisher's poem, come separately from the same wood. Along with the 'anecdotal vernacular of Jonathan Williams' and the 'urban obstinacy of Roy Fisher,' Cutts notes that 'the *pastorale* of Gael Turnbull' was 'of immense importance' to Mills ('We both had the same idea' 139, 140). Echoes of this *pastorale* are tacit in the images of the garden and the 'tree / growing birds / and the children playing' in its 'shade.' This contrasts notably with the wood appropriated by the poem's speaker that is 'shaped and polished / in a corner to touch.' This suggestion of carpentry, in the context of *Certain Trees*, draws attention to the exhibition's inclusion of wooden constructed objects made by, among others, the artists Martin Fidler, Stephen Duncalf, and Martin Rogers.

These two sensibilities and modes—the pastoral lyric and the constructed object—are, ultimately, of the same grain and, essentially, complicit in their emphasis on the root meaning of poetry as 'making' (*poiein*). This complicity also amplifies the cross-references and themes that Fisher's 'Epitaph' and Niedecker's *My Friend Tree* have suggested. For example, the concluding lines of Mills's poem—'A wood full of trees / a tree full of wood'—adumbrate the double meaning of 'wood' in Fisher's 'Epitaph' and the 'shade' of the tree recalls the reason for felling of the tree in Niedecker's 'My friend tree.' From this transtextual perspective, the epigraph of *Certain Trees* stands as a pertinent example of how the eponymous exhibition highlights 'the equivalences between books and objects, printed and constructed material' as well as demonstrating how such alliances continue to manifest 'amongst such a loose group of acquaintances' (Cutts, 'Absent Trees' 9). Serving as a tacit manifesto, therefore, the 'epigraph' to the *Certain Trees* book both outlines and practices what the exhibition surveys.

Mills's allusion to a tree 'growing birds' also recalls the origins of the name The *Jargon* Society which is also implicated in the genealogical tree of Cutts and Van Horn's exhibition. Williams has pointed out that, 'in French *jargon* means the twittering of birds' which, he claims, 'is about the best definition' (Dana 203).

Why Williams considered avian connotations the best definition for Jargon can be explained by John Bevis's books *An A–Z of Bird Song* (1995) and *Aaaaw to Zzzzzd: The Words of Birds* (2010), both of which take the 'twittering' of birds as their principal subjects. Part 'field guide,' part 'lexical curiosity,' and, arguably, part artist's book, *Aaaaw to Zzzzzd* consists of lexicons of transcribed birdcalls—the 'jargon' of the feathered tribe—from Great Britain, Northern Europe, and North America. The book also includes Bevis's own illuminating reflection on the nature of birdsong and how it has been documented or conveyed in music, poetry, field recordings, graphic notation, and mimetic oral devices (*Aaaaw* 40). The book itself came about partly through the intervention of Williams, as Bevis explains, when his earlier book *An A–Z of Bird Song*, co-published by Coracle and St Paulinus Press, 'made its way, through the mutual acquaintance of the late Jonathan Williams [...] into the hands of Roger Conover' at the MIT Press (*Aaaaw* xi).[55] Williams's role in the publication of Bevis's later book poignantly reflects the broader themes of distribution, communication, and society that *Aaaaw to Zzzzzd* and its predecessor *An A–Z of Birdsong* tacitly address through their avian subject matter.

An A–Z of Birdsong is a slim book consisting of a lexicon of transcribed birdsong and birdcalls, accompanied by a series of photos that Bevis found in Leonard Hugh Newman's book *British Moths and Their Haunts* (1949). These photos of various scenes—from woodlands, mountains and hills, and coastlines, to fields, hedgerows, ponds, and farm buildings—included by Newman are conspicuously devoid of his principal subject (moths) and instead represent the terrains of the various Lepidoptera that he describes.

In the context of Bevis's book, Newman's photos serve a similar purpose, only this time suggesting the habitat of the birds whose songs and calls form the principal subject of *An A–Z of Birdsong*. 'I thought these pictures—where the subject is not really there, where there is nothing going on, nothing for the photographer to focus on, no intention of pictorial meaning—somehow very refreshing,' Bevis has explained.[56] This absence is emphasized further by the captions that Bevis 'extracted from various ornithology books.'[57] 'This seemed a very economical device for saying something more complex,' Beavis suggests, 'the photo and text each acting both autonomously, as caption to each other, and creating something new in their relationship.'[58]

Bevis's enigmatic use of found images and text in *An A–Z of Bird Song* aligns it with certain books of Finlay's such as *Ocean Stripe Series 5*, published by Tarasque Press in 1967. Finlay's book juxtaposes quotes from the contemporary sound poets Ernst Jandl and Paul de Vree as well as extracts from Kurt Schwitters's 1924 essay 'Consistent Poetry' (all of which are taken from the third number of the magazine *Form*) with photos of fishing boats published in one of Finlay's favourite resources, the weekly trade periodical *Fishing News*. For example, an extract from Schwitters's essay—'A logically consistent poem evaluates letters and groups of letters against each other'—is presented below the photo of a fishing boat with its port registration letters clearly visible: 'GY701' (cited in Abrioux 203). This combination of avant-garde art and fishing culture, as Yves Abrioux suggests, brings 'dada into the context of

---

55 Jargon published Conover's edition of Mina Loy's *The Last Lunar Baedeker* in 1982. It is another example of how Jargon has helped in the rediscovery of important, yet neglected, writers.
56 John Bevis, email to the author, 2 June 2015.
57 Bevis, email to the author, 2 June 2015.
58 Bevis, email to the author, 2 June 2015.

Finlay's own distinctive use of letters and numbers,' just as it previously did in his earlier *Poster Poem* in 1964 (199).[59]

An A–Z of Bird Song is similarly 'composed from parallel sequences of literary and visual elements' and, like Finlay's earlier example, Bevis's use of photographs similarly subverts 'the privileged role of the photograph in reporting events' (Bann, 'Ian Hamilton Finlay's *Ocean Stripe 5*' 49). 'The image is there,' Bann observes with regard to the various *Fishing News* photos used by Finlay, 'not because of its reference to everyday life, but because it presents a de-personalised—and therefore adaptable—model of visual reality' (49). Such de-personalization is a result of the photos' lack of discursive framing or context and their juxtapositions with the equally de-personalized found texts that Finlay presents. However, like Finlay's 'Homage to Malevich', these 'model[s] of visual reality,' rather than achieving complete autonomy, establish instead a dialectical relationship with the found texts. Indeed, the adaptability that Bann identifies in *Ocean Stripe Series 5* is conveyed in terms of 'rehabilitation.' Thus, one of Finlay's found texts states: 'Selection, transformation, amputation, transplantation would, however, only yield exhibits for an anatomical museum of language, if they were not occasionally followed by a kind of rehabilitation' (cited in Abrioux 203). Thus, in their new context and their new relationship, these texts 'rehabilitate' the images in *Ocean Stripe Series 5*, and vice versa.

The use of text and image in *Aaaaw to Zzzzzd* differ with those in *An A–Z of Bird Song* (as well as Finlay's *Ocean Stripe Series 5*) because Bevis replaces Newman's photos with his own. Nevertheless, in the spirit of Newman's, Bevis's photographs of meadows, gardens, derelict 'edgelands,' bridges, train-tracks, inland waterways, and mountainous crags are notable for their absence of birds. However, where Finlay's photos in *Ocean Stripe Series 5* present de-personalized models of 'visual reality,' *Aaaaw to Zzzzzd*'s combination of text and image, as in *An A–Z of Bird Song* before it, convey a model of *aural* reality that pertinently evokes the invisible songs and calls of birds. Indeed, the lexicons that Bevis compiles imply a sound poetry akin to the one that Finlay suggests in his use of port registration letters and numbers. 'The sounds of the singing are just that,' Bevis suggests, 'sounds without semantics, making

---

59 Indeed, *Ocean Stripe Series 5* stands as a pertinent reaffirmation of Finlay's avant-garde (rather than simply 'experimental') sensibilities as they stood in the 1960s and early 1970s. As they had done previously in Finlay's *Poster Poem* and concrete poems such as *Sea-Poppy I* (1968), port letters and registration numbers become, to quote Schwitters in *Ocean Stripe Series 5*, 'the basic material,' for a poetry that, according to Abrioux, 'stresses not the disruptive energies of the [dada] movement, but rather the way its forays into para-art or anti-art can be used in the cause of cultural continuity' (cited in Abrioux 203; Abrioux 199).

what is expressed seem to me unhindered in its rawness and potency,' perhaps like Kurt Schwitters's *Ursonata* (*Aaaaw* 15).

Despite their ornithological context, Bevis's expositions of birdsong in *An A–Z of Bird Song* and *Aaaaw to Zzzzzd* might also be read as a series of reflections on, or statements about, poetry and the social dynamics of its small press networks. For example, one of the captions that Bevis provides—'Occasionally a bird will introduce some freak sound and make it part of its song'—recalls the use of found texts and speech in poetry that Niedecker, Williams, and Finlay have practiced as well as Bevis's own in *Aaaaw to Zzzzzd* (*Aaaaw* 82). 'Some species mimic the voices of other species,' evokes parody or pastiche, whereas another caption signals poetry's gender imbalances: 'In most species only the male sings, in some both male and female sing' (*Aaaaw* 44, 38). Another caption suggests how art and literary criticism tends toward its own forms of taxonomy: 'Some sounds are classified more consistently than others' (*Aaaaw* 118).

In the context of *Avant-Folk* and the small press infrastructures it has examined, the following statement seems especially pertinent: 'Each species may sing differently from place to place' (*Aaaaw* 5). This observation is reiterated by Bevis when he suggests that 'Birds belong in their landscape and help to define and distinguish one piece of land from another' (*Aaaaw* 2). As a 'solitary plover,' Niedecker's example springs immediately to mind as a 'species' very much in tune with its local place (*CW* 265). However, the wider import of Niedecker's poetry in the British Isles in the 1960s and 1970s also reflects a contrary aspect of the feathered tribe, namely, as Bevis acknowledges, 'the happy distribution of species' (*Aaaaw* 2). Adumbrating Cutts's concern for the pragmatics of 'distribution,' Bevis notes 'the fortuitous spreads of populations, frequencies of encounters, possibilities of discoveries' that the distribution of bird species likewise occasions (*Aaaaw* 4). Indeed, *Aaaaw to Zzzzzd* reiterates this idea of 'fortuitous spreads' in the division of its two lexicons (one for birds of North American and one for birds of Great Britain and Northern Europe) which encourages the reader to identify the affinities and the differences between birds across the Atlantic. These polarities—between regional locality, on the one hand, and migratory distribution, on the other—are a fitting metaphor, not only for the nature of Niedecker's poetry, but also for broader dynamics of the community in which she figures so prominently.

It is also possible to find an echo of the tacit societal dynamics of Bevis's book in Stuart Mills's comments regarding the 'consistent difference[s]' and social significance of small presses such as Jargon and Wild Hawthorn:

> In continuing to publish I continue to acknowledge theirs and similar achievements: I continue to wave a handkerchief at the world and know that, inevitably, sometime, someplace, another

> Simon Cutts will wave back with a handkerchief, though decorative, equally impractical and most probably, purchased from some small bazaar or emporium a considerable remove away from the chain stores of the high street. ('From Tarasque to *Aggie Weston's*' 141)

As well as reiterating the common currency and alternative economies of the small press community, the social gesture of publication, as Mills conceives it, is not unlike the motivations behind the calls and songs of the feathered tribe. 'Not all birds sing,' Bevis notes, 'but nearly all call, that is, they make specific sounds for warning of predators, asking for food, finding each other, and so on' (*Aaaaw* 10). Very much like the bird's call (or the wave of a handkerchief), the small press publication becomes an equivalent, and equally singular, way of 'finding each other' and acknowledging one another's presence, regardless of distance or time.

Joan Hugo has identified a similar compulsion to communicate as an integral and abiding aspect of an independent publishing ethos and economics that is traceable back to Johannes Gutenberg:

> [T]he need to communicate from one to another a variety of unaltered ideas, free of aesthetic or political censorship, in the belief that ideas have a life of their own, independent of their value as commodities, has compelled poets, artists, and all those dedicated to the life of the mind to undertake the publication of their intellectual and artistic commitments, from Luther to Thomas Paine and the Russian samizdat movement, from William Blake and William Morris to Diether Roth and Ed Ruscha. (Cited in Cutts and Lane, *The Artist Publisher* 5)

As the preceding chapters have shown, this compulsive need to communicate, exchange, and distribute—'to make things happen,' as James Jaffe remarks of Williams and The Jargon Society—underlies all of the publishing activities examined in *Avant-Folk*; from Niedecker's homemade books and Jargon's beautiful editions, to the minimal folding cards of Moschatel and the printed ephemera of Coracle (para 6). 'We're just folks you know, and we's having some fun and I think that the arts is one of the few places where this still works and it's still playful,' Williams remarks in an interview with David Annwn in 1990 (58). Yet, without the sustaining infrastructures of the small press network and the real, or imagined, communities of its participants, this creative 'fun' remains largely inconceivable. For, as facilitator *and* product of its own social events and occasions, it is the small press publication that has most emphatically and consistently reaffirmed the significance 'of one-to-one relationships, of things made by the hands and talents of persons with a feeling of kinship for you,' however remote in space or time those persons might be (*MB* 183).

Bibliography

Abrioux, Yves. *Ian Hamilton Finlay: A Visual Primer*. London: Reaktion Books, 1994. Print.

Ahearn, Barry. *William Carlos Williams and Alterity: The Early Poetry*. Cambridge: Cambridge University Press, 1994. Print.

———. 'Zukofsky, Marxism and American Handicraft.' *Upper Limit Music: The Writing of Louis Zukofsky*. Ed. Mark Scroggins. Tuscaloosa: University of Alabama Press, 1997. 80–93. Print.

Albert-Birot, Pierre. *31 Pocket Poems*. Trans. Barbara Wright. Black River Falls, WI: Obscure Publications, 2003. Print.

Allen, Donald, ed. *The New American Poetry, 1945–1960*. Berkeley: University of California Press, 1999. Print.

Allen, Vickey. Letter to Stuart Mills, 27 March 1979. *Aggie Weston's* 14 (Spring, 1979): n. pag. Print.

Alpers, Paul. 'What is Pastoral?' *Critical Inquiry*, 8.3 (1982): 437–460. Print.

Alpert, Barry. 'Jonathan Williams: An Interview (June 14, 1973).' *Vort* 4 (Fall 1973): 54–75. Print.

Anar, Anna Sigríður. *The Book as Instrument: Stéphane Mallarmé, the Artist's Book, and the Transformation of Print Culture*. Chicago: The University of Chicago Press, 2011. Print.

Andrews, Malcolm. *Landscape and Western Art*. Oxford: Oxford University Press, 1999. Print.

Annwn, David, ed. *Catgut and Blossom: Jonathan Williams in England*. London: Coracle, 1989. Print.

———. 'Interview with Jonathan Williams.' *Prospect into Breath: Interviews with North and South Writers*. Ed. Peterjon Skelt. Twickenham, Middlesex and Wakefield: North and South, 1991. 45–58. Print.

Ash, Jared. 'Primitivism in Russian Futurist Book Design.' *The Russian Avant-Garde Book, 1910–1934*. Eds. Margit Rowell and Deborah Wye. New York: Museum of Modern Art, 2002. 33–40. Print.

Augustine, Jane. Review of Lorine Niedecker, *Collected Works*. *Jacket 21* (February, 2003): n. pag. Web. 26 July 2015.

Bann, Stephen. 'A Context for Concrete Poetry.' *Studies in the Arts:*

Proceedings of St. Peter's College Literary Society. Ed. Francis Warner. Oxford: Basil Blackwell, 1968. 131–149. Print.

———. 'Coracle's Concrete Thinking.' *The Coracle: Coracle Press Gallery 1975–1987.* Ed. Simon Cutts. London: Coracle, 1989. 53–68. Print.

———. 'Ian Hamilton Finlay: An Imaginary Portrait.' *Wood Notes Wild: Essays on the Poetry and Art of Ian Hamilton Finlay.* Ed. Alec Finlay. Edinburgh: Polygon, 1995. 55–79. Print.

———. 'Ian Hamilton Finlay's *Ocean Stripe 5.*' *Scottish International* 2 (April 1968): 46–52. Print.

———. Stuart Mills Obituary. *The Independent* 21 March, 2006. Web. 17 September 2015.

———. 'Tarasque: An Introduction.' *Certain Trees: The Constructed Book, Poem, and Object 1964–2006.* Ed. Simon Cutts. Saint-Yrieix-la-Perche: Centre des livres d'artistes, 2007. 132–138. Print.

———. ed. *Midway: Letters from Ian Hamilton Finlay to Stephen Bann 1964–69.* London: Wilmington Square Books, 2014. Print.

Barrell, John, and John Bull, eds. *The Penguin Book of English Pastoral Verse.* Harmondsworth: Penguin, 1982. Print.

Bashō, Matsuo. *The Narrow Road to the Deep North and Other Travel Sketches.* Trans. Nobuyuki Yuasa. London: Penguin, 1966. Print.

Becker, Howard. S. 'Arts and Crafts.' *American Journal of Sociology* 83.4 (January, 1978): 862–889. Print.

Becker, Jane. S. *Appalachia and the Construction of an American Folk, 1930–40.* Chapel Hill and London: The University of North Carolina Press, 1998. Print.

Bell, Eleanor. '"The ugly burds without wings?" Reactions to Tradition since the 1960s.' *Modern Irish and Scottish Poetry.* Eds. Fran Brearton, Edna Longley and Peter Mackay. Cambridge: Cambridge University Press, 2011. 238–250. Print.

Bell, Millicent. *The Jargon Idea.* Providence, RI: Brown University, 1963. Print.

Bevis, John. 'A Star-gazey Pie.' *Printed in Norfolk: Coracle Publications 1989–2012.* Sheffield: RGAP, 2012. 19–79. Print.

———. *Aaaaw to Zzzzzd: The Words of Birds.* Cambridge, MA: MIT Press, 2010. Print.

———. *An A–Z of Bird Song.* Docking, Norfolk / Richmond, Yorkshire: Coracle and St Paulinus, 1995. Print.

———. Jacket note. Stephen Duncalf. *Ducts & Tracts: Notebooks 1974–1986.* Docking, Norfolk: Coracle, 1991. Print.

———. 'Stephen Duncalf: The Suburban Fauvist.' *Little Critic* 20. Tipperary: Coracle, 2014. Print.

———. 'Swings and Roundabouts.' *Certain Trees: The Constructed Book, Poem, and Object 1964–2006.* Ed. Simon Cutts. Saint-Yrieix-la-Perche: Centre des livres d'artistes, 2007. 13–24. Print.

Black, David M. 'Ian Hamilton Finlay: A Window on the Early Work.' *Chapman* 78–79 (1994): 34–37. Print.

Black Hawk. *Life of Black Hawk* (1833). Chicago, IL: Lakeside Press, 1916. Print.

Blake, Andrew. *The Land Without Music: Music, Culture and Society in Twentieth-century Britain.* Manchester: Manchester University Press, 1997. Print.

Blake, William. *The Complete Poetry and Prose.* Ed. David V. Erdman. Berkeley and Los Angeles: University of California Press, 1982. Print.

Blanton, C. D. 'Transatlantic Currents.' *A Concise Companion to Postwar British and Irish Poetry.* Eds. Nigel Alderman and C. D. Blanton. Chichester: Wiley-Blackwell, 2009. 134–154. Print.

Blaustein, Richard. *The Thistle and the Briar: Historical Links and Cultural Parallels between Scotland and Appalachia.* North Carolina and London: MacFarland and Co., 2003. Print.

Bogan, Louise. 'Popular and Unpopular Poetry in America.' *Speaking of Writing: Selected Hopwood Lectures.* Ed. Nicholas Delbanco. Michigan: University of Michigan, 1993. 84–100. Print.

Botkin, B. A. '"Folk-Say" and Folklore.' *American Speech* 6. 6 (Aug., 1931), 404–406. Print.

———. *The American People: In Their Stories, Legends, Tall Tales, Traditions, Ballads and Songs.* London and New Brunswick: Transaction Publishers, 1998. Print.

Bowlt, John E. 'Manipulating Metaphors: El Lissitzky and the Crafted Hand.' *Situating Lissitzky: Vitebsk, Berlin, Moscow.* Eds. Nancy Perloff and Brian Reed. Los Angeles, CA: Getty Publications, 2003. 129–152. Print.

———. ed. and trans. *Russian Art of the Avant-Garde: Theory and Criticism.* London: Thames and Hudson, 1988. Print.

Boyes, Georgina. *The Imagined Village: Culture, Ideology, and the English Folk Revival.* Manchester: Manchester University Press, 1993. Print.

Breunig, C. L., ed. *The Cubist Poets in Paris: An Anthology.* Lincoln, NB and London: University of Nebraska Press, 1995. Print.

Brocken, Michael. *The British Folk Revival, 1944–2002.* Aldershot, Hampshire: Ashgate, 2003. Print.

Brooker, Peter. 'In the Modernist Grain.' *The Oxford Critical and Cultural History of Modernist Magazines: Volume II: North America 1894–1960.* Eds. Peter Brooker and Andrew Thacker. Oxford: Oxford University Press, 2012. 959–965. Print.

Bunting, Basil. 'Comment on Jonathan Williams.' *JW/50: A Fiftieth Birthday Celebration for Jonathan Williams.* Eds. Thomas A. Clark and Jonathan Greene. Frankfort, Kentucky: Gnomon Press, 1979. n. pag. Print.

Burckhardt, Lucius. *Why Is Landscape Beautiful? The Science of Strollology.* Eds. Markus Ritter and Martin Schmitz. Trans. Jill Denton. Basel: Birkhäuser, 2015. Print.

Bush, Clive. *Out of Dissent: A Study of Five Contemporary British Poets.* London: Talus Editions, 1997. Print.

Byerly, Alison. 'The Uses of Landscape: The Picturesque Aesthetic and the National Park System.' *The Ecocriticism Reader: Landmarks in Literary Ecology.* Eds. Cheryll Glotfelty and Harold Fromm. Athens: University of Georgia Press, 1996. 52–68. Print.

Caddel, Richard. 'Consider: Lorine Niedecker and Her Environment.' *Lorine Niedecker: Woman and Poet*. Ed. Jenny Penberthy. Orono, ME: National Poetry Foundation, 1996. 281–286. Print.

Călinescu, Matei. *Five Faces of Modernity: Modernism, Avant-Garde, Decadence, Kitsch, Postmodernism*. Durham, NC: Duke University Press, 2003. Print.

Carlson, Prudence. 'Solitude and Renunciation.' *Solitude and Renunciation: Two Gardens. Solitude and Renunciation*. Ed. Pia Simig. Heidelberg: Kehrer Verlag, 2011. n. pag. Print.

Carruth, Allison. *Global Appetites: American Power and the Literature of Food*. Cambridge: Cambridge University Press, 2013. Print.

Charlesworth, Michael. 'Concrete to Garden.' *The Present Order: Writings on the Work of Ian Hamilton Finlay*. Eds. Caitlin Murray and Tim Johnson. Marfa, TX: Marfa Book Co., 2010. Print. 71–83. Print.

Clare, John. *The Later Poems of John Clare 1837–1864*. Volume One. Eds. Eric Robertson and David Powell. Oxford: Clarendon Press, 1984. Print.

Clark, Thomas A. *A Place Apart*. Pittenweem: Cairn Gallery, 2004. Print.

———. 'An Inconspicuous Green Flower.' *Certain Trees: The Constructed Book, Poem, and Object 1964–2006*. Ed. Simon Cutts. Saint-Yrieix-la-Perche: Centre des livres d'artistes, 2007. 143–144. Print.

———. *Folding the Last Sheep*. Nailsworth: Moschatel Press, 1973. Print.

———. 'Foreword.' *Ken Cox: Celebrating A Life's Work 1927–1968*. Gloucestershire: Family of Ken Cox, 2007. n. pag. Print.

———. 'The Gallery and the Book.' *The Coracle: Coracle Press Gallery 1975–1987*. Ed. Simon Cutts. London: Coracle, 1989. 69–73. Print.

———. *In Defence of Quiet*. Falkland: Falkland Centre for Stewardship, 2008. Print.

———. 'In Praise of Walking.' *The Unpainted Landscape*. Ed. Simon Cutts. London: Coracle Press/Edinburgh: Graeme Murray Gallery, 1987. 137–139. Print.

———. 'Openings Press: An Appreciation and Bibliography.' *Ceolfrith* 14 (Sunderland: Ceolfrith Arts Centre, 1971): 6–11. Print.

———. 'Paper and Stone, Oatmeal and Cherries.' *PN Review* 14.3 (January, 1987): 66–67. Print.

———. *Pastoral*. Pittenweem: Moschatel Press, 2010. Print.

———. 'Pastorals.' *Wood Notes Wild: Essays on the Poetry and Art of Ian Hamilton Finlay*. Ed. Alec Finlay. Edinburgh: Polygon, 1995. 152–155. Print.

———. *Pauses and Digressions*. Drawings by Laurie Clark. Nailsworth: Moschatel Press, 1983. Print.

———. 'Poetry and the Space Beyond.' *Poiesis: Aspects of Contemporary Poetic Activity*. Ed. Graeme Murray. Edinburgh: The Fruit Market Gallery, 1992. 37–45. Print.

———. *Shade at Noon*. Pittenweem: Moschatel Press, 2005. Print.

———. *The Hundred Thousand Places*. Manchester: Carcanet Press, 2009. Print.

———. *Sixteen Sonnets*. Nailsworth: Moschatel Press, 1981. Print.

————. *Some Particulars*. Kendal: Jargon Society, 1971. Print.

————. 'The Standing Poem.' *Thomas A. Clark Blog*. Thomas A. Clark, Tuesday, 13 December, 2011. Web. 26 July 2015.

————, and Simon Cutts. *Salon d'Automne: An Essay in Words & Images*. London: Coracle, 1984. Print.

Clark, Tom. *Charles Olson: The Allegory of a Poet's Life*. Berkeley, CA: North Atlantic Books, 2000. Print.

Clay, Steven, and Rodney Phillips, eds. *A Secret Location on the Lower East Side: Adventures in Writing 1960–1980*. New York: Granary Books, 1998. Print.

Cobbing, Bob, ed. *GLOUP and WOUP*. Gillingham, Kent: Arc Publications, 1974. Print.

Cockburn, Ken. 'Dancing Visions: Ian Hamilton Finlay's Early Writings.' *Folio* 10 (Summer, 2005): 6–10. Print.

————. 'Introduction.' Ian Hamilton Finlay, *The Dancers Inherit the Party: Early Poems, Stories and Plays*. Ed. Ken Cockburn. Edinburgh: Polygon, 2004. xiii–xxvi. Print.

Coleridge, Samuel Taylor. *Specimens of the Table Talk of Samuel Taylor Coleridge*. Ed. Henry N. Coleridge. London: John Murray, 1836. Print.

Colomina, Beatriz, and Craig Buckley, eds. *Clip, Stamp, Fold: The Radical Architecture of Little Magazines, 196X–197X*. Barcelona and New York: Actar, 2010. Print.

Corman, Cid. 'With Lorine: A Memorial 1903–1970.' *Truck* 16 (Summer, 1975): 57–90. Print.

Cory, Jim. 'High Art & Low Life: An Interview with Jonathan Williams.' *The James White Review: A Gay Men's Literary Quarterly* 11.1 (1992): 1, 3–4. Print.

Cosgrove, Denis. *Geography and Vision: Seeing, Imagining and Representing the World*. London: I. B. Tauris, 2008. Print.

————. 'Prospect, Perspective and the Evolution of the Landscape Idea.' *Transactions of the Institute of British Geographers* (New Series) 10.1 (1985): 45–62. Print.

Cox, Kenneth. 'The Longer Poems.' *Lorine Niedecker: Woman and Poet*. Ed. Jenny Penberthy. Orono, ME: The National Poetry Foundation, 1996. 303–310. Print.

Crawford, Robert. *Devolving English Literature*. Edinburgh: Edinburgh University Press, 2000. Print.

Creeley, Robert. *Collected Essays*. Berkeley: University of California Press, 1989. Print.

————. *Collected Poems, 1945–1975*. Berkeley: University of California Press, 2006. Print.

Creswell, Tim. 'Landscape and the Obliteration of Practice.' *Handbook of Cultural Geography*. Eds. Kay Anderson, Mona Demosh, Steve Pile, and Nigel Thrift. London: Sage Publishing, 2003. 269–283. Print.

Crichton-Smith, Ian. 'World War I.' *New Saltire 4* (Summer, 1962): 21–27. Print.

Crouch, David, and Colin Ward. *The Allotment: Its Landscape and Culture*. Nottingham: Five Leaves Press, 1997. Print.

Cutts, Simon. *A History of the Airfields of Lincolnshire.* Norfolk: Coracle, 1990. Print.

———. *A History of the Airfields of Lincolnshire II.* Glasgow: Wax 366, 2000. Print.

———. *A New Kind of Tie: Poems 1965–68.* East Markham, Nottinghamshire: Tarasque Press, 1972. Print.

———. 'Absent Trees.' *Certain Trees: The Constructed Book, Poem, and Object 1964–2006.* Ed. Simon Cutts. Saint-Yrieixla-Perche: Centre des livres d'artistes, 2007. 9–10. Print.

———. 'Allotment 3.' *Uniformagazine* 4 (Autumn 2015): 12–13.

———. *A Smell of Printing: Poems 1988–1999.* New York City: Granary Books/Coracle, 2000. Print.

———, ed. *Certain Trees: The Constructed Book, Poem, and Object 1964–2006.* Saint-Yrieix-la-Perche: Centre des livres d'artistes, 2007. Print.

———. *Eclogues: After Samuel Palmer.* Tipperary: Coracle, 2004. Print.

———. *If It Is At All.* New York and Tipperary: Granary Books and Coracle, 2007. Print.

———. 'I'm Singing and It Is A Song.' *Tarasque* 5 (c. 1965): n. pag. Print.

———. *Letterpress: New and Material Poems.* Axminster, Devon: Uniform Books, 2013. Print.

———. 'Notes on the Unpainted Landscape.' *The Unpainted Landscape.* Ed. Simon Cutts. London: Coracle Press/Edinburgh: Graeme Murray Gallery, 1987. 9–13. Print.

———. *Piano Stool: Footnotes.* Kendal: Jargon Society, 1982. Print.

———. *Some Forms of Availability: Critical Passages on the Book and Publication.* New York: Granary Books, 2007. Print.

———. 'The Aesthetic of Ian Hamilton Finlay.' *Wood Notes Wild: Essays on the Poetry and Art of Ian Hamilton Finlay.* Ed. Alec Finlay. Edinburgh: Polygon, 1995. 32–35. Print.

———, ed. *The Coracle: Coracle Press Gallery 1975–1987.* London: Coracle, 1989. Print.

———. 'The Norfolk Years.' *Printed in Norfolk: Coracle Publications 1989–2012.* Sheffield: RGAP, 2012. 11–18. Print.

———, ed. *The Presence of Landscape: Books, Cards and Printed Objects – Coracle Press 1975–2000.* Limoges: Centre Culturel Jean Gagnant, 2000. Print.

———, ed. *The Unpainted Landscape.* London and Edinburgh: Coracle Press and Graeme Murray Gallery, 1987. Print.

———. 'The Weather House and Other Works.' *The Weather House and Other Works.* London: Coracle, 1975. n. pag. Print.

———. 'We both had the same idea, of writing our names in our hats.' Stuart Mills, *Made in English: The Poems of Stuart Mills.* Ed. Simon Cutts. Ballybeg, Tipperary: Coracle, 2008. 138–141. Print.

———. and Brian Lane, eds. *The Artist Publisher: A Survey by Coracle Press.* London: Crafts Council Gallery, 1986. Print.

———. and Colin Sackett, eds. *Repetivity: Platforms and Approaches for Publishing.* Derby: Research Group for Artists' Publications, 2000. Print.

————. and Erica Van Horn. 'Coracle.' *Coracle*. Coracle, nd. Web. 26 July 2015.

Damon, Samuel Foster. *A Blake Dictionary: The Ideas and Symbols of William Blake*. Hanover, NH: University Press of New England, 1988. Print.

Dana, Robert. *Against The Grain: Interviews with Maverick American Publishers*. Iowa City: University of Iowa Press, 1986. Print.

Daniels, Stephen. 'Reviews in Brief' (*Englshpublshing: Writings and Readings 1991–2002* by Colin Sackett and *The True Line: The Landscape Diagrams of Geoffrey Hutchings* by Colin Sackett). *Cultural Geographies* 14.4 (October 2007): 629–630. Print.

Davenport, Guy. *The Geography of the Imagination*. Boston, MA: David R. Godine, 1997.

————. 'Introduction.' Jonathan Williams. *Elite/Elate Poems: Selected Poems 1971–75*. Highlands: The Jargon Society, 1979. 15–18. Print.

Davidson, Donald. *Regionalism and Nationalism in the United States: The Attack on Leviathan* (1938). Piscataway, NJ: Transaction Publishers, 1991. Print.

Davidson, Michael. *Guys Like Us: Citing Masculinity in Cold War Poetics*. Chicago, IL and London: The University of Chicago Press, 2004. Print.

————. 'Life By Water: Lorine Niedecker and Critical Regionalism.' *Radical Vernacular: Lorine Niedecker and the Poetics of Place*. Ed. Elizabeth Willis. Iowa City: University of Iowa Press, 2008. 3–20. Print.

Dennis, Victoria Solt. *Discovering Friendly and Fraternal Societies: Their Badges and Regalia*. Princes Risborough, Buckinghamshire: Shire Publications, 2005. Print.

DeSilvey, Caitlin. 'Cultivated Histories in a Scottish Allotment Garden.' *Cultural Geographies* 10.4 (October 2003): 442–468. Print.

————. 'Rewilding.' *Anticipatory History*. Eds. Caitlin DeSilvey, Simon Naylor, and Colin Sackett. Axminster, Devon: Uniformbooks, 2011. 61–62. Print.

Dewsbury, John David, Paul Harrison, Mitchell Rose, and John Wylie. 'Introduction: Enacting Geographies.' *Geoforum* 33.4 (November 2002). 437–440. Print.

Dodge, Martin. 'Land Diagram 1: Word-Geography of Cornwall.' *Land Diagrams: Twinned Studies in Landscape*, Land Diagrams: Twinned Studies in Landscape, 18 March, 2013. Web. 25 August 2015.

Dorson, Richard M. 'Introduction: Concepts of Folklore and Folklife.' *Folklore and Folklife: An Introduction*. Ed. Richard M. Dorson. Chicago, IL and London: University of Chicago Press, 1982. 1–50. Print.

Drucker, Johanna. *The Century of Artists' Books*. New York: Granary Books, 2004. Print.

————. *Figuring the Word: Essays on Books, Writing and Visual Poetics*. New York: Granary Books, 1998. Print.

————. *Theorizing Modernism: Visual Art and the Critical Tradition*. New York: Colombia University Press, 1994. Print.

Duberman, Martin. *Black Mountain: An Exploration in Community.* London: Wildwood House, 1974. Print.

Duncalf, Stephen. 'Deuteronomy.' *Anthill* 1 (January 1977): n. pag. Print.

———. *Ducts & Tracts: Notebooks 1974–1986.* Docking, Norfolk: Coracle, 1991. Print.

———. *Good Hoofs.* London: Coracle Press, 1976. Print.

———. *Huts By-way Engines Orchard.* London: Coracle Press, 1977. Print.

Duncan, Robert. 'Interview with Michael Andre Bernstein and Burton Hatlen.' *Sagetrieb* 4.2/3 (Fall & Winter, 1985): 87–135. Print.

———. *The Opening of the Field.* New York: New Directions, 1973. Print.

DuPlessis, Rachel Blau. 'Lorine Niedecker, the Anonymous: Gender, Class, Genre and Resistances.' *Lorine Niedecker: Woman and Poet.* Ed. Jenny Penberthy. Orono, ME: National Poetry Foundation, 1996. 113–138. Print.

———. 'Lorine Niedecker's "Paean to Place" and its Reflective Fusions.' *Contemporary Literature* 46.3 (2005): 393–421. Print.

———. 'Manhood and its Poetic Projects: The Construction of Masculinity in the Counter-cultural Poetry of the U.S. 1950s.' *Jacket* 31 (October, 2006): n. pag. Web. 26 July 2015.

Eaton, Allen H. *Handicrafts of the Southern Highlands.* New York: Dover Publications, 1973. Print.

Eiseley, Loren. *Darwin's Century: Evolution and the Men Who Discovered It.* New York: Anchor Books, 1961. Print.

Eliot, T. S. 'From Poe to Valery.' *The Hudson Review* 2.3 (Autumn, 1949): 327–342. Print.

Empson, William. *Some Versions of Pastoral.* London: Chatto and Windus, 1935. Print.

Epstein, Andrew. *Beautiful Enemies: Friendship and Postwar American Poetry.* Oxford and New York: Oxford University Press, 2006. Print.

Erkkila, Betsy, ed. *Walt Whitman's Songs of Male Intimacy and Love: 'Live Oak, with Moss' and 'Calamus.'* Iowa City: University of Iowa Press, 2011. Print.

Eyres, Patrick. *Arcady.* Drawings by Ian Gardner. Wilsden Bradford: New Arcadians, 1983. Print.

———. *Eye Spy Trees.* Drawings by Ian Gardner. Wilsden, West Yorkshire: Blue Tunnel Publications/Eye Spy Arcady Books, 1980. Print.

———. 'The New Arcadians: The New Arcadian Press.' *Dumbarton Oaks Research Library and Collection.* Dumbarton Oaks, n.d. Web. 26 July 2015.

———. 'On Sundials.' *Chapman,* 78/79 (1994): 99. Print.

Faranda, Lisa Pater, ed. *'Between Your House and Mine': The Letters of Lorine Niedecker to Cid Corman, 1960 to 1970.* Durham, NC: Duke University Press, 1986. Print.

Farley, Paul, and Michael Symmons Roberts. *Edgelands: Journeys into England's True Wilderness.* London: Vintage, 2012. Print.

Finlay, Alec. '"And So Books Entered Our Lives …".' *The Libraries of Thought and Imagination: An Anthology of Books and Bookshelves.* Ed. Alec

Finlay. Edinburgh: Morning Star Publications and Polygon, 2001. 13–19. Print.

———. 'The Dewy Glen.' Ian Hamilton Finlay, *The Dancers Inherit the Party and Glasgow Beasts.* Ed. Alec Finlay. Edinburgh: Polygon, 1996. 95–117. Print.

———. 'Picking the Last Wild Flower.' Ian Hamilton Finlay, *Selections.* Ed. Alec Finlay. Berkeley: University of California Press, 2012. 1–61. Print.

———. 'Shadow and Stitch.' *Chapman*, 78/79 (1994): 125–134. Print.

Finlay, Ian Hamilton. *A Calm in a Tea Cup.* Illustrated by Richard Demarco. Dunsyre: Wild Hawthorn Press, 1973. Print.

———. *A Model of Order: Selected Letters on Poetry and Making.* Ed. Thomas A. Clark. Glasgow: Wax 366, 2009. Print.

———. *A Mast of Hankies: A Celebration of the Smallest Sails Still To Be Seen On Our British Puddles and Ponds.* Photos by Dave Paterson. Dunsyre: Wild Hawthorn Press, 1975. Print.

———. *After Simon Cutts, After Samuel Palmer.* Dunsyre: Wild Hawthorn Press, 1999. Print.

———. *Capital, n. a Republican Crown.* With Lucius Burkhardt. Dunsyre: Wild Hawthorn Press, 1981. Print.

———. *The Dancers Inherit the Party and Glasgow Beasts.* Ed. Alec Finlay. Edinburgh: Polygon, 1996. Print.

———. *The Dancers Inherit the Party: Early Poems, Stories and Plays.* Ed. Ken Cockburn. Edinburgh: Polygon, 2004. Print.

———. *Domestic Pensées.* Ed. Stuart Mills. Belper, Derbyshire: Aggie Weston's Editions, 2004. Print.

———. *Evening/Sail.* Edinburgh: Graeme Murray Gallery, 1970. Print.

———. *Folding the Last Sail: After Thomas A. and Laurie Clark.* Dunsyre: Wild Hawthorn Press, 1997. Print.

———. *Found Eclogue.* Dunsyre: Wild Hawthorn Press, 1998. Print.

———. *Hints and Tips for Boat Modellers.* Little Sparta: Wild Hawthorn Press, 1999. Print.

———. *Hirtenlied/Folding the Last Sheep,* with Laurie Clark, Thomas A. Clark, and Pia Maria Simig. Dunsyre: Wild Hawthorn Press, 1999. Print.

———. *The Homeward Star.* Little Sparta: Wild Hawthorn Press, 1998. Print.

———. 'Letter to Hugh Kenner.' *Chapman* 78–79 (1994): 39–41. Print.

———. Letter to Ronald Johnson and Jonathan Williams, undated. MS 66. Box 24: 33. Spencer Research Library, University of Kansas.

———. Letter to Ronald Johnson, February 11 1970. MS 66. Box 24: 63. Spencer Research Library, University of Kansas.

———, ed. *Poor. Old. Tired. Horse.* 8 (1964). Print.

———. '*The Scots Literary Tradition* by John Speirs.' *New Saltire* (Summer 1962): 79–81. Print.

———. *Selections.* Ed. Alec Finlay. Berkeley: University of California Press, 2012. Print.

————. *They Returned Home Tired, But Happy*. Illustrated by Ian Gardner. Dunsyre: Wild Hawthorn Press, 1972. Print.

Fisher, Roy. *An Easily Bewildered Child: Occasional Prose 1963–2013*. Ed. Peter Robinson. Bristol: Shearsman, 2014. Print.

Fisher, Stephen L., ed. *Fighting Back in Appalachia: Traditions of Resistance and Change*. Philadelphia, PA: Temple University Press, 1993. Print.

————. 'Introduction.' *Fighting Back in Appalachia: Traditions of Resistance and Change*. Ed. Stephen L. Fisher. Philadelphiam PA: Temple University Press, 1993. 1–16. Print.

Foster, Hal. '"Primitive" Scenes.' *Critical Inquiry* 20.1 (Autumn, 1993): 69–102. Print.

Foucault, Michel. *The Order of Things: An Archaeology of the Human Sciences*. London: Routledge, 2002. Print.

Freeman, John. 'Paradise & The Real: The Poetry of Thomas A. Clark.' *Candid Fields: Essays and Reflections on the work of Thomas A. Clark*. Ed. Peter Dent. Budleigh Salterton, Devon: Interim, 1987. 5–18. Print.

Friedenthal, Richard, ed. *Letters of the Great Artists: From Blake to Pollock*. London: Thames and Hudson, 1963. Print.

Fry, Edward F. *Cubism*. London: Thames and Hudson, 1978. Print.

Fulton, Hamish. 'Introduction.' Robert Garioch, *Collected Poems*. Ed. Hamish Fulton. Edinburgh: Polygon, 2004. ix–xxiv. Print.

Furlani, Andre. *Guy Davenport: Postmodernism and After*. Evanston, IL: Northwestern University Press, 2007. Print.

Furnival, John. 'Openings.' *Baseline* 18 (1994): 34–38. Print.

Gappmayr, Heinz. 'sind.' *An Anthology of Concrete Poetry*. Ed. Emmett Williams. New York: Something Else Press, 1967. 122–123. Print.

Gardiner, Michael. *From Trocchi to Trainspotting: Scottish Critical Theory Since 1960*. Edinburgh: Edinburgh University Press, 2006. Print.

Gifford, Terry. *Pastoral*. London: Routledge, 1999. Print.

Gill, Eric. *An Essay on Typography*. London: Penguin, 2013. Print.

Gilonis, Harry. 'How to Read (2).' *Certain Trees: The Constructed Book, Poem, and Object 1964–2006*. Ed. Simon Cutts. Saint-Yrieix-la-Perche: Centre des livres d'artistes, 2007. 118–127. Print.

Glen, Duncan. 'Some Thoughts and Reminiscences.' *Chapman* 78–79 (1994): 23–30. Print.

Godfrey, Tony. *Conceptual Art*. London: Phaidon, 1998. Print.

Golding, Alan. 'Little Magazines and Alternative Canons: The Example of *Origin*.' *American Literary History* 2.4 (Winter, 1990): 691–725. Print.

Gombrich, E. H. 'Icones Symbolicae: The Visual Image in Neo-Platonic Thought.' *Journal of the Warburg and Courtauld Institutes* 11 (1948): 163–192. Print.

Goncharova, Nina. 'Preface to Catalogue of One-Man Exhibition.' *Russian Art of the Avant-Garde: Theory and Criticism*. Ed. and trans. John E. Bowlt. London: Thames and Hudson, 1988. 54–60. Print.

Gooding, Mel. *Songs of the Earth*. London: Thames and Hudson, 2002. Print.

Gray, Camilla. *The Russian Experiment in Art 1863–1922*. London: Thames and Hudson, 1986. Print.

Green, Rayna. 'Introduction to the Dover Edition.' Allen H. Eaton, *Handicrafts of the Southern Highlands*. New York: Dover Publications, 1973. xi–xxi. Print.

Grigson, Geoffrey. *The Englishman's Flora*. Oxford: Helicon Publishing, 1996. Print.

———. *Gardenage, or the Plants of Ninhursaga*. London: Routledge and Kegan Paul, 1952. Print.

———. *Samuel Palmer: The Visionary Years*. London: Kegan Paul, 1947. Print.

———. *Samuel Palmer's Valley of Vision*. London: Phoenix House, 1960. Print.

Gudgin, Victor. 'Situation.' *Tarasque* 3 (c. 1966): n. pag. Print.

Gurianova, Nina. 'A Game in Hell, Hard Work in Heaven: Deconstructing the Canon in Russian Futurist Books.' *The Russian Avant-Garde Book, 1910–1934*. Eds. Margit Rowell and Deborah Wye. New York: Museum of Modern Art, 2002. 24–32. Print.

Hair, Ross. 'Models of Order: Form and Cosmos in the Poetry of Ian Hamilton Finlay and Ronald Johnson.' *Texas Studies in Literature and Language* 56.2 (Summer 2014): 181–225. Print.

———. *Ronald Johnson's Modernist Collage Poetry*. New York: Palgrave Macmillan, 2010. Print.

Hall, Joan Wylie. 'Dialect Literature.' *The Companion to Southern Literature: Themes, Genres, Places, People, Movements, and Motifs*. Eds. Joseph M. Flora and Lucinda H. MacKethan. Baton Rouge: Louisiana State University Press, 2002. 206–207. Print.

Hamilton, Alfred Starr. *A Dark Dreambox of Another Kind*. Eds. Ben Estes and Alan Felsenthal. Brooklyn, New York: The Song Cave, 2013. Print.

———. *Poems*. Penland, North Carolina: The Jargon Society, 1970. Print.

Hardie, Philip R. *Virgil*. Oxford: Oxford University Press, 1998. Print.

Harkey, John. 'Usable Dimensions: An Afterword.' Lorine Niedecker, *Homemade Poems*. New York: Center for the Humanities, Graduate Center, City University of New York, 2012. 1–12. Print.

Harley, J. B. 'Deconstructing the Map.' *Writing Worlds: Discourse, Text and Metaphor in the Representation of Landscape*. Eds. Trevor J. Barnes and James S. Duncan. Oxon: Routledge, 2006. 231–247. Print.

Harrison, Stephan, Steve Pile, and Nigel Thrift, eds. *Patterned Ground: Entanglements of Nature and Culture*. London: Reaktion Books, 2004. Print.

Hart, Matthew. *Nations of Nothing But Poetry: Modernism, Transnationalism, and Synthetic Vernacular Writing*. New York: Oxford University Press, 2010. Print.

Havlick, David. 'Logics of Change for Military-to-Wildlife Conversions in the United States.' *GeoJournal* 69 (2007): 151–164. Print.

Henderson, Hamish. *The Armstrong Nose: Selected Letters of Hamish Henderson*. Ed. Alec Finlay. Edinburgh: Polygon, 1996. Print.

Avant-Folk

———. *Alias MacAlias: Writings on Songs, Folk and Literature.* Edinburgh: Polygon, 1992. Print.

Heraclitus. *Fragments.* Trans. T. M. Robinson. Toronto: University of Toronto Press, 1987. Print.

Herd, David. 'Making Spaces: An Interview with Thomas A. Clark.' *Oxford Poetry* II. 3 (1993): 97–102. Print.

Hirsch, Jerrold. 'Folklore in the Making: B. A. Botkin.' *The Journal of American Folklore* 100.395 (January– March, 1987): 3–38. Print.

———. *Portrait of America: A Cultural History of the Federal Writers' Project.* Chapel Hill and London: The University of North Carolina Press, 2003. Print.

Hollo, Anselm. *Braided River: New and Selected Poems 1965–2005.* Cambridge: Salt Publishing, 2005. Print.

Horovitz, Michael. 'Afterwords.' *Children of Albion: Poetry of the Underground in Britain.* Ed. Michael Horovitz. Harmondsworth: Penguin, 1969. 316–377. Print.

Houédard, Dom Sylvester. 'The Wider Ecumenism.' *The Aylesford Review* 7.2 (Summer 1965): 118. Print.

Howe, Susan. 'Foreword.' Erica Van Horn, *Living Locally.* Axminster, Devon: Uniformbooks, 2014. 5–6. Print.

———. 'The End of Art.' *Archives of American Art Journal* 14.4 (1974): 2–7. Print.

Hubbard, Thomas K. *The Pipes of Pan: Intertextuality and Literary Filiation in the Pastoral Tradition from Theocritus to Milton.* Ann Arbor: University of Michigan Press, 2001. Print.

Hunt, John Dixon. *Nature Over Again: The Garden Art of Ian Hamilton Finlay.* London: Reaktion Books, 2008. Print.

'Ian Hamilton Finlay.' *The Tate Gallery 1974–6 Illustrated Catalogue of Acquisitions.* London: The Tate Gallery, 1978. 91–93. Print.

Innes, Sue. 'Man of Sparta.' *Wood Notes Wild: Essays on the Poetry and Art of Ian Hamilton Finlay.* Ed. Alec Finlay. Edinburgh: Polygon, 1995. 9–15. Print.

Irby, Kenneth. '"america's largest openair museum."' *Parnassus: Poetry in Review* 8.2 (1980): 307–328. Print.

Jaffe, James. 'Jonathan Williams, Jargonaut.' *Jacket* 38 (Late 2009): n. pag. Web. 26 July 2015.

James, David, and Philip Tew. 'Introduction: Re-envisioning Pastoral.' *New Versions of Pastoral: Post-Romantic, Modern, and Contemporary Responses to the Tradition.* Eds. David James and Phillip Tew. Cranbury, NJ: Associated University Presses, 2009. 13–30. Print.

Jennison, Ruth. 'Waking Into Ideology: Lorine Niedecker's Experiments in the Syntax of Consciousness.' *Radical Vernacular: Lorine Niedecker and the Poetics of Place.* Ed. Elizabeth Willis. Iowa City: University of Iowa Press, 2008: 131–150. Print.

Johnson, Ronald. 'Jonathan Williams.' *American Poets since World War II: Dictionary of Literary Biography* Vol. 5. Ed. Donald J. Greiner. Detroit, MI: Gale Research, 1980. 406–409. Print.

260

————, and Jonathan Williams. 'Nearly Twenty Questions.' *Conjunctions* 7 (Spring, 1985): 225–238. Print.

————. 'Six, Alas!' *Chicago Review* 37.1 (Winter, 1990): 26–41. Print.

Johnson, Samuel. *The Lives of the Poets: A Selection*. Ed. Roger Lonsdale. Oxford: Oxford World's Classics, 2009. Print.

Jones, Gavin Roger. *Strange Talk: The Politics of Dialect Literature in Gilded Age America*. Berkeley: University of California Press, 1999. Print.

Jones, Jonathan. 'The Artistic Jingoism of the Bomber Command Memorial.' *The Guardian*, June 29, 2012. Web. 26 July 2015.

Kahnweiler, Daniel-Henry. *The Rise of Cubism*. Trans. Henry Aronson. New York: Wittenborn, Schulz, 1949. Print.

Kane, Daniel. *All Poets Welcome: The Lower Eastside Poetry Scene in the 1960s*. Berkeley: University of California Press, 2003. Print.

Keir, W. A. S. 'Poets, Poetasters, Bards and/or Makars.' *New Saltire* 4 (Summer, 1962): 82–85. Print.

Kenedy, R. C. 'Ian Hamilton Finlay.' *Wood Notes Wild: Essays on the Poetry and Art of Ian Hamilton Finlay*. Ed. Alec Finlay. Edinburgh: Polygon, 1995. 39–44. Print.

Kenner, Hugh. *A Homemade World: The American Modernist Writers*. New York: Alfred A. Knopf, 1975. Print.

————. Dust jacket blurb. Ian Hamilton Finlay, *Domestic Pensées*. Ed. Stuart Mills. Belper, Derbyshire: Aggie Weston's Editions, 2004. Print.

————. *The Elsewhere Community*. Oxford and New York: Oxford University Press, 2000. Print.

Killian, Kevin 'Jack Spicer's Secret.' *Jacket* 37 (early 2009): n. pag. Web. 26 July 2015.

Kuhl, Nancy. *The Book Remembers Everything: The Work of Erica Van Horn*. Tipperary/New York: Coracle/Granary Books, 2010. Print.

Kusano, Shimpei. *Asking Myself Answering Myself*. Trans. Cid Corman. New York: New Directions, 1984. Print.

Lanier, Sidney. *Poems of Sidney Lanier*. Ed. Mary Day Lanier. Athens: University of Georgia Press, 1999. Print.

Latter, Alex. *Late Modernism and The English Intelligencer: On the Poetics of Community*. London: Bloomsbury, 2015. Print.

Lawson, Andrew. 'On Modern Pastoral.' *Fragmente* 3 (Spring, 1991): 34–41. Print.

Leibowitz, Herbert. '*Blues & Roots, Rue & Bluets, The Appalachian Photographs of Doris Ulmann*.' New York Times Book Review (21 November 1971): 54, 56, 58. Print.

————. 'Introduction.' Jonathan Williams. *Blues & Roots/Rue & Bluets: A Garland for the Southern Appalachians* (second edition). Durham, NC: Duke University Press, 1985, n. pag. Print.

Lewis, Wyndham, ed. *Blast* 1 (June, 1914). Reprint. Berkeley, CA: Gingko Press, 2009. Print.

LeWitt, Sol. 'Paragraphs on Conceptual Art.' *Conceptual Art: A Critical Anthology*. Eds. Alexander Alberro and Blake Stimson. Cambridge, MA: MIT Press, 1999. 12–16. Print.

Lindsay, Maurice. 'The Ant-Renaissance Burd, Inseks an Haw.' *New Saltire* 4 (Summer, 1962): 61–67. Print.

Lippard, Lucy R. 'Conspicuous Consumption: New Artists' Books.' *Artists' Books: A Critical Anthology and Sourcebook.* Ed. Joan Lyons. Rochester, NY: Visual Studies Workshop Press, 1985. 49–58. Print.

———. 'Escape Attempts.' *Six Years: The Dematerialization of the Art Object from 1966 to 1972.* Ed. Lucy R. Lippard. Berkeley and Los Angeles: University of California Press, 1997. vii–xxii. Print.

Lister, Raymond. 'Francis Oliver Finch.' *Studies in the Arts: Proceedings of St. Peter's College Literary Society.* Ed. Francis Warner. Oxford: Basil Blackwell, 1968. 99–115. Print.

Livingston, Robert Eric. 'Glocal Knowledges: Agency and Place in Literary Studies.' *PMLA* 116.1 (January, 2001): 145–157. Print.

Lodder, Christina. 'Russian Avant-Garde Art: From Neoprimitivism to Constructivism.' *Russian Painting of the Avant-Garde 1906–1924.* Edinburgh: Scottish National Gallery of Modern Art, 1993. 11–21. Print.

Loewinsohn, Ron. 'After the (Mimeograph) Revolution.' *TriQuarterly* (Spring, 1970): 221–236. Print.

Long, Richard. *Selected Statements and Interviews.* Ed. Ben Tufnell. London: Haunch of Venison, 2007. Print.

Lorimer, Hayden. 'Cultural Geography: The Busyness of Being "More-than-Representational."' *Progress in Human Geography February* 29.1 (February, 2005): 83–94. Print.

———. 'Telling Small Stories: Spaces of Knowledge and the Practice of Geography.' *Transactions of the Institute of British Geographers* 28.2 (June, 2003): 197–217. Print.

Loughrey, Brian. *The Pastoral Mode: A Casebook.* Basingstoke: Macmillan, 1984. Print.

Lowell, Amy, ed. *Some Imagist Poets: An Anthology.* Boston, MA and New York: Houghton Mifflin Company, 1915. Print.

MacDiarmid, Hugh. *Albyn: Shorter Books and Monographs.* Ed. Alan Riach. Manchester: Carcanet, 1996. Print.

———. *Selected Prose.* Ed. Alan Riach. Manchester: Carcanet Press, 1992. Print.

McGann, Jerome. *Black Riders: The Visible Language of Modernism.* Princeton, NJ: Princeton University Press. 1993. Print.

McClure, J. Derrick. *Language, Poetry, and Nationhood: Scots as a Poetic Language from 1878 to the Present.* East Lothian: Tuckwell Press, 2000. Print.

Mabey, Richard. *The Unofficial Countryside.* Introduced by Iain Sinclair. Stanbridge, Dorset: Little Toller Books, 2010. Print.

Malevich, Kasimir. 'From Cubism and Futurism to Suprematism: The New Painterly Realism.' *Russian Art of the Avant-Garde: Theory and Criticism.* Ed. and trans. John E. Bowlt. London: Thames and Hudson, 1988. 116–135. Print.

Markov, Vladimir. *Russian Futurism: A History.* London: Macgibon and Kee, 1969. Print.

Martin, Robert K., ed. *The Continuing Presence of Walt Whitman: The Life After the Life*. Iowa City: University of Iowa Press, 1992. Print.

Massey, Doreen. *For Space*. Los Angeles and London: Sage, 2005. Print.

Matless, David. *In The Nature Of Landscape Cultural Geography On The Norfolk Broads*. Chichester: Wiley Blackwell, 2014. Print.

Maud, Ralph. *What Does Not Change: The Significance of Charles Olson's 'The Kingfishers.'* Cranbury, NJ: Associated University Presses, 1998. Print.

Mayakovsky, Vladimir. *Listen! Early Poems 1913–1918*. Trans. Maria Enzensberger. San Francisco, CA: City Lights Books, 1991. Print.

Mays, J. C. C. 'Rare Sighting in the Haldon Hills.' *artcornwall*. artcornwall.org, nd. Web. 26 July 2015.

Mellers, Wilfrid. *Vaughan Williams and the Vision of Albion*. London: Barrie & Jenkins, 1989. Print.

Meyer, Thomas. 'JW Gent & Epicurean.' *Jacket* 38 (Late 2009): n. pag. Web. 26 July 2015.

Meyrick, Robert. 'In Pursuit of Arcadia: British Printmaking in the 1920s.' *Poets in the Landscape: The Romantic Spirit in British Art*. Ed. Simon Martin. Chichester: Pallant House Gallery, 2007. 59–82. Print.

Middleton, Peter. 'The British Niedecker.' *Radical Vernacular: Lorine Niedecker and the Poetics of Place*. Ed. Elizabeth Willis. Iowa City: University of Iowa Press, 2008. 247–270. Print.

———. 'Lorine Niedecker's "Folk Base" and Her Challenge to the American Avant-Garde.' *The Objectivist Nexus: Essays in Cultural Poetics*. Eds. Rachel Blau DuPlessis and Peter Quartermain. Tuscaloosa: University of Alabama Press, 1999. 160–188. Print.

'Migrant Press.' Promotional flyer c. 1965. Print.

Mills, Stuart. *A Far Distant Landscape*. Illustrations by Ian Gardner. *New Arcadian Journal* 22 (1986). Print.

———. 'Coracle.' *The Coracle: Coracle Press Gallery 1975–1987*. Ed. Simon Cutts. London: Coracle, 1989. 14. Print.

———. 'Foreword.' *Tarasque* 6: n. pag. Print.

———. 'From Tarasque to *Aggie Weston's*.' *Certain Trees: The Constructed Book, Poem, and Object 1964–2006*. Ed. Simon Cutts. Saint-Yrieix-la-Perche: Centre des livres d'artistes, 2007. 141. Print.

———. *Made in English: The Poems of Stuart Mills*. Ed. Simon Cutts. Ballybeg, Tipperary: Coracle, 2008. Print.

———, and Simon Cutts. Untitled. *Tarasque 5*, n. pag. Print.

———, and Simon Cutts. 'some pointers taken at random from notebooks, and other sources.' *Tarasque* 2 (c. 1964): n. pag. Print.

Milton, John. *The Major Works*. Eds. Stephen Orgel and Jonathan Goldberg. Oxford: Oxford World's Classics, 2003. Print.

Mingus, Charles. *Blues & Roots*. Atlantic, 1960. LP.

Mitchell, Georgina. *The North American Folk Music Revival: Nation and Identity in the United States and Canada, 1945–1980*. Aldershot, Hampshire: Ashgate, 2007. Print.

Moeglin-Delcroix, Anne. *Ambulo ergo sum: Nature as Experience in Artists' Books*. Koln: Verlag dr Buchenhandlung Walther Konig, 2015. Print.

————. 'Little Books & Other Little Publications.' Trans. Patricia Railing. *Little Critic* 15. Tipperary: Coracle, 2001. Print.

————. 'Poet or Artist?' Trans. Jessica Moore. *The Present Order: Writings on the Work of Ian Hamilton Finlay*. Eds. Caitlin Murray and Tim Johnson. Marfa, TX: Marfa Book Company, 2010. 31–69. Print.

Monk, Geraldine. 'A Working Class Elitist Is Something to Be.' *Cusp.* Ed. Geraldine Monk. Bristol: Shearsman, 2012. 182–190. Print.

Morgan, Edwin. *Essays*. Chaedle: Carcanet, 1974. Print.

————. *The Midnight Letterbox: Selected Correspondence (1950–2010)*. Eds. James McGonigal and James Coyle. Manchester: Carcanet, 2015. Print.

————. 'Poor. Old. Tired. Horse.' *Wood Notes Wild: Essays on the Poetry and Art of Ian Hamilton Finlay*. Ed. Alec Finlay. Edinburgh: Polygon, 1995. 26–27. Print.

Morris, William. *Hopes and Fears for Art: Five Lectures Delivered in Birmingham, London, and Nottingham, 1878–1881*. London: Ellis & White, 1882. Print.

Mottram, Eric. 'Jonathan Williams.' *VORT* 4 Number (Fall, 1973): 102–111.

Nadel, Ira B. '"A Precision of Appeal": Louis Zukofsky and the *Index of American Design*.' *Upper Limit Music: The Writing of Louis Zukofsky*. Ed. Mark Scroggins. Tuscaloosa: University of Alabama Press, 1997. 112–126. Print.

Neate, Hannah. 'Because the Trent Bookshop is in Nottingham.' *Cusp.* Ed. Geraldine Monk. Bristol: Shearsman, 2012. 35–50. Print.

Nicholls, Peter. 'Lorine Niedecker: Rural Surreal.' *Lorine Niedecker: Woman and Poet*. Ed. Jenny Penberthy. Orono, ME: National Poetry Foundation, 1996. 193–217. Print.

Nichols, Miriam. *Radical Affections: Essays on the Poetics of Outside*. Tuscaloosa: University of Alabama Press, 2010. Print.

Niedecker, Lorine. *A Cooking Book*. Brattleboro, VT: Longhouse, 2014.

————. *Collected Works*. Ed. Jenny Penberthy. Berkeley: University of California Press, 2002.

————. 'Extracts from Letters to Kenneth Cox.' *The Full Note: Lorine Niedecker*. Ed. Peter Dent. Budleigh Salterton, Devon, Interim, 1983. 36–42. Print.

————. 'Letters.' *Truck* 16 (Summer 1975): 41–54. Print.

————. 'Lorine's home-made book for Aeneas' (1956). *The State of Wisconsin Collection*. University of Wisconsin Digital Collections, n.d. Web. 3 August 2015.

————. *New Goose*. Ed. Jenny Penberthy. Berkeley, CA: Listening Chamber, 2002. Print.

North, Michael. *The Dialect of Modernism: Race, Language and Twentieth-Century Literature*. New York and Oxford: Oxford University Press, 1994. Print.

Norvig, Gerda S. *Dark Figures in the Desired Country: Blake's Illustrations to The Pilgrim's Progress*. Berkeley: University of California Press, 1993. Print.

'Notes on Contributors.' *Mica* 5 (Winter, 1962): 28. Print.

Olson, Charles. *Collected Prose.* Eds. Donald Allen and Benjamin Friedlander. Berkeley and Los Angeles: University of California Press, 1999. Print.

————. *The Maximus Poems.* Ed. George F. Butterick. Berkeley and Los Angeles: University of California Press, 1984.

Owens, Richard, and Jeffery Beam. 'The Lord of Orchards: Jonathan Williams at 80.' *Jacket 38* (2009): n. pag. Web. 26 July 2015.

Palmer, A. H., ed. *The Life and Letters of Samuel Palmer.* London: Seeley and Co.: 1892. Print.

Palmer, Samuel. *The Parting Light: Selected Writings.* Ed. Mark Abley. Manchester: Carcanet, 1985. Print.

Panofsky, Erwin. *Meaning in the Visual Arts: Papers in and on Art History.* New York: Doubleday, 1955. Print.

Patterson, Tom. 'O For A Muse of Fire: The Iconoclasm of Jonathan Williams and the Jargon Society.' *Afterimage* 23 (March/April, 1996): 8–12. Print.

Pattison, Neil. 'All Flags Left Outside.' *Certain Prose of The English Intelligencer.* Eds. Neil Pattison, Reitha Pattison, and Luke Roberts. Cambridge, MA: Mountain Press, 2012. i–xxiv. Print.

Peebles, Alistair. 'Labour, Blossom: Ian Hamilton Finlay and Orkney.' *Painted Spoken* 7 (2011): 8–21. Print.

Penberthy, Jenny. 'A Posse of Two: Lorine Niedecker and Ian Hamilton Finlay.' *Chapman* 78–79 (1994): 17–22. Print.

————. 'Next Year or I Fly my Rounds, Tempestuous.' Ed. Jenny Penberthy. *Sulfur* 41 (Fall, 1997). 42–71. Print.

————. *Niedecker and the Correspondence with Zukofsky 1931–1970.* Cambridge: Cambridge University Press, 1993. Print.

Perloff, Marjorie. 'From "Suprematism" to Language Game: *The Blue and Brown Poems* of Ian Hamilton Finlay.' *The Present Order: Writings on the Work of Ian Hamilton Finlay.* Eds. Caitlin Murray and Tim Johnson. Marfa, TX: Marfa Book Company, 2010. 85–103. Print.

————. *The Futurist Moment: Avant-Garde, Avant Guerre, and the Language of Rupture.* Chicago, IL: University of Chicago Press, 1986. Print.

Peters, Margot. *Lorine Niedecker: A Poet's Life.* Madison: University of Wisconsin Press, 2011. Print.

Peterson, Jeffrey. 'Lorine Niedecker: "Before Machines."' *Lorine Niedecker: Woman and Poet.* Ed. Jenny Penberthy. Orono, ME: The National Poetry Foundation, 1996. 245–279. Print.

Petty, Antje. '"*Dies schrieb Dir zur Erinnerung …*" From *Album Amicorum* to Autograph Book.' *Max Kade Institute for German-American Studies.* Max Kade Institute for German-American Studies, April, 2007. Web. 26 July 2015.

Phillpot, Clive. *Booktrek: Selected Essays on Artists' Books (1972–2010).* Zurich: JRP/Ringier, 2013. Print.

Poe, Edgar Allan. *Selected Writings.* Ed. David Galloway. Harmondsworth: Penguin, 1967. Print.

Pound, Ezra. *The Cantos.* London: Faber and Faber, 1996. Print.

————. *Literary Essays.* Ed. T. S. Eliot. London: Faber and Faber, 1960. Print.

Power, Kevin. 'Jonathan Williams: Car Cum.' *Truck 21: A 50th Birthday Celebration for Jonathan Williams.* Eds. Thomas A. Clark and Jonathan Greene. Frankfort, KY: Truck/Gnomon Press, 1979. n. pag. Print.

Price, Richard. 'Migrant the Magnificent.' *PN Review* 33.4 (March–April, 2007): 29–33. Print.

————. 'Some Questions about Literary Infrastructure in the 1960s.' *The Scottish Sixties: Reading, Rebellion, Revolution?* Eds. Eleanor Bell and Linda Gunn. Amsterdam and New York: Rodopi, 2013. 93–114. Print.

Prynne, J. H. 'From a Letter.' *Mica* 5 (Winter, 1962): 2–3, 28. Print.

Pursglove, Glyn. 'Thomas A. Clark Interviewed by Glyn Pursgrove.' *Poetry Information* 18 (1978): 12–20. Print.

Putnam, Michael. C. J. *Virgil's Pastoral Art: Studies in the Eclogues.* Princeton, NJ: Princeton University Press, 1970. Print.

Quartermain, Peter. 'Reading Niedecker.' *Lorine Niedecker: Woman and Poet.* Ed. Jenny Penberthy. Orono, ME: The National Poetry Foundation, 1996. 219–227. Print.

Rasula, Jed. *Destruction Was My Beatrice: Dada and the Unmaking of the Twentieth Century.* New York: Basic Books, 2015. Print.

Reason, David. 'A Hard Country Singing.' *The Unpainted Landscape.* Ed. Simon Cutts. London: Coracle Press/Edinburgh: Graeme Murray Gallery, 1987. 24–87. Print.

————. 'Line And Line About.' Thomas A. Clark, *About Nothing In Particular.* A Morning Star Folio, 1990. n. pag. Print.

Renteln, Alison Dundes, and Alan Dundes. 'What Is Folk Law?' *Folk Law: Essays in the Theory and Practice of Lex Non Scripta, Volume 1.* Eds. Alison Dundes Renteln and Alan Dundes. Madison: University of Wisconsin Press, 1994. 1–4. Print.

Reverdy, Pierre. 'On Cubism.' Edward F. Fry *Cubism.* London: Thames and Hudson, 1978. 143–146. Print.

————. 'Some Advantages of Being Alone.' Edward F. Fry *Cubism.* London: Thames and Hudson, 1978. 149. Print.

Rhodes, Colin. *Primitivism and Modern Art.* London: Thames and Hudson, 1994. Print.

Riley, Denise. *Selected Poems.* Hastings: Reality Street Editions, 2000. Print.

Roberts, Kay. 'House as Format.' *The Coracle: Coracle Press Gallery 1975–1987.* Ed. Simon Cutts. London: Coracle, 1989. 9–12. Print.

Rose, Gillian. *Feminism and Geography: The Limits of Geographical Knowledge.* Minneapolis: University of Minnesota Press, 1993. Print.

Rosenmeyer, Thomas G. *The Green Cabinet: Theocritus and the European Pastoral Lyric.* Berkeley: University of California Press, 1973. Print.

Rothenberg, Jerome. 'Pre-Face.' *A Secret Location on the Lower East Side: Adventures in Writing 1960–1980.* Eds. Steven Clay and Rodney Phillips. New York: Granary Books. 9–11. Print.

Roub, Gail. 'Getting to Know Lorine Niedecker.' *Lorine Niedecker: Woman and Poet.* Ed. Jenney Penberthy. Orono, ME: National Poetry Foundation, 1996. 79–86. Print.

Roy, Bonnie. 'Niedecker Blue: Proofs and Poetics.' *Contemporary Literature* 56.3 (Fall 2015): 476–504. Print.

Sackett, Colin. 'Allotment.' *The Coracle: Coracle Press Gallery 1975–1987.* Ed. Simon Cutts. London: Coracle, 1989. 74–84. Print.

———. 'Bibliopoly: Interview with Cathy Courtney.' 1995. *Colin Sackett.* Colin Sackett, n.d. Web. 26 July 2015.

———. 'Collection.' *Anticipatory History.* Eds. Caitlin DeSilvey, Simon Naylor, and Colin Sackett. Axminster, Devon: Uniformbooks, 2011. 29–30. Print.

———. *Englshpublshing: Writings and Readings 1991–2002.* Tipperary: Coracle/Limoges: Sixtus/Éditions / Exeter: Spacex, 2004. Print.

———. *Geeooggrraapphhyy.* Axminster, Devon: Colin Sackett, 2009. Print.

Saito, Yuriko. *Everyday Aesthetics.* Oxford: Oxford University Press, 2010. Print.

Saper, Craig. J. *Networked Art.* Minneapolis and London: University of Minnesota Press, 2001. Print.

Saroyam, Aram. *Door to the River: Essays and Reviews from the 1960s into the Digital Age.* Jaffrey, NH: David R. Godine/Black Sparrow, 2010. Print.

Saunders, Timothy. '"Using Green Words" or "Abusing Bucolic Ground."' *Pastoral and the Humanities: Arcadia Re-inscribed.* Eds. Mathilde Skoie and Sonia Bjørnstad-Velázquez. Exeter: Bristol Phoenix Press, 2006. 3–13. Print.

Schlesinger, Kyle. 'The Jargon Society.' *Jacket* 38 (Late 2009): n. pag. Web. 8 Sep 2016.

Schumacher, E. F. *Small is Beautiful: A Study of Economics as if People Mattered.* New York: Random House: 1993. Print.

Scobie, Stephen. *Earthquakes and Explorations: Language and Painting from Cubism to Concrete Poetry.* Toronto: Toronto University Press, 2012. Print.

Scroggins, Mark. 'The Piety of Terror: Ian Hamilton Finlay, the Modernist Fragment, and the Neo-classical Sublime.' *Jacket* 15 (2001): n. pag. Web. 26 July 2015.

Sheeler, Jessie. *Little Sparta: The Garden of Ian Hamilton Finlay.* London: Frances Lincoln, 2003. Print.

Shelley, Percy Bysshe. *The Selected Poetry and Prose of Shelley.* Ware, Hertfordshire: Wordsworth Editions, 2002. Print.

Shepherd, Nan. *The Living Mountain.* Edinburgh: Canongate, 2011. Print.

Sheppard, Robert. *The Poetry of Saying: British Poetry and Its Discontents 1950–2000.* Liverpool: Liverpool University Press, 2005. Print.

Shevchenko, Aleksander, 'Neo-Primitivism: Its Theory, Its Potentials, Its Achievements.' Ed. Paul E. Bowlt. *Russian Art of the Avant-Garde: Theory and Criticism.* London: Thames and Hudson, 1988. 41–54. Print.

Shoard, Marion. 'Edgelands.' *Remaking the Landscape: The Changing Face of Britain*. Ed. Jennifer Jenkins. London: Profile Books, 2002. 117–146. Print.

Sikelianos, Eleni. 'Life Pops from a Music Box Shaped Like a Gun: Dismemberment and Mendings in Niedecker's Figures.' *Radical Vernacular: Lorine Niedecker and the Poetics of Place*. Ed. Elizabeth Willis. Iowa City: University of Iowa Press, 2008. 31–40. Print.

Sikes, E. E. *Lucretius, Poet and Philosopher*. Cambridge: Cambridge University Press, 1936. Print.

Sinclair, Iain. 'Introduction.' *The Unofficial Countryside*. Richard Mabey. Stanbridge, Dorset: Little Toller Books, 2010. 7–13. Print.

———. *London Orbital: A Walk Around the M25*. London: Penguin, 2003. Print.

Sitwell, Edith. *A Poet's Notebook*. London: Macmillan, 1944. Print.

———. *Collected Poems*. London: Sinclair-Stevenson, 1993. Print.

Skinner, Jonathan. 'Particular Attention: Lorine Niedecker's Natural Histories.' *Radical Vernacular: Lorine Niedecker and the Poetics of Place*. Ed. Elizabeth Willis. Iowa City: University of Iowa Press, 2008. 41–59. Print.

Smith, Dale, 'Devotion to the Strange: Jonathan Williams and the Small Press.' *Jacket* 38 (Late 2009): n. pag. Web. 26 July 2015.

Snell, Bruno. *The Discovery of the Mind in Greek Philosophy and Literature*. Trans. Thomas. G. Rosenmeyer. Mineola, NY: Dover Editions, 1982. Print.

Solt, Mary Ellen. *Concrete Poetry: A World View*. Bloomington: Indiana University Press, 1968. Print.

Sorrentino, Gilbert. 'Misconstruing Lorine Niedecker.' *Lorine Niedecker: Woman and Poet*. Ed. Jenny Penberthy. Orono, ME: The National Poetry Foundation, 1996. 287–292. Print.

Spragg, Andy. 'Tom Raworth Speaks to Andy Spragg.' *Miso Sensitive*, Friday, 21 January, 2011. Web. 26 July 2015.

Stacey, Robert. '"Into the Order of Things": The Relations of Painting to the Poetry of Thomas A. Clark.' *Candid Fields: Essays and Reflections on the Work of Thomas A. Clark*. Ed. Peter Dent. Budleigh Salterton, Devon: Interim, 1987. 24–36. Print.

Stein, Gertrude. *Picasso*. New York: Dover Publications, 1984. Print.

Stewart, Susan. 'Garden Agon.' *Representations* 62 (1998): 111–143. Print.

Tait, Robert. 'The Concreteness of a Wild Hawthorn.' *Extra Verse* 15 (Spring, 1965): 1–13. Print.

Theocritus. *Idylls*. Trans. Anthony Verity. Oxford: Oxford World's Classics, 2008. Print.

Thiselton-Dyer, T. F. *The Folk-lore of Plants*. (1889). Middlesex: The Echo Library, 2008. Print.

Thrift, Nigel. *Non-representational Theory: Space, Politics, Affect*. Abingdon, Oxfordshire: Routledge, 2008. Print.

Tomlinson, Charles. *American Essays: Making It New*. Manchester: Carcanet, 2001. Print.

————. 'Introduction.' Simon Cutts, *A New Kind of Tie: Poems 1965–68*. East Markham: Nottinghamshire, 1972. n. pag. Print.

Tuan, Yi-Fu. *Space and Place: The Perspective of Experience*. Minneapolis: University of Minnesota Press, 1977. Print.

————. 'Thought and Landscape: The Eye and the Mind's Eye.' *The Interpretation of Ordinary Landscapes*. Ed. D. W. Meinig. New York: Oxford University Press, 1979. 89–102. Print.

Tucker, Alan. 'Moschatel Press.' *Certain Trees: The Constructed Book, Poem, and Object 1964–2006*. Ed. Simon Cutts. Saint-Yrieix-la-Perche: Centre des livres d'artistes, 2007. 142. Print.

Tucker, Susan, Katherine Ott and Patricia P. Buckler, eds. *The Scrapbook in American Life*. Philadelphia: Temple University Press, 2006. Print.

Tuma, Keith. *Fishing By Obstinate Isles: Modern and Postmodern British Poetry and American Readers*. Evanston, IL: Northwestern University Press, 1999. Print.

Turnbull, Gael. *More Words: Gael Turnbull on Poets and Poetry*. Eds. Jill Turnbull and Hamish Whyte. Bristol: Shearsman, 2012. Print.

Turnbull, Jonnie. 'The Migrant Years.' *PS (Painted Spoken Prose Supplement)* 1 (2006): n. pag. Print.

Twiddy, Iain. *Pastoral Elegy in Contemporary British and Irish Poetry*. London: Continuum, 2012. Print.

Van Horn, Erica. 'A healthy rosemary plant.' Postcard. Clonmel, Tipperary: Coracle, 2008. Print.

————. *Living Locally*. Axminster, Devon: Uniformbooks, 2014. Print.

————. *Stiles & The Pennine Way*. Docking, Norfolk: Coracle, 1993. Print.

Vernon, John. 'The Cry of Its Occasion: Robert Creeley.' *Boundary 2* 6.3/7.1 (Spring–Autumn, 1978): 309–328. Print.

Virgil. *The Eclogues*. Trans. G. Lee. Harmondsworth: Penguin, 1984. Print.

————. *The Pastoral Poems*. Trans. E. V. Rieu. Harmondsworth: Penguin, 1967. Print.

Volk, Douglas. 'The Human Element in Arts and Crafts.' *Brush and Pencil* 11.6 (March, 1903): 443–444. Print.

Wain, John. 'Foreword' Jonathan Williams. *Lines About Hills Above Lake*. Fort Lauderdale: Roman Books, Inc, 1964. 5–8. Print.

Ward, Geoff. *The Writing of America: Literature and Cultural Identity from the Puritans to the Present*. Cambridge: Polity Press, 2002. Print.

Warren, Rosanna. *Fables of the Self: Studies in Lyric Poetry*. New York: W. W. Norton, 2008. Print.

Watten, Barrett. *The Constructivist Moment: From Material Text to Cultural Poetics*. Middleton, CT: Wesleyan University Press, 2003. Print.

Weaver, Mike. 'Ian Hamilton Finlay.' *Extra Verse* 15 (Spring, 1965): 13–19. Print.

Wheatley, David. Review of *Rays* by Richard Price and *The Hundred Thousand Places* by Thomas A. Clark. *The Guardian Review* (31 October, 2009): 14. Print.

White, Eric B. *Transatlantic Avant-Gardes: Little Magazines and Localist Modernism*. Edinburgh: Edinburgh University Press, 2012. Print.

Whitfield, Sarah. *Fauvism*. London: Thames and Hudson, 1991. Print.

Whitman, Walt. *Poetry and Prose*. New York: Literary Classics of the United States, 1982. Print.

Williams, Jonathan. *An Ear in Bartram's Tree: Selected Poems 1957–1967*. New York: New Directions, 1972. Print.

———. *Blackbird Dust: Essays, Poems, and Photographs*. New York: Turtle Point Press, 2000. Print.

———. *Blues & Roots/Rue & Bluets: A Garland for the Southern Appalachians*. Photographs by Nicolas Dean. New York: Grossman Publishers, 1971. Print.

———. *Blues & Roots/Rue & Bluets: A Garland for the Southern Appalachians* (second edition). Durham, NC: Duke University Press, 1985. Print.

———. 'Colonel Colporteur's Winston-Salem Snake Oil.' *VORT* 4 Number (Fall, 1973): 76–83. Print.

———, ed. *Epitaphs for Lorine*. Penland, NC: The Jargon Society, 1973.

———. Jacket endorsement for Lorine Niedecker, *T &G: Collected Poems (1936–1966)*. Penland, North Carolina: Jargon Society, 1969. Print.

———. *Jubilant Thicket: New and Selected Poems*. Port Townsend, WA: Copper Canyon Press, 2005. Print.

———. 'Jonathan Williams's Nation Of Has, For Those Who Haven't: Interview by Jeffery Beam for *Rain Taxi* 2003.' *The Jargon Society*. The Jargon Society, 2003. Web. 26 July 2015.

———. *The Magpie's Bagpipe: Selected Essays*. Ed. Thomas Meyer. San Francisco, CA: North Point Press, 1982. Print.

———. *Uncle Gus Flaubert Rates the Jargon Society In One Hundred One Laconic Présalé Sage Sentences*. Chapel Hill, NC: Rare Book Collection/ University Library, 1989. Print.

Williams, Raymond. *The Country and the City*. Oxford: Oxford University Press, 1975. Print.

Williams, William Carlos. *Selected Essays*. New York: New Directions, 1969.

———. *Spring and All*. New York: New Directions, 2011. Print.

Willis, Elizabeth. 'Introduction.' *Radical Vernacular: Lorine Niedecker and the Poetics of Place*. Ed. Elizabeth Willis. Iowa City: University of Iowa Press, 2008. xiii–xxiii. Print.

———. 'Possessing Possession: Lorine Niedecker, Folk, and the Allegory of Making.' *XCP: Cross-Cultural Poetics* 9 (2001): 97–106. Print.

———. 'The Poetics of Affinity: Lorine Niedecker, William Morris, and the Art of Work.' *Contemporary Literature* 46.4 (Winter, 2005): 579–603. Print.

Winkfield, Trevor. 'An Example to Follow.' *The Coracle: Coracle Press Gallery 1975–1987*. Ed. Simon Cutts. London: Coracle, 1989. 7–8. Print.

———. *Georges Braque and Others: The Selected Art Writings of Trevor Winkfield (1990–2009)*. Brooklyn, NY: The Song Cave, 2014. Print.

Wordsworth, William, and Samuel Taylor Coleridge. *Lyrical Ballads: 1798 and 1802*. Ed. Fiona Stafford. Oxford: Oxford World's Classics, 2013. Print.

Wright, Edward. *Graphic Work & Painting*. St Albans: Priory Press, 1985. Print.

Writers' Program of the Work Projects Administration in the State of Wisconsin. *Wisconsin: A Guide to the Badger State*. New York: Duell, Sloan and Pearce, 1941. Print.

Wylie, John. *Landscape*. London and New York: Routledge, 2007. Print.

Young, Alan. *Dada and After: Extremist Modernism and English Literature*. Manchester: Manchester University Press, 1981. Print.

Zukofsky, Louis. *'A'*. Baltimore and London: The Johns Hopkins University Press, 1993. Print.

———. *A Useful Art: Essays and Radio Scripts on American Design*. Ed. Keith Sherwood. Middletown, CT: Wesleyan University Press, 2003. Print.

———. *Prepositions +: The Collected Critical Essays*. Middletown, CT: Wesleyan University Press, 2000. Print.

Zurbrugg, Nicholas. 'Ian Hamilton Finlay and Concrete Poetry.' *Contemporary British Poetry: Essays in Theory and Criticism*. Eds. James Acheson and Romana Huk. Albany: State University of New York, 1996. 113–141. Print.

Index

Printed and bound by CPI Group (UK) Ltd, Croydon, CR0 4YY

24/04/2025

14661359-0001